Lecture Notes in Computer Science   8937

Commenced Publication in 1973
Founding and Former Series Editors:
Gerhard Goos, Juris Hartmanis, and Jan van Leeuwen

More information about this series at http://www.springer.com/series/7410

Massimo Felici · Carmen Fernández-Gago (Eds.)

Accountability and Security in the Cloud

First Summer School,
Cloud Accountability Project, A4Cloud
Malaga, Spain, June 2–6, 2014
Revised Selected Papers and Lectures

 Springer

Editors
Massimo Felici
HP Labs
Bristol
UK

Carmen Fernández-Gago
University of Malaga
Malaga
Spain

ISSN 0302-9743   ISSN 1611-3349   (electronic)
Lecture Notes in Computer Science
ISBN 978-3-319-17198-2   ISBN 978-3-319-17199-9   (eBook)
DOI 10.1007/978-3-319-17199-9

Library of Congress Control Number: 2015935047

LNCS Sublibrary: SL4 – Security and Cryptology

Springer Cham Heidelberg New York Dordrecht London
© Springer International Publishing Switzerland 2015

Printed on acid-free paper

Springer International Publishing AG Switzerland is part of Springer Science+Business Media
(www.springer.com)

Preface

Cloud computing is a key technology that is being adopted progressively by companies and users across different application domains and industries. Yet, there are emerging issues such as security, privacy, and data protection. The first A4Cloud[1] summer school was one of the first in the area of accountability and security in the cloud. The main aim of the summer school was to establish a reference event for sharing with young researchers and practitioners research insights in the areas of accountability and security in the cloud. This first summer school was organized by the EU-funded A4Cloud project, in collaboration with the European projects CIRRUS[2], CocoCloud[3], CUMULUS[4], and SPECS[5]. The school was held in Malaga (Spain) during June 2–6, 2014 and hosted PhD students from Greece, UK, Italy, Spain, The Netherlands, Sweden, Norway, and Germany.

Thematic Areas

The program of the school was multidisciplinary including lectures on technical and socio-legal aspects of accountability and security in the cloud. The school program included the following thematic contributions:

- Accountability in the Cloud
- Security in the Cloud
- Privacy and Transparency in the Cloud
- Empirical Approaches for the Cloud
- Socio-Legal Aspects of the Cloud
- Cloud Standards
- Accountability Glossary of Terms and Definitions.

Besides these themes, participants were encouraged to contribute to the school program by presenting their works on related topics. This collection consists of papers related to the lectures presented during the school. These papers provide a reading list and reference capturing the state of the art on topics such as accountability, security, privacy, metrics, and standards in the cloud. Alongside the lecture papers, this

---

[1] Cloud Accountability Project (A4Cloud) – http://www.a4cloud.eu/

[2] Certification, InteRnationalisation and standaRdization in cloUd Security (CIRRUS) – http://www.cirrus-project.eu/

[3] Confidential and compliant clouds (CocoCloud) – http://www.coco-cloud.eu/

[4] Certification infrastrUcture for MUlti-Layer cloUd Services (CUMULUS) – http://www.cumulus-project.eu/

[5] Secure Provisioning of Cloud Services based on SLA Management (SPECS) – http://specs-project.eu/

collection also includes (three) selected and peer-reviewed papers (submitted to the school) that provide further examples of ongoing research work in the areas of accountability and security in the cloud.

Target Audience

This edited collection brings together the main school contributions covering the state of the art and research insights on accountability and security in the cloud. For this reason, the volume will be a reference for anyone interested in knowing about the topics of accountability and security in cloud computing. The contents of this edited collection could serve as a course book for graduate, postgraduate, and professional courses concerned with accountability and security in cloud computing, which is currently the focus in the curricula for new BSc, MSc, and PhD programs as well as extensive research and development as a consequence of the increasing importance of the topic.

Acknowledgments

We would like to thank the lecturers for attending the school and delivering such magnificent lectures, the Program Committee members for their hard work during the review process, and the school participants for their interests and contributions to the school. Furthermore, we would like to thank the organizing projects mentioned above for their support, which was of paramount importance. We particularly appreciate the work done by the local organization team from the NICS group at the University of Malagá.

January 2015   Massimo Felici
                                                        Carmen Fernández-Gago

Organization

Program Chairs

Massimo Felici   HP Labs, UK
Carmen Fernández-Gago   University of Malaga, Spain

Organizing Committee

Marina Egea   ATOS, Spain
Massimo Felici   HP Labs, UK
Carmen Fernández-Gago   University of Malaga, Spain
Julie Grady   HP Labs, UK
Aljosa Pasic   ATOS, Spain
Vasilis Tontopoulos   Athens Technology Center S.A., Greece
Nick Wainwright   HP Labs, UK

Program Committee

Ludo Block   Grant Thornton, The Netherlands
Valentina Casola   University of Naples, Italy
Erdal Cayirci   University of Stavanger, Norway
Brian Dziminski   Queen Mary University of London, UK
Marina Egea   ATOS, Spain
Massimo Felici   HP Labs, UK
Carmen Fernández-Gago   University of Malaga, Spain
Simone Fischer-Huebner Karlstad University, Sweden
Maartje Niezen   Tilburg University, The Netherlands
Alain Pannetrat   Cloud Security Alliance, UK

Contents

Accountability in the Cloud

Accountability for Data Governance in the Cloud

Massimo Felici[(⊠)] and Siani Pearson

Security and Cloud Lab, Hewlett-Packard Laboratories, Long Down Avenue,
Bristol BS34 8QZ, UK
{massimo.felici,siani.pearson}@hp.com

Abstract. Cloud computing represents a major shift in the way Information and Communication Technology (ICT) is deployed and utilised across industries. Alongside the technological developments, organisations need to adapt to emerging operational needs associated with data governance, policy and responsibility, as well as compliance with regulatory regimes that may be multi-jurisdictional in nature. This paper is concerned with data governance in cloud ecosystems. It characterises the problem of data governance due to emerging challenges (and threats) in the cloud. It advocates an accountability-based approach for data stewardship. It defines accountability and introduces a model consisting of attributes, practices and mechanisms. The accountability model underpins an accountability framework supporting data governance. This paper also discusses emerging relationships between accountability, risk and trust. The overall objective of the proposed accountability-based approach to data governance is to support a transparent and trustworthy cloud.

Keywords: Accountability · Cloud computing · Data protection · Governance

1 Introduction

Cloud computing is transforming the way Information and Communication Technology (ICT) is deployed and consumed across different application domains. Cloud computing is defined as *"a model for enabling ubiquitous, convenient, on-demand network access to a shared pool of configurable computing resources (e.g., networks, servers, storage, applications, and services) that can be rapidly provisioned and released with minimal management effort or service provider interaction"* [1]. Different service and deployment models enable various customer-provider relationships depending on the types of cloud services procured (see [2] for examples of some generic cloud use cases). With the adoption of cloud computing and the transfer of data to the cloud, accountability has emerged as a critical concept related to data protection in cloud ecosystems Note that accountability is a notion that is used in slightly different senses in different contexts, and hence there is no uniformly accepted definition [3]. It is necessary to maintain chains of accountability across cloud ecosystems. This is to enhance the confidence in the trust that cloud actors have while operating in the cloud.

In the context of this paper, we focus on accountability for protection of data (e.g. personal and/or confidential data) [4], in which it is among the identified *"technical*

© Springer International Publishing Switzerland 2015
M. Felici and C. Fernández-Gago (Eds.): A4Cloud 2014, LNCS 8937, pp. 3–42, 2015.
DOI: 10.1007/978-3-319-17199-9_1

and organisational measures of data protection and data security" [5]. Unfortunately, despite its relevance for supporting governance of privacy [6], data protection and security in the cloud, the concept of accountability is difficult to define and operationalize (that is, to put into practice) uniformly across cloud ecosystems because *"defining what exactly accountability means in practice is complex"* [4]. In the context of privacy and data protection, accountability is used in the sense (following the OECD, Organisation for Economic Co-operation and Development, guidelines on privacy and data protection [7]) of an *"accountability principle"* that *"a data controller should be accountable for complying with measures which give effect to the"* privacy principles (i.e. collection limitation, data quality, purpose specification, use limitation, security safeguards, openness and individual participation). Various elements have been identified as characterising a general accountability principle. The Article 29 Data Protection Working Party in [4] identifies various elements defining the general principle of accountability (namely, reinforcing obligations, appropriate measures implementing the Data Protection Directive, the role of data protection authorities, sanctions, and the development and regulation of certification schemes). In addition, the Galway Project has identified five essential elements of an accountable organisation [8]. Accountability might provide a means to unlock the potential of cloud computing by helping to address relevant problems of data protection emerging in cloud ecosystems [9, 10]. This approach has been further explored within the EU Cloud Accountability Project (A4Cloud). A4Cloud focuses on accountability for cloud (and other future internet services) as the most critical prerequisite for effective governance of personal and confidential data processed by cloud-based services. Accountability helps to align cloud ecosystems with relevant regulatory regimes [11] like the ones defined by the EU Data Protection Directive [12].

This paper presents a conceptual model, consisting of attributes, practices and mechanisms for accountability in the cloud [13]. The proposed model forms the basis for characterising accountability relationships between cloud actors, and hence chains of accountability in cloud ecosystems [13]. The accountability model enables a framework for supporting accountability in cloud ecosystems. This paper is structured as follows. Section 2 provides a rationale for an accountability-based approach to data governance in the cloud. It discusses the main drivers for accountability. Section 3 defines accountability. Section 4 contextualises and explains the main characteristics of an accountability-based approach. Section 5 defines cloud and data protection roles. It describes what being accountable means in cloud ecosystems. Section 6 introduces a conceptual model consisting of accountability attributes, practices and mechanisms. The accountability model underpins the framework presented in Sect. 7 that supports accountability in the cloud. Section 8 describes accountability governance in the cloud. Section 9 discusses emerging threats in cloud ecosystems and discusses relationships between accountability, risk and trust. This paper therefore provides an analysis of accountability for data governance in the cloud. The paper defines the concept of accountability tailored to the cloud, an accountability model and an accountability framework, which enable accountability governance. These provide the foundations for an accountability-based approach for data governance in the cloud.

2 Problem of Data Governance

Cloud computing is one of the most relevant recent shifts in the way Information and Communications Technology (ICT) is provided and utilised. This technological change concerns data governance, because large amounts of personal and confidential data are steadily transferred to the cloud. Stakeholder interactions and responsibilities vary across the entire cloud supply chain. This is manifested in different ways to the stakeholders. Data subjects are no longer co-located with their data, leading to uncertainty due to lack of transparency and loss of control. Cloud customers and providers may act as controller and/or processor of personal and confidential data (Article 29 Data Protection Working Party's Opinion [14] clarifies the concepts of controller and processor, and provides some examples of organisations taking these roles, e.g. telecom operators, e-government portals, social networks). Such organisations have the responsibility of protecting data from privacy and security breaches, including due to unintended usage [12]. Governance in the cloud therefore requires understanding, moderating and regulating the relationships between cloud consumers (cloud customers) and providers. The NIST guidelines and recommendations (*"on how organisations should consider the relative opportunities and risks of cloud computing"*) highlight the relationship between cloud customers and providers as critical for security and privacy [15]. Clarifying the roles and responsibilities between customers and providers is important when considering moving to the cloud – *"The partnership between providers and consumers in designing, building, deploying, and operating clouds presents new challenges in providing adequate security and privacy protection. It becomes a collaborative process between providers and consumers to share the responsibilities in implementing the necessary controls"* [15]. Figure 1 shows a generic representation of the problem of data governance in a cloud ecosystem.

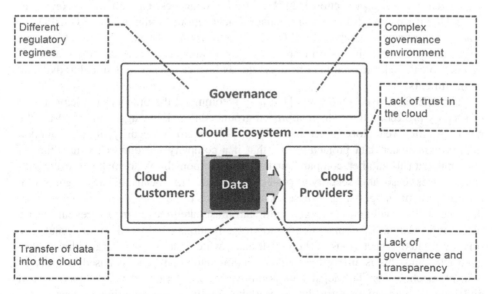

Fig. 1. Problem of data governance in a cloud ecosystem

Different data protection requirements arise in the relationships between cloud customers and providers [5]. Accountability is among the identified *"technical and organisational measures of data protection and data security"* [5]. Unfortunately, despite its relevance for supporting governance of privacy, data protection and security in the cloud [6], the concept of accountability is difficult to define and operationalize (that is, put into practice) uniformly across cloud ecosystems as *"defining what exactly accountability means in practice is complex"* [4]. The remainder of this section discusses some drivers for an accountability-based approach to data governance in the cloud.

2.1   Regulatory Complexity

The collection and processing of personal information is subject to regulation in many countries across the world. There are many different national data protection legislations in place. For example, the United States (US) does not have a comprehensive regime of data protection but instead has a variety of laws targeted at the protection of particularly sensitive types of information that tend to be sector-based or enacted at the state level. This (sometimes inconsistent) matrix of national laws can make it really hard for businesses to ensure full compliance if they are operating in multiple jurisdictions. There is pressure from organisations for greater global interoperability to be achieved via development of a clear and consistent framework of data protection rules that can be applied, in order to reduce unnecessary administrative burdens and risks.

Transborder flow of personal information, including access to this information, is restricted by some of these laws. For example, the European Data Protection Directive 95/46/EC (DPD) is an important piece of privacy legislation that restricts the movement of data from EU to non-EU countries that do not meet the European adequacy standard for privacy protection [12]. Many other countries, e.g. Australia, New Zealand, Hong Kong and Japan, have enacted legislation similar to the EU DPD. In practice, contractual mechanisms like Binding Corporate Rules or Model Contracts might need to be put in place in order to allow data access. However, these arrangements typically take several months to set up, and hence are not well suited to dynamic environments.

The OECD revised guidelines [16] now recommend the practical implementation of privacy protection through an approach grounded in risk management and stress the need for improved global interoperability. With regard to security, it is a common requirement under data protection law that if a company outsources the handling of personal data to another company, it has some responsibility to make sure the outsourcer uses reasonable security to protect those data. This means that any organisation creating, maintaining, using or disseminating records of personal data must ensure that the records have not been tampered with, and must take precautions to prevent misuse of the information. Of course, in addition, organisations need to take into account the privacy-related expectations of their customers, which may be specified within private contracts, and this is likely to involve a combination of process-based and access control mechanisms. The legal obligations vary according to the regulatory context and indeed there are likely to be some quite significant changes in the near future.

Once these changes are implemented, many service providers will gain a range of data security obligations including adopting risk management practices and reporting major security incidents to competent authorities and affected parties.

In order to harmonise data protection and to take into account new technologies including cloud computing, the European Commission (EC) has been working on a new General Data Protection Regulation (GDPR) [17], which will replace the DPD. In the proposed GDPR, which is currently being discussed and revised, accountability features and privacy by design take further precedence. Amongst other things, the proposed GDPR imposes new obligations and liabilities for data processors, new requirements on data breach notification and stricter rules on international data transfers. It also empowers National Regulatory authorities to impose significantly higher fines. In addition, a European Cloud Computing Strategy [18] has been launched aiming at more clarity and knowledge about the applicable legal framework and making it easier to verify compliance with the legal framework (e.g. through standards and certifications). Furthermore, the European Commission has also published a cybersecurity strategy [19] alongside a draft directive on a Network and Information Security (NIS) Platform [20]. Once the GDPR combined with the cybersecurity strategy will be implemented, many service providers will need to comply with a range of data security obligations including adopting risk management practices and reporting major security incidents.

The emerging regulatory complexity and the difficulty of compliance with different regulatory regimes represent barriers to migration to the cloud. A major reason for this is that data flows tend to be global and dynamic. As discussed above, the collection and processing of personal information is subject to regulation in many countries across the world and some national laws restrict transborder flow of personal information, including access to this information. This matrix of (sometimes inconsistent) national laws can make it difficult for businesses that wish to provide effective stewardship of the data that they handle to ensure full compliance when operating in multiple jurisdictions. It can be difficult even to determine which laws apply and which courts should preside. There is pressure from organisations for greater harmonisation to reduce unnecessary administrative burdens and risks. These two issues – *trust* and *complexity* – are closely linked. Both legal and ethical obligations arise to ensure privacy and protect data, and these need to be built upon to demonstrate the trustworthy nature of cloud services.

2.2 Challenges in Cloud Ecosystems

There are a variety of data protection concerns related to cloud computing that include ongoing questions of jurisdiction and exacerbation of privacy risk through sub-processing and de-localisation, as well as legal uncertainty. For example, the NIST guidelines on security and privacy in public cloud computing point out concerns for cloud adoption that include governance over data use and processing, the compliance to laws, regulations, standards and specifications, the management of risks to assess trust and trustworthiness along the cloud service chains and the effective implementation of incidence response mechanisms [21]. Table 1 lists key issues and links them to features characterising the cloud that can potentially increase data protection risks.

Table 1. Cloud features and issues

CLOUD FEATURES	POTENTIAL DATA PROTECTION ISSUES
Multi-tenancy	• Data of co-tenants may be revealed in investigations • Isolation failure • Proper deletion of data and virtual storage devices
Elasticity	• Multiplies attack surfaces • De-anonymisation facilitated
Abstraction	• Cannot rely upon physical security controls
Automation	• Ensuring appropriate data protection when data flows are dynamic • Decrease in human involvement in data protection
Data duplication	• Detecting and determining who is at fault if privacy breaches occur • Difficulty in knowing geographic location and which specific servers or storage devices will be used
Easy data access from multiple locations	• Data access from remote geographic locations subject to different legislative regimes, and transborder data flow compliance issues • Potential for risky usage by employees without due consideration
Subprocessing	• Potential complexity of cloud service delivery chains, both horizontally and vertically • Lack of transparency or compliance by subprocessors • Unauthorized data access from employees of CSPs • Risks to confidentiality from subpoenas or access by foreign governments • Overlapping responsibilities in data management • Unauthorized secondary usage and profiling • Vendor demise

For example, cloud vulnerabilities include the multi-tenancy of cloud applications, in which co-tenants may gain inappropriate access to the data of another application instance and the simplification of data access from multiple geographic locations, but with completely different legislative regimes. Also, data duplication and proliferation in the cloud create problems in terms of compliance, since the loss of control and transparency significantly affect the data lifecycle management across various involved providers in a service provisioning chain.

A categorisation of risks from an EU perspective has been made according to lack of transparency or control by the Article 29 Working Party in their Opinion on Cloud Computing [5]. Similar risks were highlighted by the French data protection authority [22], with the addition of ineffective or non-secure destruction of data, or excessive data retention periods, and of takeover of the cloud provider by a third party. A detailed analysis of cloud computing risks has been provided by European Union Agency for Network and Information Security (ENISA) [23].

2.3   Drivers for Accountability

This section has discussed some of the drivers for accountability. Cloud computing represents the most significant shift in ICT deployments. The globalisation of businesses and the new technologies create global ecosystems that pose new challenges. Among the challenges is the regulatory complexity that is inherent in many cloud environments. Accountability potentially allows avoidance of the complex matrix of national laws and reduces unnecessary layers of complexity for cloud providers [10]. Additionally, cloud features expose, in particular, cloud customers and providers to new emerging challenges exacerbating data protection risks. Relationships among cloud stakeholders, e.g. customers, providers and regulators, are characterised by uncertainty resulting in a lack of trust in the cloud. In response to the seemingly insufficient reflection of EU data protection principles and obligations in concrete measures and practices used by organisations, the Article 29 Data Protection Working Party advocated in its opinion on the principle of accountability [4] that such a general principle could help move data protection *from theory to practice*, as well as provide a means for assisting data protection authorities in their supervision and assessment tasks: *"EU data protection principles and obligations are often insufficiently reflected in concrete internal measures and practices. Unless data protection becomes part of the shared values and practices of an organisation, and responsibilities for it are expressly assigned, effective compliance will be at considerable risk, and data mishaps are likely to continue."* Therefore, a major driver for an accountability-based approach is to provide an incentive for organisations *to do the right thing*, in terms of providing appropriate and adequate data protection in the sense described above, by means of decreasing regulatory complexity, easing transborder data flow restrictions while avoiding increased privacy harm, encouraging best practice, using strong punishment as a deterrent and allowing organisations to choose what measures they will use, so long as they can show that these are effective and appropriate for the context.

3 Accountability Definitions

Accountability is becoming an important notion, defining the relations between various stakeholders and their behaviours towards data in the cloud. In cloud ecosystems, the accountors are cloud actors (organisations or individuals with certain responsibilities) acting as a data steward (for other people's personal and/or confidential data). The accountees are other cloud actors, that may include private accountability agents, consumer organisations, the public at large and entities involved in governance. Building on our analysis of the problem of data governance (and an analysis of different understandings of accountability [3]), a definition of accountability that is applicable across different domains and that captures a shared multidisciplinary understanding is:

> **Definition of Accountability:** *Accountability consists of defining governance to comply in a responsible manner with internal and external criteria, ensuring implementation of appropriate actions, explaining and justifying those actions and remedying any failure to act properly.*

Internal criteria are not necessarily visible to stakeholders external to that organisation, as they might for example reflect the risk appetite of that organisation or known security vulnerabilities; external criteria could include best practice on security, data protection and breach notification, as well as privacy regulatory and contractual requirements and societal expectations. However, given the scope of the project, we need to refine this definition to reflect our project focus. We look at accountability in the context of a cloud ecosystem, which is a business ecosystem of interacting organisations and individuals – the actors of the cloud ecosystem – who provide and consume cloud services. In other words, the main stakeholders in the cloud ecosystem are cloud providers and cloud users. In this ecosystem the stakeholders interact in a constant process of change. Moreover the stakeholders within the ecosystem are controlled not only by the internal factors of the system, such as codes of conduct and existing relations, but also by external factors such as regulations, the wider environment or even required skills.

Accountability, in general, is used prescriptively, that is, accountability of some agent to some other agent for some state of affairs. It reflects an institutional relation arrangement in which an actor can be held to account by a forum (for example, a customer organisation, business association or even the public at large). Accountability then focuses on the specific social relation or the mechanism that involves an obligation to explain and justify conduct. Subsequently, accountability is *"a relationship between an actor and a forum, in which the actor has an obligation to explain and to justify his or her conduct, the forum can pose questions and pass judgement, and the actor can be sanctioned"* [24]. In an accountability relationship thus two parties and an object can be distinguished: (a) the steward or **accountor**, (b) **accountee** or forum, and (c) the codes or **norms** on the basis of which the relationship is struck. The latter are the shared framework for explanation and justification that are negotiated between the accountor (to answer, explain and justify) and accountee (to question, assess and criticise). An accountability code then is a system of signals, meanings and customs, which binds the parties in a stewardship relation. There are different stages in accountability relations:

- information in which explanation is given and one's conduct is justified
- debate, in which the adequacy of the information and /or the legitimacy of conduct is debated (answerability)
- the forum must pass judgement and sanction whether formally (for example, via fines, disciplinary measures and unwritten rules leading to resignation) or informally (for example, having to render account in front of television cameras or via disintegration of public image and career).

Accountability as a mechanism thus can be used as a tool to induce reflection and learning. It provides external feedback on (un)intended effects of an organisation's actions. However, accountability is also used in a more normative way – *accountability as a virtue* [25]. Accountability as a virtue is largely defined by bad governance: what is irresponsive, opaque, irresponsible, ineffective or even deviant behaviour. Accountability as a virtue, a normative concept, entails the promise of fair and equitable governance. Behaving in an accountable or responsible manner then is perceived as a desirable quality and laid down in norms for the behaviour and conduct of actors. Moreover, accountability then is not something imposed upon someone or an organisation by another actor, but an inherent feeling, the feeling of being morally obliged to be responsive, open, transparent and responsible. Hence, accountability as a virtue is a normative concept whereby a set of standards is provided for the evaluation of behaviour of public actors, and being accountable is seen as a positive quality in organisations or officials [25], while accountability as a mechanism is used in a narrower, descriptive sense, to describe an institutional relation or arrangement in which an actor can be held to account by a forum.

Our understanding of cloud accountability combines the notions introduced earlier of accountability as a mechanism and accountability as a virtue within the private sector of cloud computing and its cloud ecosystem. Our approach is to build on these notions to incorporate accountability in the cloud ecosystem by allowing for a mechanism that ensures the possibility of giving account ex post facto (via accountability tools) and steering accountability behaviour ex ante (via accountability as a virtue). Accountability as a virtue is extended to apply to cloud actors including cloud service providers, and accountability as a mechanism entails the social relation between the accountor and accountee that involves an obligation to explain and justify conduct. A definition of accountability within cloud ecosystems that we have produced, again through consideration of relevant interdisciplinary literature, is the following:

Definition of Accountability (for Cloud Ecosystems): *Accountability for an organisation consists of accepting responsibility for data with which it is entrusted in a cloud environment, for its use of the data from the time it is collected until when the data is destroyed (including onward transfer to and from third parties). It involves the commitment to norms, explaining and demonstrating compliance to stakeholders and remedying any failure to act properly.*

This definition differs slightly from the more generic one, for the following reasons. Security and privacy management is evolving into an information stewardship problem. In the cloud, it is harder to establish the risks and obligations, implement appropriate operational responses and deal with regulatory requirements. Notions of transparency and assurance receive more emphasis and it is necessary to ensure *chains of accountability*. Accountability places a responsibility upon an organisation that uses personal information to ensure that the contracted partners to whom it supplies the personal information are compliant, wherever in the world they may be. So, the communities responsible for data stewardship place responsibilities/constraints on other individuals or on the way systems operate, and these constraints are met along the chain of provision. Furthermore, we focus on governance of personal and/or confidential data in the cloud.

4 From Accountability to Being Accountable

Accountability complements the usage of appropriate privacy and security controls [26] in order to support democratically determined principles that reflect societal norms, regulations and stakeholder expectations (Fig. 2). Governance and oversight of this process is achieved via a combination of Data Protection Authorities, auditors and Data Protection Officers within organisations, the latter potentially supplemented by private accountability agents acting on their behalf. As shown in Fig. 2, accountability and good systems design (in particular, to meet privacy and security requirements) are complementary, in that the latter provides mechanisms and controls that allow implementation of principles and standards, whereas accountability makes organisations responsible for providing an appropriate implementation for their business context, and addresses what happens in case of failure (that is, if the account is not provided, is not adequate, if the organisation's obligations are not met, e.g. there is a data breach).

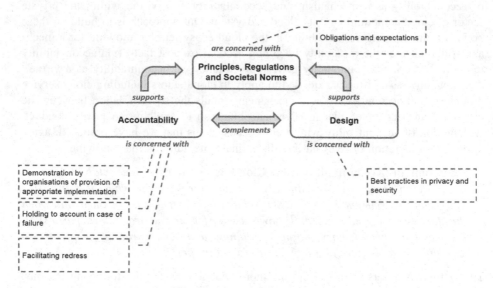

Fig. 2. Accountability framing

Although organisations can select from accountability mechanisms and tools in order to meet their context, the choice of such tools needs to be justified to external parties. A strong accountability approach would include moving beyond accountability of policies and procedures, to accountability of practice. There is an associated requirement for data controllers to be able to demonstrate compliance to supervisory authorities upon request. Hence, organisations are allowed increased control over aspects of compliance (i.e. which tools and mechanisms to use in order to achieve compliance), but at the expense of having to demonstrate on an ongoing basis that these mechanisms are appropriate for their business context, and operationally work as expected (Fig. 3). The legal and contractual context defines the norms applicable to actors in a given cloud ecosystem, and their associated obligations, responsibilities and liabilities.

Businesses need to meet these obligations, as well as obligations and requirements imposed by other stakeholders that include customers and data subjects. Accountability aims to entrust organisations with the practical aspects of complying with data protection obligations. This involves clarification of requirements of the different cloud actors within cloud ecosystems, as well as transparency and provisions of trustworthy accounts by organisations that collect or handle personal information. Cloud actors may select mechanisms and tools to support accountability practices, and thereby help them to comply with relevant regulatory regimes within specific application domains.

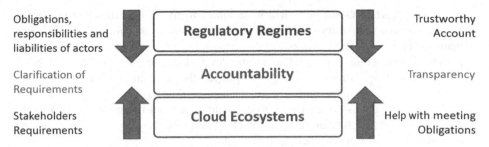

Fig. 3. Accountability context

4.1 Accountability-Based Approach

We argue that an accountability-based approach should have a number of characteristics that include a notion of *strong accountability*. This term has recently been proposed in [27] to describe an approach that applies not only to policies and procedures, but also to practices, so that the effectiveness of the processing of personal data can be overseen (this stresses a distinction between *reporting* and *demonstrating*). This is supported by precise binding commitments enshrined in law and involves regular audits by independent entities. However, this should not be contradictory with the need for flexibility that is required by the industry. Similarly, in order to avoid charges of *privacy whitewashing* whereby apparent accountability encourages a false basis for trust in data controllers by data subjects, we argue that an accountability-based approach (such as the one of the Cloud Accountability Project) should have the following characteristics:

- **Supporting externally agreed data protection approach:** Accountability should be viewed as a means to an end (i.e. that organisations should be accountable for the personal and confidential information that they collect, store, process and disseminate), not as an alternative to reframing basic privacy principles or legal requirements. Thus, the accountability elements in the GDPR provide a certain assurance of compliance with the data protection principles, but do not replace them.
- **Trust in the verification process:** There needs to be a strong enough verification process to show the extent to which commitments have been fulfilled. Missing evidence can pose a problem, and guarantees are needed about the integrity and authenticity of evidence supporting verification. In addition, the actor carrying out the verification checks needs to be trusted by the data subject and to have the appropriate authority and resources to carry out spot checking and other ways of asking organisations to demonstrate compliance with regulatory and contractual obligation by providing accounts that may take various forms (e.g. certificates, seals and audit reports). This is why the data protection authorities will need to play a key role in the trust verification, for example in data protection certification. In terms of external governance mechanisms, strong enforcement strategies, not only in terms of verification, but also in terms of increasing the likelihood of detection of unlawful practices and strong penalties if caught, seem to be a necessary part of accountability. Data protection impact assessments, codes of conduct and certifications are proposed

to increase trust in cloud providers who adhere to them. It is thus of the utmost importance that regulatory and supervisory bodies have a primary role in the verification of the level of compliance of these tools. Furthermore, to give data subjects give back some control it would be another level of interaction if the data subjects' comments and needs receive a response and ideally even show some fundamental development in the application or organisational data processing. This form of feedback to the data subjects (in response to their feedback) is another form of verification. There are further related aspects supporting this approach in terms of responsibility and transparency, as listed below.

- **Clarity and acceptance of responsibility:** The relationship between controllers and processors in cloud service provision chains can sometimes be complex. The commitments of the data controller need to be well defined – this is (part of) the aspect of responsibility, that is an element of accountability. The respective responsibility of cloud customers and cloud providers will need to be defined in contracts and the definition of standard clauses by the industry, as validated by regulators, will help cloud customers with lower negotiation capabilities. The commitments of the data controller should include all applicable legal obligations, together with any industry standards (forming part of the external criteria against which the organisation's policies are defined) and any other commitment made by the data controller. Once again, the responsibilities of the entities along the cloud provider chain need to be clearly defined, including relative security responsibilities. On the other hand, certain tasks will need to be jointly carried out to be effective, such as risk assessment and security management. In this case there is a clear need for cooperation and coordination. Note that to what extent cloud providers should be considered as controllers or processors remains questionable [28].
- **Transparency:** A main goal of accountability is to go beyond regulation through fostering transparency about actual practices and thus enabling promotion of good data handling practices, in a proactive sense. The commitments of the data controller(s) need to be expressed in an understandable language by the data subjects affected and other parties as appropriate – this is a key transparency aspect. In addition, the mechanisms used and relevant properties of the service providers in the provision chain need to be clarified as appropriate to cloud customers and regulators. It would also be beneficial to integrate social interaction between data subjects and the cloud infrastructure and service providers, for example via feedback mechanisms that enable comments on privacy policies and data usage reports [29]. Furthermore, data protection impact assessments and privacy impact assessments are forms of verification for accountability (that should be used in conjunction with others) that can be used to help provide transparency about the nature of the risks, including the criteria used in the risk assessment, how decisions are made to mitigate risk, and whether the mechanisms to be used and implemented are appropriate for the context. Comprehensive obligations for controllers to inform supervisory authorities and data subjects of personal data breaches would further increase transparency.
- **Avoidance of increased risk:** Technical security measures (such as open strong cryptography) can help prevent falsification of logs, and privacy-enhancing techniques and adequate access control should be used to protect personal information

in logs. Note however that data that is collected for accountability might be itself data that can be abused and hence needs to be protected as much as the processed data. The potential conflict of accountability with privacy is somewhat reduced as the focus in data protection is not on the accountability of data subjects but rather of data controllers, which need to be accountable towards data subjects and trusted *intermediaries*.

- **Avoidance of increased burden:** Accountability must deliver effective solutions whilst avoiding where possible overly prescriptive or burdensome requirements.
- **Avoidance of social harm:** Accountability should have democratic and ethical characteristics. Transparency should be as high as possible, in balance with other interests (as considered above while describing transparency). Mechanisms should also be developed to help regulators do their job, notably with respect to enhancement of the verification process as discussed above.

4.2 Accountability Evidence

Accountability evidence, as illustrated in Fig. 4, needs to be provided at a number of layers. At the policies level, this would involve provision of evidence that the policies are appropriate for the context, which is typically what is done when privacy seals are issued. But this alone is rather weak. In addition, evidence can be provided about the measures, mechanisms and controls that are deployed and their configuration, to show that these are appropriate for the context.

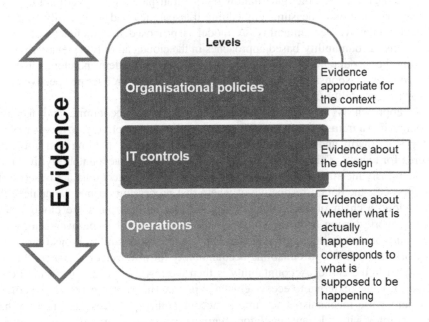

Fig. 4. Accountability evidence

For example, evidence could be provided that Privacy Enhancing Technologies (PETs) have been used, to support anonymisation requirements expressed at the policy level. For higher risk situations continuous monitoring may be needed to provide evidence that what is claimed in the policies is actually being met in practice. Even if this is not sophisticated, some form of checking the operational running and feeding this back into the accountability management program in order to improve it is part of accountability practice, and hence evidence will need to be generated at this level too. In particular, technical measures should be deployed to enhance the integrity and authenticity of logs, and there should be enhanced reasoning about how these logs show whether or not data protection obligations have been fulfilled. The evidence from the above would be reflected in the account, and would serve as a basis for verification and certification by independent, trusted entities. Accountability is particularly hard to achieve in the cloud context, but that is actually a context where it is strongly needed. The main factors contributing to this difficulty are:

- The complexity of technology offers.
- The necessity to split responsibilities depending on the service delivery model.
- Potential weak links in dynamically formed cloud provider chains, and
- The current shallowness of transparency and verifiability in the cloud context.

If the data controller is ultimately made accountable for meeting obligations right along the service provision chain, they should try to obtain contractual assurances that lessen the risk of potential weak links in dynamically formed cloud provider chains. That is, contractual agreements between the series of actors taking part in the cloud chain should provide for the accountability obligations of data controllers owed to data subjects. Regarding the potential shallowness of transparency and verifiability, technical and organisational measures embedding transparency and verifiability by design are key for effective accountability. A model is proposed that includes such tools. Without this, accountability-based approaches in the cloud can only be relatively weak. Extending the accountability relationship between cloud providers and cloud customers to the provider's responsibility to society at large provides a broader perspective on the need for accountability in the cloud.

Our approach is to integrate legal, regulatory, socio-economic and technical approaches into a framework to provide accountability pre-emptively, to assess risk and avoid privacy harm and reactively to provide transparency, auditing and corrective measures for redress. This enables us to implement chains of accountability, including interdisciplinary mechanisms to ensure that obligations to protect data are observed by all who process the data, irrespective of where that processing occurs. To achieve this for the cloud a chain of accountability needs to be built through the cloud service supply network starting from the cloud service users, which can be overseen by regulators, auditors and business governance. The Cloud Accountability Project provides a framework and technologies enabling accountability for how personal and confidential data is used in the cloud. Accountability is then the result of complying with a combination of public (external to ecosystems) and private (internal to ecosystems) criteria. Cloud actors use mechanisms to support accountability practices, and thereby help them to comply with relevant regulatory regimes within specific application domains.

5   Accountability in Cloud Ecosystems

There is a need to clarify actor roles in cloud ecosystems from an accountability perspective, using a terminology that is applicable both to data protection and business confidentiality domains. The cloud taxonomy defined by NIST [30], as most relevant for cloud computing terminology, has been extensively adopted by practitioners and researchers (both in Industry and Academia) to described cloud supply chains in terms of cloud computing roles (i.e. *consumers, providers, brokers, auditors* and *carriers*). In order to take into account accountability (and in particular, its emphasis on responsibility), it is necessary to extend and to refine the cloud computing roles. For example, end-users (one of the end points of cloud supply chains) who ultimately own the data or have some other interest or rights over its dissemination and usage are misrepresented (or undermined) by cloud computing roles. Another example of misrepresented role is the lack of representation for relevant supervisory authorities. Rather than creating a novel taxonomy, we extended and refined the existing NIST cloud computing terminology in [30] (maintaining an alignment with its mail roles) with roles that support a systematic analysis of accountability in the cloud ecosystems.

We extend the cloud computing roles (defined by NIST in [30]) creating a taxonomy of (seven) cloud actor roles tailored to accountability in the cloud (Table 2). We briefly examine some of the key reasons that motivated us to adopt the taxonomy in Table 2. The NIST cloud taxonomy defines a cloud customer as an entity that both (1) has a business relationship with, and (2) uses the services of, a cloud provider. We observe that in the data protection domain, the data subject does not always fit that definition: the data subject may not have a business relationship with a cloud provider directly (or through a broker), but rather with a cloud customer. In the business confidentiality domain, a similar situation may also materialise – e.g. a business will provide data to another business, which itself uses the service of a cloud provider. This has conducted us to add the cloud subject as a distinct actor to our extended taxonomy. All actors in the supply chain are ultimately accountable to the cloud subject. Once we add a cloud subject in our model, we need to also consider the role of the relevant supervisory authority. This is particularly clear in the data protection domain. Although Data Protection Authorities (DPAs) or telecom regulators (NRAs) may be seen as cloud auditors in the NIST model, they also have the distinct characteristic of holding enforcement powers. This has similarly conducted us to include the cloud supervisory authority in our extended taxonomy. In some cases, in order to facilitate the discussion, we found it useful to further distinguish both cloud subjects and cloud customers as individuals or organisations. Furthermore, some actors may endorse more than one role. For example, in the original NIST model, cloud customers may also act as cloud providers. This is also true in our taxonomy where additionally cloud subjects may act as cloud customers, and the supervisory entity may act also as an auditor in some situations. We also slightly refined the definition of cloud auditor proposed by NIST to better encompass accountability, which is also concerned with compliance.

The revision of cloud actor roles allows us to structure the discussion of the chains of accountability enabling the comparison of different cloud ecosystems and identification of accountability relationships supported by different mechanisms. The analysis

Table 2. Cloud actor roles

1. **Cloud Subject:** An entity whose data are processed by a cloud provider, either directly or indirectly. When necessary we may further distinguish: (a) **Individual Cloud Subject**, when the entity refers to a person. (b) **Organisational Cloud Subject**, when the entity refers to an organisation.
2. **Cloud Customer:** An entity that (a) maintains a business relationship with, and (b) uses services from a Cloud provider. When necessary we may further distinguish: (a) **Individual Cloud Customer**, when the entity refers to a person. (b) **Organisational Cloud Customer**, when the entity refers to an organisation.
3. **Cloud Provider:** An entity responsible for making a [cloud] service available to Cloud Customers
4. **Cloud Carrier:** The intermediary entity that provides connectivity and transport of cloud services   between Cloud providers and Cloud Customers.
5. **Cloud Broker:** An entity that manages the use, performance and delivery of cloud services, and   negotiates relationships between Cloud providers and Cloud Customers.
6. **Cloud Auditor:** An entity that can conduct independent assessment of cloud services, information system operations, performance and security of the cloud implementation, with regards to a set of requirements, which may include security, data protection, information system management, regulations and ethics.
7. **Cloud Supervisory Authority:** An entity that oversees and enforces the application of a set of rules.

of any particular cloud ecosystem should identify specific accountability relationships among actors and how they relate to the elements of accountability in high level scenarios relating to the treatment of personal and of business sensitive information within service provision chains. The discussion of such roles in terms of accountability allows us to identify specific responsibilities. Moreover, the identified cloud computing roles extend the ones identified from technical considerations of cloud computing. The discussion of specific scenarios further points out roles and responsibilities in cloud ecosystems. We can then extend the analysis of accountability relationships by a data protection perspective, in terms of data protection roles [28]. Table 3 summarises the roles identified from both perspectives (i.e. cloud computing and data protection) and their possible mapping.

According to the current European data protection directive, a data controller (DC) essentially determines the purposes for which and the manner in which personal data are processed. A data processor (DP) processes personal data upon the instructions of

Table 3. Data protection roles

CLOUD ACTOR ROLES	DATA PROTECTION ROLES
Cloud subject	Data subject
Cloud customer	Data controller or Data processor
Cloud provider	Data processor or Data controller
Cloud carrier	Data processor or Data controller (unlikely) or Not applicable
Cloud broker	Data processor or Data controller
Cloud auditor	Not Applicable
Cloud supervisory authority	Supervisory authority (DPA or NRA)
(Not Applicable)	Third party
(Not Applicable)	Recipient

the data controller. The data subject is the living person that can be identified by personal data, and the data protection authority (DPA) is the supervisory body. In other regulatory contexts, different roles may apply to entities, such as data owner, in a similar manner. In the cloud context, cloud subjects may be data subjects, cloud customers and cloud providers would be Data Controllers (DCs) or Data Processors (DPs), and cloud carriers and cloud brokers may be DPs, or possibly DCs or else fall outside the controller/processor distinction, depending upon their function. The organisational cloud customer is in general considered to be the DC and is regulated by the DPA. Even though in most cases organisational cloud customers are not in a position to negotiate with cloud providers, they may still choose amongst offerings and hence are still considered a DC [5]. An individual cloud customer is likely to be considered to be a data subject, although there are situations where they would be considered as a DC, for example where they use a cloud service for professional purposes involving processing data of other data subjects. Cloud providers are nearly always a DP but could be a DC. They may need to assume co-controllership respon- sibilities, but may not know who the users are or what their services are being used for. If they process personal data which is not provided by a cloud customer, acting autonomously to define the means and the purpose of the processing, the cloud pro- vider is a DC. The cloud provider is a DP if it processes personal data to provide a service requested by a cloud customer and does not further process the data for its own purposes. There are also cases where the cloud provider can be a joint DC, namely when it processes data to provide a service requested by a cloud customer but in addition further processes the data for its own purposes (e.g. advertising). In the pro- posed EU General Data Protection Regulation (GDPR), DPs who process data beyond the DC's instructions would be considered as a joint DC. This case might include changing security measures or data handling practices.

6 Accountability Model

Building on the concept of accountability, we introduce a model of accountability for data stewardship. The model expands upon the definition of accountability by introducing accountability practices, attributes and mechanisms. Accountability attributes encompass the numerous elements and properties of accountability at the conceptual level. Accountability practices characterise organisational behaviour, and hence define what it means to be an accountable organisation. Diverse mechanisms are used in order to support such practices. Accountability is interpreted in terms of accountability attributes. These accountability attributes are operationalised (that is, put into practices) by organisational accountability practices. Accountability practices need to comply with and mediate between external (drawn from relevant regulatory regimes and ethical attitudes) and internal criteria (characterising organisational culture). In order to implement such practices, organisations use different accountability mechanisms tailored to their domains. Organisations adopt mechanisms and shape (that is, adapt or modify) them in order to address their needs as well as embed organisational knowledge derived from experience. These mechanisms therefore constrain and support accountability practices, and the operational interpretation of the accountability attributes. Figure 5 illustrates how attributes, practices and mechanisms form a model of accountability for cloud ecosystems. The accountability model consists of:

- **Accountability attributes** – conceptual elements of accountability applicable across different domains (i.e. the conceptual basis for our definition, and related taxonomic analysis)
- **Accountability practices** – emergent behaviour characterising accountable organisations (that is, how organisations operationalise accountability or put accountability into practices)
- **Accountability mechanisms** – diverse processes, non-technical mechanisms and tools that support accountability practices (that is, accountability practices use them).

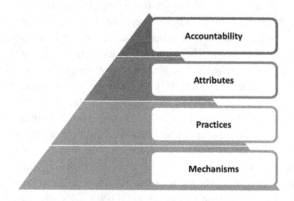

Fig. 5. Accountability attributes, practices and mechanisms

The emerging relationships between accountability attributes, practices and mechanisms give rise to an operational interpretation of accountability. This characterisation explains how organisations may attain accountability in different ways (that is, instantiate this accountability model differently according to their particular contexts).

6.1 Accountability Attributes

Accountability attributes capture concepts that are strongly related to and support the principle of accountability. We propose a number of attributes, coming from our analysis at the topmost layer, i.e. from our definition and related literature. The core (key) attributes are: *transparency, responsiveness, responsibility* and *remediability*. In addition, as we shall see, *verifiability* is a key property of an object of accountability, and accountability indicators about the measures used by an organisation include the key attributes of *appropriateness* and *effectiveness*. We now consider these notions in more detail. We shall distinguish between attributes that we consider to be key to the concept of accountability, in the sense that they are most associated with our definition of accountability and related notions in the literature, and those that we consider to be of secondary relevance, in the sense that they are not necessary elements of accountability or have a strongly overlapping meaning to a key attribute. We identify the objects that a cloud actor is accountable for within a cloud ecosystem to be [31]:

- **Norms:** *the obligations and permissions that define data practices; these can be expressed in policies and they derive from law, contracts and ethics.*
- **Behaviour:** *the actual data processing behaviour of an organisation.*
- **Compliance:** *entails the comparison of an organisation's actual behaviour with the norms.*

From our definition of accountability, the core attributes are suggested in a direct way: *"commitment to norms"* and *"demonstrating compliance"* suggest that transparency is an important element; *"explaining to stakeholders"* suggests responsiveness; *"accepting responsibility"* suggests responsibility; *"remedying failure to act properly"* suggests remediability. More specifically, these key attributes refer to:

- **Transparency:** *the property of a system, organisation or individual of providing visibility of its governing norms, behaviour and compliance of behaviour to the norms.*
- **Responsiveness:** *the property of a system, organisation or individual to take into account input from external stakeholders and respond to queries of these stakeholders.*
- **Responsibility:** *the property of an organisation or individual in relation to an object, process or system of being assigned to take action to be in compliance with the norms.*
- **Remediability:** *the property of a system, organisation or individual to take corrective action and/or provide a remedy for any party harmed in case of failure to comply with its governing norms.*

By *system* here we mean (parts of) the accountable cloud ecosystem, which could for example be a chain of cloud providers or an IT process, which should be accountable to humans. However, since in a legal sense the entities further down the chain are not accountable to cloud customers, but rather to the entity one step up the chain, often in our domain of interest the accountability property will relate to a single cloud provider.

Being transparent is required not only with respect to the identified objects of the cloud ecosystem (i.e. norms, behaviour and compliance) but also with respect to remediation. Transparency can be argued to be the most important attribute of accountability. A stronger definition would require demonstration of the governing norms, behaviour and compliance of behaviour as part of the definition of transparency. However, we hold that it is more natural for this aspect of demonstration to be captured mainly within the verification attribute given below. A weaker definition of transparency would only require visibility of the governing norms, but we consider this interpretation of the notion of transparency in the context of accountability to be too weak.

Responsiveness is a key element of the notion of accountability in the relation between government and electorate because ultimately, it is the electorate that mandates what happens (for example, via a social contract). In the context of cloud computing the providers are private entities that determine their own actions, between the boundaries set by regulation, and if users do not like this, they can refuse to use the service. However, responsiveness is required even in the relation between cloud providers and their users. It refers to the two-way communication relation between cloud providers and external stakeholders (such as individual cloud customers and regulators) needed within the cloud ecosystem to define part of the governing norms. Generally speaking, the audience for an organisation's account should somehow be involved with the process by which the account is produced, and not only with the product.

Responsibility is revealed through being an attribute of the accountability objects, so is slightly different from the other attributes listed here, in that for each object, process or system within an accountable ecosystem a responsible entity (i.e. cloud actor that here would be the accountor) should be provided.

The remediability attribute provides assurance that being responsible, etc. is not sufficient and further action is required in order to be accountable; although legal responsibility, namely liability, leads to remedies, accountability equally puts emphasis not only on whom to blame but how to heal. An attribute that is a property of the objects of accountability (i.e. norm, behaviour, compliance) is:

- **Verifiability:** *the extent to which it is possible to assess norm compliance.*

This is a property of the behaviour of a system, service or process that it can be checked against norms. We consider this to be a core attribute because of our explanation of accountability in terms of defining and displaying relevant norms, behaviour and compliance to the norms. Other attributes that are properties of accountability objects but are of secondary relevance are:

- **Attributability:** *the possibility to trace a given action back to a specific entity.*

This is a property of behaviour or of a norm violation. Attributability is considered of secondary relevance as it is not explicit in our definition of accountability, but is implied in the notions of responsibility and transparency. For responsibility to materialise in a meaningful way, actions have to be attributable to those responsible for them. Furthermore demonstration of this responsibility through transparency allows for accountability.

- **Observability:** *the extent to which the behaviour of the system is externally viewable.*

This is a property of behaviour of a system, service or process which describes how well the internal behaviour of a system, service or process can be described by observing the external outputs of the system, service or process. Observability is considered of secondary relevance as it is not necessary for accountability (as observability implies transparency and verifiability but the opposite is not true), even though if organisations know that they are likely to be observed then they may be more likely to behave in a responsible manner. While transparency requires an actor taking actions to be transparent, observability is more passive and the actor may not even be aware of it. It is possible to be transparent (and accountable) and non-observable, by the intervention of a third party that can observe a party instead and transfer the element of transparency.

Accountability is not a binary state, but often has many factors indicating the extent of accountability of an organisation. If accountability is seen as a process in which an organisation can mature, accountability indicators can assess the maturity of the organisation, with a focus on the mechanisms used and resultant behaviour. Accountability attributes may be defined to capture the important aspect of deployment of 'appropriate and effective measures' that meet technical, legal and ethical compliance requirements, and act as this type of indicator:

- **Appropriateness:** *the extent to which the technical and organisational measures used have the capability of contributing to accountability.*
- **Effectiveness:** *the extent to which the technical and organisational measures used actually contribute to accountability.*

By *contribute to accountability*, we mean (in the light of the analysis above) contribute to defining and displaying relevant norms, behaviour and compliance to the norms. We believe that it is acceptable to refer to accountability within these definitions since they are accountability indicators (properties of the measures used to support organisational accountability).

The cloud ecosystem not only has internal factors steering accountability, there are also some external factors that have the ability or are needed to keep the process of accountability in motion. These external factors often relate to governance mechanisms that, for example, sanction when compliance is not met. Hence there are accountability attributes that relate to the process by which the accountee holds the accountor to account. One of these is punishability, which is achieved through sanctions. Another attribute relevant to this process is verifiability, which, as already considered above, allows for the provision of evidence that compliance to the norms is (or is not) met. A further relevant attribute is liability. When an actor becomes liable for his actions, one could perceive this as a form of sanctioning. Liability is the legal obligation (either financially or with some other penalty) in connection with failure to apply the norms. It is closely related to legal responsibility (although being held liable does not necessarily mean that the same entity is actually responsible, for example, according to the DPD, data controllers are always held liable towards data subjects, even in connection with a damage actually caused by data processors), and is not referred to directly in our definition, and so could be considered to be a secondary attribute.

- **Liability:** *the state (of an organisation or individual) of being legally obligated or responsible in connection with failure to apply the norms.*

There exist emerging relationships (e.g. implication and inclusion) among the concepts described above dependent on different viewpoints of analysis (related to societal, legal and ethical aspects of accountability). For example, from a legal perspective, responsibilities imply obligations, which consequently may involve sanctions; liability is based upon the establishment of norms, allowing the request for remedies and the imposition of sanctions should these norms not be met. If the norms are not met it is not necessarily the case that all related failures can be entirely remedied (e.g. in case of a data breach the harm resulting from the disclosure of information is done and that cannot be entirely corrected). Table 4 summarises the core accountability attributes.

Table 4. Core accountability attributes

ATTRIBUTES OF (ELEMENTS OF) ACCOUNTABLE SYSTEMS	
Transparency	A property of a system, organisation or individual of providing visibility of its governing norms, behaviour and compliance of behaviour to the norms.
Responsiveness	A property of a system, organisation or individual of taking into account input from external stakeholders and responding to queries of these stakeholders.
Responsibility	A property of an organisation or individual in relation to an object, process or system of being assigned to take action to be in compliance with the norms.
Remediability	A property of a system, organisation or individual of taking corrective action and/or providing a remedy for any party harmed in case of failure to comply with its governing norms.
ATTRIBUTES OF ACCOUNTABILITY OBJECTS	
Verifiability	The extent to which it is possible to assess norm compliance.
ACCOUNTABILITY INDICATORS	
Appropriateness	The extent to which the technical and organisational measures used have the capability of contributing to accountability.
Effectiveness	The extent to which the technical and organisational measures used actually contribute to accountability.

6.2 Accountability Practices

Accountability practices, derived directly from the given definitions, characterise emerging behaviour (highlighting operational and organisational objectives to be met) manifested in accountable organisations. Specifically, an accountable organisation:

- Defines governance to responsibly comply with internal and external criteria, particularly relating to treatment of personal data and/or confidential data.
- Ensures implementation of appropriate actions.
- Explains and justifies those actions, namely, demonstrates regulatory compliance that stakeholders' expectations have been met and that organisational policies have been followed.
- Remedies any failure to act properly, for example, notifies the affected data subjects or organisations, and/or provides redress to affected data subjects or organisations, even in global situations where multiple cloud service providers are involved.

6.3 Accountability Mechanisms

The accountability model highlights 'what' needs to be implemented. Within the model, accountability mechanisms (cf. the 'how') are instances of tools and techniques supporting accountability practices (that is, high level objectives that accountable organisations need to achieve). Organisations can adopt different available accountability mechanisms as appropriate for their contexts. They will use what is best suited to their particular processes, demonstrating at the same time that the appropriate mechanisms have been selected. Accountability mechanisms focus on the core aspects of accountability (e.g. remediation, notification and risk assessment) and are expected to be used in conjunction with separate privacy and security mechanisms [26].

Mechanisms (e.g. security controls, policies, tools, standards, legal mechanisms, penalties), from a social science viewpoint, are accountability objects (*"that both inhabit several communities of practice and satisfy the information requirements of each of them"* [32]). Accountability mechanisms (developed by A4Cloud) complement others that are available from third parties. They may be used individually or in combination. Organisations may select from different alternatives. For example, they may choose to use the Privacy Level Agreement format specified by the Cloud Security Alliance (CSA) to express privacy-related obligations [33] or the Cloud Trust protocol [34] to ask for and receive information from cloud service providers about the elements of transparency, or they may take another approach to do so.

7 Accountability Framework

This section presents an accountability framework for the cloud. It describes our high level approach and how a combination of legal, governance and technical measures are used to enable chains of accountability to be built along cloud service provision chains. This section highlights that the emerging accountability framework enables cloud ecosystems to comply with relevant regulatory regimes within specific application domains. This section also explains how the emerging accountability framework supports the analysis of cloud ecosystems and emerging issues (e.g. data protection issues). The aim in particular is to strengthen the accountability of organisations that use cloud services and organisations that provide cloud services to data subjects and regulators. This section introduces an accountability framework that is based upon the defined accountability model. The accountability framework supports:

- assessment of potential *co-design* of mechanisms from different disciplines (i.e. legal, regulatory, procedural and/or technical)
- provision of *flexibility* in our approach, including 'intelligent accountability' in complex environments and incorporation of varying degrees of accountability according to the context
- assessment of *accountability in different cloud delivery and deployment models*; possibly, this could include identification of patterns and capabilities that are suitable for specific cloud computing contexts (e.g. private cloud vs. public cloud, storage-based cloud vs. flexible computing ones, etc.)
- contribution towards high-level design and architecture– mapping across to *requirements for functional components* within systems that provide accountability and starting to build a high-level, logical design structure and explaining how the component parts work together.

Accountability promotes implementation of practical mechanisms whereby legal requirements and guidance are translated into effective protection for data. Legislation and policies tend to apply at the data level, but the mechanisms can be at various levels, including the system level and data level. A toolbox of measures could be provided for data controllers, to allow construction of custom-built solutions, whereby the controllers might tailor measures to their context (e.g. taking into account consideration of the systems involved, type of data and data flows). We can co-design legal mechanisms, procedures and technical measures to support this approach. We may integrate design elements to support: prospective (and proactive) accountability, using preventive controls, and retrospective (and reactive) accountability, using detective controls.

- **Preventive Controls** – These can be used to mitigate the occurrence of an action for continuing or taking place at all (e.g. an access list that governs who may read or modify a file or database, or network and host firewalls that block all but allowable activity). The cloud is a special example of how businesses need to assess and manage risk better [35]. Preventive controls for cloud include risk analysis and decision support tools (for example, Privacy Impact Assessments), policy enforcement (for example, machine readable policies, privacy-enhanced access control and obligations), trust assessment, obfuscation techniques and identity management.
- **Detective Controls** – These are used to identify the occurrence of a privacy or security risk that goes against the privacy or security policies and procedures (for example, intrusion detection systems, policy-aware transaction logs, language frameworks and reasoning tools). Detective controls for the cloud include audit, tracking, reporting, and monitoring.
- **Corrective Controls** – These (e.g. an incident management plan, dispute resolution) are used to fix an undesired result that has already occurred.

Preventive, detective and corrective controls complement each other: a combination of these would ideally be required in order to provide accountability. Provision of accountability would not just be via procedural means, especially for cloud, which is such an automated and dynamic environment. Technology can play an important role in enhancing the solution (e.g. by enforcing policies). Procedural measures for accountability include determining the capabilities of Cloud Service Providers (CSPs) before selection, negotiating contracts and Service Level Agreements (SLAs), restricting the transfer of confidential data to CSPs and buying insurance. Organisations should also appoint a Data Protection Officer, regularly perform privacy impact assessments on new products and services, and put mechanisms in place to allow quick response to data subject access and deletion requests. Technical measures for accountability can include encryption for data security mitigation, privacy infomediaries and agents to help increase trust. We also need to be able to rely on infrastructure to maintain appropriate separations, enforce policy and report information accurately. It could be argued that the current regulatory structure places too much emphasis on remediation of problems (e.g. privacy breaches), and not enough on trying to get organisations to *do the right thing* for data protection in the first place.

Our approach involves the provision of hybrid accountability mechanisms via a combination of policies, regulatory and technical means. It is a co-regulation strategy based on a corporate responsibility model underpinned primarily by contract. This approach places the onus upon the data controller to take a more proactive approach to ensuring compliance, and encourages cloud service vendors and subcontractors to compete in providing services on the basis of evolving better privacy and security enhancing mechanisms and processes. We build upon the accountability definitions and model discussed and extend these to include prospective effects, that is to say, proactive rather than just reactive measures. This is because the policies by which we are judging our actors are constantly changing, the context and technological environment is changing and privacy-related harms to individuals are not equal. It is necessary to provide mechanisms to determine liability in the event of a breach, but we also (from the point of view of the data controller) build in processes and reinforce good practices such that the liability does not arise in the first place. We suggest ways in which an organisation might take an accountability approach further in order to develop a reflexive privacy process that is not simply a static compliance mechanism but rather that involves an on-going process of data protection monitoring and review and improvement throughout the contractual chain. Figure 6 shows examples of services supporting accountability. The identified services map to the trusted services supporting accountability that are developed by the Cloud Accountability Project or that relate directly to those. Other services could be provided and would fit into this framework, such as incident management, identity management services and certification. We provide benefits and tools for a range of different stakeholders (Fig. 6).

This model would vary according to context and depend on relevant parameters. Related questions include investigating: *To what extent do the same mechanisms apply for personal data, confidential data, sensitive info, location info, and other sensitive information? How can we put intelligence into accountability? What should underlie all scenarios? What should vary, in terms of accountability? What guidance can be given in terms of appropriate levels of external assessment and certification for different contextual types?* The functional aspects of accountability may be achieved by mechanisms in the following way:

- **Proper allocation of responsibilities** – via management support, allocation of responsibilities for data protection within an organisation and clarification of responsibilities across supply chains.

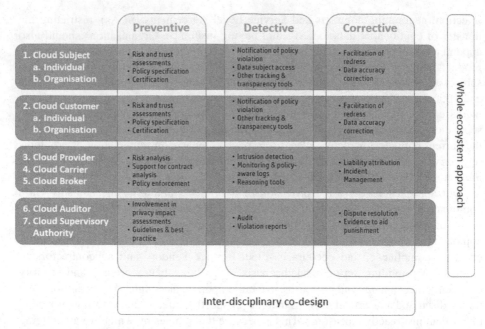

	Preventive	Detective	Corrective
1. Cloud Subject **a. Individual** **b. Organisation**	• Risk and trust assessments • Policy specification • Certification	• Notification of policy violation • Data subject access • Other tracking & transparency tools	• Facilitation of redress • Data accuracy correction
2. Cloud Customer **a. Individual** **b. Organisation**	• Risk and trust assessments • Policy specification • Certification	• Notification of policy violation • Other tracking & transparency tools	• Facilitation of redress • Data accuracy correction
3. Cloud Provider **4. Cloud Carrier** **5. Cloud Broker**	• Risk analysis • Support for contract analysis • Policy enforcement	• Intrusion detection • Monitoring & policy-aware logs • Reasoning tools	• Liability attribution • Incident Management
6. Cloud Auditor **7. Cloud Supervisory Authority**	• Involvement in privacy impact assessments • Guidelines & best practice	• Audit • Violation reports	• Dispute resolution • Evidence to aid punishment

Whole ecosystem approach

Inter-disciplinary co-design

Fig. 6. Accountability framework

- **Definition of the contextual obligations to be followed** (carried out by organisations and reflecting stakeholder and regulatory requirements) – via formation of appropriate organisational policies, contracts, stakeholder engagement.
- **Risk and trust assessment to decide which mechanisms to use in the given context to meet the policies** – via risk identification/assessment, trust assessment, appropriate choice of business partners.
- **Deployment of appropriate privacy and security controls** (these are the mechanisms determined above and include means to make uses transparent to individuals and to assure that their rights are respected) – via security and privacy best practice, including transparency tools.
- **Monitoring data practices** (by organisations and by regulatory oversight) – via tracking tools.
- **Detection of policy violations** – via audit and violation detection tools (e.g. evidence collection).
- **Correction of policy violations** – via remediation and/or compensation.
- **Reporting of policy violations** – via breach notification and transparency tools.
- **Demonstration of policy compliance** (including that policies defined by organisations are appropriate, the mechanisms used are appropriate for the context and that the operational environment is satisfying the policies) – via provision of trustworthy account, verification (about appropriate use of privacy and security controls), certification, provision of evidence about satisfaction of obligations along service provision chains, transparency tools.

Not only are mechanisms to achieve this run within different types of organisation, but others are kinds of meta-mechanisms that can bridge across organisations, for example helping with clarifying responsibilities, or with the verification process.

8 Accountability Governance

Accountable organisations need to define and implement appropriate governance mechanisms relating to treatment of personal and/or confidential data in cloud environments. *"Cloud governance encompasses two main areas: internal governance focuses on a provider's technical working of cloud services, its business operations, and the ways it manages its relationship with customers and other external stakeholders; and external governance consists of norms, rules, and regulations which define the relationships between members of the cloud community and attempt to solve disputes between them"* [36]. All actors involved in the cloud – customers, service providers, and supervisory authorities (whether individual cloud customers, businesses, public organisations and even other cloud service providers) – and those directly involved in governance have a role to play in making cloud services accountable for how data is used and managed in the cloud. Inspired by the NIST definition of Information Security Governance [37], accountability governance can be defined as the process of establishing and maintaining a framework and supporting management structure and processes, as well as accepting and providing assignment of responsibility to:

- provide stewardship of personal and confidential data with which the organisation is entrusted,
- processing, sharing, storing and otherwise using said data according to contractual and legal requirements, from the time it is collected until when the data is destroyed (including onward transfer to and from third parties),
- comply with legal, ethical and moral obligations, policies, procedures and mechanisms,
- explain and demonstrate ethical implementation to internal and external stakeholders and remedy any failure to act properly.

In essence, accountability governance consists in accepting responsibility for accountability objectives, and in establishing and sponsoring the operational structure and process to meet these objectives. The board (or equivalent executive leadership) of the organisation is responsible for governance. It can (and usually does) create management structures to assign authority in the implementation of the oversight and processes identified. However, it ultimately remains responsible and accountable for meeting these objectives [38]. Nothing in this definition is dependent on the mechanisms used to store or process the data. The accountability governance objectives do not depend on whether data processing uses cloud computing. However, cloud has a strong impact on how governance is implemented. In a simplified view, accountability is modelled as a relationship between two parties: the first party (the application provider) is accountable to another party (the customer) for something (in this case, handling data in a defined manner). These roles bear a strong relationship to the roles defined in data protection legislation; the first party might be a data controller and the second a data subject. This relationship can be defined across multiple dimensions:

- **Legal:** laws and regulations assign responsibilities and obligations to both parties.
- **Contractual:** the use of cloud services is done in the context of an agreement between the cloud customer and the cloud provider. This agreement can take many forms, for example, a negotiated contract or terms and conditions applicable to all cloud users.
- **Technical:** the cloud service offers a set of functionalities, which are accessed through a defined interface. This interface is provided by the cloud provider and is invoked by the cloud customer, hence creating the relationship.
- **Administrative:** operators and administrators can only manage the resources placed under their administrative control. Administrative domains define which resources are in the control of which party.

Figure 7 shows the interaction between two organisations (as a continuous process) driven by accountability governance (constrained by external criteria and regulatory regimes but orchestrated independently by organisations). Organisation A could be part of a service provision chain that involves cloud service providers and Organisation B is actually an oversight and enforcement actor (e.g. regulator) in the chain. Organisation A defines and implements appropriate governance mechanisms, which enable demonstration of governance. Organisation B, in holding to account Organisation A, can ask for further clarification, engage in discussions and also (request to) apply sanctions. As a result, Organisation A may modify its own organisational governance. In summary, accountability governance consists of taking responsibilities for specific accountability criteria, ensuring them by deploying suitable mechanisms and demonstrating their appropriateness and effectiveness by evidence.

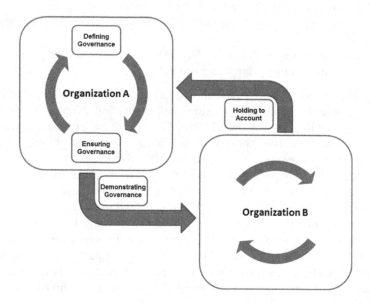

Fig. 7. Accountability Governance

Organisations need to provide transparency of those actions taken in order to show that stakeholders' expectations have been met and that organisational policies have been followed. They also need to remedy any failure to act properly (e.g. by notifications, remedies, sanctions) even in cloud-supply chains involving multiple service providers. Accountability governance redefines interactions between providers and regulators as well as between providers themselves. The ethical nature of an accountability-based approach and the organisational obligations that result from taking this approach represent a shift from reactive to proactive governance of personal and/or confidential data. Organisations commit to the stewardship of personal and/or confidential data by addressing legal, contractual and ethical obligations. Organisations deploy and use different mechanisms (e.g. policies), take into account social norms, provide evidence to internal and external stakeholders, and remedy any failure to act properly. While accountability may not typically be composed; i.e. it is primarily a bilateral relationship, the ability to behave in an accountable manner in the context of the cloud depends on cloud services supporting accountability attributes, such as transparency.

9 Dealing with Emerging Threats in Cloud Ecosystems

Let us now consider the accountability relationships between the various actors in a cloud ecosystem (such as those illustrated by Fig. 8). Every party of the cloud service is called to be accountable to other parties. Figure 8 shows some examples of threats (e.g. loss of governance, lock in hazard, incomplete data deletion) in cloud ecosystems. The threats are drawn from existing risk analyses of cloud computing [23, 39–41]. ENISA further reviewed emerging threats in order to point out potential risks and highlight areas for mitigations [42].

Cloud customers and providers are exposed to various problems. For instance, from a resource viewpoint, an increasing amount of data and resources may require new mechanisms enabling cost-effective management while guaranteeing critical features like security and privacy. From the viewpoint of security, privacy or trustworthiness, some of the issues that consumers and regulators are mostly concerned about are things like lack of transparency and control in cloud service provision [39], as well as worries about increased unwanted access to their data by third parties, including governments. The compliance with multiple jurisdictional requirements may also exacerbate complexities from a legal perspective [11]. Such challenges are perceived as barriers to the adoption of cloud computing.

There are different obligations according to the roles that apply in a given scenario. The DC is accountable for applicable data protection measures. The cloud providers as DPs must provide security measures, and their responsibilities will vary according to the combination of cloud service and deployment models. For example, Platform as a Service (PaaS) providers are responsible for the security of the platform software stack and Software as a Service (SaaS) providers are responsible for security applications delivered to end users. The lower down the stack the cloud provider stops, the more security the consumer is tactically responsible for implementing and managing. The liabilities involved are expressed within contracts as there can be ramifications of failure within cloud ecosystems, affecting other parties. The DPs are accountable for

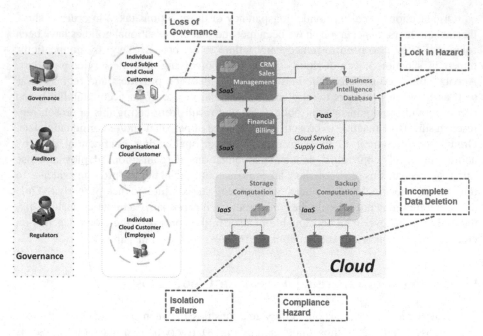

Fig. 8. Emerging threats in cloud ecosystems

co-operation with the DC to meet data subjects' rights, assist the DC in providing security measures, and should act only on the DC's behalf. Thus, there are chains of accountability through the cloud service supply chains to the cloud customer.

In addition, cloud providers and customers are accountable to the actors involved in governance and enforcement (as shown on the left hand side of Fig. 8). These include regulators, stakeholders and society, as well as auditors and business governance. These are especially interested in monitoring and measuring non-functional aspects, leaving it to the service providers to determine how they actually want to achieve those. The organisational cloud customer is in general accountable to these governance entities for applicable data protection measures. All actors in the supply chain are ultimately accountable to the cloud subject. Extending the accountability relationship between cloud providers and cloud consumers to the provider's responsibility to society at large provides a broader perspective on the need for accountability in the cloud. Hence, most of the data protection risks associated with cloud should be reduced by contractual provisions that can include penalties for the service provider, and by technical and organisational measures for the customer and the service provider. If the DC is ultimately made accountable for meeting obligations right along the service provision chain, it should try to obtain contractual assurances that lessen the risk of potential weak links in dynamically formed cloud provider chains. That is, contractual agreements between the series of actors taking part in the cloud chain should provide for the accountability obligations of DCs ultimately owed to data subjects.

Accountability can be achieved via a combination of public accountability – derived from transparent interaction (between subjects of personal data, supervisory authorities, regulatory bodies and DCs), legislation, soft regulation, on-going Privacy Impact Assessments (PIAs), certification, audit and public policy – and private accountability –derived from interactions between DCs and data processors (premised on contract law, technological processes and practical internal compliance requirements) [10]. Furthermore, we advocate the combination of a strong and soft approach to support accountability provision. The soft approach relates to addressing how accountability can be achieved in a socially beneficial way, including ethical governance and the democratic aspect. The strong approach involves supporting accountability of practice, provision and analysis of trusted evidence to show whether or not data protection obligations have been fulfilled, verification by independent, trusted entities and certification based on such verification.

9.1   Risk Assessment

Accountability, as articulated by the Article 29 Working Party [4], begins to shift our thinking from only having an obligation to comply with a principle, to an obligation to prove that you can put those principles into effect. Risk assessment is therefore particularly important for accountability, because it is a central part of the process used to determine and demonstrate that the policies (whether reflected in corporate privacy and security policies or in contractual obligations) that are signed up to and the corresponding practices that are implemented by an organisation (adopting an accountability-based approach) are effective and appropriate to the context [43, 44]. On-going risk assessment and mitigation relating to new products or processes, as well as regular risk assessment and validation of the accountability program, are captured within the core elements of implementing an accountability project within an organisation specified within the Galway Project [8]. These core elements of implementing an accountability project within an organisation [8], are very similar to the guidance provided by the Privacy Commissioners of Canada, Alberta and British Columbia [45], which also emphasises the need for risk assessment, as does the revised OECD guidelines [16], which now recommend the practical implementation of privacy protection through an approach grounded in risk management and stress the need for improved global interoperability. The type of procedures and mechanisms employed by an organisation could vary according to the risks represented by the processing and the nature of the data [22, 23, 26, 46, 47]. Automation can enhance this process [9]. Data impact assessment may also become an obligation for some high risk contexts within the GDPR [17].

Risk assessment within an organisation can potentially be extended to encompass both pre-emptive approaches (to assess risk and avoid privacy harm) and reactive approaches that provide transparency and audit. Furthermore, the privacy policies and mechanisms need to take into account the entire life cycle. Companies need to think about what data they will collect and how they plan to use it, but also what the potential harms are for individuals. It is the data subject that is in a sense the real owner of data, who ultimately is harmed in case of failure and who should be empowered and supported. For example, if you are tracking someone online then under an accountability approach you might include clear notice that tracking is happening, how the tracking data will be used, as a mechanism for individuals to choose not to be tracked and to request previous tracking data to be deleted.

The Privacy Impact Assessment (PIA) process (incorporating privacy by design to help organisations assess the impact of their operations on personal privacy) assesses the privacy requirements of new and existing systems. It is primarily intended for use in public sector risk management, but is increasingly seen to be of value to private sector businesses that process personal data. Similar methodologies exist and can have legal status in Australia, Canada and the US [48]. The methodology aims to combat the slow take-up to design in privacy protections from first principles at the enterprise level. Usage is increasingly being encouraged and even mandated in certain circumstances by regulators [48].

PIAs are regarded as an essential tool for implementing the accountability principle and demonstrating compliance [4, 17], where PIAs based on self-verification by or on behalf of data controllers are proposed for higher risk data processing operations. The Article 29 WP Opinion 3/2010 on the Principle of Accountability states that [4]: *"As a complement to the principle, specific additional requirements aiming at putting into effect data protection safeguards or at ensuring their effectiveness could be set up. One example would be a provision requiring the performance of a privacy impact assessment for higher risk data processing operations"*. In addition to this, data impact assessment may also become an obligation for some high risk contexts within the forthcoming GDPR [17]. The proposed GDPR [17] introduces a risk-based approach to PIAs (namely, Data Protection Impact Assessments, or DPIAs). Prior to processing of personal data, a DPIA is required if the processing is likely to present specific risks for the rights and freedoms of data subjects, taking into account the nature, scope and purpose of the data processing.

However, there is still no consensus on the final legal provisions. Existing organisational risk assessment processes need to be enhanced to meet the requirements above, or else supplemented with separate privacy-specific risk assessment [48]. The UK Information Commissioners' Office (ICO) – an organisation responsible for regulating and enforcing access to and use of personal information – have already rolled out a process to encourage privacy by design guidelines on privacy impact assessments [49], and a number of standards and tools related to PIAs exist [50].

Risk assessment must be extended right along the service provision chain: in order to implement a chain of accountability for the non-functional attributes of an ICT system, it must be possible to measure those attributes in a meaningful way. However, this is non-trivial. For example, liability assignment is currently particularly difficult in an international context where business relations are negotiated and regulated by contracts, and there are differences among the countries with respect to legal framework and regulations. Furthermore, it is very difficult and resource-demanding to detect and then prove that electronic data has been compromised and to identify the perpetrator. What is reported to the police is just a small percentage of all violations detected. In addition, risk allocation is (for large deals) negotiated individually in contracts, so that a single provider will have a different risk allocation scheme with each of its major customers. Law and regulation differs between countries, so that there is no single scheme of risks to be addressed, or single view on liability if those risks eventuate (note that there are also worries about how exactly privacy impacts would be measured and taken into account, even if a PIA were carried out).

Current risk assessment methods have not been designed for use in a cloud computing setting, and there is at the moment no methodology or tool developed for assessing and predicting risks related to accountability of cloud services. Even in a non-cloud environment, automation of privacy impact assessment is not yet mature [51]. Practical challenges include whether objective or subjective harm (e.g. material tangible harm to individuals, moral non-tangible harm to individuals, and harm to democratic and societal values of a free society) can be used as a basis for evaluation, and how this could be encoded. An additional challenge relates to what the evidence looks like that is provided by DPIAs to external parties, and how important organisational criteria and choices in this decision making process can get exposed to other parties. Related to this issue, self-verification through PIAs could involve a transparency duty with regard to the outcome of the PIAs (e.g. public PIA registers), but this is not even specified from the regulatory side and the situation is unclear.

A further challenge relates to the way in which verification is provided that the measures used (potentially across a supply chain network) are appropriate for the context. The intention of using risk management is to mitigate risks and to identify operational trade-offs, that is, what it is reasonably feasible to achieve in terms of protections with respect to emerging security and privacy threats [39]. Within organisational risk management processes, security and privacy policies are translated into implementable solutions that make use of specific mechanisms (e.g. security controls) in order to monitor and enforce operationally the implementation of such policies. Detected policy violations are then assessed as part of the risk management. Gathering evidence is central for organisational risk management processes [45]. On the one hand, evidence provides valuable information to risk management. On the other hand, evidence would support assurance – *"Assurance is about providing confidence to stakeholders that the qualities of service and stewardship with which they are concerned are being managed and maintained appropriately"* [35]. This is also particularly important when dealing with emergent digital risk [52] due (to a certain extent) to the shift required while deploying new technological paradigms like cloud computing. This is also relevant in the case of supply chain risk management [53].

Risk assessment is a preventative accountability measure that helps prevent risky actions happening. It is also used to demonstrate how the security and privacy mechanisms used are appropriate for the context. Cloud Service Provider (CSP) chains should be taken into account within the analysis. Accountability functionality must also be part of the solution, so accountability requirements should be part of the output of the risk assessment process – *"can we predict how risky it is to provide our personal data to an entity or organisation?"* [54]. Among the main challenges of risk assessment are: risk assessment across CSP chains [53], assessment of social harms (different *"types of harm may directly or indirectly affect individuals"* [54]), output as part of a design process and output as part of the account/verification process. Risk assessment is also concerned with the problem of lack of trust in the cloud, as discussed in the next section.

9.2   Accountability, Risk and Trust

The relationship between risk and trust has been considered (in particular, from social and policy perspectives) to underpin the governance of privacy [55]. Both risk (management) and trust (promotion) provide alternative viewpoints of analysis. Having recognized that *"the problem of privacy is socially and politically constructed"* [55], it is necessary to balance objective evidence with subjective perceptions while dealing with policy governance. Objective evidence is derived from mechanisms that can be implemented and monitored in the cloud [56]. For instance, the work in [57] provides an example of a mechanism that may be implemented by cloud providers and used by cloud customers in order to gather objective evidence and obtain assurance about running services (e.g. assurance that cloud services comply with relevant national jurisdictions). Other similar mechanisms can be utilized to provide further transparency, which is part of accountability, to cloud customers. Approaches (like risk assessment) promoting transparency (of information) would support *"better understanding of exposures to privacy dangers, the distribution of risks, and the patterning of trusting [that] may be worth seeking"* [55]. In this respect, accountability (as promoting transparency) is critical for supporting governance of privacy, data protection and security in the cloud [6]. In general, accountability needs to mitigate risk, hence suggesting trust or mistrust depending on the supported accountability in practice. The problem then is to understand how accountability mechanisms mitigate specific risks – *How does accountability address emerging threats?*

In particular, we need to make explicit the relationships between the different aspects of the accountability model (and the associated framework) mitigating the emerging threats in the cloud. For instance, the CSA Cloud Control Matrix [58] identifies specific controls (e.g. Governance and Risk Management, Legal & Standards Compliance, Supply Chain Management, Transparency and Accountability) that relate directly to aspects of accountability. Mapping accountability to specific mechanisms (and explaining how they mitigate risks) highlights how accountability (if successfully supported) contributes to mitigate a broad range of risks, encompassing privacy and security. Accountability mechanisms complement privacy and security controls. Therefore, a combination of accountability, privacy and security controls are necessary in order to mitigate and address emerging risks. An accountability assessment with respect to risk then consists in assessing whether or not relationships between assets and accountability are successfully supported. If accountability is successfully supported, the result would be to mitigate risks and to enhance trustworthiness and transparency.

We have collected and analysed stakeholders' feedback in order to gather accountability requirements for cloud services [31]. The analysis of the accountability requirements points out emerging relationships between accountability, risk and trust and the way in which they underpin accountability governance. Stakeholders, attending dedicated workshops, involved organisational cloud customers, cloud providers, data protection authorizes and researchers [59]. Stakeholders agree that trust facilitates interactions between cloud actors. They additionally point out that trust is related to the context of the interaction (that is, the actors in a cloud supply chain, cloud ecosystem), whereas risk is context free (that is, risks are perceived to be independent from the specific cloud ecosystem, not necessarily the likelihood and or the impact of such risks).

High risk levels would affect trustworthiness. The relationship between accountability and risk stimulated interesting discussions too.

Stakeholders affirmed that accountability will enhance trustworthiness and change risk perception [59] – *"responding to perceived risk can lead to less secure solutions, instead of optimal controls"*, hence *"reduced perceived risk will increase cloud adoption, increased transparency will mean increased usage"*. On the relationship between accountability and trust, stakeholders agreed that accountability supports trust decisions and enhances cloud trustworthiness. They also highlighted that *"accountability is a good starting point to trust but not the answer"*, that is, being accountable for specific actions is essential but not sufficient for being trusted. Stakeholders confirmed that *"accountability is very important"* and influences trust in cloud services. Enhancing trustworthiness will have also an effect on risk due to trust decisions. In summary, stakeholders articulated accountability, risk and trust as follows:

- **Accountability** – The term accountability is understood differently by stakeholders. There is not yet a shared understanding of the accountability concept itself. Stakeholders recognize different attributes (or elements) such as responsibility and liability contributing to accountability. However, they understand the contributions of such attributes toward accountability in different ways. This depends on their background and expertise. There were no major objections about the presented accountability model. A structured representation of accountability would support discussions on accountability and building a shared understanding of the concept itself. Other comments were concerned with the relationship between accountability, risk and trust. There was a convergent understanding that the relationships between accountability and risk and accountability and trust are different (in the sense of having a different nature).
- **Accountability and Risk** – Although accountability addresses risk, it is as yet unclear how. The relationship between accountability and risk is a generalized one. That is, it is believed that accountability addresses emergent risks affecting security and privacy in cloud ecosystems. However, stakeholders had difficulties in figuring out in which way. This is probably due to the fact that the concepts were presented in general terms and in the context of an accountability-based approach to risk and trust. Future work would need to identify clear examples of the effect of accountability on risk. Stakeholders questioned whether accountability addresses risk (by modifying risk profiles in terms of likelihood of occurrence or severity of impact) or changes risk perception of emerging threats in cloud ecosystems. This is another interesting aspect of the relationship between accountability and risk that requires further investigation.
- **Accountability and Trust** – The relationship between accountability and trust seems to be more context-dependent than the one with risk. Accountability helps to make trust decisions. However, accountability itself seems to be necessary but not sufficient for trust (or to imply trust unconditionally). This agrees with research on the data protection implications of accountable surveillance practices – *"Accountability is however only part of the solution and only contributes to generate trust in institutions and market players engaged in surveillance to the extent that these are compelled to give an account of their practices."* [60]. A critical aspect of trust

seems to be related to the evidence provided to stakeholders. Such accountability evidence is often associated to the implementation of privacy by design principles and the adoption of specific mechanisms [61]. Therefore, accountability (in particular transparency) plays an important role in trust decisions and can support trustworthiness (in particular based on accountability evidence).

The emerging relationships between accountability, risk and trust underpin the accountability-based approach to data governance in the cloud.

10 Concluding Remarks

This paper has discussed various drivers for accountability in the cloud. Adopting the cloud involves transfers of personal and/or confidential data, hence a loss of governance over the way data is managed and controlled in the cloud. Different regulatory regimes at the national and international level combined with potential threats affecting the cloud represent barriers to cloud adoption. Accountability has emerged as a critical aspect of data governance in the cloud. This paper introduces the foundations of an accountability-based approach to data governance in the cloud. Based on our accountability definitions, one independent from the application domain and another tailored to the cloud, the paper introduces an accountability model consisting of accountability attributes, practices and mechanisms. The model provides the basis for an accountability framework supporting cloud actors by different means across cloud supply chains and hence supporting accountability chains. The analysis of accountability provided across cloud supply chains points out various aspects concerned with the different cloud roles and data protection roles of cloud actors.

The discussion of emergent threats in cloud ecosystems highlights the role of risk assessment within an accountability-based approach. It also points out insights about how accountability, risk and trust relate to each other. In order to be accountable, organisations need to deploy mechanisms (e.g. tools and controls) that are suitable for cloud ecosystems and proportionate to the threats. The deployment of such mechanisms intends to mitigate the risks, and to enhance transparency of data stewardship in the cloud. Risk assessment has a critical role in identifying suitable mechanisms. In addition, certification involves scrutiny by third parties that the identified mechanisms are implemented and that organisational practices comply with regulatory regimes [62]. For instance, the CSA STAR (Security, Trust & Assurance Registry) relies on a three-level Open Certification Framework [63], which assesses and documents how organisations implement security controls identified by the Cloud Control Matrix [58]. However, in order to maintain continuous monitoring as well as to enhance transparency and assurance, specific mechanisms supporting automation and evidence gathering are necessary [64]. An accountability-based approach, such as the one introduced in this paper, is necessary in order to support data stewardship in the cloud. In summary, this paper introduces and discusses an accountability-based approach to data governance in the cloud. The proposed approach is based on an accountability model and framework enabling accountability in cloud ecosystems.

Acknowledgements. This work has been partly funded from the European Commission's Seventh Framework Programme (FP7/2007-2013), grant agreement 317550, Cloud Accountability Project – http://www.a4cloud.eu/ – (A4Cloud). We would like to thank our project partners and colleagues who contributed to the accountability-based approach presented in this paper, in particular, we acknowledge the contributions of Brian Dziminski, Carmen Fernandez Gago, Simone Fischer-Hübner, Frederic Gittler, Martin Jaatun, Theo Koulouris, Ronald Leenes, Jesus Luna, Maartje Niezen, David Nuñez, Alain Pannetrat, Jenni Reuben Shanthamoorthy, Jean-Claude Royer, Anderson Santana de Oliviera, Dimitra Stefanatou and Vasilis Tountopoulos.

References

1. Mell, P., Grance, T.: The NIST Definition of Cloud Computing. National Institute of Standards and Technology, NIST Special Publication 800-145 (2011)
2. Cloud Computing Use Case Discussion Group: Cloud Computing Use Cases White Paper, Version 4.0 (2010)
3. Papanikolaou, N., Pearson, S.: A cross-disciplinary review of the concept of accountability: a survey of the literature. In: International Workshop on Trustworthiness, Accountability and Forensics in the Cloud (TAFC), Malaga (2013)
4. Article 29 Data Protection Working Party: Opinion 3/2010 on the Principle of Accountability, 00062/10/EN WP 173 (2010)
5. Article 29 Data Protection Working Party: Opinion 05/2012 on Cloud Computing, 05/12/EN WP 196 (2012)
6. Guagnin, D., et al. (eds.): Managing Privacy Through Accountability. Palgrave Macmillan (2012)
7. Organisation for Economic Co-operation and Development (OECD): OECD Guidelines on the Protection of Privacy and Transborder Flows of Personal Data (1980)
8. Galway Project: Accountability: A Compendium for Stakeholders. The Centre for Information Policy Leadership LLP (2011)
9. Pearson, S.: Toward accountability in the cloud. IEEE Internet Comput. **15**(4), 64–69 (2011). IEEE
10. Charlesworth, A., Pearson, S.: Developing accountability-based solutions for data privacy in the cloud. Innovation, Spec. Issue Priv. Technol. Eur. J Soc. Sci. Res. **26**(1), 7–35 (2013). Taylor & Francis
11. Felici, M., Jaatun, M.G., Kosta, E., Wainwright, N.: Bringing Accountability to the Cloud: Addressing Emerging Threats and Legal Perspectives. In: Felici, M. (ed.) CSP EU FORUM 2013. CCIS, vol. 182, pp. 28–40. Springer, Heidelberg (2013)
12. Directive 95/46/EC of the European Parliament and of the Council of 24 October 1995 on the protection of individuals with regard to the processing of personal data and on the free movement of such data. Official Journal L 281, 23 Nov 1995, pp. 0031–0050 (1995)
13. Felici, M., Koulouris, T., Pearson, S.: Accountability for data governance in cloud ecosystems. In: 2013 IEEE 5th International Conference on Cloud Computing Technology and Science (CloudCom 2013), vol. 2, pp. 327–332. IEEE (2013)
14. Article 29 Data Protection Working Party: Opinion 1/2010 on the concepts of "controller" and "processor", 00264/10/EN (2010)
15. Badger, L., et al.: Cloud Computing Synopsis and Recommendations. NIST Special Publication 800-146 (2012)
16. OECD: The OECD Privacy Framework. Organisation for Economic Co-operation and Development (2013)

17. European Commission: Proposal for a directive of the European Parliament and of the council on the protection of individuals with regard to the processing of personal data by competent authorities for the purposes of prevention, investigation, detection or prosecution of criminal offences or the execution of criminal penalties, and the free movement of such data (2012)
18. European Commission: Unleashing the Potential of Cloud Computing in Europe (2012)
19. European Commission: Cybersecurity Strategy of the European Union: An Open, Safe and Secure Cyberspace (2013)
20. European Commission: Directive on Network and Information Security (2013)
21. Jansen, W., Grance, T.: Guidelines on Security and Privacy in Public Cloud Computing, NIST SP 800-144 (2011)
22. CNIL: Recommendations for Companies Planning to Use Cloud Computing Services, Commission nationale de l'informatique et des libertés (2012)
23. Catteddu, D., Hogben, G. (eds.): Cloud Computing: Benefits, Risks and Recommendations for Information Security. ENISA Report (2009)
24. Bovens, M.: Analysing and assessing accountability: A conceptual framework. Eur. Law J. 13(4), 447–468 (2007)
25. Bovens, M.: Two concepts of accountability: accountability as a virtue and as a mechanism. Spec. Issue Account. Eur. Gov. West Eur. Politics 33(5), 946–967 (2010)
26. Pearson, S.: On the relationship between the different methods to address privacy issues in the cloud. In: Meersman, R., Panetto, H., Dillon, T., Eder, J., Bellahsene, Z., Ritter, N., De Leenheer, P., Dou, D. (eds.) ODBASE 2013. LNCS, vol. 8185, pp. 414–433. Springer, Heidelberg (2013)
27. Butin, D., Chicote, M., Le Métayer, D.: Strong accountability: beyond vague promises. In: Gutwirth, S., Leenes, R., De Hert, P. (eds.) Reloading Data Protection: Multidisciplinary Insights and Contemporary Challenges, pp. 343–369. Springer, Netherlands (2014)
28. Van Alsenoy, B.: Allocating responsibility among controllers, processors, and "everything in between": the definition of actors and roles in Directive 95/46/EC. Comput. Law Secur. Rev. 28(1), 25–43 (2012)
29. Guagnin, D., Hempel, L., Ilten, C.: Bridging the gap: We need to get together. In: Guagnin, D., et al. (eds.) Managing Privacy through Accountability, pp. 102–124. Palgrave (2012)
30. Liu, F., et al.: NIST Cloud Computing Reference Architecture. National Institute of Standards and Technology, NIST Special Publication 500-292 (2011)
31. Jaatun, M.G., Pearson, S., Gittler, F., Leenes, R.: Towards strong accountability for cloud service providers. In: 2014 IEEE 6th International Conference on Cloud Computing Technology and Science (CloudCom 2014). IEEE (2014)
32. Bowker, G.C., Star, S.L.: Sorting Things Out: Classification and Its Consequences. The MIT Press, Cambridge (1999)
33. CSA: Privacy Level Agreement Outline for the Sale of Cloud Services in the European Union. Cloud Security Alliance, Privacy Level Agreement Working Group (2013)
34. Knode, R., Egan, D.: Digital Trust in the Cloud: A Precis for the CloudTrust Protocol, v2.0. Computer Science Corporation (2010)
35. Baldwin, A., Pym, D., Shiu, S.: Enterprise information risk management: Dealing with cloud computing. In: Pearson, S., Yee, G. (eds.) Privacy and Security for Cloud Computing. Springer, Heidelberg (2013)
36. Reed, C.: Cloud Governance: The Way Forward. In: Millard, C. (ed.) Cloud Computing Law. Oxford University Press, Oxford (2013)
37. Bowen, P., Hash, J., Wilson, M.: Information Security Handbook: A Guide for Managers. National Institute of Standards and Technology, NIST Special Publication 800–100 (2006)
38. De Clercq, J., et al.: The HP Security Handbook. HP publication 4AA1-7729EEW (2008)

39. CSA: The Notorious Nine: Cloud Computing Top Threats in 2013. Cloud Security Alliance, Top Threats Working Group (2013)
40. CSA: Top Ten Big Data Security and Privacy Challenges. Cloud Security Alliance (2012)
41. CSA: Security Guidance for Critical Areas of Focus in Cloud Computing V3.0, Cloud Security Alliance (2011)
42. ENISA: ENISA Threat Landscape 2013 – Overview of current and emerging cyber-threats. European Network and Information Security Agency (2013)
43. Article 29 Data Protection Working Party: Statement on the role of a risk-based approach in data protection legal frameworks, 14/EN WP 218 (2014)
44. CIPL: A Risk-based Approach to Privacy: Improving Effectiveness in Practice. Centre for Information Policy Leadership (2014)
45. Office of the Information and Privacy Commissioner of Alberta, Office of the Privacy Commissioner of Canada, Office of the Information and Privacy Commissioner for British Colombia: Getting Accountability Right with a Privacy Management Program (2012)
46. ENISA: Privacy, Accountability and Trust – Challenges and Opportunities. European Network and Information Security Agency (2011)
47. Pearson, S.: Privacy management in global organisations. In: De Decker, B., Chadwick, D.W. (eds.) CMS 2012. LNCS, vol. 7394, pp. 217–237. Springer, Heidelberg (2012)
48. Tancock, D., Pearson, S., Charlesworth, A.: Analysis of privacy impact assessments within major jurisdictions. In: Proceedings of the 2010 Eighth Annual International Conference on Privacy Security and Trust (PST), pp. 118–125. IEEE (2010)
49. Trilateral Research & Consulting: Privacy Impact Assessment and Risk Management. UK Information Commissioner's Office (ICO) (2013)
50. ICO: Data Protection Act – Conducting privacy impact assessments code of practice. UK Information Commissioner's Office (ICO) (2013)
51. Pearson, S., Sander, T.: A decision support system for privacy compliance. In: Gupta, M., Walp, J., Sharman, R. (eds.) Data Mining: Concepts, Methodologies, Tools, and Applications, pp. 1496–1518. IGI Global, New York (2013)
52. Lloyd's: Lloyd's 360° Risk Insight Managing Digital Risk: Trends, Issues and Implications for Business (2010)
53. Boyens, J., et al.: Supply Chain Risk Management: Practices for Federal Information Systems and Organizations, pp. 800–161. NIST Special Publication (2013)
54. Robinson, N., et al.: Review of the European Data Protection Directive. RAND Europe, Cambridge (2009)
55. Bennett, C.J., Raab, C.D.: The Governance of Privacy: Policy Instruments in Global Perspective. The MIT Press, Cambridge (2006)
56. Pearson, S.: Privacy, security and trust in cloud computing. In: Pearson, S., Yee, G. (eds.) Privacy and Security for Cloud Computing, Computer Communications and Networks, pp. 3–42. Springer, Heidelberg (2013)
57. Schiffman, J., et al.: Cloud Verifier: Verifiable Auditing Service for IaaS Clouds. In: IEEE Ninth World Congress on Services (SERVICES 2013), pp. 239–246, IEEE Computer Society (2013)
58. CSA: Cloud Control Matrix. Cloud Security Alliance, CSA CCM v3.0 (2013)
59. Felici, M., Pearson, S.: Accountability, risk, and trust in cloud services: Towards an accountability-based approach to risk and trust governance. In: 2014 IEEE World Congress on Services (SERVICES), pp. 105–112. IEEE (2014)
60. Coudert, F.: Accountable surveillance practices: Is the EU moving in the right direction? In: Preneel, B., Ikonomou, D. (eds.) APF 2014. LNCS, vol. 8450, pp. 70–85. Springer, Heidelberg (2014)

61. Antignac, T., Le Métayer, D.: Privacy by design: From technologies to architectures. In: Preneel, B., Ikonomou, D. (eds.) APF 2014. LNCS, vol. 8450, pp. 1–17. Springer, Heidelberg (2014)
62. Sunyaev, A., Schneider, S.: Cloud services certification. Commun. ACM **56**(2), 33–36 (2013). ACM
63. CSA: CSA STAR – Security, Trust and Assurance Registry (STAR) Overview. Cloud Security Alliance (2014)
64. Anisetti, M., et al.: A test-based security certification scheme for web services. ACM Trans. Web (TWEB) **7**(2), 1–41 (2013). Article 5, ACM

Security in the Cloud

On the Adoption of Security SLAs in the Cloud

Valentina Casola[1]([⊠]), Alessandra De Benedictis[1], and Massimiliano Rak[2]

[1] Universita' di Napoli Federico II, Naples, Italy
{valentina.casola,alessandra.debenedictis}@unina.it
[2] Seconda Universita' di Napoli, Caserta, Italy
massimiliano.rak@unina2.it

Abstract. Can security be provided as-a-Service? Is it possible to cover a security service by a proper Service Level Agreement? This paper tries to reply to these questions by presenting some ongoing research activities from standardization bodies and academia, trying to cope with the open issues in the management of Security Service Level Agreement in its whole life cycle, made of negotiation, enforcement and monitoring phases.

Keywords: Service Level Agreement · Security SLA · Cloud computing · SLA life cycle

1 Introduction

Security still represents one of the main limits in the adoption of cloud computing. It is not rare the case where cloud service providers (CSPs) offer *non-transparent* security mechanisms, embedded in the systems, which are non-negotiable and, above all, vulnerable. The common approach followed by CSPs is a yes/no solution: they provide (or they declare that they provide) the higher security level available with their technological solutions. As a consequence, customers have a very limited set of offerings in terms of security features, often without real grants about the way in which such mechanisms are actually implemented and granted. Nonetheless, it would be desirable to have security being considered exactly as all the other parameters: we want to negotiate security like all other service terms, and we need a way to let users be aware of what kind of security mechanisms are being put in place to protect their data and applications. At the end of the day, we want to offer Security-as-a-Service and, as for all the other services, we want to deliver it under the control of SLAs. The problem is that currently the SLAs are mainly focused on service-related aspects such as performance and availability, and very few terms are related to security (mainly disaster recovery and business continuity). Indeed, many European initiatives have been activated by the European Community to define a common understanding and semantic of SLAs for cloud computing [15], and specific subgroups are working on security-related aspects but, up to date, security is not under negotiation.

The idea of Security-as-a-Service implies that we can dynamically "add security" to services even when they are offered by public, potentially untrusted,

M. Felici and C. Fernández-Gago (Eds.): A4Cloud 2014, LNCS 8937, pp. 45–62, 2015.
DOI: 10.1007/978-3-319-17199-9_2

CSPs. Indeed, to do this, we would need mechanisms that are able to: (i) automatically enforce security mechanisms and controls; (ii) automatically monitor the "security level" promised in the SLA; (iii) face the problem of negotiation, taking in consideration that, typically, users sign the SLAs but, while they understand the concepts of "response time", "availability of a system" or "offered functionalities", they are not security experts, as they usually understand and express very general security needs (e.g., "I want a secure system, always available") but they are not able to translate general terms in actual security mechanisms and controls to enforce.

Indeed, it is up to a security administrator to translate user security requirements, standard guidelines and compliance policies into low-level security mechanisms, policies and configurations, able to cover all security related points that are addressed in those high-level document-based requirements and procedures. So, what are the problems associated to finding and signing an agreement in terms of security requirements? We can face the problem from two different perspectives: from (i) a semantic point of view, there is the need for a common vocabulary to express and evaluate security parameters, while from (ii) an operational point of view, we have to consider automatic mechanisms that from one side are able to enforce proper security mechanisms to meet specific security requirements, and from the other side are able to continuously monitor the security requirements that have been promised.

As for negotiation, there is the need for mechanisms to specify cloud security requirements, and to let users understand the standalone and comparative security features offered by different CSPs. As for the enforcement of security, from a technological point of view, there are no difficulties in enforcing service-based mechanisms once the list of mechanisms, their configurations and how to enforce them are available. As for the monitoring, due to the gap between the actual security mechanisms adopted and user expectations, it is common practice for cloud users to "blindly trust" their CSPs, and to react (e.g., closing subscriptions and changing their provider) only after a security incident has occurred.

How to monitor security and security SLAs when they affect services offered by public, external CSPs? Which are the parameters to monitor? The problem is still open and few dedicated solutions exist. Furthermore, the monitoring problem is even worse in cloud than for traditional outsourcing providers, especially if we take in consideration the different cloud deployment models (IaaS, PaaS and SaaS), where responsibilities are shared among customers and providers in different ways, according to what is offered as-a-service and what is under the control of the customers. Traditional SIEM systems, Intrusion Detection Systems and Vulnerability Assessment tools may not suffice in the cloud.

Despite the state of the art efforts, aiming to build and represent security parameters in cloud SLAs (e.g., the CSA SLA and PLA working groups, or research projects as A4cloud, CUMULUS, Tclouds and Contrail), there are no available user-centric solutions offering systematic mechanisms to manage the whole SLA life-cycle. In this paper, we are going to present a number of international initiatives related to standardization efforts for a common SLA vocabulary and related to research project results, and we will present the original approach provided by the SPECS project [6], whose main goal is just to provide security-as-a-service in the cloud environment, with an approach based on the management of the SLA life cycle. We will focus our attention on one of the main problems that is faced within the project, namely the quantitative evaluation of security. Indeed, we will present two different techniques (namely the Reference Evaluation Methodology and the AHP-based evaluation technique) to evaluate security, starting from the security parameters described in a formalized SLA and how they can be evaluated.

The remainder of the paper is structured as follows: in Sects. 2 and 3 we will provide an overview of the motivation to reasoning about the SLAs and in particular the Security SLAs, and we will discuss a number of initiatives from standardization bodies and from the scientific community towards the Security SLA and the concept of metrics to evaluate security. In Sect. 4, we will present the SLA-based approach provided by the SPECS project and in particular we will present the main features and issues associated to the SLA life cycle management; we will present two techniques to evaluate the security provided by CSP that help in the negotiation phase and we will illustrate some mechanisms and approach toward automatic enforcement and monitoring. Finally, in Sect. 5 some conclusions will be drawn.

2   Reasoning on SLA

As discussed in the Introduction, an SLA is a contract among a provider and its customers stating the quality level of the services offered. In addition to the list of covered services and to the service terms guarantees, an SLA should clearly state how to determine whether the provider is delivering the service as promised or not. Moreover, it should include the responsibilities of both the provider and the consumer of the services, and the remedies to be applied by the provider or the customer in case some terms are not respected. In the practice, this rarely happens in state of art SLAs, which are often legal documents, written in natural language and including the above discussed concepts only in an informal way.

When moving towards automatic reasoning on SLAs, which requires the SLAs to be expressed in a machine readable format, the side effect is that, usually, service providers focus on technical aspects and on what they are actually able to measure, while customers focus on the requirements they have with respect to their usage of the application.

When applying these concepts to security, the complexity grows easily, as there is a *semantic gap* between the customer, which has specific security requirements, but often does not have expertise on security terminology, and the provider, which aims at expressing the security level of its services with respect to very detailed technical terms, with focus on the service behaviour and not on how it will be used by (one of) its customers. The issue becomes even more complex when considering a typical cloud customer, which acquires resources from one or more CSPs in order to build up a cloud application to sell services to other customers.

Such kind of customers have clear responsibilities over the security of the services they offer, but do not have full control over the resources on top of which they run such services. In such scenario, the cloud customer requirements may be specified in a *Security SLA*: as an example, the customer may require that data confidentiality is granted, implying that data must be encrypted both while in motion and at rest, and in such cases the details of the encryption algorithms and access control policies should be specified in the SLA. Moreover, privacy requirements should be taken into account: basic privacy concerns are addressed by requirements such as data encryption, retention, and deletion. An SLA should make it clear how the CSP isolates data and applications in a multi-tenant environment. Even management of data over CSP resources should be clearly stated: how does CSPs prove they comply with retention laws and deletion policies? In cases when regulations must be enforced because of the type of involved data, CSPs should be able to prove compliance. Moreover, for critical data and applications, CSPs should be proactive in notifying customers when the terms of an SLA are violated or at risk, due to infrastructure issues, performance problems and security incidents. Finally, as another example, audit rights should be defined, in order to enable monitoring for any data breaches including loss of data and availability issues. In this case, SLAs should clarify when and how the audits will take place.

Currently, the standard contracts offered by CSPs are one-sided and service provider-friendly, with little opportunity to change terms. Few CSPs offer meaningful service levels or assume some responsibility for legal compliance, security or data protection. Many permit suspension of service or unilateral termination, and disclaim all or most of the provider's potential liability. In this scenario, there is no space for customer requirements. This is contradictory with the cloud computing paradigm, which assumes the *On-demand self-service* as one of the basic characteristics of cloud computing: the customer should be able to select and activate services without any human interaction. The side effect, from an SLA point of view, is that the SLAs should be automated, facing the problems outlined above, trying to adapt the requests to the actual state of the provider resources, in order to grant the respect of agreed terms.

A solution can be provided by filling the semantic gap between CSPs (good practices, guidelines, compliance policies,) and security mechanisms to enforce (technology specific) and monitor to guarantee security levels (Fig. 1). As outlined in Fig. 1, the goal of the Security SLAs should be to fill the gap between the typical mechanisms and solutions adopted in security, the security control models and the cloud architecture.

In order to meet such goal, it is fundamental to have a common and standardized security vocabulary that helps in a clear mapping between requirements, security controls and cloud architecture. As it will be shown in the next section, at the state of art such shared and standard vocabulary does not exist. The second relevant aspect is the capability to quantitatively evaluate the security offering in order to define the *security levels*, which will be addressed in Sect. 4.1.

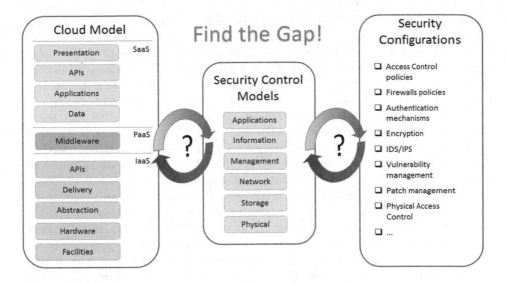

Fig. 1. The semantic gap among security requirements, guidelines and configuration

3 Related Work

As outlined in Sect. 2, the lack of a shared and standard vocabulary for both security and cloud concepts is one of the main limits for the adoption of Security SLAs. Actually, the cloud computing paradigm is relatively young: only in September 2011 the widely accepted cloud definition from NIST [20] was considered definitive, but up to that moment dozen of different definitions were proposed. The state of art of standardization in the cloud context is well outlined by the European Commission in the *Unleashing the Potential of Cloud Computing in Europe* Directive [15]. Currently, two main proposals have been released to define a cloud reference architecture, namely the *NIST Cloud Reference Architecture* [19] and the *ISO Reference Architecture and Vocabulary* [1,2].

For what regards the adoption of SLAs, the state of art is in a similar condition: the only (de facto) standard for a machine readable format is WS-Agreement [5], born in the GRID context, while more high-level standards aiming at defining in detail what an SLA should contain are the *ISO 19086* [3], still not definitive, and the initiative from the European Commission, i.e., the Cloud Selected Industry Group on Service Level Agreement (C-SIG SLA), which released a guideline for the production of standards on SLAs [23].

As for the security field, the main reference for security controls definition and best practices is the set of standards proposed by NIST and ISO. In particular, the NIST 800-53 and 800-53A documents offer guides for assessing security controls and ISO recommendations 20000-1, 20000-7, 27036-4, 27001, 27002, 27017 and 27018 comprise aspects such as service management of cloud services, guidelines for suppliers regarding Information Security, requirements and metrics for security management also applied to cloud computing. ISO has recently started an initiative in order to identify specific security controls for the cloud context (ISO 27017).

For the cloud specific environment, it is relevant to outline the role of Cloud Security Alliance, which provided set of questionnaires to evaluate the security level of cloud providers through a three layer approach to Security Certification named STAR, whose starting is a publicly available self-assessment questionnaire (CAIQ) [14]. In such context, CSA proposed a Cloud Control Matrix (CCM) [13] which lists the possible security controls to be adopted in the cloud context.

From the research activities point of view, the cloud security and Security SLA problem is addressed directly and indirectly in many active research projects. As an example, Accountability for Cloud (A4Cloud[1]) aims to improve the acceptability of cloud-based infrastructures where critical data is perceived to be at risk. CUMULUS[2] develops an integrated framework of models, processes and tools to support the certification of security properties of multi-layer cloud services using multiple types of evidence for security, including service testing, monitoring data and trusted computing proofs. CIRRUS[3] is one more project focusing mostly on certification and standardization in cloud. In the cloud context, CONTRAIL [18] is an IP project that addresses, among a lot of other issues, the SLA management in Cloud Federations, topic that was addressed even in mOSAIC[4]. Finally, TClouds[5] is the first EC-ICT project that deeply analyzes the security issues. It has until now delivered a set of solutions belonging to the IaaS level.

4   The SLA-Based Approach to Cloud Security

Starting from the previous consideration, we are going to propose an innovative approach to provide security services in the cloud that are offered under the control of SLAs with security parameters. At this aim, we need to be able to manage an SLA in its whole life cycle and to automatically enforce security by implementing security mechanisms that cover the desired security parameters.

Figure 2 illustrates a simplified view of the SLA life cycle management with a flow chart diagram, which is mainly based on five different activities:

- *negotiation:* to cope with users and providers needs and requirements and find an agreement;
- *enforcement:* to implement proper security mechanisms and controls;
- *monitoring:* to be able to continuously monitor the security parameters to guarantee;
- *remediation:* to provide proper actions in case of some alert conditions;
- *re-negotiation:* to change the SLA in case some security provision has been violated.

---

[1] The A4Cloud project web site, http://www.a4cloud.eu/.
[2] The CUMULUS project web site, http://www.cumulus-project.eu/.
[3] The CIRRUS project web site, www.cirrus-project.eu.
[4] The mOSAIC project web site, http://www.mosaic-cloud.eu/.
[5] The TClouds project web site, http://www.tclouds-project.eu/.

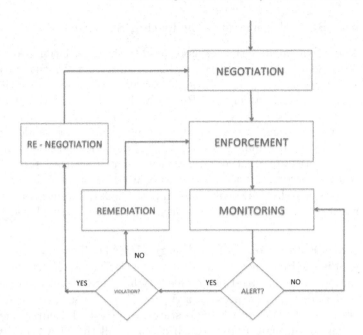

Fig. 2. The SLA life cycle management

In particular, in the negotiation phase there is the need for tools that support users to express their security requirements, and for methodologies to evaluate the security provided by different providers. In the enforcement phase, there is the need to properly plan the activation of security mechanisms to be able to build secure service invocations. In the monitoring phase, there is the need to guarantee security by continuously monitoring security parameters. Remediation and re-negotiation apply only when some alert or violation conditions occur, and should be managed properly. Indeed, the SPECS (Secure Provisioning of cloud Services based on SLA management) project [6] goals are mainly related to cope with these problems in order to provide and control security through proper services. In fact, SPECS aims at supporting both cloud customers and CSPs to respectively access and provide a secured target service. SPECS Security Services provide security guarantees to cloud customers, by using specific services to negotiate, enforce and continuously monitor the security parameters included in the SLA (SLA-based approach).

In next subsections, we are going to provide some in-sight on the research ongoing activities on negotiation, and in particular on the methodologies to evaluate the security provided by a CSP, on the enforcement and on the monitoring of security services, giving an overview on what is actually available in the literature and what are the future works to be done to effectively implement the SLA-based approach.

4.1 Security SLA Negotiation: Evaluating Security

As already said, of the main activities associated to the negotiation process is the assessment and evaluation of security. In this section, we will focus our analysis on two security evaluation methodologies to express and evaluate security terms included in an SLA [10], namely the Reference Evaluation Model (REM) [11] and an AHP-based evaluation methodology [8]. Thanks to these, we are able to (i) express security through a semi-formal and not ambiguous model (Security SLA) where the chosen formalization is easy to adopt for both customers and security experts; (ii) evaluate the security level that a security service is able to guarantee by aggregating the security associated to all SLA security terms (multi-decision approach); (iii) evaluate/compare/rank different providers offering different systems according to the measured quality/security level.

The Reference Evaluation Methodology (REM). The first methodology that we present is the Reference Evaluation Model (REM) [9,12], whose goal is to provide an automatic means to state the security level provided by a service. The methodology defines how to express in a rigorous way the security SLA, how to evaluate a formalized SLA, and how to state the provided security level. Any SLA is represented through a tree, which contains all the SLA security terms (intermediate nodes and leaves). In Fig. 3 the three methodology phases are shown: **Policy Structuring**, **Policy Formalization** and **Policy Evaluation**:

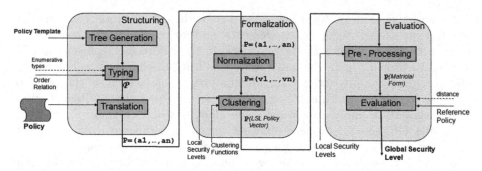

Fig. 3. Phases of the evaluation methodology

1. The goal of the **Structuring** phase is to associate an enumerative and ordered data type K_i to the n leave-security terms of the SLA. An SLA space "P" is defined as $P = K_1 \times K_2 \times \ldots \times K_n$, i.e., the vector product of the n security terms K_i. The space is defined according to an SLA template that strongly depends on the application context.
2. The main goal of the **Formalization** phase is to turn the SLA space "P" into a homogeneous space "PS". This transformation is accomplished by a normalization and clusterization process which allows to associate a Local Security Level (LSL) to each provision; after that, the security terms may be compared by comparing their LSLs.

3. The main goal of the **Evaluation** phase is to pre-process the *"PS"* vector of LSLs in order to represent it by a $n \times 4$ matrix whose rows are the single security terms K_i and the number of columns is the chosen number of LSLs for each provision. For example, if the number of LSL is four and the LSL associated to a provision is l_2, the row in the matrix associated to the provision in the matrix will be: (1,1,0,0). Finally, a distance criteria for the definition of a metric space is applied. REM adopts the Euclidean distance among matrices:
$d(A, B) = \sqrt{(\sigma(A - B, A - B))}$
where $\sigma(A - B, A - B) = Trace((A - B)(A - B)^T)$

To define the Global Security Level L_{Px} associated to the SLA P_x, we have introduced some reference levels and adopted the following metric function:

$$L_{Px} = \begin{cases} L_0 \; if f d_{x0} \leq d_{10} \\ L_1 \; if f d_{10} < d_{x0} < d_{20} \\ L_2 \; if f d_{20} < d_{x0} < d_{30} \\ L_3 \; if f d_{30} < d_{x0} < d_{40} \\ L_4 \; if f d_{40} \leq d_{x0} \end{cases}$$

where $d_{i,0}$ are the distances among the references and the origin of the metric space (denoted as $\emptyset$). This function gives a numerical result to the security; the idea is to evaluate the security associated to a service through the evaluation of its security SLA.

The GSL is a measure of the security provided by an service according to its security SLA; it is obtained by formalizing the process that is manually performed by security experts while trying to extend trust to other domains. The details of the methodology are out of the scope of this paper, and they can be found in [9].

The AHP Based Methodology. To satisfy the flexibility, adaptability, and interoperability requirements that are necessary in SLA stipulation and monitoring processes, we propose to formalize SLA policies according to hierarchical Quality Models whose structure must be defined according to the rules of the following Quality meta-model [7].

The SLA Quality meta-model comprehends some fundamental concepts:

- Quality Characteristic: any quality requirements, such as Performance, Security, Cost, Maintainability
- Characteristics may be arranged in a hierarchy (Measurable Characteristics are the leaves)
- Measurable Characteristic: a Quality Characteristic that can directly be measured

In Fig. 4 we reported the quality meta-model and we formally express service SLAs as an instance of the meta-model.

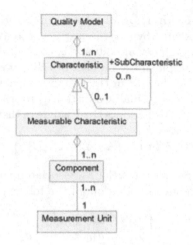

Fig. 4. The SLA quality meta-model

The evaluation process is made of two different steps:

1. A security expert *designs the decision model*;
2. The decision maker evaluates the quality by *applying the decision model*.

The **decision model design activity** includes three main steps, i.e., Weight Assignment, Clustering, and Rating. They are preliminarily performed just once, independently of the number of evaluations that will be performed. In the Weight Assignment step, the relative importance of the characteristics is rated; in the Clustering step, for each measurable characteristic, the sets of values that will be considered equivalent for the aims of the evaluation are defined; finally, in the Rating Step, each set is associated to a rating value. In the following, an example of these three steps is reported:

Step 1: Weight Assignment. For each Characteristic not directly measurable, the decision process designer will estimate the relative *Intensity of Importance* of any pair of its n Sub-Characteristics, by defining a matrix of $n*n$. Then, the designer has to build the *Comparison matrix* and then *Normalize* the matrix to define security parameters weights, as illustrated in Fig. 5.

Steps 2 and 3: Clustering e Rating. To cluster the possible values of an SLA offering, the designer has to define a *Utility Function R* to order the possible values on the basis of relative (and not absolute) preferences (as the Local Security Levels of the REM methodology): given two values x and y of the set, if x is preferred to y then $R(x) > R(y)$. Let us consider, as an example, the *Average Response Time* Characteristic, we can define the utility function as follows:

$$R = Offered_{value}/Requested_{value} \tag{1}$$

Then, all possible solutions to this function are clustered in three levels according to this meaning: {very fast response, sufficiently fast response, quite slow response}:

Intensity of Importance and its interpretation	
Intensity of Importance	**Interpretation**
1	Equal Importance
3	Moderate Importance
5	Strong Importance
7	Very strong Importance
9	Extreme Importance

1. Build the Comparison matrix

2. Normalize The matrix

	Average Response Time	Standard Deviation Response Time	Maximum Response Time	Weights
Average Response Time	21/31	15/21	7/13	0.64
Standard Deviation Response Time	7/31	5/21	5/13	0.28
Maximum Response Time	3/31	1/21	1/13	0.07

Fig. 5. Weight assignment

$$UF = \begin{cases} R < 0.5 \\ 0.5 <= R < 1 \\ 1 <= R < 2 \end{cases} \qquad (2)$$

After clustering each possible value, the designer rates all clusters according to their *Goodness* (the Goodness of a cluster is defined in the same way as the weight) and defines the following *Satisfaction Function* that represents the relative rate/evaluation of a cluster:

$$Ssc(R) = \begin{cases} 0.63 \ if f R < 0.5 \\ 0.26 \ if f 0.5 <= R < 1 \\ 0.11 \ if f 1 <= R < 2 \end{cases} \qquad (3)$$

In the *decision making activity*, a customer can easily compare the security of an offered service (expressed in the Quality Offer Model) against his needs (expressed in the Quality Request Model); the security of different services is compared by evaluating:

1. a *Satisfaction Function* for each Measurable Characteristic;
2. a *Satisfaction Function* for each non-Measurable Characteristic;
3. the *Overall Satisfaction Function* that aggregates all evaluations.

In particular, for each Characteristic c, the *Satisfaction Function* can be evaluated as the weighted sum of the Satisfaction of its Sub-Characteristics:

$$S_C(req.off) = \sum_{sc \in C(c)} w_{SC} S_{SC}(req, off) \qquad (4)$$

where $C(c)$ is the set of Sub-Characteristics affecting the Quality Characteristic; w_{SC} is the weight of the Sub-Characteristic sc and $S_{SC}(req, off)$ is the value of the Satisfaction Function of the Sub-Characteristic sc.

Finally, the *Overall Satisfaction* of a service offering is given by:

$$S(req.off) = \sum_{c \in C} w_c S_c(req, off) \qquad (5)$$

where the set C includes all the higher level Characteristics of the customer Quality Model, while wc is the weight of that Characteristics and $S_c(req, off)$

is the Satisfaction value of the Characteristic c. We invite the interested reader to refer to [7] for a more detailed discussion of this technique.

The two proposed techniques have many points in common: indeed, the security terms and associated metrics are closely connected with services, system parameters and configuration mechanisms, and they are always pre-evaluated by security experts in order to let the evaluation process be automatic. Among the positive aspects, they always take into account both the user requirements and evaluators perspectives (weight definition, cluster assignment, security level definition). As for the drawbacks, the security is evaluated starting from a static evaluation of enforced security mechanisms (but the security provided changes with time due to new attacks and vulnerability), and there is the need for automatic monitoring systems to assure the respect of security parameters. Once the different providers' offerings are evaluated, the customer can choose the one that best fits his needs and, finally, he can sign the SLA. Moreover, there is the need for automatic mechanisms to enforce security mechanisms and, possibly, redress security mechanisms to react to some alert and there is the need for monitoring systems that are targeted to security parameters. In the next two sections we will present an overview of current open issues and available solutions on these last points, too.

4.2   Security SLA Enforcement

After the negotiation phase, a signed SLA must be implemented. SLA implementation involves making sure that the negotiated service levels are correctly set up and monitored, in order to report possible failures and trigger proper reactions. SLA monitoring will be discussed in the next subsection, while in the following we provide an overview of the issues related to the configuration and activation of a negotiated service fulfilling specific security requirements, and to the management of possible violations.

The basic requirement to provide cloud end-users with the services they requested in the negotiation phase, is the availability of security mechanisms, protocols and tools offered according to an as-a-service approach. Indeed, in non-trivial cases where the target services are not yet offered with the desired guarantees by any provider, such *security services* may be integrated into the target services' supply chains (i.e., the chains of service invocations involved in the provisioning of the target services), to add the missing features.

Several security-as-a-service products are being currently offered by some vendors, which mainly deal with identity and access management, intrusion detection, encryption etc. In the context of research projects, we can mention the Consec framework defined within the Contrail project, aimed at providing a stack of software components for the federation of independent clouds. ConSec is a framework that enables any infrastructure provider to make use of federated (i.e., external) identity management with authorization and auditing features. This solution may be useful to enrich the catalog of security services available for the enforcement of SLOs with specific pluggable services for identity federation, authorization and auditing.

While the identification of proper supply chains able to guarantee the requested secure services is a task to be accomplished during the negotiation phase (to determine whether a solution exists to satisfy the end-user requests), the actual set up of the supply chain acknowledged by the end-user is performed during the SLA implementation. It involves retrieving, configuring and activating all services/resources needed to have the desired service up and running, and requires a planning activity aimed at defining a complete workflow. Once set up, the services should be monitored in order to detect possible violations of the signed SLA, which would imply the application of penalties or other actions taken against the provider. In this scenario, from the perspective of both the customer and the provider, it would be desirable to be warned about a possible incoming violation, in order to take proper countermeasures and avoid it. At this aim, enforcement should also envision a diagnosis activity, for the analysis of monitoring data, and include the capability of identifying, if possible, the best reaction strategy to implement.

An example of security management framework aimed at mediating between cloud services and security mechanisms is described in [4]. The proposed framework is composed of three layers, namely the management layer, the enforcement layer, and the feedback layer, which are respectively responsible of: (i) defining the security specifications of the cloud service providers and customers, (ii) planning security and selecting security controls based on identified risks, and (iii) collecting and analyzing measurements related to security metrics to ensure that the system is operating within the defined boundaries, by triggering configuration updates in case of deviations from the defined boundaries.

The described approach is followed by other projects, which also adopt SLAs for security specification and assurance. As an example, we mention SLA@SOI[6], that proposes a solution for orchestrating services on the basis of SLAs. In SLA@SOI, the enforcement of the quality characteristics is tightly connected to an SLA manager, a complex software component in charge of the whole management of SLAs.

The SPECS project[7] is also working on improving cloud services' security by adopting an SLA-based approach. The SPECS framework is aimed at managing the whole SLA life-cycle. In particular, the enforcement of SLAs is addressed by a complex module which includes, on the one hand, all components needed to plan and realize the SLA implementation, to reason on monitoring data for diagnosis purposes and to react in case of alerts or violations, and, on the other hand, a catalogue of security services available to improve the security provided by third-parties.

4.3 Security SLA Monitoring

When talking about security monitoring, many questions and open issues should be addressed. As outlined in this section, the problem should be faced by many

---

[6] The SLA@SOI project web site, http://sla-at-soi.eu/.

[7] The SPECS project web site, http://specs-project.eu/.

point of views. In particular, any monitoring solution should cope with the following questions: *What to monitor?* Physical resource? Physical infrastructures? Or even Virtual Machines and related Software assets? *Where are the monitoring agent?* Many options are configurable in the cloud (monitoring on-premises, monitoring on hosting IaaS, monitoring via SaaS or via other third parties), so which is the configuration that best fits the signed SLA? and *What data* should be monitored? How to manage the huge amount of data? Last, but not least, which security metrics to monitor?

Cloud monitoring typically involves dynamically tracking the Quality of Service (QoS) parameters related to virtualized resources (e.g., VM, storage, network, appliances, etc.), the physical resources they share, the applications running on them and the hosted data. The continuous monitoring of the cloud and of its SLAs, mostly expressed in terms of performance-related guarantees, is of paramount importance for both cloud providers and customers. As for providers in particular, they both aim at preventing SLA violations to avoid penalties, and at ensuring an efficient resource utilization to reduce costly maintenance.

While several tools exist for performance and QoS monitoring in cloud environments, both open source and commercial, security-related monitoring tools are less developed, and current monitoring infrastructures lack appropriate solutions for adequate SLA monitoring. As for security monitoring, few tools exist (many of them are represented by research results), which are typically represented by intrusion detection systems. Therefore, covering all aspects of cloud security SLA monitoring necessarily requires a combination of several monitoring tools.

Most of the current cloud monitoring tools is focused on specific aspects of cloud operation, providing only a partial solution for the cloud monitoring problem. For example, the open source tool Nagios[8] offers complete monitoring and alerting for servers, switches, applications, and services, while Ganglia[9] is a scalable distributed monitoring system for high-performance computing systems such as clusters and Grids, which collects dozens of system metrics related to CPU, memory, disk, network and process data. Other examples of popular monitoring tools are the commercial Amazon CloudWatch[10], AzureWatch[11] and OPNET[12].

All mentioned tools are general purpose and have not been designed to directly cope with SLAs. Examples of SLA-oriented monitoring tools are represented by CloudComPaaS[13], LoM2HiS [16] and CASViD [17] or the solution proposed in mOSAIC [22]. CloudComPaaS is an SLA-aware PaaS for managing a

---

[8] Nagios - The Industry Standard In IT Infrastructure Monitoring, http://www.nagios.org/.

[9] Ganglia Monitoirng System, http://ganglia.sourceforge.net/.

[10] Amazon CloudWatch, http://aws.amazon.com/cloudwatch.

[11] AzureWatch, www.paraleap.com/azurewatch.

[12] OPNET, www.opnet.com.

[13] GRyCAP CloudComPaaS, http://www.grycap.upv.es/compaas/about.html.

complete resource lifecycle, and features an extension of the WS-Agreement SLA specification for cloud computing. The monitor module performs the dynamic assessment of the QoS rules from active SLAs. The three basic operations of the monitor are updating the SLA terms state, checking the guarantees state and performing self-management operations. SLAs registered in the monitor are set to be updated every certain period of time, commonly defined as monitoring cycle. The monitor evaluates the formulas of the guarantee terms and sets the value of the guarantees to either Fulfilled or Violated. CASViD (cloud application SLA violation detection) [17] aims at monitoring and detecting SLA violations at the application layer, and includes tools for resource allocation, scheduling, and deployment. It is an SNMP-based monitoring approach for SLA violation. Service requests are placed through a defined interface to the front-end node, acting as the management node. The VM configurator sets up the cloud environment by deploying pre-configured VM images. The request is received by the service interface and delivered to the SLA management framework for validation, then it is passed to the application deployer for resource allocation and deployment. CASViD monitors the application and sends information to the SLA management framework for detection of SLA violations.

Enabling SLA Monitoring. The first challenge to face to enable security SLA monitoring is to provide a mapping between the application-level security SLOs specified in an SLA and the related measurable low-level metrics. For instance, let us consider the *availability* high-level SLO referred to a cloud application. The application is actually running on physical or virtual resources, which are characterized by low-level metrics such as CPU, memory, uptime, downtime, etc., which are those actually measurable. Thus, there is a gap between the low-level resource metrics and the high-level SLA parameters.

According to ENISA [21], the security parameters for a security monitoring framework can be classified as in Fig. 6. For each parameter, the monitoring and testing methodology, as well as the related thresholds to trigger events (e.g., incident reports or response and remediation) have to be defined. In terms of security requirements, the monitoring tests are quite complex. One of the reasons is the restricted access to the monitoring data, represented in Fig. 7.

Once the security parameters to monitor have been defined, it is necessary to determine appropriate monitoring intervals at the application level, keeping the balance between the early detection of possible SLA violations and the intrusiveness of the monitoring tools on the whole system. With the monitoring of the cloud infrastructure resources, the provider gains information about the usage of the resources and the current resource availability status. The rate of acquiring this information is an important factor influencing the overall performance of the system and the profit of the provider. On the one hand, monitoring at a high rate delivers fast updates about the resource status to the provider, but it can results in a high overhead, which eventually degrades the performance of the system. On the other hand, monitoring at a low rate causes the miss of information such as missing to detect SLA violation, which results in paying

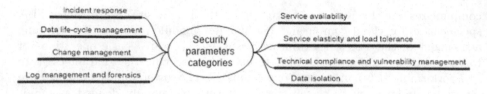

Fig. 6. ENISA security parameters

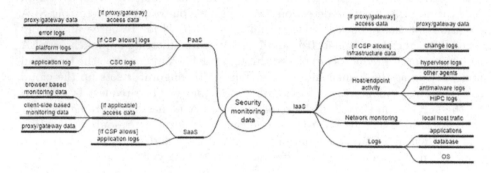

Fig. 7. Security monitoring data

of SLA penalties by the provider. Therefore, to address this issue, techniques to determine the optimal measurement intervals to efficiently monitor to detect SLA violations are required.

A key issue related to the selection of the parameters to monitor is the monitoring granularity. Three main options are possible: client-oriented monitoring, virtual system monitoring and physical system monitoring. Finally, another related issue is the approach adopted to gather monitoring data. Again, three options are possible: use proper APIs offered by the public cloud providers themselves to collect logs, install custom monitoring agents on the monitored infrastructure, or use third-party tools able to gather information on the services under monitoring from the outside.

The adoption of the best configuration of monitoring system to activate, should be automatically related to the security parameters included in the SLA and affect both infrastructures that host many user virtual resources (multi-tenancy) and user-specific resource to protect. Indeed, the SPECS project is trying to cope with this problem by defining during the SLA enforcement phase the number and typology of monitoring services to activate according to the specific security mechanisms and controls to activate.

5   Conclusions

A Service Level Agreement is a contract among the customer and the provider that states the quality level of the services offered. The scientific and industrial communities are recently investigating the possibility to offer Security-as-a-Service and, above all, to provide such kind of services under specific guarantees formalized in proper SLAs, as done for other services. To reply to this question, many open issues should be addressed, that can be summarized as: (i) it is difficult to express security requirements, (ii) it is difficult to evaluate security and (iii) it is difficult to monitor and guarantee security. These three points represent the main limitation to adopt security SLAs and, even worse, in the cloud environment. In this paper, we tried to address the main research initiatives that face these problems and even presented the SLA-based approach proposed by the SPECS project. In particular, we illustrated different techniques to quantitatively evaluate security, and automatically enforce and monitor the security of cloud services.

Acknowledgment. This research is partially supported by the grant FP7-ICT-2013-11-610795 (SPECS).

References

1. ISO/IEC 17788:2014. Information Technology-Cloud Computing-Overview and Vocabulary. Technical report, International Organization for Standardization (2014)
2. ISO/IEC 17789:2014. Information Technology-Cloud computing-Reference architecture. Technical report, International Organization for Standardization (2014)
3. ISO/IEC NP 19086-1. Information Technology-Cloud computing-Service level agreement (SLA) framework and technology-Part 1: Overview and concepts. Technical report, International Organization for Standardization (2014)
4. Almorsy, M., Ibrahim, A., Grundy, J.: Adaptive security management in saas applications. In: Nepal, S., Pathan, M. (eds.) Security, Privacy and Trust in Cloud Systems, pp. 73–102. Springer, Heidelberg (2014)
5. Andrieux, A., Czajkowski, K., Dan, A., Keahey, K., Ludwig, H., Nakata, T., Pruyne, J., Rofrano, J., Tuecke, S., Xu, M.: Web Services Agreement Specification (WS-Agreement). Technical report, Global Grid Forum, Grid Resource Allocation Agreement Protocol (GRAAP) WG, September 2005
6. Casola, V., De Benedictis, A., Rak, M., Villano, U.: Preliminary design of a platform-as-a-service to provide security in cloud. In: CLOSER 2014 – Proceedings of the 4th International Conference on Cloud Computing and Services Science, pp. 752–757, Barcelona, Spain, April 3–5 (2014)
7. Casola, V., Fasolino, A.R., Mazzocca, N., Tramontana, P.: An ahp-based framework for quality and security evaluation. In: Proceedings of the 2009 International Conference on Computational Science and Engineering, CSE 2009, vol. 03, pp. 405–411. IEEE Computer Society, Washington, DC (2009)
8. Casola, V., Fasolino, A.R., Mazzocca, N., Tramontana, P.: A policy-based evaluation framework for quality and security in service oriented architectures. In: Proceedings – 2007 IEEE International Conference on Web Services, ICWS 2007, pp. 1181–1182 (2007)
9. Casola, V., Mazzeo, A., Mazzocca, N., Rak, M.: An innovative policy-based cross certification methodology for public key infrastructures. In: Chadwick, D., Zhao, G. (eds.) EuroPKI 2005. LNCS, vol. 3545, pp. 100–117. Springer, Heidelberg (2005)

10. Casola, V., Mazzeo, A., Mazzocca, N., Rak, M.: A sla evaluation methodology in service oriented architectures. In: Gollmann, D., Massacci, F., Yautsiukhin, A. (eds.) Advances in Information Security, pp. 119–130. Springer, USA (2006)

11. Casola, V., Mazzeo, A., Mazzocca, N., Vittorini, V.: A policy-based methodology for security evaluation: a security metric for public key infrastructures. J. Comput. Secur. 15(2), 197–229 (2007)

12. Casola, V., Mazzocca, N., Luna, J., Manso, O., Medina, M., Rak, M.: Static evaluation of certificate policies for grid pkis interoperability. In: Proceedings - Second International Conference on Availability, Reliability and Security, ARES 2007, pp. 391–399 (2007)

13. Cloud Security Alliance. Cloud Control Matrix v3.0. https://cloudsecurityallia nce.org/download/cloud-controls-matrix-v3/

14. Cloud Security Alliance. Consensus Assessment Initiative Questionnaire V1.1. https://cloudsecurityalliance.org/research/cai/

15. European Commission. SWD(2012) 271 final. Unleashing the Potential of Cloud Computing in Europe. Technical report, September 2012

16. Emeakaroha, V.C., Brandic, I., Maurer, M., Dustdar, S.: Low level metrics to high level slas - lom2his framework: bridging the gap between monitored metrics and sla parameters in cloud environments. In: 2010 International Conference on High Performance Computing and Simulation (HPCS), pp. 48–54, June 2010

17. Emeakaroha, V.C., Ferreto, T.C., Netto, M.A.S., Brandic, I., De Rose., C.A.F.: Casvid: Application level monitoring for sla violation detection in clouds. In: 2012 IEEE 36th Annual Computer Software and Applications Conference (COMPSAC), pp. 499–508, July 2012

18. Harsh, P., Jegou, Y., Cascella, R.G., Morin, C.: Contrail virtual execution platform challenges in being part of a cloud federation. In: Abramowicz, W., Llorente, I.M., Surridge, M., Zisman, A., Vayssière, J. (eds.) ServiceWave 2011. LNCS, vol. 6994, pp. 50–61. Springer, Heidelberg (2011)

19. Liu, F., Tong, J., Mao, J., Bohn, R.B., Messina, J.V., Badger, M.L., Leaf, D.M.: NIST SP - 500–292. Cloud Computing Reference Architecture. Technical report, National Institute of Standards & Technology, September 2011

20. Mell, P.M., Grance, T.: SP 800–145. The NIST Definition of Cloud Computing. Technical report, National Institute of Standards & Technology, Gaithersburg, MD, United States (2011)

21. European Network and Information Security Agency (ENISA). Procure secure. a guide to monitoring of security service levels in cloud contracts, April 2012

22. Rak, M., Venticinque, S., Mahr, T., Echevarria, G., Esnal, G.: Cloud application monitoring:the mosaic approach. In: 2011 IEEE Third International Conference on Cloud Computing Technology and Science (CloudCom), pp. 758–763, November 2011

23. European Commission C-SIG (Cloud Select Industry Group) subgroup. IP/14/743. New guidelines to help EU businesses use the Cloud. Technical report, June 2014

A Certification Framework for Cloud Security Properties: The Monitoring Path

Marina Egea[2]([⊠]), Khaled Mahbub[1], George Spanoudakis[1],
and Maria Rosa Vieira[2]

[1] Department of Computer Science, City University London, London, UK
{K.Mahbub,G.E.Spanoudakis}@city.ac.uk
[2] Atos, Research and Innovation, Madrid, Spain
{marina.egea,maria.vieira}@atos.net

Abstract. In this paper we describe the structure and functionality of a certification integrated framework aimed to support the certification of security properties of a Cloud infrastructure (IaaS), a platform (PaaS), or the software layer (SaaS). Such framework will bring service users, service providers and cloud suppliers to work together with certification authorities in order to ensure security properties and certificates validity in the continuously evolving cloud environment. For this purpose, the framework relies on multiple types of evidence gathering with respect to security, e.g., testing services, monitoring agents or trusted computing proofs. In this paper we will focus only on the monitoring case and will illustrate its use. Yet, this framework is designed to be able to follow models for hybrid, incremental and multi-layer security certification since cloud security has to build upon the entire cloud stack.

Keywords: Cloud security · Monitoring tools · Monitoring based certification models

1 Introduction

The very nature of Cloud computing makes the systems deployed in such environment more exposed than ever before. The surface of attacks targeting applications and data has expanded from Web into mobile and cloud systems. As a consequence, the rapid adoption of detection and protection mechanisms for companies' assets along with the assurance of the resources they consume or provide in Cloud has turned out in one of highest priorities for companies using cloud support. Yet, this situation has also made other companies reluctant of migrating their systems to cloud due to the feel of losing control of their systems and becoming exposed.

But, not only the increased level of exposure but also the complexity in understanding the underlying infrastructure, platform or services delivering the required functionality to the consumers have made different organizations to classify cloud security properties or risks to both guide cloud vendors in their

© Springer International Publishing Switzerland 2015
M. Felici and C. Fernández-Gago (Eds.): A4Cloud 2014, LNCS 8937, pp. 63–77, 2015.
DOI: 10.1007/978-3-319-17199-9_3

road to meet security, and to assist prospective cloud customers in assessing the overall security risk of a cloud provider. These taxonomies usually reference the security requirements of the global ISO/IEC 27001. For instance, the Cloud Control Matrix [1] that is designed to provide fundamental security principles to guide cloud vendors and to assist prospective cloud customers in assessing the overall security risk of a cloud provider.

However, how companies or individual customers get assurance that an IT product meets its security objectives is a further question. According to Common Criteria [6], assurance can be derived from reference to sources such as unsubstantiated assertions, prior relevant experience, specific experience, or active investigation. The framework described in this paper supports the philosophy of providing (continuous) independent assurance by active investigation. Namely, it offers support for a (constant) evaluation of an IT resource in order to determine whether certain security property hold from a given point in time on, in a particular context. The security certification scheme is so conceived to create transparency in the industry, helping business to evaluate the security risks they may accept when working with a particular cloud service provider.

Organization. We start by briefly summarizing off-the-shelf monitoring tools in Sect. 2. In Sect. 3 we explain the infrastructure and functionality of a certification framework for Cloud security. In Sect. 4 we explain a monitoring based certification process. We illustrate this process in Sect. 5 using an example from the e-Health domain. Taking into account the state of the art of monitoring tools, we outline future work in Sect. 6. Finally, we draw conclusions in Sect. 7.

2 State of the Art of Cloud Monitoring Tools

To the best of our knowledge, there is no other certification infrastructure similar to the framework that we describe in Sect. 3, i.e., there is no other framework able to manage monitoring based certification, testing based certification and, in an immediate future, also TPM based and hybrid certification (to combine both monitoring and testing approaches).

Regarding cloud infrastructure monitoring, there are a number of open source versions of industrial strength cloud monitoring tools that could be used by the CUMULUS framework as external evidence collectors (once that we have also certified their reliability). First of all, we note that most of these off-the-shelf tools are dealing with performance, availability, or resource consumption. This fact leaves most of the security properties listed in [11] as not addressed by state of the art tools. Later, in Sect. 6 we report on security properties coverage (with respect to the list in [11]) that seems to be reached with the tools described here. This report is based on a preliminary suitability desktop analysis of these tools to monitor evidences related to the security properties.

Zenoss Core. Reference [5] is an enterprise network and systems management application written in Python that can monitor availability, performance, events and configuration across layers and platforms. It has an open source version, Zen Pack, that makes possible to monitor the capacity and performance of applications running on a Cloud Foundry platform. This pack allows monitoring metrics like, for example, memory or disk consumption or utilization, CPU average usage across instances, or total and running application instances.

Nagios Core. Reference [7] is an open source system and network monitoring application originally designed to run under Linux. It watches hosts (e.g., processor load, disk usage), applications, services, OS, network protocols and is able to provide notifications. Nagios allows defining macros that can be instantiated as monitoring metrics for particular services. E.g., a time-stamp in time format indicating the time at which the service was last detected as being in an 'OK' state. Moreover, it provides a powerful API allowing easy monitoring of custom applications, services, and systems since it has a simple plugin design that allows users to easily develop their own service checks.

Hyperic. Reference [14] provides proactive performance management with constant visibility into applications and infrastructure, and a notification service. The key monitoring and management capabilities of Hyperic are resource discovery, metric collection, and event tracking. Regarding resource discovery, the Hyperic agent managing a platform automatically discovers the resources, e.g., architecture, RAM, CPU speed, IP address or domain name, and software on the platform, e.g., web servers, application servers or database servers. Regarding metric collection, the Hyperic agent can collect metrics for the resource targeting availability, performance, utilization, and throughput for each supported resource type. Regarding event tracking, Hyperic can monitor log and configuration files and record events of interest for most server types. For instance, user logins, windows registry key changes or error logs.

New Relic. Reference [10] delivers software as a service which monitors web and mobile applications in real-time that run in cloud, on-premise, or hybrid environments. The New Relic Platform allows user to write plugin agents using Java or Ruby that can be run anywhere to collect metrics from any available system and report them to New Relic for customized dashboard visualization. A distinctive feature of New relic is that it provides metrics from end-user monitoring, e.g. apdex score; application monitoring, e.g., response times, performance of external services, most time consuming transactions; database monitoring, e.g., time spent in database calls; infrastructure monitoring, e.g., server resources monitoring, analysis of CPU, disk or memory; availability and error monitoring, e.g., application availability monitoring and alerting, incident or error detection, alerting and analysis.

Ganglia. Reference [8] is a scalable distributed monitoring system for high-performance computing systems such as clusters and grids. Ganglia is an open-source project, that allows monitoring the following metrics: system load averages that indicate the average number of processes running on the systems; memory usage averages that indicate the average usage of memory, in the form of user process or shared memory areas, system cache, buffer or swap areas; % CPU utilization across all processes on all systems; and network bandwidth usage averages that indicates the average use of network bandwidth across the nodes.

Less oriented towards performance or availability monitoring, *OSSEC* [13] is an Open Source Host-based Intrusion Detection System that performs log analysis, file integrity checking, policy monitoring, rootkit detection, real-time alerting and active response. It has a centralized manager that receives information from agents which may be running simultaneously for different operating systems, e.g., Linux, MacOS, Solaris, HP-UX, AIX and Windows.

In contrast with the monitoring tools that we have described before, the *EVEREST* monitoring framework [12] that is the one that we are currently employing to monitor evidences in the CUMULUS project, supports a *formal approach* for the specification and constant checking of a wide range of monitoring rules with precise time constraints, and can deal with events that may be captured and notified from distributed sources and through different communication channels. EVEREST can also support the monitoring of conditions at various levels (e.g. network and application levels).

3 Infrastructure of a Cloud Security Certification Framework

The certification infrastructure presented here is the core layer of the CUMULUS framework [2] since it is responsible for issuing, maintaining, or revoking certificates according to the different types of certification models that it can be provided with, e.g. testing-based, monitoring-based certification models or, as a refinement, trusted computing monitoring-based certification models. More details about the use of these types of models in the framework can be found in [2,3,11]. The framework components that are described next are in charge of managing the evidence gathered to assure a certain resource's security property, and accordingly the certificates that are issued, maintain or revoked based on the collected proofs. The security properties that we aim to address with the framework are those contained in the security property vocabulary specified in [11, Annex A]. Each subsection of this annex represents one of the control domains of the Cloud Control Matrix [1][1].

3.1 Framework Components

Next, we describe the components of the certification framework that are depicted in Fig. 1.

---

[1] The list of security properties contained by deliverable D2.1 [11, Annex A] was specified by the Cloud Security Alliance that is part of the CUMULUS project consortium.

- **Certification Manager.** This component communicates with a CA through a Management API so as the CA can upload or delete new certification models. It is also connected with the Certification and Security Models databases and it delegates the management to the testing or monitoring manager according to the type of model the CA selects through a corresponding API. Moreover, it provides information stored in Certification Models to the 'Certification Generator/Attestation' component through the 'Generation API'.
- **Certificate Generator/Attestation.** This component issues certificates when enough and appropriate evidences are collected, according to the information of the Certification Models and based on the evidences stored in the 'Evidence Database (DB)'. It also stores the issued Certificates into the 'Certificates DB'.
- **Certification Communicator.** This component provides the 'Retrieval API' that allows the actors to retrieve certificates. This component also provides a 'Notification API' to notify actors about the status of certificates. Moreover, from the 'Certificates Registry DB,' the certification communicator collects all information about the requested certificates.
- **Certificates DB.** This is the database that stores the certificates: it acts as a blackboard architecture for the 'Certification Communicator' and the 'Certificate Generator/Attestation' components. This repository is connected and properly related to the 'Certified Services DB.'
- **Evidence DB.** This database stores the aggregated evidence collected that sustain that a given security property holds for a resource. It plays the role of a blackboard architecture for the four types of Managers and the 'Certificate Generator/Attestation' components.
- **Security Models DB.** This database stores the security models defined by security experts.
- **Certification Models DB.** This database stores the certification models defined by security experts.
- **Monitoring Manager.** This component is responsible for planning and setting up the monitoring infrastructure when the 'Certification Manager' calls it through the 'Monitoring Manager API' according to a request from a Certification Model.
- **Testing Manager.** This module is responsible for planning and setting up the testing infrastructure when the Certification Manager calls it through the 'Testing Manager API', according to a request from a Certification Model.

3.2 Interactions and Usage

The information exchange with the certification infrastructure is mainly performed through the Retrieval API, and the Management API that are described next.

- **Management API.** This is a provided interface that enables to carry out framework management tasks, like adding and updating certification models in the 'Certification models DB', as well as requesting to issue a certificate for a specific service.

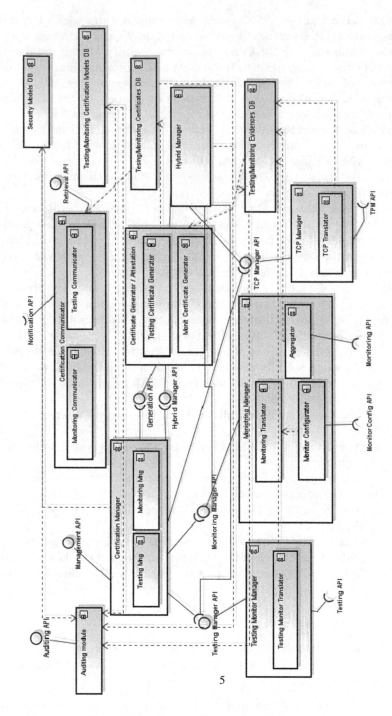

Fig. 1. Cumulus framework architecture

– `Retrieval API`. This is a provided interface that enables the communication with the framework: sending requests for certified components, checking the validity of certificates and getting run-time-related information.

There are other APIs, i.e., Notification API, and Auditing API that are not yet implemented but planned for future development. The `Notification API` will be an interface that deals with subscriptions and notifications for receiving certificates that fulfill the specified requirements at run-time. The `Audit API` will be an interface that allows cloud auditors to review the certification process supported by the framework.

In Fig. 2 we illustrate at a high level how the process of certificate creation is supported by the interaction of the framework components, and driven through the Management API. Note that a CA directly interacts with a dashboard that is not part of the framework but allows user friendly interaction with it. The certificate creation process starts when a CA selects a resource (namely, a target of certification-TOC), e.g. a service, and a security property to be certified for this cloud resource, e.g. it stores data encrypted. For this combination, the CA also has to select a certification model (from those retrieved from the certification models database). Once these parameters have been instantiated, a certificate is requested to the certification manager that passes this request into the testing or the monitoring manager (depending on the certification model that was selected). Either of these managers uses external but trusted cloud testing or monitoring modules to gather and store evidences that can sustain the security property chosen for the selected resource. When these evidences are sufficient,

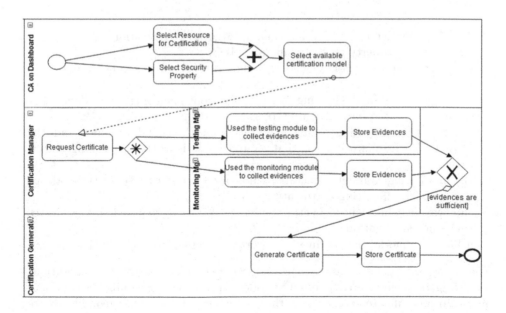

Fig. 2. Certificate creation process

a certificate is generated by the Certification Generator component that, in addition, stores the new certificate that it has generated based on the evidences. In the following sections, we will provide more details of the certification process, placing the focus on the monitoring case.

We describe next the stakeholders that were identified for the CUMULUS framework [2]. Ultimately, all of them have to interact with the infrastructure explained in this section. *Cloud Service Consumers* use the framework either to develop an application fulfilling some security requirements, to retrieve a certified service, or to check the validity of a certificate; *Certification Authorities (CA)* use the framework either to issue a certificate for cloud services, or to define or validate a certification model (that can be used afterwards to certify various services); *Cloud Service Providers* use the framework either to specify a service to be certified, to issue a certificate for a service, or to define or check the validity of a certification model; *Cloud Auditors* use the framework to check the security compliance of a given application based on the documentation provided by the framework; and *Security Experts* that use the framework to define security properties and related certification requirements for a certain domain.

4   Monitoring Based Certificate Creation Process

The certification management process in the case of monitoring based certificates is handled by the monitoring manager. The whole process is driven by the monitoring based certification model (MBCM) that is passed to the manager. This model is defined in XML according to the schema shown in Fig. 3. A MBCM specifies:

1. the cloud service to be certified (i.e., a Target of Certification (ToC));
2. the security property to be certified for ToC;
3. the certification authority who will sign the certificates generated by the model;
4. an assessment scheme defining general conditions regarding the evidence that must be collected for being able to issue a certificate;
5. validity tests regarding the configuration of the cloud provider and the CUMULUS framework itself that should be satisfied before issuing certificates;
6. the monitoring configurations that will be used in order to collect the evidence required for generating certificates;
7. the way in which the collected evidence will be aggregated in certificates (evidence aggregation); and
8. a life cycle model that defines the overall process of issuing certificates.

The assessment scheme in an MBCM (see Fig. 4) defines general conditions regarding the evidence that must be collected in order to be able to issue and maintain a certificate according to the particular MBCM. These conditions are related to:

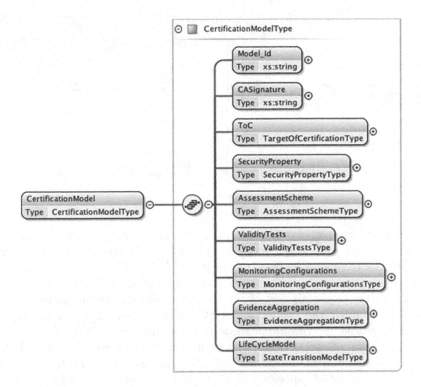

Fig. 3. MBCM overall schema

i. the sufficiency of the collected evidence collection (e.g., minimum period over which a target of certification must be monitored before a certificate for the particular property of it can be issued) and are specified by evidence sufficiency condition elements,

ii. the absence of conflicting evidence regarding the property to be certified, i.e., evidence that the security property of interest would have been violated if the assessment were to be made over a different time period (specified as conflict elements), and

iii. the absence of any anomalies, i.e., indications of potential attacks or operating conditions which despite of not having affected yet the security property that is assessed, may do so in the future (specified by anomalies elements).

These conditions must be satisfied, in addition to the guarantee states that are part of the assertion definition of the property, for the certificate to be issued[2].

Once it receives an MBCM, the monitoring manager checks whether the security property that is to be certified can be monitored for the given TOC. This is performed by parsing the property, creating an abstract syntax tree (AST) for it and using AST to establish whether the TOC is placed on a cloud

---

[2] A full description of the schema for specifying MBCMs is available in [3].

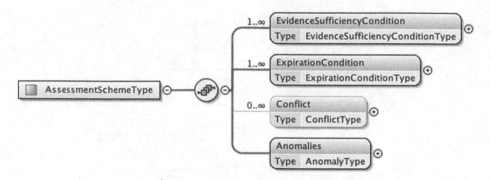

Fig. 4. MBCM assessment scheme

infrastructure that can provide the raw monitoring events required in order to check the security property. This check is performed by checking the monitoring capabilities of the cloud where TOC is placed [4,9]. If this check is successful, the monitoring manager creates a concrete monitoring configuration as part of the MBCM, i.e., a description of the event captors and the monitor that will be used to monitor the property and the subscriptions that will be required in order to enable the communication of events from the former to the latter. The transmission of events from event captors to the monitor of the CUMULUS framework takes place through an event bus (events are encrypted). Depending on the validity tests specified in MBCM, the monitoring manager may also require that the event captors and the event bus used for the capture and transmission of monitoring events run also on infrastructures that are enabled by a trusted platform module (TPM) and that their implementations at the outset have integrity. Subsequently, the monitoring manager initiates the monitoring process by: (a) activating the event captors, and (b) translating the security property that is to be certified into observable assertions and passing them to the monitor to start the run-time checking. Following the above, steps the monitoring manager polls the monitor at regular intervals to collect any monitoring results, which are relevant to the security property that is being assessed. These results are stored in the evidence DB of the framework.

When the collected evidence is sufficient for making an assessment about the property, i.e., it satisfies the evidence sufficiency conditions of the MBCM, two further checks are performed to establish if a certificate can be issued for the TOC:

1. A check of whether the collected evidence shows any violations of the monitored security property;
2. A check of whether any additional validity conditions specified in the MBCM are satisfied. Such conditions may, for example, require a TPM-enabled confirmation of the integrity of the components used to collect and analyze the monitoring evidence, as well as the components of the CUMULUS framework itself throughout the monitoring process.
3. A check of whether any detected anomalies and conflicts are acceptable to the certification authority that will sign of the certificate.

These checks are performed by the certificate generator and if 1 and 2 are successful, the generator aggregates the accumulated monitoring evidence and creates a certificate of the security property for the TOC incorporating the aggregated evidence with it. The aggregation of monitoring evidence takes place as described by the evidence aggregation element of MBCM. Once generated, a certificate is stored in the certificates DB and can be retrieved by any external party that has (read) access rights to it. The retrieval of certificates is supported by the certification communicator component of the CUMULUS framework.

In the current implementation, we are using EVEREST (EVEnt REaSoning Toolkit [12]) as a key component of the certificate generator to perform the monitoring required during the certification process. EVEREST is an open-source monitoring framework developed by the authors of this paper that are working for City University to support the monitoring of service-based systems. EVEREST supports the monitoring of properties expressed in a first order temporal logic language based on Event Calculus.

5   An Example: Certificate Issuing in an e-Health Scenario

An example of security property that could be certified through a monitoring based certificate in the e-Health scenario is an instance of an integrity requiring that a TOC should protect that data that it stores from unauthorised alterations. This property corresponds to `AIS:integrity:data-alteration-prevention` in the catalog of properties that the Cloud Security Alliance has defined [11]. In the CUMULUS framework this property is specified as an assertion in SecureSLA* as shown in Fig. 5. The description of SecureSLA* is beyond the scope of this paper and can be found in [11]. The above definition of the integrity property uses the variable autop which indicates an invocation of the authorisation operation of `authorisation::interface::authorise` to check if cns has appropriate authorisation rights (successful authorisation is indicated by requiring the output result of the authorisation operation to be true). The property of protected (i.e., authorised) alteration is then specified by a guarantee state which requires that for each invocation of a data alteration operation, the authorisation operation has been invoked prior to it and it has responded with an output that indicates the authorisation of the particular consumer. The temporal sequence of the two operations is indicated by the condition less_than (request (autop), request (altop)) and less_than (reply(autop), request(altop)). The correlation of the requester of the alteration operation and the agent whose credentials are checked by the authorisation operation is ensured by using the same value for the requester parameter of the data alteration operation and the agent parameter of the authorisation operation (i.e., credentials). In the case of the above property the CUMULUS framework would first check if the cloud infrastructure where the specific TOC whose integrity is to be certified can provide primitive events capturing the calls of the operations `dataalteration::interface::deletepatient` and `authorisation::interface::authorise` and the responses

```
assertion {
   sla_ template { ...
   altop is invocation [ invoke {
      endpoint = endpoint::id::a
      operation = dataalteration::interface::deletepatient
      param { name = requester value = credentials } } ]
   autop is invocation [ invoke {
      endpoint = endpoint::id::b
      operation = authorisation::interface::authorise
      param { name = agent value = credentials }
      param { name = result value = true } } ]

/* —AGREEMENT TERM — */

   agreement_ term { id = agreement::term::1 guaranteedstate
      { id = guaranteedstate1
      ( less_ than (request(autop),(request(altop)) ) and
      (less_ than (reply(autop),request(altop)) ) } }
      }
}
```

Fig. 5. Assertion for data alteration prevention

to these calls, i.e., events matching the terms request(autop), request(altop), reply(autop), and request(altop) in the above assertion. If such event captors exist the monitoring process can start. The evidence sufficiency conditions in this case could, for example, require that the considered event log should include at least 10,000 invocations of each of the operations `dataalteration::interface::deletepatient` and `authorisation::interface::authorise`, gathered over a period of at least 1 year. Based on these conditions, if after collecting evidence satisfying the above conditions, there are no instances of violation of the assertion in Fig. 5, a certificate for the relevant TOC and the property can be generated.

6   Future Work

In this section we report on a preliminary suitability desktop analysis of the state of the art Cloud monitoring tools to address security properties. Namely, we have performed an initial prospective analysis regarding which of these *off-the-shelf* monitoring tools seem to support evidence gathering in order to validate that any of the properties in the catalog defined in [11] are present. In [11] the interested reader can find more details about property definition. For our analysis, we have inspected the metrics that these monitoring tools could collect and judged whether their reported values could be used as evidence for the security properties in [11]. The result of this analysis is summarized in Table 1. Notice that we omit completely in the discussion those categories from [11] that

Table 1. Security properties coverage by SotA Cloud monitoring tools (Desktop analysis)

	Zenoss core	Nagios core	Hyperic	New relic	Ganglia	OSSEC
A.1 (18)						
A.1.2						✓
A.1.4						✓
A.1.9		✓	✓	✓		
A.1.17				✓		
A.2 (2)						
A.2.1		✓				
A.4 (3)		✓	✓	✓		✓
A.9 (5)						
A.9.1				✓		
A.11 (7)						
A.11.3						✓
A.11.6				✓		
A.14 (11)		✓	✓	✓		
A.15 (4)						
A.15.3	✓	✓	✓	✓	✓	
A.15.4	✓	✓	✓	✓	✓	

do not seem to be supported by any monitoring tool. This result will be our starting point for a *hands-on* evaluation of some of these Cloud monitoring tools both regarding evidence gathering and how difficult or easy it is to use them as external monitoring tools that can gather evidence for our infrastructure in order to issue or maintain certificates.

Next, we will name the category, the number of its properties breakdown between parenthesis, and which monitoring tools seem able to gather evidences at any of the cloud levels in relation to one property in that category. In short, based on the number of security properties covered, Nagios, Hyperic and New Relic are those tools that are able to gather evidences that could help CUMULUS to certify a major number of security properties. For these tools, we will perform a *hands on* analysis in the immediate future. This analysis will also consider how easy or hard is to achieve a proper interplay of these tools with the CUMULUS monitoring infrastructure.

We explain next what is shown briefly in Table 1. This table shows which monitoring tools seem to support which security properties from [11, Annex A] according to their provided descriptions:

- *A.1.AIS: Application & Interface Security* (18). OSSEC seems suitable to check both `A.1.2 Software alteration detection` and `A.1.4 Data alteration detection`. Nagios, Hyperic and New Relic could help to validate the property `A.1.9 network authenticated server access`. In addition, New Relic could help to validate the property `A.1.17 user traceability`.

- *A.2 IVS: Infrastructure & Virtualization Security* (2). Nagios seems useful to validate `A.2.1 Tenant isolation level`.
- *A.4 SEF: Security Incident Management, E-Discovery & Cloud Forensics* (3). Nagios, Hyperic, New Relic and OSSEC seem to offer support for validating the properties in this category.
- *A14. Business Continuity Management & Operational Resilience* (11). Nagios, Hyperic and New Relic seem suitable to address this category.
- *A9. Legal & Standards Compliance* (5). New Relic seems suitable to address in particular, the property `A.9.1 Country level anchoring`.
- *A.11 DSI (Data Security & Information Life cycle Management)* (7). New Relic seems suitable to address the property `A.11.6 Storage retrieveability`. Also, OSSEC seems suitable for `A.11.3 Data leakage detection`.
- *A15. Change Control & Configuration Management* (4). Zenos, Hyperic, Nagios, New Relic, and Ganglia seem specifically adequate to validate some properties in this category. In particular, the properties `A.15.3 Percentage of timely configuration change notifications` and `A.15.4 Configuration change reporting capability`.

7 Conclusions

In this paper we have presented a certification infrastructure that is able to manage monitoring based certification, testing based certification and, in an immediate future, as we explain below, also TPM based and hybrid certification (to combine both monitoring and testing approaches). We have focused on the monitoring based certification and have illustrated our approach to address it with an example from the e-Health domain. The infrastructure described in this paper is intended to offer support for a (constant) evaluation of an IT resource in order to determine whether certain security property hold from a given point in time on, in a particular context. In this manner we try to reinforce transparency in the industry, helping business to evaluate the security risks they may accept when working with a particular cloud service provider.

We have also reported on off-the-shelf tools for cloud infrastructure monitoring, and have identified a number of open source versions of industrial strength tools that could be used by the CUMULUS infrastructure as external evidence collectors. Finally, we have reported on the results of a preliminary suitability desktop analysis to address the catalog of the security properties in [11]. This analysis was based on the inspection of the metrics collected by these tools, and their potential use as evidences supporting these security properties.

We conclude noting that, in addition to the infrastructure described in Sect. 3, there are some components that are not currently part of the framework but are planned to be implemented in the future. For example, an `Auditing Module` will allow cloud auditors to analyze the entire certification process, including the certifications models, the processed evidences and the issued certificates.

Also, a `Trusted Computing manager` component will be integrated to provide authentication and measurement functions based on the Trusted Computing platform for both the Monitoring and Testing Monitor Managers. Finally, an `Hybrid Manager` component will be designed and implemented so as it can be responsible to handle hybrid certificates (e.g., certificates based upon both types of evidences gathered by monitoring and testing or TC) when the Certification Manager calls it through the 'Hybrid Manager API.' It should probably communicate with the other managers, in order to collect all required information for hybrid certification.

Acknowledgment. The work presented in this paper has been partially funded by the EU FP7 project CUMULUS (grant no. 318580).

References

1. Cloud Security Alliance. Cloud control matrix v. 3.0.1 (2014). https://cloudsecurityalliance.org/research/ccm/
2. CUMULUS. Deliverable D5.1 'CUMULUS framework architecture', June 2013. http://www.cumulus-project.eu/
3. CUMULUS. Deliverable D2.3 'Certification Models v2', May 2014. http://www.cumulus-project.eu/
4. Foster, H., Spanoudakis, G.: Advanced service monitoring configurations with sla decomposition and selection. In: Chu, W.C., Wong, W.E., Palakal, M.J., Hung, C.-C. (eds.) Proceedings of the 2011 ACM Symposium on Applied Computing (SAC), TaiChung, Taiwan, 21–24 March, pp. 1582–1589. ACM (2011)
5. Zenoss Inc. Cloud Foundry Zen Pack (2014). http://www.zenoss.com/solution/awareness
6. ISO/IEC. Common Criteria-ISO/IEC 15408 (2014). http://standards.iso.org/ittf/PubliclyAvailableStandards/index.html
7. Nagios Enterprises LCC. Nagios core, GNU License (2014). http://nagios.sourceforge.net/docs/nagioscore/4/en/about.html#whatis
8. BSD license open source software. Ganglia Monitoring System (2014). http://ganglia.info/
9. Spanoudakis, G., Krotsiani, M., Mahbub, K.: Incremental certification of cloud services. In: 7th International Conference on Emerging Security Information, Systems and Technologies (SECUREWARE 2013) (2013). http://openaccess.city.ac.uk/3236/
10. New Relic. New Relic-Server, Browser, APM (2014). http://newrelic.com/products
11. Pannetrat, A., Hogben, G., Katopodis, S., Spanoudakis, G., Sánchez, C.: Deliverable D2.1 'Security Aware SLA Specification Language and Cloud Security Dependency Model', May 2013. http://www.cumulus-project.eu/index.php/public-deliverables
12. Spanoudakis, G., Kloukinas, C., Mahbub, K.: The serenity runtime monitoring framework. In: Kokolakis, S., Gómez, A.M., Spanoudakis, G. (eds.) Security and Dependability for Ambient Intelligence, vol. 45, pp. 213–238. Springer, USA (2009)
13. OSSEC tem. OSSEC-Open source security (2014). http://www.ossec.net/
14. VMWare. Hyperic HQ-open source edition (2014). http://www.hyperic.com

Privacy and Transparency in the Cloud

HCI Requirements for Transparency
and Accountability Tools
for Cloud Service Chains

Simone Fischer-Hübner[(⊠)], John Sören Pettersson, and Julio Angulo

Karlstad University, Universitetsgatan 2, 651 88 Karlstad, Sweden
{simone.fischer-huebner, john_soren.pettersson,
julio.angulo}@kau.se

Abstract. This paper elaborates HCI (Human-Computer Interaction) requirements for making cloud data protection tools comprehensible and trustworthy.
The requirements and corresponding user interface design principles are derived
from our research and review work conducted to address in particular the following HCI challenges: How can the users be guided to better comprehend the
flow and traces of data on the Internet and in the cloud? How can individual end
users be supported to do better informed decisions on how their data can be used
by cloud providers or others? How can the legal privacy principle of transparency and accountability be enforced by the user interfaces of cloud inspection
tools? How can the user interfaces help users to reassess their trust/distrust in
services? The research methods that we have used comprise stakeholder
workshops, focus groups, controlled experiments, usability tests as well as literature and law reviews. The derived requirements and principles are grouped
into the following functional categories: (1) ex-ante transparency, (2) exercising
data subject rights, (3) obtaining consent, (4) privacy preference management,
(5) privacy policy management, (6) ex-post transparency, (7) audit configuration, (8) access control management, and (9) privacy risk assessment. This broad
categorization makes our results accessible and applicable for any developer
within the field of usable privacy and transparency-enhancing technologies for
cloud service chains.

Keywords: Usable privacy · HCI requirements · Cloud service · Transparency ·
Accountability

1 Introduction

Responsibilities of cloud services are complicated and difficult to comprehend due to
the drive to make service delivery to companies and other organisations on heavily
automatised subscriptions processes. Privacy principles and questions of accountability
are thus hidden in standardized policy documents that furthermore may change every
year or so when new possibilities are available for one or several of the cloud services
that together make up a cloud service for a particular organisation. Organisations
relying on cloud services for their own activities towards customers, members, or
employees, are thus risking to not being able to fulfill their obligations concerning data

© Springer International Publishing Switzerland 2015
M. Felici and C. Fernández-Gago (Eds.): A4Cloud 2014, LNCS 8937, pp. 81–113, 2015.
DOI: 10.1007/978-3-319-17199-9_4

processing and are thus also risking their reputation. A whole range of functions are needed to make data processing transparent to data subjects[1] as well as to privacy officers and privacy auditors. Moreover, however advanced these functions must be, they also have to be available to private persons, to officers at the companies using the cloud services, and to the cloud service providers as well as to privacy auditors and data protection board officers. Thus, the user interfaces for such functionality must meet each user at his/her level of competence and responsibility.

This paper reports on requirements collected and structured for the development of user interface guidelines for tools that will enhance transparency and accountability in cloud service chains. The work has been conducted within the EU7FP project A4Cloud – Cloud Accountability project (www.a4cloud.eu) and reported in more detail in the A4Cloud project Deliverable D:C-7.1 on "General HCI principles and guidelines for accountability and transparency in the cloud" [1].

The relation of this work to the A4Cloud project is given in the following section after which the general research questions motivating our work and the specific functionality framework employed for the present paper are stated.

1.1   Relations to the A4Cloud Project

The A4Cloud project deals with accountability for the cloud and other future Internet services. It conducts research with the objective of increasing trust in cloud computing by developing methods and tools for different stakeholders through which cloud providers across the entire cloud service value chains can be made accountable for the privacy and confidentiality of information held in the cloud. The A4Cloud stakeholders, for whom methods and tools will be developed, comprise cloud customers in the form of *individual end users* and *business end users* (i.e., service providers outsourcing data processing to the cloud), *data subjects* whose data have been outsourced to the cloud (and who may or may not be individual end users), as well as *regulators*, such as data protection commissioners, and *cloud auditors*. The methods and tools that are developed are combining risk analysis, policy enforcement, monitoring and compliance auditing with tailored IT mechanisms for security, assurance and redress. In particular, the A4Cloud project is creating solutions to support cloud users in deciding and tracking how their data are used by cloud service providers [2].

A4Cloud solutions thus also include tools for enhancing transparency of data processing for the different stakeholders, so-called transparency-enhancing tools or transparency tools. The concept of transparency, as it is considered by us in A4Cloud, comprises both 'ex ante transparency', which enables the anticipation of consequences before data are actually disclosed (e.g., with the help of privacy policy statements), as well as 'ex post transparency', which informs about consequences if data already has been revealed (what data are processed by whom and whether the data processing is in conformance with negotiated or stated policies) (compare [3]).

---

[1] A 'data subject' is a natural person about whom personal data are processed.

1.2   Research Questions

This paper results from the work aimed at providing a set of general HCI principles and guidelines, which have a basis in human-centered design and which should support User Interface (UI) design for transparency functions in cloud services.

For deriving the requirements for such HCI principles and guidelines, our group conducted research and review work for addressing particularly the following HCI challenges that are of relevance for tools for different cloud stakeholders:

- How can users be guided to better comprehend the flow and traces of data on the Internet and in the cloud?
- How can individual end users (i.e. data subjects) be supported to do better informed decisions on how their data can be used by cloud providers or others?
- How can the legal privacy principle of transparency and accountability be enforced by the user interfaces of A4Cloud or other transparency and accountability tools?
- How can the user interfaces help users (in particular individual end users) to reassess their trust/distrust in services?

This paper summarizes the work conducted for addressing these challenges and the results achieved in the form of HCI requirements for user interfaces for tools for accountability and transparency in cloud service ecology.

1.3   Framework of Functional Categories for Presenting the Derived Requirements

In order to make use of the requirements brought forth by our data collection and analysis, the resulting requirements have to be inserted in a framework of function categories where each category conceivably could be handled by different but inter-acting tools within a future highly integrated framework for accountable and transparent cloud services. The set of broadly defined functions we will use in the concluding presentation in Sect. 5 have been worked out in the planning and on-going work of A4Cloud and find close parallels in other projects. In short, we categorize the transparency and accountability functionality in the following nine groups:

- Ex ante transparency (policy display incl. policy mismatches, mediating of trust-worthiness or risks to individual end users).
- Exercising data subject rights (permitting data subjects to access or to delete, block, correct their data).
- Obtaining informed consent (from data subjects for the processing of their personal data).
- Privacy preference management (helping individual end users to manage their privacy preferences).
- Privacy policy management (for business end users).
- Ex post transparency (incl. display of policy violations and help with risk mitigation).
- Audit configuration (help with settings in regard to collection of evidences).

- Access control management.
- Privacy risk assessment (for business end users).

1.4 Outline

The remainder of this paper is structured as follows:

Section 2 presents related previous work on HCI principles and guidelines for Privacy-Enhancing Technologies (PETs) and privacy-enhancing identity management including transparency-enhancing tools and functions. It is discussed how far these guidelines can also be applied within the cloud context, and what the limitations of these guidelines are.

Section 3 motivates the choice of HCI challenges addressed in our approach, mostly as an answer to the limitations found in Sect. 2. It also discusses the research questions that those challenges imply in more detail.

Then Sect. 4 presents and motivates the different research methods we applied when addressing these HCI challenges and deriving HCI requirements. The actual research work has been reported in various publications and is not reported here (see esp. [4–6]. For a comprehensive summary, see A4Cloud Deliverable D-C.7.1 [1]).

Section 5, "Mapping Requirements to Functional Categories", presents the "grand total" of elicited HCI requirements by sorting them into the nine functional categories mentioned in 1.3. Moreover, for each requirement, the observation(s) behind the requirement is (are) mentioned as well as suggestions for possible HCI design guidelines.

Finally, Sect. 6, "Concluding Remarks", will provide conclusions of this work and provide an outlook into the future HCI work.

2 Related Work

In this section, we present an overview of related HCI principles, recommendations and guidelines for usable privacy and security, which are based on earlier research and that can be of relevance for cloud technologies. We point out how far existing guidelines need further enhancements for the context of accountability and transparency in the cloud.

HCI guidelines for both security and privacy technologies have to address specific HCI challenges, as noted first by [7] for security, and later by many others for privacy:

- Security and privacy protection are typically secondary goals for ordinary users;
- They contain difficult concepts that may be unintuitive to lay users;
- True reversal of actions is not possible.

Jakob Nielsen published one of the most referred to collection of general HCI principles, his so-called 10 Usability Heuristics for User Interface Design [8], which are called "heuristics" because they are rather rules of thumb than specific usability guidelines. These HCI heuristics, which were originally derived from an analysis of 249 usability problems, comprise: "Visibility of system status", "Match between system and the real world", "User control and freedom", "Consistency and standards", "Error prevention", "Recognition rather than recall", "Flexibility and efficiency of use", "Aesthetic and minimalist design", "Help users recognize, diagnose, and recover from errors", "help and documentation."

Johnston et al. expanded and modified the Nielsen's list of principles to derive criteria for a successful HCI applied in the area of IT security ("HCI-S"; [9]).

Further relevant HCI guidelines for aligning security and usability for secure applications were for instance proposed by Yee [10] and by Garfinkel [11]. Even though these guidelines are related to secure applications, some of them can be interpreted and adapted to privacy-enhancing transparency and accountability. For instance, Yee's guideline of "Explicit authorization" stating that "a user's authority should only be granted to another actor through an explicit user action understood to imply granting" can be translated to the guideline that informed consent to personal data disclosure should require an explicit user action understood to imply disclosure. Similarly, also his principles of "Visibility" and "Revocability" of authority could be applied to personal data disclosures. Dhamija and Dusseault [12] discussed flaws of identity management posing HCI and security challenges, and provide some HCI-related recommendations how to address them, which are partly based on Yee's guidelines.

Important domain-specific HCI requirements can be derived from privacy legislation. In the EU FP5 project PISA (Privacy Incorporated Software Agents), Patrick et al. [13, 14] have studied in detail how legal privacy principles derived from the EU Data Protection Directive 95/46/EC [15] can be translated into HCI requirements and what are possible design solutions to meet those requirements. Their research focused on legal privacy principles of (a) transparency, (b) purpose specification and limitation and (c) data subject rights, as well as (d) informed consent as a basis for legitimate data processing. As concluded by the project, these legal principles "have HCI implications because they describe mental processes and behaviours that the data subject must experience in order for a service to adhere to the principles. For example, the principles require that users understand the transparency options, are aware of when they can be used, and are able to control how their personal data are handled. These legal requirements are related to mental processes and human behaviour, and HCI techniques are available to satisfy these requirements" [13]. Therefore, the HCI requirements that were derived comprised requirements on comprehension (to understand, or to know), consciousness (to be aware of or to be informed), control (to manipulate, or be empowered) and consent (to agree) in relation to the selected legal principles.

As a possible HCI solution for achieving informed consent and (ex ante) transparency, the PISA project proposed the concept of 'Just-In-Time-Click-Through Agreements' (JITCTAs), which instead of providing complex and lengthy service terms, should confirm the users' understanding or consent on an as-needed basis. JITCTAS therefore provide small agreements that are easier for the user to read and process, and that facilitate a better understanding of the decision being made in context.

The Art. 29 Data protection Working Party[2] has in its opinion on "More Harmonised Information Provisions" given the recommendation of providing information

---

[2] Under Article 29 of the Data Protection Directive, a Working Party on the Protection of Individuals with regard to the Processing of Personal Data is established, made up of the Data Protection Commissioners from the Member States together with a representative of the European Commission. The Working Party is independent and acts in an advisory capacity. The Working Party seeks to harmonize the application of data protection rules throughout the EU, and publishes opinions and recommendations on various data protection topics.

in a "multi-layered format under which each layer should offer individuals the information needed to understand their position and make decisions" [16]. They suggest three layers of information provided to individuals, which include the short privacy notice (basically corresponding to JITCTAs), the condensed notice and the full privacy notice. The short notice (layer 1) must offer individuals the core information required under Article 10 of the EU Data Protection Directive 95/46/EC, which includes at least the identity of the controller and the purpose of processing. In addition, a clear indication must be given as to how the individual can access additional information. The condensed notice (layer 2) includes in addition all other relevant information required under Art. 10, such as the recipients or categories of recipients, whether replies to questions are obligatory or voluntary and information about the data subject's rights. The full notice (layer 3) includes in addition to layers 1 and 2 also "national legal requirements and specificities."

In the EU FP6 PRIME project on "Privacy and Identity Management for Europe", one built upon the legal privacy principles and HCI requirements from the PISA project along with HCI requirements for socio-cultural privacy principles to derive proposed UI design solutions for privacy-enhancing Identity Management systems [17].

The PRIME project has also followed the Working Party's recommendations to use multi-layered privacy notices and the concept of a JITCTA in its design proposals for "Send Data?" dialogue boxes for obtaining the user's informed consent. However, a problem with click-through agreements including JITCTAs is that users have the tendency to automate behaviours so that the individual parts of an action are executed without conscious reflection [18]. The PRIME HCI work package therefore also developed the alternative concept of Drag-And-Drop-Agreements (DaDAs), by which users have to express consent by moving graphical representations of their data to a graphical representation of the receiver, and thus forces users to make better informed decisions while also allowing the system to detect erroneous conceptions of the user if data are dropped on the wrong recipient (e.g. credit card symbol is dropped on web shop symbol instead of on pay service symbol) [19].

Based on experiences gained from developing UIs for privacy-enhancing identity management systems over several years, the EU FP7 project PrimeLife provided an experience report *"Towards Usable Privacy Enhancing Technologies: Lessons Learned from the PrimeLife Project"* (Graf et al. 2011) which discusses HCI fallacies and provides HCI heuristics, best practice solutions and guidance for the development of usable PETs, which will be of relevance for A4Cloud. This report started with identifying major HCI fallacies that were experienced, which included the problem of many users to differentiate whether data are stored on the user side (under the user's control) and to comprehend to which network entities personal data flows during online transactions. Furthermore, the mediation of trustworthiness, intercultural differences and a well comprehensible terminology to be used in UIs are challenges to be taken into consideration. Many of the HCI issues that were experienced are mental model issues which are difficult to solve for novel PET concept, which are unfamiliar for the users. This is especially true for those PETs, for which no obvious real world analogies exist. Based on those experiences and lessons learned, the report provides HCI heuristics for PETs, which adapt, extend and exemplify the classical list of Nielsen's Usability Heuristics for the PET domain. Finally, the report also provides some evaluation guidelines for PET user interfaces, and what needs to be considered for the preparation and performance of usability tests.

In particular, *PET-USES* (Privacy-Enhancing Technology Users' Self-Estimation Scale) is introduced, which was developed in PrimeLife as a post-test questionnaire that enables users to evaluate PET-User Interfaces both in terms of the primary task and specific PET related secondary tasks [21].

In complementation to the HCI heuristics, the PrimeLife project also developed *HCI Patterns for PETs* which provide best practice solutions ("design patterns", after Alexander et al. [22]) for the PET user interface design [23]. Relevant also is the on-going Privacy Design Pattern project described by Doty and Gupta (http://privacypatterns.org/).

Finally, a couple of recent reports on trust marks and privacy seals should be mention as these also deals with HCI questions for transparency in the web. The recent recommendations in ECC-Net's Trust mark report ([24], pp. 54ff) does not give specific details on graphics and interaction design, but lists a number of criteria that should be easy to check for consumers, and it is noted that presently trust marks are not well-known or easily identified. Besides being easily identifiable, the standards of a trust mark must also be easily understood. Finally it can be mentioned that the report stresses a number of criteria that "give a trust mark the 'added value' beyond the legal requirements that companies are forced to meet anyway." These criteria are often directly related to HCI questions: easy access to member-checkups, access to multilingual information and service, access to each trader's internal complaint handling system and also to alternative dispute resolutions, especially online dispute resolution. These recommendations have much in parallel to work done in PRIME and PrimeLife on DataTrack. Referring to the ECC-Net's report and some other sources, ENISA [25] identifies five challenges in communicating privacy seals to ordinary web users and then presents directions to go in order to find solutions to these challenges.

While the existing HCI principles and guidelines presented in this section are still valid and applicable to cloud PET, some work is needed to elaborate and derive further HCI principles and guidelines addressing specifically HCI challenges for transparency and accountability technologies in the cloud context. Most HCI fallacies identified by the PrimeLife project in regard to the users' comprehension of his personal data flows and traces, trust in PETs and comprehension of novel PET concepts will also be important to address when designing user interfaces for privacy-enhancing transparency and accountability tools for the cloud. Legal privacy principles may be interpreted differently for the cloud and are currently re-discussed under the proposed reform of data protection legislation in Europe. Therefore, we have specifically researched related HCI challenges on comprehension of personal data flows, PET concepts such as policy notices, trust and the interpretation of legal privacy principles in the cloud context to derive further specific HCI principles and guidelines for the cloud context.

3 HCI Challenges and Related Research Questions

This section presents the HCI challenges and related research questions that we regard as fundamental and which therefore have motivated the research methodology accounted for in Sect. 4.

As discussed above, previous HCI research has revealed that many users have problems to differentiate whether data are stored on the user side (under the user's control) or on a remote services side and the problem to comprehend to which network entities personal data flows during online transactions (e.g. [23]). Evoking the correct mental model in regard to where data are transferred to and where they are processed will be a particularly pertinent challenge for cloud computing because one or several chains of cloud service providers may be involved:

How can users be guided to better comprehend the flow and traces of data on the Internet and in the cloud?

- What are the mental models of different stakeholders and types of users in regard to the distribution of personal data in a complex cloud ecosystem?
- What HCI concepts are suitable for evoking the correct mental models of data flows and traces?

These questions will be significant for both ex ante technologies for transparency, e.g. in the form of privacy policy tools, as well as for ex-post transparency enhancing technologies, which will allow users to track their data in the cloud.

However, for supporting individual users in making decisions on how their data are used by cloud providers, it has to be taken into consideration that previous research has shown that lay users often do not behave rationally with regard to decisions on personal data disclosure [26, 27] meaning that we cannot assume either that they will do so when deciding on the disclose or outsourcing their data to the cloud. In order to design usable tools that offer transparency and accountability of the users' data in the cloud, we have to understand their attitudes, behaviours and mental models in relation to cloud services. Having these understandings can help to reveal what these users value, what they think is important, and what useful features that can be included in the user-friendly tools for transparency and accountability and how these features can be designed to be valued and well understood by individual users.

When it comes to the business end users, their security officers face the challenge generating and managing access control rule sets for controlling the use of data in the cloud.

These aspects have motivated us to research also the following:

How can end users be supported to make more informed decisions on how their data can be used by cloud providers or others?

- How much cognitive effort or time are people willing to spend in order to understand what happens to different types of personal information in the cloud?
- How can the user interfaces of ex ante transparency tools be designed to support and motivate users to take more rational and informed decisions?

- How can service providers obtain usable access control rule sets for data outsourced to the cloud that are reflecting the organisation's access control policy and are easy to understand and manage?

The EU Legal Data Protection Directive has defined legal principles for providing transparency and control to users. In the context of cloud computing, the existing legal requirements may partly need some re-interpretation. Currently, also new legal principles for providing better transparency and control for individual cloud users and increasing accountability for cloud providers have been discussed as part of the proposed EU data protection regulation [28]. Therefore, a third HCI challenge that we addressed, which is also related to the other two HCI challenges mentioned above, is:

How can the legal privacy principles of transparency and accountability be enforced by the user interfaces of A4Cloud tools?

- What legal privacy principles for transparency and accountability for the cloud need to be taken into consideration by the HCI design of A4Cloud tools?
- How can legal privacy principles for transparency and accountability for the cloud be mapped to HCI principles and solutions?

Finally, as concluded in the recent ECC-Net [24] and ENISA [25] reports, trust plays a key role in the acceptance and uptake of PET solutions. The ISO 25010:2011 definition of *trust* runs: "Degree to which a user or other stakeholder has confidence that a product or system will behave as intended." [29]. From this definition it may appear as if people's notions of trustworthiness in an electronically delivered service were simply an issue of how well they trust an automaton. However, there is ample evidence that trust stems from a range of sources – previous encounters with the service provider (possibly in non-electronic form), the general reputation of the brand of the service provider, as well as statements made by friends – rather than from any direct understanding of the privacy and security reliability of the service in question. In addition, users may lack trust in novel PETs with functionality which may not fit their mental models of how the technology works. For this reason, one more challenge to be tackled is:

How can the user interfaces help users (in particular individual end users) to reassess their trust/distrust in services?

- What are suitable HCI means for mediating trust in trustworthy services?
- How can user interfaces connect to known reliable sources for trust?

Thus, these were the questions motivating our research. In the next section we will discuss the methodology that was developed to start to address these challenges. Several methods were used, each generating a set of specific requirements and HCI design suggestions. Section 5 makes a comprehensive summary of the requirements (and in brief also of proposed HCI principle and design suggestions) by presenting them in relation to the functional categories identified in Sect. 1.3.

4 Research Methods

This section discusses and motivates our research methodologies and ethical considerations.

4.1   Human-Centred Design

We strived to follow a human-centred design approach for eliciting and testing HCI requirements and guiding the development of user interface design principles. Human-centred design is defined by ISO 9241-210 as "an approach to interactive systems development that aims to make systems usable and useful by focusing on the users, their needs and requirements, and by applying human factors/ergonomics, and usability knowledge and techniques" [30]. In the research reported here we have elicited and refined user requirements and related HCI principles through methods including stakeholder focus groups, controlled usability testing and other methods described in the subsection below.

For the choice of methods, we have taken into consideration that important concepts for the comprehension of transparency and related risks, such as what information is stored and where it is processed, are usually difficult to understand for the lay users, while other end user groups such as regulators or security administrators usually have a clearer understanding. Therefore, different user-groups require different interfaces and interaction paradigms. This also means that the different user groups have to be involved using different approaches to human-centred design. For this reason, we have used controlled experiments and mock-up-based evaluations in addition to focus groups in order to explore the needs of lay users, while the needs of professional stakeholder groups were mainly investigated by means of stakeholder workshops and focus groups. The controlled experiments and mock-up-based evaluations had as an objective to analyse lay users' mental models of cloud-related technical concepts, since our earlier work has shown that many HCI issues are mental model issues which are difficult to solve for novel PET concepts [20, 31].

The following subsection briefly describes the methodologies applied and the reason they were regarded as suitable approaches for eliciting HCI requirements. The sequence of methods applied during the first 12 months of the project is also depicted in Fig. 1.

4.1.1   Methods Employed

This subsection discusses and motivates the different research methods that we have applied when addressing these HCI challenges and deriving HCI principles while following a human-centred design approach.

Stakeholder workshop. Stakeholder workshops provide the opportunity for active face-to-face interactions between different influential actors who can express their opinions and needs for a system being developed. This method is strongly encouraged during the initial design processes, as a way of ensuring that the needs of those who might be impacted by the system are taken into account, as well as trying to achieve a common vision of the system [32]. An important step of this method is identifying those stakeholders that can have a say on the development of the system. Typically one stakeholder representative is selected from a user group and invited to participate in a workshop.

Once the stakeholders have been identified different approaches can be followed during the meeting in order to incite discussions, to promote the exchange of ideas and

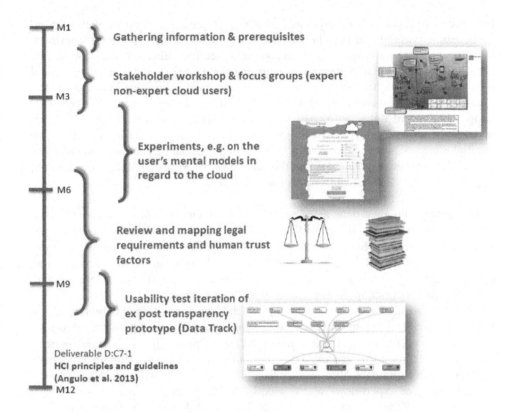

M1

Gathering information & prerequisites

M3

Stakeholder workshop & focus groups (expert non-expert cloud users)

Experiments, e.g. on the user's mental models in regard to the cloud

M6

Review and mapping legal requirements and human trust factors

M9

Usability test iteration of ex post transparency prototype (Data Track)

Deliverable D:C7-1
HCI principles and guidelines
(Angulo et al. 2013)
M12

Fig. 1. Methods used during A4Cloud's first project year for eliciting HCI requirements and principles

to identify the needs of the different user groups being represented by invited stakeholders. Such approaches can include general discussions, moderated interviews, focus groups, as well as Open Space [33] and World Cafés [34] methodologies, and others. Depending on the approach taken and the number of participants, the discussions might derive from one main question (as is often the case of Open Space), or from a series of questions. Also, participants might be divided into groups trying to identify challenges related to different themes, or they can be all exchanging ideas while a moderator leads the discussions. The results from the discussions can then be compiled, interpreted and expressed as a set of system requirements. Follow-up interviews or feedback from participants can also be setup in case the researchers need to complement or correct the information acquired during the workshop session.

We have carried out a stakeholder workshop concentrating on the HCI aspects of cloud services. Participants came from the Swedish Data Inspection Board, the Swedish branch of the European Consumer Centre Network, IT service and planners from the region of Karlstad (the University, the Public Health Care provider, the Municipality), and from two IT companies. The purpose of running such a workshop was to discover HCI requirements. These initial requirements also served as the basis and motivations for our subsequent experiments and tests. The workshop was divided into two main sessions, a morning and an afternoon session. A moderator encouraged participants, without biasing the discussions, to elaborate on common questions, concerns and decisions regarding cloud computing services, such as client opinions, the considerations that are important when acquiring cloud services, the decision process of business and individual users surrounding adopting and using cloud computing services, as well as the issues encountered during the use of these services. Observers were assigned to record notes and occasionally ask questions to clarify points or to keep discussions alive. During the afternoon session participants were divided into two parallel groups, where the discussions in one group concentrated on business end users and on the other group focused on individual end users. Workshop notes were later put together to a list of HCI requirements and principles.

Focus groups. Focus groups are appropriate for bringing together a cross-section of users so that they can collaboratively unveil their opinions and needs regarding particular challenges foreseen in the design of a system. Moderators of a focus group can stimulate participants to discuss these opinions with the other group members by using different approaches, such as asking direct questions to participants, encouraging brainstorming, instructing them to work with various probes, etc.

To understand the different ways in which individuals with different levels of familiarity with technology perceive cloud services and comprehend the flow of their personal data on the Internet and in the cloud and vulnerabilities in Internet services, we conducted three focus groups session (including a pilot session with undergraduate students) with participants that were considered expert and non-expert users.

The group of expert users was formed of 16 Ph.D. students in computer science coming from different Swedish Universities (but with different nationalities) who were taking a graduate course on the topic of Privacy Enhancing Technologies. The non-expert users consisted of a group of 15 individuals from different age ranges, cultural and educational backgrounds, who were participants of a project for personal development towards employment opportunities.

Semi-structured Interviews. Semi-structured interviews are interviews where not all questions are designed or planned before the interview, allowing the interview to follow and explore new directions as they come up in the interview process [35].

Semi-structured interviews were considered a good method for capturing the challenges regarding the management of access control lists by system administrators, and how those challenges are commonly handled in their field of work. The results were used as the base for Experiment 4 described below.

Controlled experiments. In experimental studies so-called dependent variables of interest are identified. Then the factors in the study, or independent variables, can be controlled for checking the level of influence of these factors on the variables of interest. By performing experiments using control groups, different hypotheses about people's behaviours, actions, attitudes, opinions and performance can be tested. The ecological validity in an experiment measures the extent to which the setup of the experiment matches real world situations.

We designed and carried out four controlled experiments in order to study the mental models, motivations, and needs of lay users when subscribing to cloud storage services.[3] In order to improve the ecological validity of the experiments, participants were deceived into believing that the cloud service was a real service but afterwards informed about the experimental nature.

Experiment 1: Understanding willingness to distribute personal data to cloud services. **Participants:** 120. **Hypothesis:** End users are more willing to release personal data to a cloud service in exchange for observable valuables (such as free cloud storage). This was confirmed, especially as concerns what end users themselves perceive as non-sensitive.

Experiment 2: Framing and terminology. **Participants:** 190. **Hypothesis:** End users willingness to release personal data depends on how the cloud service expresses benefits at the moment of releasing data. This hypothesis was indeed confirmed.

Experiment 3: Desired cloud services' features. **Participants:** 179. **Hypothesis:** End users would have preferences over certain features for managing their data released to a cloud service. Results in short: users did not show a strong willingness to spend cognitive efforts setting privacy controls, but transparency features are appealing features.

Details and results of the first three experiments are found in Angulo et al. [5].

Experiment 4: A between-subjects experiment design was deployed to gather evidence for the accuracy of the metrics proposed by Beckerle and Martucci [6]. This type of experiment was chosen because a control group was needed for comparing the results of the participants that were assisted by a tool that provided them with measurements regarding the security and usability of their access control rule sets with the results of the participants that didn't have such a support. **Participants:** 12. Eight were non-experts regarding access control configuration and management. The other 4 participants were IT support professionals (experts), who manage access control mechanisms on a regular basis. Four experienced system administrators were then used to rank the results. This evaluation showed that the participants in the group that had the support from our formal tool, rule sets, and metrics performed significantly better than those in the group without this support ($t(3.629) = 7.621$, $p = 0.007$; details of this fourth experiment are published in Beckerle and Martucci [6]).

Usability evaluation. Usability testing is a technique that can measure the actual performance of users when trying to achieve a tasks with a given user interface. During a usability test session test participants are given a set of tasks and a test moderator guides the participant through the tasks while at the same time observing and annotating the interactions of the participants with the interface. The moderator also encourages participants to express aloud their opinions, actions and reactions to the prototype, in an approach commonly referred to as the "think aloud" protocol (Jaspers et al. [43]).

---

[3] These areas were motivated by a range of studies, in particular Brandimarte et al. [36], Gross and Acquisti [27], Hoadley et al. [37], Ion et al. [38], Langer [39], Marshall and Tang [40], Tversky and Kahneman [41], and Xu [42].

Usability testing of low-fidelity prototypes was considered a suitable method for our purposes because it has the advantage of letting lay users communicate their needs, opinions and expectations about new technologies. Expressing this in the open format of the "think aloud" protocol rather than by questionnaires is important as such users might not be very familiar with the terminologies and technologies related to cloud computing, and might not have a clear understanding of how Internet technologies and data handling works either. (We also used the technique of counterbalancing to minimize the introduction of cofounding variables; Rubin and Chisnell [44]).

The objective of the usability test was to test whether graphical illustrations of data flows can improve the lay users' understanding of their personal data traces. Earlier studies of a transparency-enhancing tool called *Data Track* carried out during the PRIME and PrimeLife projects (Pettersson et al. [45]; Wästlund and Fischer-Hübner [46]) had revealed the difficulty for lay users to comprehend the flow and traces of their data on the Internet. In addition, recent work has shown a privacy-friendly mechanism in which data could be stored remotely, for instance, at a cloud service, but still under the users' control [47]. Therefore, in A4Cloud we have tested alternative HCI concepts consisting of graphical UI illustrations of where data are stored and to which entities data have been distributed. Based on the usability heuristic suggesting a "match between the system and the real world" [8], graphical illustrations of data storage and data flows have a potential to display data traces more naturally as in real world networks, as discussed in the PRIME deliverable D06.1.f, Sect. 5.8.1 [17]. Besides, previous research studies suggest that network-like visualizations provide a simple way to understand the meaning behind some types of data [48, 49], and other recent studies claim that users appreciate graphical representations of their personal data flows in forms of links and nodes [50, 51]. The results of usability evaluations that we performed in A4Cloud for graphical user interfaces of the Data Track trace view as depicted in Fig. 2 are reported in Fischer-Hübner et al. [4].

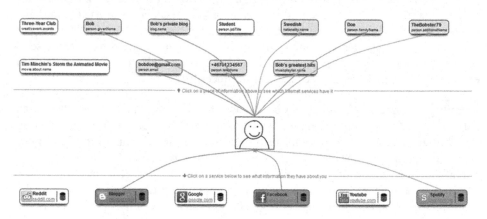

Fig. 2. The user interface of the Data Track trace view that was subject to usability evaluations.

Eliciting and mapping legal requirements. Legal principles will have to be enforced by the user interfaces of transparency and accountability tools. Such principle were elicited in four ways: from the stakeholder group workshops, by a review of relevant legal documents (including the EU Data Protection Directive 95/46/EC [15], the newly proposed EU data protection regulation [28], and relevant opinions published by Art. 29 Data Protection Working Party [16] and [52]), by interviews with legal experts from the A4Cloud project, as well as from input from the A4Cloud advisory board. The mapping of these legal principles to HCI principles and proposed design solutions were partly based on, and partly extending the work of, the PISA project [13], the PrimeLife HCI patterns [23], as well as other relevant HCI guidelines and heuristics. Detailed results are published in Fischer-Hübner et al. [4].

Eliciting requirements from trust issues mentioned in studies and surveys on cloud and Internet use. For eliciting HCI requirements for mediating trustworthiness of services, including cloud services when they (in the future) have been evaluated by transparency-enhancing tools, a literature review was conducted. Many studies on Internet services and users, in particular those involving individual end users, have focused on the degree of confidence people have in e-commerce web sites and more recently in cloud services. Our literature review concentrated on a number of studies from which it has been possible to crystallise HCI requirements and, to some extent, map onto tentative HCI principles or UI examples. Many of the studies refer to other works on trust but it has not been within the scope to follow up on every work. Rather, only one or a few references for an interesting trust-related phenomenon have been deemed sufficient to motivate the discussion of the phenomenon in question and its possible inclusion in the collection of requirements and this is reflected in Sect. 5. We acknowledge that for many of the "observations" derived from publications, more references could possibly have been provided.

4.2   Ethical Consideration

Before the work with external participants in tests, experiments, focus groups, and workshops commenced a description of the work planned and the relation to the A4Cloud project in large was sent to the local board for ethical evaluations at Karlstad University. The plan described the recruitment of participants of focus groups, work-shops, tests, and experiments where we only involved "adult (healthy) volunteers" who provided their informed consent. The plan furthermore described routines for handling and anonymising data at the earliest possible time, providing transparency, and guaranteeing all participants the rights they should have as data subjects. As no sensitive data were obtained and rules of the Swedish data protection act and the EU Data Protection Directive 95/46/EC were clearly followed, no ethical or legal privacy concerns were found by the board.

5   Mapping HCI Requirements to Functional Categories

In order to propose a concise set of HCI principles and guidelines for cloud service chain transparency tools, we group the HCI requirements and related HCI principles obtained from the different research activities indicated in Sect. 4 into general categories related to required functionality of possible accountable and transparent tools. This categorization is on a high functional level and is of the general applicability for tools developed to make cloud service chains transparent and service providers accountable.

From the analysis provided in A4Cloud and other projects, we recognize functionality for:

1. Ex ante transparency (policy display incl. policy mismatches, mediating of trustworthiness or risks to individual end users);
2. Exercising data subject rights;
3. Obtaining consent;
4. Privacy preference management (helping individual end users to manage their privacy preferences)
5. Privacy policy management (for business end users)
6. Ex post transparency (incl. display of policy violations and help with risk mitigation)
7. Audit configuration (help with settings in regard to collection of evidences)
8. Access control management
9. Privacy risk assessment (for business end users)

Below in Sects. 5.1–5.9, we map the obtained HCI requirements and related HCI principles and design suggestions onto these functional categories. This mapping has the objective to show for each type of functionality what HCI requirements need to be met and what HCI principles should be followed during the UI design. For each requirement we list one or several observations noted in our studies. For each observation we attempt to formulate an HCI principle as well as one or several suggestions for UI design solutions. (To lessen the complexity of presentation, we do not refer to our own published results; the interested reader is directed to [1]).

5.1 Ex Ante Transparency

Ex ante transparency tools should meet the HCI requirements motivated and discussed in the following subsections.

5.1.1 Make Explicit Data Disclosures and Implicit Data Collections Transparent

This requirement is based on four observations made in our focus groups and in the usability test.

Focus group observation: Non-expert users believe that acting entities are more related to each other than they might be in reality. Tendency to believe that personal information is distributed among many of the entities represented: "All internet companies can share information about me". **HCI Principle:** The interface should clearly show the different entities that could get a hold of which kind of personal information. **Design suggestion:** Create a network visualization that clearly shows the entities (nodes) getting users' information and the pieces of information that each entity has (as the links).

Focus group observation: Both non-experts and advanced users are aware that service providers can do analysis of their data to find out more information about them. However, non-expert users are less aware of the consequences of the possible misuse of their data. **HCI Principle:** Users could be informed about some of the possible inferences that a service provider (or a group of service providers) can make based on their previous and current data disclosures. **Design suggestion:** Show how different data items can be linked together to form new information or deduce information about them which they might not like to disclose. A series of small network visualisation can be done showing common examples of combinations of data that can reveal more than people tend to imagine.

Focus group observation: Both groups are aware that it is not only the explicit release of personally identifiable information that is important, but also what can be deduced from the data (like behaviours, attitudes, etc.). Information about such inferred data is even less transparent than explicitly disclosed data. **HCI Principle:** Show people the data that they have disclosed explicitly, and show some of the possible inferences that a service can do based on that data. **Design suggestion:** Show a form where people enter data. Then a tool will present a list that shows the possible inferences about their behaviour and personal data based on simple searches that can be conducted.

Usability test observation: There is a difference in the understanding of explicit and implicit collection of data. **HCI Principle:** Users should be made aware of implicit collection of data done by the service provider. **Design suggestion:** When informing about explicit, implicit and inferred personal data, make the look of the explicitly sent (i.e. information that user sent explicitly, for example during registration to a service) information different from the look of implicitly collected information or inferred information (i.e. information that the service provider collects without the user being fully aware of it, such as location, browser version, whether the customer is reliable, etc.).

5.1.2   Make Data Sharing and Data Processing Along the Cloud Chain Transparent, and Provide the Means to Verify It

This requirement is based on four observations from different studies.

Workshop note: There is a lack of transparency along the chain of (cloud) service providers in regard to their location and applicable laws. The main services providers that are contacted may be located in Sweden, while back-end (cloud) service providers are located in another country (Cf. also [53]). **HCI Principle:** Users have to be informed about the country and legal regime of the data controller and data processors and/or the contract's explicit choice of law along the cloud chain. **Design suggestion:** Policy icons illustrating the storage location (e.g., inside or outside EEA) and/or legal rules or practices.

Workshop note: It is difficult for individual and business end users as well as auditors to track data in the cloud and to find out who has or has had access to the data for what purposes. **HCI Principle:** There should be usable and selective audit and transparency tools which even make the handling of explicitly and implicitly collected data (e.g. via the Facebook Like button) transparent (incl. information about data processing purposes). **Design suggestion:** Different visualisations of the users' previous implicit and explicit data disclosures and of the data flows to different service providers could be applied, using, for instance, a timeline view or a trace view. Information about agreed-upon policies can be provided by clicking on service provider representations in a trace view visualisation.

Focus group observation: Both non-experts and advanced users have an idea that data are being forwarded to third parties by service providers. However, non-expert users seem to have a less clear idea of who these third parties may be. **HCI Principle:** (i) The interface should put emphasis on explaining the distribution of information to third parties in a clear way. (ii) Present the purposes for which these third parties are allowed to use the data. (iii) The interface should also explain that sometimes the third parties are not specified or identified by service providers in their policies. (**No specific principle suggested.**)

Trust review: Well-placed trust grows out of active enquiry [54–56]. **HCI Principle:** Users should be able to pursue experimentation and enquiring. Users should be guided beyond enquiring only of friends and relatives. **Design suggestion:** (i) Safe environments for experimentations and enquiries (the environments must not oversimplify the complex cloud service ecology). (ii) Make it possible to enquire "good sources".

5.1.3   Provide Indicators for the Trustworthiness of Nodes Along the Cloud Chain

Workshop note: Services (such as hotels.com, resia.se) operate only as a media-tor/broker, but take no responsibility if something goes wrong. Service brokers have to inform the users about who is the responsible data controller/service provider, with whom the agreement/service contract is actually made. **HCI Principle:** User interfaces of service brokers have to clearly inform the users about the identity of responsible data controller/service provider with whom the contract is made. (**No specific principle suggested.**)

Focus group observation: Expert users have a clearer idea of where attacks can happen and of possible counter measures. Non-expert users had an idea that information can be at risk, but it is very unclear for them what can be attacked, why the information is vulnerable, and the approaches to mitigate the problems. **HCI Principle:** Lay users need help creating correct mental models of what is vulnerable/risky and what is safe. They should be able to understand when they are performing risky actions and feel comfortable or confident when their risks are minimal. Risks should be communicated to users by showing consequences of behaviours in a minimalistic way. **Design suggestion:** Indicate different risk levels with colours and clear explanations. Use adequate language that would communicate the right message to the right user group. Provide layered explanations in an understandable way that can be read in more detail if users are interested, thus catering for the different experience of users.

5.1.4   Policies Need to Make Transparent the Possible Consequences of Data Disclosures in Different Recurrent Situations

Experiment result: Perceived sensitivity of data can influence people's behaviours in regard to exercising control. However, data that might be perceived as non-sensitive (or harmless) can become sensitive with changes in time and/or context. **HCI Principle:** (i) Users should be informed about possible scenarios in which data items could become sensitive. (ii) Users should also be aware about the different purposes for which their information might be used, as well as the possible recipients of their data, since this can affect their behaviour. The perceived sensitivity of data can be dependent on the context in which it is used. **Design suggestion:** (i) In the user interface, provide inline examples of data aggregation or misuse of seemingly harmless data. (ii) Provide a visual indication of how their data might be transferred across the cloud chain or shared with third party services. Icons for data processing purposes could indicate context information in regard to the potential use of the data by these services.

Experiment result: Users are willing to disclose personal data that are perceived as non-sensitive in exchange for a reward that seems valuable. **HCI Principle:** Users should be made aware of the risk and benefits of disclosing their data to a service. **Design suggestion:** Make users conscious about the value of the data they are releasing comparable to something they can relate to, like the estimated monetary value (that the data has for the service providers).

5.1.5 Make Explicit that a Service Is a Cloud-Based Service and What This Implies in Terms of Privacy/Security for the Intended User

Experiment result: Users are unaware or not well informed about the types of online services they subscribe to in regards to the handling of their data and personal privacy. **HCI Principle:** (i) Cloud providers should inform individual end users about the services' privacy policies and make the implications of data disclosures transparent to these users. (ii) Ex ante transparency awareness should be promoted, in order for users to know what type of service they are subscribing to. **Design suggestion:** Make it explicit through the wording and the use of standard icons the consequences in terms of benefits and risks of having personal data in the cloud.

Trust review: Transfer of trust: trust in the company itself is often transferred to trust in the security of company's cloud services [40]. **HCI Principle:** Users should be clear about the difference between service performance and privacy performance. **Design suggestion:** Make evaluation results concerning trustworthiness prominent.

5.1.6 Provide Easily Comprehensible Policies Informing Data Subjects at Least About the Identity of the Controller, Other Responsible Parties, for What Purposes the Data Will Be Used Plus Other Details Needed, so that They Can Understand the Implications

Four observations motivate this requirement:

Workshop note: It is unclear for individual users how they can get redress or compensation if something goes wrong, and whom they should contact in this case, especially if sub cloud providers are used (for instance, a user signs up with the service "Box" providing a cloud service, and Box uses Amazon as a sub cloud provider). **HCI Principle:** It has to be clear and understandable for the user who the responsible parties are and how they can be contacted in case of disputes. **Design suggestion:** (i) Clearly display the contact address of responsible parties on the top layer of multi-layered policies. (ii) Redress tools have to support end users in contacting the data controller or responsible party.

To this problem comes the workshop note enlisted under Sect. 5.1.2 (lack of transparency along the chain of services as regards applicable laws).

Experiment result: Knowing who is able to view/access and see users' data stored in the cloud as well as how the data are used are appealing features. **HCI Principle:** It should be easy for users to find and adjust functionality related to the visibility and usage of their data for specific purposes. **Design suggestion:** Provide privacy-friendly default settings for data access controls and usage that can be easily adapted "on the fly" (as for instance suggested in [57]).

Legal considerations: Data subjects have the right to be informed at least about the controller's identity, purposes and other details as required under Art. 10 EU Data Protection Directive 95/46/EC and should also be informed about any further information needed for making data processing in the cloud transparent and compliant with data protection laws. **HCI Principle:** The data subjects know at least who is the controller of their data, for what purposes the data are obtained plus other details (e.g., contacts and geographic locations of data centres along the cloud chain, applicable laws, how requests by law enforcement are handled, etc.), so that they can understand the implications. **Design suggestion:** Policy information is (i) provided in a way that accounts for the users' mental models; (ii) structured in multiple layers following the recommendation by the Art. 29 Data Protection Working Party [16]; (iii) complemented with suitable policy icons.

5.1.7   Make Trust-Enhancing Indicators Intuitive, Consistent and Believable, as Well as Be Appealing for the Appropriate User Group

Workshop note: There are no commonly used seal/labels for security and trustworthiness for cloud services (apart from the more recent CSA and Cloud Industry Forum certifications). If there were, how would the users know what labels to trust? (ii) Individuals are often not interested in understanding all details of trust seals, but would rather like to know in general whether their data are "secure". **HCI Principle:** Information about trust seals should be displayed in an understandable manner. Further information about the meaning of the seal should be easily accessible. **Design suggestion:** (i) Information about trust-related aspects of seals can be hierarchically structured in different layers (similarly as multi-layered privacy policies – cf. [16]). (ii) Standardized and broadly used seals can be more easily recognized and understood. (iii) In-place information about what a seal means can be provided, e.g. via tooltips or information dialogs and/or links to official information regarding the seals.

Experiment result: People may become skeptical towards unknown services that promise them to guard their privacy. **HCI Principle:** The cloud provider should explain not only the benefits for users, but also the benefits for the cloud provider itself when offering accountable and privacy-friendly features to its customers. (**No specific principle suggested.**)

Experiment result: Trust regarding unknown cloud services might have a cultural component to it. Users from different cultures exhibit different levels of trust. **HCI Principle:** Cloud provider should consider their customers in terms of the culture, location of service, and legislative regimes and cater for their collective mental models and attitudes towards data in the cloud. **Design suggestion:** (i) When users are about to subscribe to a cloud service, appeal to their cultural background by emphasizing features of security, access policies and the like. (ii) Accountability and transparency features might balance the level of trust across different cultures.

Trust review: Internet is regarded as intrinsically insecure ([58]; cf. the cloud study by Ion et al. [38]; cf. also Tsai et al. [59] and the ECC-Net report [24]). **HCI Principle:** "Users needed more accurate and robust models to be able to discover and trust cloud computing services." (Marshall and Tang 2012) **Design suggestion:** In the user interface: users should be directed to sources they would normally rely on. The *Trustguide* speaks of the necessity of taking measures also outside the user interface; this does not directly translate into HCI requirements, but the UI should relate to it [56].

Trust review: "...perceived availability, access, security, and reliability would be key variables of cloud computing acceptance in public sectors since they were found to be influential in predicting the behavioural intention to use cloud technologies" Shin ([60], p. 200). Stakeholder workshop: A "business first attitude" in cloud adoption where economic considerations far outweigh privacy concerns. **HCI Principle:** Business end users need to be correctly informed about cloud security, performance, and availability for individual cloud services they consider. This requirement holds for private sector [61] and public sector [60] alike. For private sector this requirement also meets the problem of the business first attitude if accountability measurements are included in the information so that such aspects can easily be included in the decision process. **Design suggestion:** If available, display trustworthiness by evaluation results in regard to security, privacy, performance, and availability. Use visualisation of an accountability model and match with visualisation of current chain.

5.1.8 Users Should Be Able to Know the Approach and Consequences When Deciding to End the Service

Workshop note: At the time of service registration, end users do not think about how to end the service in the future. While the registration for a service is usually made easy, it is often (made) difficult for end users/organizations to unregister/terminate a service contract, delete data or transfer data to other service providers. It is not always clear to end users whether they "own" their data (or are still in control of their data), as they do not check the terms and conditions carefully. **HCI Principle:** Information about service termination, any continued use of the data by the provider or others even after the termination, data deletion and portability should be easily accessible and comprehensible for end users. **Design suggestion:** Clearly present information about the option and rights of deletion and data portability in the context when it is relevant (e.g., when a service is terminated).

Trust review: Perceived lack of longevity of identifiers makes users blur partial identities: preference for long-lasting identifiers (such as personal email addresses rather than appropriate work-related email addresses; [62]). **HCI Principle:** Users must trust that they can manage in a life-long way the information associated with different identities (implications for transparency and restitution controls). **Design suggestion:** (No obvious way to bridge the trust gap or where to bridge it.)

5.1.9   Users Should Be Aware of the Extent to Which They Can Act
Under Pseudonyms

Trust review: Anonymity option unknown: unawareness of options for identity management has negative effects on trust in privacy-enhancing technology [58]. **HCI Principle:** Users must be able to understand the extent to which they can act under pseudonyms and that they could also access to transparency information when acting under a pseudonym. **Design suggestion:** Within the user interface demonstrate how pseudonymity and anonymity options work, and how users could access their data under a pseudonym.

5.1.10   Inform Users About the Termination of Their Contract in a Clear
and Straight-Forward Manner

See the workshop note under Sect. 5.1.8.

5.1.11   Make Reasonable Claims About the Privacy and Security Policies
and Technical Capabilities of the Service to Promote Trust

Trust review: Unsubstantiated claims do not build trust ([56]: this issue concerns a long-term perspective; one company's misconduct can affect a whole sector). **HCI Principle:** Users must be able to put the right scope to their distrust. **Design suggestion:** Make privacy and security statements short and very clear, and make the scope (i.e. to whom they apply) very explicit.

5.2   Exercising Data Subject Rights

Tools for exercising data subject rights should meet the HCI requirements motivated and discussed in the following subsections.

5.2.1   Make Users Aware of Their Data Subject Rights, and Support
Them to Exercise Their Rights; in Particular, Make Control
Options that Are Relevant in Certain Situations More Obvious
at Those Particular Situations

We refer to several observations here. As in Sect. 5.1.6, there are the rights to be informed but also the problem that redress and compensations are unclear to users. In additions, the following three observations motivate Sect. 5.2.1:

   Focus group observation: Expert users' concerns go beyond the use of personal data, but deal also with people's rights and democratic governments. Non-expert users are less aware of their rights concerning the protection of their data. **HCI Principle:** Interested users should be able to audit the chain of cloud services. Who has accessed data, for what purpose, why did they access those data a particular occasion, with whom data were shared with, etc. It should be easy for people to exercise their rights regarding data protection and handling practices. **Design suggestion:** Make users aware of their rights with links to information (in further policy layers), and help them exercise them by providing them with clear options for action and show a list of logged data that users can query with various questions related to their personal information. Queries can help to filter results that are of relevance for the users. Display a visualization of the chain of clouds and their potential vulnerabilities.

Legal considerations: Data subjects have the right to access their data pursuant to Art. 12 EU Data Protection Directive. Data subjects may have further rights in regard to the processing of their data according to that Directive and more specific laws, e.g. in Sweden a data subject has the right to information on who have accessed the data subject's data according to the Swedish Patient Act. **HCI Principle:** Data subjects are conscious of their ex post transparency rights, understand and can exercise their rights. **Design suggestion:** (i) Ex ante Transparency functions are displayed prominently and obvious to operate. (ii) Transparency functions are based on a suitable metaphor and/or account for the user's mental models. (iii) Transparency functions are made available at the right time/in the right context, e.g. tracking logs should display online functions to exercise the right to access. A "right of access button" could be provided that if clicked allows to see list of what info can be accessed including tracking logs.

Legal considerations: Data subjects have the right to correct, delete or block their data pursuant to Art. 12 (b) EU Data Protection Directive. Further rights, such as the data erasure or the right to data portability, are currently proposed. **HCI Principle:** Data subjects are conscious of their control rights, understand and can exercise their rights. **Design suggestion:** (i) Functions for exercising data subject rights are displayed prominently and obvious to operate. (ii) Transparency functions are based on a suitable metaphor and/or account for the user's mental models. (iii) Transparency functions are made available at the right time/context, e.g. at the time when users are accessing their data locally or online.

5.2.2 Provide Clear Statements of What Rights Apply to Individual Users Considering Different Factors, Such as the Users' Culture or Location and Applicable Legal Regime

Again, we refer as in 5.1.6 to the data subjects' rights. In addition, we refer:

Workshop note: Web services that target their business to Swedish customers (by having a Swedish website, a Swedish telephone support number, using SEK as a currency, etc.) fall under Swedish consumer and data protection laws, even if the business is located outside of Sweden and independent of what contracts say. **HCI Principle:** User should be informed about the applicable consumer rights. Redress tools should (at least in these cases) allow users to contact the data controller in their native language. **(No specific principle suggested.)**

Trust review: "Users from different countries may have different privacy expectations and understanding of privacy guarantees offered by the cloud storage system" [38]. **HCI Principle:** Internationalisation "involves going beyond just translating the service interface and privacy policy" [38]. **Design suggestion:** When seeking customers outside EEA, seek expertise to cover different populations' expectations.

Trust review: Restitution measures have positive trust effects [56]. **HCI Principle:** Clearly mark the possibility and ways of redress. **Design suggestion:** Users' interfaces for transparency tools, such as the Data Track, could mark restitution measures.

5.3 Obtaining Consent

Tools for obtaining consent should meet the HCI requirements motivated and discussed in the following subsections.

5.3.1 Make Users Aware of Pros and Cons of Their Possible Choices in an Unbiased Manner

Experiment result: Users' willingness to release personal data is influenced by the description of alternatives (users tend to prefer short-term benefits). **HCI Principle:** Make users aware of all pros and cons of their choice in an unbiased fashion. **Design suggestion:** Tooltips and/or help texts to clarify consequences of actions.

Trust review: Unsubstantiated claims build trust [63]: the problem here is that well-articulated privacy assurances make many individual end users trust a service' competence and intentions. **HCI Principle:** As users do not scrutinise privacy statements etc., users must be made aware of trustworthy assessments of trustworthiness. **Design suggestion:** Make evaluation results concerning trustworthiness as prominent as cloud providers' privacy and security claims.

5.3.2 Obtain Users' Informed Consent by Helping and Motivating Them to Understand Policies and Service Agreements, so that They Understand the Implications

Workshop note: Often individual end users do not make a really informed choice. It is easy to deceive people because they often neither read nor understand the agreements. **HCI Principle:** Display privacy policies in a simple and understandable manner. **Design suggestion:** (i) Privacy policy statements could be explained in short videos clips (produced by consumer organizations), at the time when the user has to make choices. (ii) Display a graph view of personal data flow, showing how the service provider that users are contacting is connected to other services and the possible distribution of users' data for different purposes. (iii) Drag-and-drop data handling agreements (DaDAs (Drag and Drop Agreements), c.f. Sect. 2) can also help users to consciously understand what they are agreeing to.

Workshop note: Individual users find it difficult to read and understand long and complicated contracts/terms and conditions that are posted online. Often data loss, i.e. unavailability of their data, is the greatest of the consumers' concerns, but limitations of availability (in terms of the amounts of time that data are accessible) mentioned in terms and conditions are not transparent to them. **HCI Principle:** Users have to be aware of and understand important service limitations. **Design suggestion:** Use of UI elements for making users aware, e.g. suitable icons.

Legal considerations: Personal data processing in the cloud can be legitimised by the data subject's unambiguously given consent pursuant Art. 7 (a) EU Directive. **HCI Principle:** Users give informed consent and are understanding the implications. **Design suggestion:** Consent is obtained by click-through agreements associated to short privacy notices (top layer notices of multiple-layered policies), or via DaDAs as discussed in Sect. 2.

5.4 Privacy Preference Management

Privacy preference management tools should meet the HCI requirements motivated and discussed in the following subsections.

5.4.1   UIs for Preference Settings Need to Make Consequences in Different Recurrent Situations and Risks and Benefits of Disclosure Transparent

Two observations: Lay users need help creating correct mental models of what is vulnerable/risky as noted in Sect. 5.1.3 above, and users must be able to understand the extent to which they can act under pseudonyms and that such identification schemas can provide access to transparency information, as noted in Sect. 5.1.9.

5.4.2   Make Users Aware of Pros and Cons of Choices in a Comprehensible and Unbiased Manner

Same as Sect. 5.3.1 under "Obtaining consent".

5.4.3   Offer Appropriate Default Settings and Choices that Are Privacy-Friendly and Reflect the Users Preferred Options

Workshop note: Users have the need to classify their data or groups of data (e.g., by marking sensitive personal data, confidential data). Data classification is needed in particular for risk analysis and by policy tools. **HCI Principle:** Users should be guided when defining and editing labels to classify their data in an easy and meaningful way. Moreover, the user should be able to browse through these data by the defined categories. **Design suggestion:** Provide a filter that allows users to select which categories (labels) are displayed. A tree view can be provided where users can check/uncheck the data to be shown. Alternatively, use tabs to divide the different categories.

Workshop note: Security and privacy risks are not very clear and comprehensible to many individual end users. Even security incidents have no long lasting impacts on the user's risk awareness. On the other hand, they are not interested in policy details but just would like to know whether their data are "safe". **HCI Principle:** Users should be able to understand risk evaluation results, especially if these describe serious risks of non-compliance. They must be informed about privacy breaches/non-compliance in regard to data that they have already disclosed, in such a way that they are aware of and understand those risks. **Design suggestion:** An overall risk evaluation results can be displayed in a prominent way, using a multi-layered structure as suggested by the Art. 29 Data Protection Working Party [16]. The presentation should be based on suitable metaphors.

5.4.4   Let Users Do Settings at the Moment When It Is Relevant ("on-the-Fly" Management of Privacy Settings)

Experiment result: Users are unmotivated to spend cognitive effort or time at setting up privacy controls. **HCI Principle:** Users should be motivated to spend the necessary cognitive effort or time in adjusting their privacy preferences at a moment that is relevant to them and meaningful to their actions. Consequences are easier to grasp than technical features and terms. Inform users not only about how settings can be adjusted, but the consequences of adjusting such settings. **Design suggestion:** (i) Provide appropriate privacy-friendly defaults for a set of situations in order to ease the users' burden of setting privacy preferences. (ii) Let users adjust their preferences "on the fly" as needed. Providing brief but meaningful explanations in terms of the privacy consequences might motivate users to care about adjusting. (iii) In order to enhance users' comprehension and motivation, a cloud provider should present its privacy-enhancing features in a way that relates to users' everyday reality and strive to put technical explanations in secondary information layers.

5.4.5 Explain Consequences not in Technical Terms, but in Practical Terms ("speak the user's language")

Workshop note: It is often unclear for individual users what cloud providers really do with the data (e.g., if they are linking and merging different registers) and whether they are following negotiated or agreed-upon policies and contracts **HCI Principle:** Users should understand data processing purposes and consequences. And, as in Sect. 5.4.3, users must be informed about serious risks of non-compliance and what this may imply when they set preferences, and about privacy breaches/non-compliance in regard to data that they disclosed. **Design suggestion:** Present consequences by "speaking the user's language".

5.5 Privacy Policy Management

Privacy Policy management tools should meet the HCI requirements motivated and discussed in the following subsections.

5.5.1 Make It Possible for Business End Users to Negotiate What Is Negotiable, and Make Negotiation Clear and Simple

Workshop note: In contrast to traditional outsourcing, standard contracts are usually used for cloud computing, which are often less negotiable for business end users in terms of security and privacy and indeed most other matters. **HCI Principle:** Make it possible for users to negotiate what is negotiable, and make the negotiation process clear and simple. **Design suggestion:** Provide opt-in alternatives, e.g. in regard to the country/legal regime of the data storage location.

5.5.2 Provide Opt-in Alternatives, E.G. in Regard to the Country/Legal Regime of the Data Storage Location

We have the same motivating observation as for the requirement immediately above, but here we raise the suggested HCI design to a requirement.

5.6 Ex Post Transparency

Ex post transparency tools should meet the HCI requirements motivated and discussed in the following subsections.

5.6.1 Make Users Conscious of Their Ex Post Transparency Rights, so that They Understand and Can Exercise Their Right of Access

The motivating facts behind this requirement is of course that data subjects have the right to access their data pursuant Art. 12 EU Data Protection Directive etc., as mentioned in Sect. 5.2.1 above.

5.6.2 Make Users Aware of What Information Services Providers Have Implicitly Derived from Disclosed Data

As in Sect. 5.1.1, we noted in focus groups that non-expert users are less aware of the possibility of further data about them being derived or inferred from their explicitly-disclosed data, and of the consequences of possible misuse of their data.

5.6.3 Make Users Aware of the Data Processing and Sharing Practices of the Service Provider

One should observe that it is often unclear for individual users what cloud providers really do with the data as mentioned in Sect. 5.4.5; cf. also Sect. 5.1.1 on non-expert users' belief that acting entities are more related to each other than they might be in reality, and Sect. 5.1.2 on non-expert users do not appear to have a clear idea of who third parties may be.

5.6.4 Help Users Making Data Traces Transparent, E.G. by Providing Interactive Visualisations

The general problem is the one quoted in Sect. 5.1.2 that it is difficult for individual end users, business end users as well as auditors to track data in the cloud and to find out who has or has had access to the data for what purposes. In addition to the obvious requirement deriving from this, we add the suggestion about interactive visualisations from the following experimental results:

Usability test observation: Visualizing data releases through a trace view was found useful, intuitive and informative. It seems to be preferred over a timeline view. **HCI Principle:** Users should have an intuitive and interactive way of visualising previous disclosures of personal data. **Design suggestion:** Data releases could be visualised as a bipartite network, with one possibility having the user as a node in the centre and links branching on one side to the different services (and chain of services) with whom he has had a relationship, and on the other side linking to the data items that have been released.

5.7 Audit Configuration

Audit configuration tools should meet the HCI requirements motivated and discussed in the following subsections.

5.7.1 Provide a Standard Way to Perform Audits Across the Chain of Services. In Particular, Provide Audit Functions that Visualise Differences of SLAs Along the Cloud Chain

Workshop note: Service Level Agreements (SLAs) of different cloud services along the chain may not match (in addition to the problem that SLAs aren't even defined in the same way). **HCI Principle:** Tools for auditors and business users should visualize the differences between different SLAs. **Design suggestion:** Display a visual chain of SLAs and indicate with colors or icons when there is a mismatch of SLAs. Let users click on a particular mismatching connection to see the details and support his decisions.

5.7.2   Provide Audit Functions that Make also Implicitly Collected Data Transparent

As in Sects. 5.1.2 and 5.6.4, there is a notable difficulty for auditors (among others) to follow up data collection and processing.

5.8   Access Control Management

Access control management tools should meet the HCI requirements motivated and discussed in the following subsections.

5.8.1   Allow Users to Classify Their Data Items and Easily Provide Access Control Rules for These Data

See Sect. 5.4.3, the first workshop note.

5.8.2   Allow System Administrators to Verify the Accuracy of Access Control Rules in a Straightforward and Simple Manner

Experiment result: It is very difficult for system administrators to verify the accuracy of access control rule sets regarding the access control policy. Thus rule sets need to be understandable and manageable to assist system administrators in their task. **HCI Principle**: (i) Concise rule sets are better than large sets. (ii) Redundant/contradicting rules are to be avoided. (iii) Rule sets need to be designed to facilitate tasks for administrators. **Design suggestion:** Tools, sets, and metrics that can support administrators to evaluate and compare the security and usability properties of different rule sets.

5.9   Privacy Risk Assessment

Privacy Risk assessment tools should meet the HCI requirements motivated and discussed in the following subsections.

5.9.1   Provide Different Types of User (Business End Users Versus Individual End Users) with Appropriate Indicators Obtained from Risk Assessment Activities. Make Risk Awareness Long Lasting

Cf. Sect. 5.4.3, second note, and Sect. 5.1.7 for the problem that many lay users regard Internet as intrinsically insecure.

5.9.2   Provide Clear Visualizations of Vulnerability of Private Data Depending on Different Situations

As noted in the focus group observation quoted in Sect. 5.1.3, it is very unclear for non-expert users what can be attacked, why is the information vulnerable and the approaches to mitigate the problems.

6 Concluding Remarks

In comparison to traditional forms of outsourcing and internet services, transparency and control in the cloud requires that more complex information about the data handling along the cloud chain is provided to data subjects and other stakeholders. The items presented in Sects. 5.1–5.9 are in their objective similar to those for other kinds of 'usable privacy' ecologies, even though transparency-enhancing tools for the cloud have to inform users about some additional aspects and it is important that developers apply them against the background of the complex picture of the cloud service chain.

To conclude, in this work we have elaborated HCI requirements for making transparency-enhancing tools comprehensible and trustworthy in order to make them useful for analysing cloud service chains. The paper reports on how we have applied human-centred design methods to derive HCI requirements and related HCI principles. The analyses conducted provided requirements on how users can be guided to better understand their data traces, how they can be supported to make better informed decisions in regard to the use of their data by cloud and other service providers, how legal privacy principles and social trust requirements can be enforced by e.g. transparency-enhancing tools. The different studies have been published in different papers [4–6]. Here a set of high level guidelines was presented that summarises the derived HCI principles.

This work has also revealed more specific open HCI research challenges to be addressed within the A4Cloud project and beyond. In particular, we identified the following research questions: How can ex ante transparency tools better inform users about the *consequences* of data disclosures? How can one derive good privacy *default* settings that are both privacy friendly and matching the user's preferences? How can ex ante transparency tools best illustrate and make obvious who will be in control of the data and/or who will be processing data under which conditions, and what means of legal or technical control exist in which situations? How can mismatches of policies or SLAs along the cloud chain best be presented to individual and business end users?

Acknowledgements. This work has in part been financed by the European Commission, grant FP7-ICT-2011-8-317550-A4CLOUD.

We thank project co-workers that have contributed to the research with the help of whom these requirements were derived, especially Erik Wästlund, Leonardo Martucci, and Tobias Pulls. Besides, we thank W Kuan Hon from Queen Mary University London for very helpful comments.

References

1. Angulo, J., Fischer-Hübner, S., Pettersson, J.S.: General HCI principles and guidelines for accountability and transparency in the cloud. A4Cloud Deliverable D:C-7.1, September 2013 (2013)
2. Pearson, S., Tountopoulos, V., Catteddu, D., Sudholt, M., Molva, R., Reich, C., Fischer-Hübner, S., Millard, C., Lotz, V., Jaatun, M.G.: Accountability for cloud and other future Internet services. In IEEE 4th International Conference on Cloud Computing Technology and Science (CloudCom), 2012. IEEE (2012)

3. Hildebrandt, M.: Behavioural biometric profiling and transparency enhancing tools. FIDIS Deliverable D7.12, March 2005. FIDIS EU project (2009)
4. Fischer-Hübner, S., Angulo, J., Pulls, T.: How can cloud users be supported in deciding on, tracking and controlling how their data are used? In: Hansen, M., Hoepman, J.-H., Leenes, R., Whitehouse, D. (eds.) Privacy and Identity 2013. IFIP AICT, vol. 421, pp. 77–92. Springer, Heidelberg (2014)
5. Angulo, J., Wästlund, E., Högberg, J.: What would it take for you to tell your secrets to a cloud? - studying decision factors when disclosing information to cloud services. In: Bernsmed, K., Fischer-Hübner, S. (eds.) NordSec 2014. LNCS, vol. 8788, pp. 129–145. Springer, Heidelberg (2014)
6. Beckerle, M., Martucci, L.A.: Formal definitions for usable access control rule sets from goals to metrics. In: Proceedings of the Ninth Symposium on Usable Privacy and Security (SOUPS 2013), New Castle, UK, 24–26 July. ACM (2013)
7. Whitten, A., Tygar, J.D.: Why Johnny can't encrypt: a usability evaluation of PGP 5.0. In: The Proceedings of the 8th USENIX Security Symposium (1999)
8. Nielsen, J.: Usability inspection methods. In: Conference Companion on Human Factors in Computing Systems. ACM (1995)
9. Johnston, J., Eloff, J.H., Labuschagne, L.: Security and human computer interfaces. Comput. Secur. **22**(8), 675–684 (2003)
10. Yee, K.: Aligning security and usability. IEEE Secur. Priv. **2**(5), 48–55 (2004)
11. Garfinkel, S.: Design principles and patterns for computer systems that are simultaneously secure and usable. Massachusetts Institute of Technology (2005)
12. Dhamija, R., Dusseault, L.: The seven flaws of identity management: usability and security challenges. IEEE Secur. Priv. **6**(2), 24–29 (2008)
13. Patrick, A.S., Kenny, S.: From privacy legislation to interface design: implementing information privacy in human-computer interactions. In: Dingledine, R. (ed.) PET 2003. LNCS, vol. 2760, pp. 107–124. Springer, Heidelberg (2003)
14. Patrick, A.S., Kenny, S., Holmes, C., van Breukelen, M.: Human computer interaction. In: van Blarkom, G.W., Borking, J.J., Olk, J.G.E. (eds.) Handbook of Privacy and Privacy-Enhancing Technologies: The Case of Intelligent Software Agents, pp. 249–290. College Bescherming Persoonsgegevens, Den Haag (2003)
15. European Commission: Directive 95/46/EC of the European Parliament and of the Council of 24 October 1995 on the protection of individuals with regard to the processing of personal data and on the free movement of such data. Office Journal L. 281. 23.11.1995 (1995)
16. Art. 29 Data Protection Working Party: Opinion 10/2004 on More Harmonised Information Provisions, 25 November 2004. European Commission (2004)
17. Pettersson, J.S.: HCI Guidelines. PRIME Deliverable D06.1.f. Final Version. PRIME project (2008)
18. International Standard Organization (ISO): Ergonomic requirements for office work with visual display terminals (VDTs)-Part 11: guidance on usability-Part 11 (ISO 9241-11:1998) (1998)
19. Pettersson, J.S., Fischer-Hübner, S., Danielsson, N., Nilsson, J., Bergmann, M., Clauss, S., Kriegelstein, T., Krasemann, H.: Making PRIME usable. In: Proceedings of the 2005 Symposium on Usable Privacy and Security (SOUPS 2005), Pittsburg, PA, USA. ACM (2005)
20. Graf, C., Hochleitner, C., Wolkerstorfer, P., Angulo, J., Fischer-Hübner, S., Wästlund, E., Hansen, M., Holtz, L.: Towards Usable Privacy Enhancing Technologies: Lessons Learned from the PrimeLife Project. PrimeLife Deliverable D4.1.6. PrimeLife (2011)

21. Wästlund, E., Wolkerstorfer, P., Köffel, C.: PET-USES: privacy-enhancing technology – users' self-estimation scale. In: Bezzi, M., Duquenoy, P., Fischer-Hübner, S., Hansen, M., Zhang, G. (eds.) IFIP AICT 320. IFIP AICT, vol. 320, pp. 266–274. Springer, Heidelberg (2010)
22. Alexander, C., Ishikawa, S., Silverstein, M.: Pattern Languages. Center for Environmental Structure. Oxford University Press, New York (1977)
23. PrimeLife WP4.1: HCI Pattern Collection – Version 2. In: Fischer-Hübner, S., Köffel, C., Pettersson, J., Wästlund, E., Zwingelberg, H. (eds.) PrimeLife Deliverable D4.1.3. PrimeLife (2010). http://www.primelife.eu/results/documents
24. ECC-Net: Trust marks report 2013: "Can I trust the trust mark?". The European Consumer Centres, Network (2013). www.konsumenteuropa.se/PageFiles/159275/Trust%20Mark%20Report%202013.pdf
25. ENISA: On the security, privacy, and usability of online seals. An overview Version December 2013. European Union Agency for Network and Information Security (2013). www.enisa.europa.eu
26. Spiekermann, S., Grossklags, J., Berendt, B.: E-privacy in 2nd generation e-commerce: privacy preferences versus actual behavior. In: Proceedings of the 3rd ACM Conference on Electronic Commerce, Tampa, Florida, USA. ACM (2001)
27. Gross, R., Acquisti, A.: Information revelation and privacy in online social networks. In: Proceedings of the 2005 ACM Workshop on Privacy in the Electronic Society, Pittsburg, PA, USA. ACM (2005)
28. European Commission: Proposal for a Regulation of the European Parliament and of the Council on the protection of individuals with regard to the processing of personal data and on the free movement of such data (General Data Protection Regulation). COM (2012) 11 Final. Brussels, 25.1.2012 (2012)
29. International Standard Organization (ISO): 25010-2011. Systems and software engineering – Systems and software Quality Requirements and Evaluation (SQuaRE) – System and software quality models (2011)
30. International Standard Organization (ISO): 9241-210: 2009. Ergonomics of human system interaction-Part 210: Human-centred design for interactive systems (formerly known as 13407) (2010)
31. Wästlund, E., Angulo, J., Fischer-Hübner, S.: Evoking comprehensive mental models of anonymous credentials. In: Camenisch, J., Kesdogan, D. (eds.) iNetSec 2011. LNCS, vol. 7039, pp. 1–14. Springer, Heidelberg (2012)
32. Maguire, M., Bevan, N.: User requirements analysis. In: Hammond, J., Gross, T., Wesson, J. (eds.) Usability. IFIP — The International Federation for Information Processing, vol. 99, pp. 133–148. Springer, New York (2002)
33. Owen, H.: Open Space Technology: A User's Guide. Berrett-Koehler Publishers, San Francisco (2008)
34. Brown, J., Isaacs, D.: The World Café: Shaping Our Futures Through Conversations that Matter. Berrett-Koehler Publishers, San Francisco (2005)
35. Bernard, H.R.: Research Methods in Cultural Anthropology. Sage, Newbury Park (1988)
36. Brandimarte, L., Acquisti, A., Loewenstein, G.: Misplaced confidences: privacy and the control paradox. Social Psychological and Personality Science 4(3), 340–347 (2012). SAGE Publications
37. Hoadley, C.M., Xu, H., Lee, J.J., Rosson, M.B.: Privacy as information access and illusory control: The case of the Facebook News Feed privacy outcry. Electron. Commer. Res. Appl. 9(1), 50–60 (2010)

38. Ion, I., Sachdeva, N., Kumaraguru, P., Capkun, S.: Home is safer than the cloud!: privacy concerns for consumer cloud storage. In: Proceedings of the Seventh Symposium on Usable Privacy and Security, Pittsburg, PA, USA, p. 13:1. ACM (2011)
39. Langer, E.J.: The illusion of control. J. Pers. Soc. Psychol. **32**(2), 311 (1975)
40. Marshall, C., Tang, J.C.: That syncing feeling: early user experiences with the cloud. In: Proceedings of the Designing Interactive Systems Conference. ACM (2012)
41. Tversky, A., Kahneman, D.: The framing of decisions and the psychology of choice. In: Wright, G. (ed.) Behavioral Decision Making, pp. 25–41. Springer, New York (1985)
42. Xu, H.: The effects of self-construal and perceived control on privacy concerns. In: Proceedings of the 28th Annual International Conference on Information Systems (ICIS 2007) (2007)
43. Jaspers, M.W.M., Steen, T., van den Bos, C., Geenen, M.: The think aloud method: a guide to user interface design. Int. J. Med. Inform. **73**(11–12), 781–795 (2004)
44. Rubin, J., Chisnell, D.: Handbook of Usability Testing: How to Plan, Design, and Conduct Effective Tests. Wiley Publ., Indianapolis (2008)
45. Pettersson, J.S., Fischer-Hübner, S., Bergmann, M.: Outlining "Data Track": privacy-friendly data maintenance for end-users. In: Wojtkowski, W., Wojtkowski, W.G., Zupancic, J., Magyar, G., Knapp, G. (eds.) Advances in Information Systems Development, pp. 215–226. Springer, New York (2007)
46. Wästlund, E., Fischer-Hübner, S.: End User Transparency Tools: UI Prototypes. PrimeLife Deliverable D.4.2.2. PrimeLife project (2010)
47. Pulls, T.: Privacy-friendly cloud storage for the data track. In: Jøsang, A., Carlsson, B. (eds.) NordSec 2012. LNCS, vol. 7617, pp. 231–246. Springer, Heidelberg (2012)
48. Freeman, L.C.: Visualizing social networks. J. Soc. Struct. **1**(1), 4 (2000)
49. Becker, R.A., Eick, S.G., Wilks, A.R.: Visualizing network data. IEEE Trans. Vis. Comput. Graph. **1**(1), 16–28 (1995)
50. Kani-Zabihi, E., Helmhout, M.: Increasing service users' privacy awareness by introducing on-line interactive privacy features. In: Laud, P. (ed.) NordSec 2011. LNCS, vol. 7161, pp. 131–148. Springer, Heidelberg (2012)
51. Kolter, J., Netter, M., Pernul, G.: Visualizing past personal data disclosures. In: ARES 2010 International Conference on Availability, Reliability, and Security, 2010, p. 131. IEEE (2010)
52. Art. 29 Data Protection Working Party (2012). Opinion 5/2012 on Cloud Computing. European Commission, 1 July 2012
53. Art. 29 Data Protection Working Party (2010). Opinion 1/2010 on the concepts of "controller" and "processor". European Commission, 16 February 2010
54. O'Neill, O.: A Question of Trust. CUP, Cambridge (2002)
55. Wamala, C.: Does IT count?: complexities between access to and use of information technologies among Uganda's farmers. Luleå Tekniska universitet, Luleå (2010)
56. Lacohée, H., Crane, S., Phippen, A.: Trustguide: Final report. Trustguide, October 2006 (2006)
57. Angulo, J., Fischer-Hübner, S., Wästlund, E., Pulls, T.: Towards usable privacy policy display and management. Inf. Manag. Comput. Secur. **20**(1), 4–17 (2012)
58. Andersson, C., Camenisch, J., Crane, S., Fischer-Hübner, S., Leenes, R., Pearson, S., Pettersson, J.S., Sommer, D.: Trust in PRIME. In: Proceedings of the Fifth IEEE International Symposium on Signal Processing and Information Technology. IEEE (2005)
59. Tsai, J.Y., Kelley, P., Drielsma, P., Cranor, L.F., Hong, J., Sadeh, N.: Who's viewed you?: the impact of feedback in a mobile location-sharing application. In: CHI 2009 Proceedings of the SIGCHI Conference on Human Factors in Computing Systems, ACM (2009)

60. Shin, D.: User centric cloud service model in public sectors: policy implications of cloud services. Gov. Inf. Q. **30**, 194–203 (2013)
61. Pearson, S.: Privacy, security and trust in cloud computing. In: Pearson, S., Yee, G. (eds.) Privacy and Security for Cloud Computing, pp. 3–42. Springer, London (2013)
62. Voida, A., Olson, J.S., Olson, G.M.: Turbulence in the clouds: challenges of cloud-based information work. In: CHI 2013 Proceedings of the SIGCHI Conference on Human Factors in Computing Systems, ACM (2013)
63. Joinson, A.N., Reips, U.-D., Buchanan, T., Paine Schfield, C.B.: Privacy, trust, and self-disclosure online. Hum.-Comput. Interact. **25**(1), 1–24 (2013)

Privacy-Preserving Identity Management as a Service

David Nuñez[✉], Isaac Agudo, and Javier Lopez

Universidad de Málaga, Málaga, Spain
{dnunez,isaac,jlm}@lcc.uma.es

Abstract. In this paper we tackle the problem of privacy and confidentiality in Identity Management as a Service (IDaaS). The adoption of cloud computing technologies by organizations has fostered the externalization of the identity management processes, shaping the concept of Identity Management as a Service. However, as it has happened to other cloud-based services, the cloud poses serious risks to the users, since they lose the control over their data. As part of this work, we analyze these concerns and present a model for privacy-preserving IDaaS, called BlindIdM, which is designed to provide data privacy protection through the use of cryptographic safeguards.

Keywords: Identity Management as a Service · Cloud computing · Privacy · Cryptography

1 Introduction

The benefits of adopting cloud computing technologies are widely-known nowadays. Some of these benefits are on-demand provisioning of high-quality services, flexibility, redundancy and cost reduction. Companies and organizations from a wide variety of sectors and sizes are gradually embracing the cloud and externalizing some of their internal processes. Within these processes, identity management stands out for its ubiquitous nature, as it plays a key role in authentication and access control. However, it also introduces an overhead in cost and time, and in most cases, specialized applications and personnel are required for setting up and integrating identity management systems.

As has already happened for other services, the cloud paradigm represents an innovative opportunity to externalize the identity management processes. *Identity Management as a Service (IDaaS)* is the cloud industry's response to the problem of identity management within organizations, allowing them to outsource these services from their internal infrastructures (*on-premise model*) and deploy it in the cloud (*on-demand model*). Although IDaaS offers organizations a great opportunity to reduce costs and simplify business processes, it also introduces a variant of one of the classic problems of cloud computing, namely, the loss of control over outsourced data. Moreover, in this case it is information about users' identity, which is inherently sensitive.

© Springer International Publishing Switzerland 2015
M. Felici and C. Fernández-Gago (Eds.): A4Cloud 2014, LNCS 8937, pp. 114–125, 2015.
DOI: 10.1007/978-3-319-17199-9_5

The principal motivation behind this work is enabling the provision of identity services by the cloud, where data storage and processing could be offered by possibly untrusted cloud providers, but still offering an identity management service that guarantees user's privacy and control. To this end, we present BlindIdM [1], a privacy-preserving IDaaS system where identity information is stored and processed in a blind manner, removing the necessity of trusting that the cloud identity provider will not read the data.

Organization. The rest of this paper is organized as follows: In Sect. 2, we describe what are the main research challenges that we face in this work. In Sect. 3, we present some of the work that is relevant to this research, mainly centered on privacy in identity management. In Sect. 4, we describe the BlindIdM model and explain our approach for proposing an instantiation of it, as well as some experimental results. Finally, Sect. 5 concludes the paper.

2   Research Challenges

The work presented here aims to tackle the following research challenges:

- Leveraging user-centricity in identity management: Most current identity management systems are provider-centric, so identity providers are in a privileged position to learn information about users. We want to create means for empowering the users with respect identity providers.
- Enhancing users' privacy in digital transactions that involve their identity: Privacy and confidentiality of identity information is threatened on a daily basis. Strong safeguards for protecting this information should be in place. We believe that cryptographic tools are needed for solving this issue.
- Interoperability of the solutions: Any new solution to these problems should take open standards in consideration in order to facilitate and enhance interoperability.
- Solutions that reduce the trade-off between anonymity and accountability: It is a big challenge to design solutions that support both aspects; we need to enhance accountability in digital transactions, but at the same time, it is necessary to respect users' privacy.
- Applicability of this approach to other cases of study. At this stage we are focusing on Identity Management as a Service, but this solution can be adapted to other contexts, such as those that involve data sharing in the cloud.
- Exploring and devising new cryptographic techniques for protecting privacy on cloud-based settings.

3   Related Work

The problem of privacy in identity management is a widely studied subject. In particular, much work has been carried out regarding unlinkability of users with respect to the other entities involved in the identity management processes. For example, in [2], the authors present PseudoID, a model for private federated login that achieves unlinkability of users to visited sites. To this end, a blind signature service participates during the generation of an access token that is handed to the identity provider; this access token consists of a pseudonym and a secret value, that are both used to authenticate the user anonymously. Although this work presents an interesting contribution to privacy-enhanced identity providers, it is centered on the unlinkability aspects of the authentication of users. Moreover, this model is not suitable for maintaining users information in the identity providers, since the providers are unable to correlate users to their pseudonyms.

With regard to the intersection of identity management, privacy and cloud computing, there has also been some research done. In [3], the authors propose SPICE, an identity management system for cloud environments whose main goal is to preserve users privacy. SPICE satisfies a set of properties that the authors claim an identity management system in the cloud should fulfill, such as unlinkability and delegatable authentication. In order to accomplish this, SPICE uses a re-randomizable group signature scheme. However, the aim of SPICE is not the same as ours, since we are not tackling unlinkability, but data confidentiality. In [4], a privacy-preserving identity management system for cloud environments is presented; this system is based on zero-knowledge proofs that allow the user to prove the knowledge of a set of attributes without revealing their value. However, the authors do not tackle the privacy issues that are the concern of our work, since in their setting, identity providers store in clear the values of the attributes of the users.

In [5], the authors propose a solution based on the deployment of active bundles in the cloud provider. An active bundle is a mobile agent, in this case a virtual machine, which contains the identity information of the user and that is protected by cryptographic means. Every time an operation involves the use of identity information, the cloud provider interacts with an active bundle to retrieve this information. However, this approach seems to be impractical because of the large overhead that introduces the use of a large container for data, such as a VM. Moreover, the proposal does not detail any procedure to transport these active bundles to the cloud in an efficient manner.

Another proposal, based on the use of sticky policies and trusted computing, is presented in [6]. This work presents an interesting approach where information, along with a specific policy that should be enforced in order to disclose the data, is obfuscated before leaving users domain. In this approach, a trusted authority is in charge of giving the receiver the means to de-obfuscate the information, after verifying that the receiver complies with its associated policy; trusted computing is used to ensure the integrity of both software and hardware environments of the receiver. However, this work is focused on the direct sharing of information, which makes it unusable in an identity management setting, where an identity provider is used as an intermediary and must somehow manage this information.

4   BlindIdM: Privacy-Preserving IDaaS

In an IDaaS scenario, organizations entrust their corporate identity information to cloud identity providers, which are then responsible for storing and managing this information. It follows then that cloud identity providers are in a privileged position in order to read users' data that is in their custody. Although there are several regulatory, ethical and economic reasons for discouraging this possibility, the fact is that nothing actually prevents identity providers from accessing users' information at will. Traditional IDaaS relies on the existence of a strong trust link between the organizations and the cloud identity providers, since organizations *trust* that their identity information will be managed properly and that the provider will respect the confidentiality; however, current cloud providers do not implement real mechanisms for preventing themselves from betraying this trust. Even if we assume that the identity provider is not dishonest and that its internal policy is respectful regarding identity information, there are other factors that could lead to privacy disclosure, such as security breaches, insider attacks, or legal requests [7].

Traditionally, cloud providers have tackled these problems defining Service Level Agreements (SLAs) and internal policies; however, these measures keep this issue as a trust problem. Nothing actually prevents providers from breaking these agreements and policies; users simply *trust* them not do it. In other words, there is an important trust problem, inherent to cloud computing – users want to have access to services but, at the same time, they are unwilling to provide their data to entities that they do not necessarily trust. It is therefore desirable to count with more advanced security mechanisms that enable users to benefit from cloud computing and still preserve their privacy and the control over their information, ideally through cryptographic means [8].

The aforementioned concerns led us to conceive of the concept of *Blind Identity Management* (BlindIdM) [1], a model whereby the cloud identity provider is able to offer an identity information service, without knowing the actual information of the users; that is, it provides this service in a *blind* manner. This is a great innovation with respect to current identity management systems, where users' identity information is managed by the identity provider and the user is obliged to trust that the provider will make proper use of his data and will guarantee its protection. Our intention is that this model will enable organizations to choose a cloud identity provider without necessarily establishing a strong bond of trust with it; i.e., they do not have to trust that the cloud identity provider will respect data privacy. Instead, the sturdiness of the underlying cryptographic schemes should be sufficient to guarantee such protection. The novel aspect of our proposal lies in the protection of data: the host organization encrypts users' identity information prior to outsourcing it to the cloud, in such a way that it is still manageable by the cloud identity provider, without being able to be read. The next subsections describe our proposal in more detail.

4.1   Incentives

In this section we explore what incentives may motivate a cloud identity provider to offer its services in a blind manner. From a strictly economic point of view, it may not make sense to still provide these services for free, since they will probably incur more expenses as a result of implementing additional security mechanisms. Furthermore, they will lose control over the user's data, which is currently a valuable asset, for instance, used for marketing purposes. Still, there are some incentives that certainly could encourage cloud identity providers to offer such a blind service. Among them we find:

– Compliance with data privacy laws and regulations: In an IDaaS setting, one of the consequences for cloud identity providers is that they can be seen in the eyes of the law as stewards and processors of *Personal Identifiable Information(PII)*. As a consequence, they are obliged to comply with specific laws and regulations regarding data protection, such as the EU Data Protection Directive. Some of these regulations demand that personal identifiable information must be protected using appropriate encryption techniques. A privacy-preserving approach like ours, which achieves data confidentiality through encryption mechanisms, could be very useful to help cloud identity providers to comply with data protection regulations. We argue that, given the proper cryptographic safeguards, encrypted data is not private anymore, and could even be freely distributed without compromising users' privacy.
– Minimization of liability: Currently there is a lot of discussion, especially from the cloud industry and lawmakers, with regard to liability in cloud computing due to its nature of outsourced service provision. Although cloud providers currently try to reduce their liability through specific clauses in SLAs, legal responsibility for the data in the cloud also lies on the side of the cloud provider. There are a lot of examples from blog sites, Internet forums, or file hosting services (such as the Megaupload case in 2012 [9]), where the owners of these services are indicted for hosting illegal or defamatory material, even though they have not generated said content. Since in our proposal, outsourced data is encrypted prior to arriving the cloud and the cloud provider does not hold the decryption keys, liability is drastically minimized, as cloud identity providers are unable to read user's data. We can take a shipping service as an analogy: they will not be liable for any illegal or dangerous item delivered through their service, since they cannot open the packages and inspect their content (or at least, every delivered package). Instead, users should be the ones designated as liable and subject to the enforcement of key disclosure laws.
– Data confidentiality as an added value: Offering secure data processing and confidentiality could be considered as a competitive advantage over the rest of identity services, and in the future can lead to a business model based on the respect for users' privacy and data confidentiality. We foresee the model of Blind Identity Management as a technical starting point for a business model centered on data confidentiality as a core value.

4.2   Identity Management Setting

Before going into further details, it is necessary to explain the setting where identity interactions occur. Federated Identity Management is a set of distributed technologies and processes that enable information portability between different domains, which permits both a dynamic distribution of identity information and delegation of associated tasks, such as authentication or user provisioning. Thus, organizations coordinate with each other to form federations for exchanging identity information. One of the key aspects of this model is the establishment of trust relationships between the members of the federation, which enables them to believe the statements made within the federation. This way, although users are authenticated by their local organization, they are able to access services and resources from other organizations of the federation. The parties involved in a federated identity interaction are required to mutually exchange identity information for identification and authentication purposes regardless of whether they have previous knowledge of each others' identity information or not. The main actors that participate in these interactions are [10,11]:

- *Users*, the subjects of the identity information; most of the times they are also the principal source of this information. Users are generally the actors that request resources and services through their interaction with applications and online services. Users perform this interaction through a *user agent*, which is usually a browser, but it could also be a specific application.
- *Service Providers* (*SP*), the entities that provide services and resources to users or other entities. In a federated identity management context, service providers outsource the processes of authentication and management of users to identity providers. Because of this, service providers act as consumers of user's identity information, following a determined identity management protocol.
- *Identity Providers* (*IdP*), which are specialized entities that are able to authenticate users and to provide the result of this authentication to service providers, without revealing additional information about the user. The information that they exchange with service providers may even be just a statement about the success of the authentication of the user, enabling the user to access the service anonymously. Identity providers are also responsible for managing the identity information of their associated users, and in some cases, they may certify it.

Figure 1a shows a high-level view of a federated identity setting, where a host organization acts as a federated identity provider. In a regular FIM setting, an employee from the host organization requests a service from the service provider, who in turn asks the organization for identity information about its employee. However, in our setting we will assume that the host organization partially outsources the identity management processes to a cloud identity provider, while retaining the authentication service on-premises. The cloud identity provider now acts as an intermediary in the identity interactions, and is also in charge for storing and supplying identity information; Fig. 1b shows this setting.

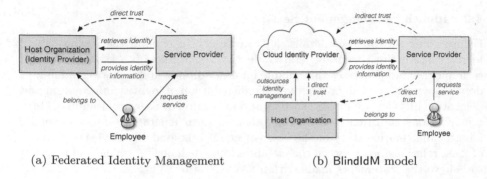

(a) Federated Identity Management   (b) BlindIdM model

Fig. 1. Relation between entities in different models

Optionally, other kinds of actors may come into play such as attribute issuing authorities, certification providers, identity brokers, etc.; however, we will restrict the scope of this work to the basic case.

With regard to trust assumptions, we consider the cloud identity provider as an adversary, and in particular, we will assume it to be *data-curious*, a type of honest-but-curious adversary, which behaves correctly with respect to protocol fulfillment, but has no hindrance to try to access users' data.

4.3   Supporting Mechanisms

Proxy Re-Encryption. From a high-level viewpoint, a proxy re-encryption scheme is an asymmetric encryption scheme that permits a proxy to transform ciphertexts under a public key into ciphertexts encrypted under another public key. In order to do this, the owner of the data gives a re-encryption key to the proxy that makes this process possible, without learning anything about the underlying plaintexts and the private keys. Besides defining encryption and decryption functions, like any traditional public key scheme, a proxy re-encryption scheme also defines a re-encryption function for executing the transformation. Proxy re-encryption schemes are of particular interest in cloud computing, specially when one considers scenarios that deal with the sharing of confidential or sensitive data. Data in the cloud can always be in an encrypted form, and the possibility of re-encrypting it to different actors facilitates the sharing.

Identity Management Protocols. In order to instantiate BlindIdM, it is necessary to use a standard identity management mechanism. We now describe two of the most used protocols: OpenID and SAML.

OpenID is a decentralized model for identity management, which allows service providers to delegate the authentication of users to identity providers. In this model, the identity of a user is represented by a URI, called OpenID identifier. Hence, users dont need to create a separate account for each site; instead, they just have to use their OpenID identifier, and the authentication procedure will be conducted through the users identity provider. The OpenID 2.0 specification

[12] enables the exchange of users attributes within the OpenID protocol flow, through the OpenID Attribute Exchange extension (OpenID AX) [13]. In the OpenID context, the identity provider is usually called *OpenID provider* (*OP*) and the service provider, *relying party* (*RP*); however, we will adhere to the common convention, and we will refer to them as identity provider (IdP) and service provider (SP), respectively.

SAML 2.0 (Security Assertion Markup Language) [14] is a standard XML-based framework that enables the description and exchange of identity information between different security domains. With SAML, identity information is expressed in the form of assertions, which are a set of statements about a subject; these statements cover different aspects, such as authentication, authorization and identity attributes. SAML attributes are used to express identity information about the subject of the assertion. In our proposal, we make extensive use of this construction, as we take it as the basic medium for conveying encrypted identity information.

4.4   Instantiation of the BlindIdM Model

In [1], we describe a particular instantiation of BlindIdM that uses SAML 2.0 as the underlying identity management protocol and proxy re-encryption techniques to achieve end-to-end confidentiality of the identity information, while allowing the cloud to provide an identity service.

In the scenario proposed by this model, the host organization (including all the employees) acts as the user, and the identity management of the organization is outsourced to a cloud identity provider. Identity information flows from the user (in our case, from the host organization), acting as a source of information, to the service provider, acting as a consumer of information. Specifically, the host organization encrypts the identity information under its public key p_H prior sending it to the cloud identity provider. The use of proxy re-encryption enables the identity provider to transform these ciphertexts into encrypted attributes under the public key of the service provider, p_{SP}; in order to do so, the identity provider needs a re-encryption key $r_{H \to SP}$ generated by the host organization and provided beforehand. Figure 2 shows how the SAML Authentication protocol can be extended for supporting the BlindIdM model; in particular, the steps highlighted in grey are the extension points over the original protocol. More details are given in [1] on how this process is framed within the SAML protocol using standard extension mechanisms.

The first ideas towards our proposal were presented in [15], where we describe a user-centric IDaaS system based in OpenID and proxy re-encryption. Figure 3 shows a diagram of the proposed system, and the main information flows. Although conceived as a proof of concept, this is the first work that achieves blind processing of identity information; however, trust issues arise as OpenID does not provide proper mechanisms for establishing trust. The work in [1] solves these problems and provides more solid mechanisms of integration with the identity management protocol.

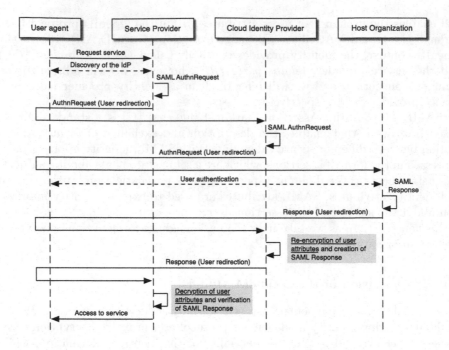

Fig. 2. Extending the SAML Authentication protocol in our solution

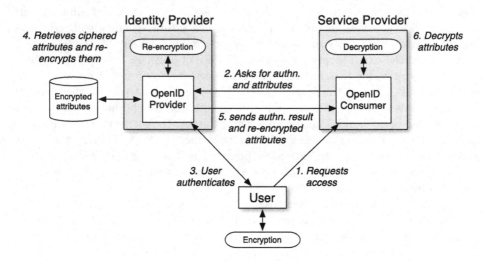

Fig. 3. Integration of our solution with OpenID

4.5   Implementation and Performance Evaluation

In order to make a quantitative evaluation of our proposal, we developed a prototype implementation using Java as coding language. Our execution environment was an Apple Macbook Pro laptop, with a 2.66 GHz Intel Core 2 Duo processor and 4 GB of RAM, running Mac OS X 10.6.8. We implemented the proxy re-encryption scheme using the jPBC library [16], a pairing-based cryptography library for Java. As for the cryptographic details, we used a Type A elliptic curve with a 256-bit group order and 3072 bits for the field size, which achieves a 128-bit security level. Additionally, we have made extensive use of exponentiation preprocessing of frequently-used elements for efficiency reasons.

The median execution times for the main operations, as well as an estimate of the number of cycles, are presented in Table 1. Note that although the re-encryption operation is slower than encryption and decryption, in a real setting it would be performed by a cloud provider that presumably counts on a much more powerful computing environment. In a realistic scenario, re-encryption and decryption are the most frequent operations, since they constitute the equivalent to a 'read' operation. The number of cycles gives an approximation of the workload involved in the main operations, independently of the frequency of the CPU; this metric will be of use in the next subsection. In order to estimate the number of cycles per operation, we simply multiply the time of execution by the frequency of the CPU of the experimental machine; however, note that this approach give us an overestimation of the number of cycles, as it is difficult to isolate the execution from other environmental interferences such as multitasking and I/O operations, therefore the actual figures are probably lower.

Table 1. Performance results for the main operations

Operation	Time (ms)	Cycles
Generation of global parameters	7279.98	1.94E+10
Generation of a secret key	0.01	1.86E+04
Generation of a public key	20.05	5.33E+07
Generation of re-encryption key	139.66	3.72E+08
Encryption	23.31	6.20E+07
Re-encryption	90.09	2.40E+08
Decryption	14.28	3.80E+07

From a practical point of view, it is also crucial to determine whether our proposal is economically feasible. Most of cryptography-based proposals only provide theoretical analysis of security and complexity, but do not tackle the economic viability. In [1], we provide an economic assessment of our proposal and estimate the cost of proxy re-encryption operations in USD cents; these expenses are a consequence of the incurred cost of the cryptographic computations in a

Table 2. Costs for the main operations

Operation	Cost per operation	Operations per cent
Encryption	4.34E+08	2304
Re-encryption	4.79E+08	2087
Decryption	5.70E+08	1755

cloud environment. For a detailed description of this analysis and the rationale behind these estimations, we refer the reader to this text. The costs of these operations, presented in Table 2, are the same as in our system since we are using the same proxy re-encryption scheme. For instance, it can be seen that the re-encryption operation, which is the one executed by the cloud provider, has an estimated cost of 4.79E-04 USD cents; in other words, the cloud identity provider can perform approximately 2087 re-encryptions for one USD cent. From these figures we can conclude that the cryptographic overhead is reasonable, as it permits an IDaaS system to serve thousands of encrypted attributes for a few cents, considering the costs that an organization could incur in the case of a disclosure or security breach; although these costs are difficult to estimate due to their business and legal nature, at the very least such incidents would have a negative impact with regard to reputation and loss of customers. As an illustrative example, let us suppose that the IDaaS system receives a million attribute requests per day, which implies a million re-encryptions per day. This represents an additional expense of approximately 2000 USD on a yearly basis, since the cost for a re-encryption is 4.79 E-04 cents. We think these figures are reasonable for an average-sized organization, but ultimately it would depend on the savings from outsourcing their identity services to the cloud.

5   Conclusions

In this paper we present a solution to the problem of privacy for Identity Management as a Service. IDaaS is a recent trend, powered by cloud computing technologies, that allows companies and organizations to benefit from outsourcing identity management processes. The reduction of costs and time-consuming tasks associated with managing identity services are the main reasons behind this externalization. However, as is the case for other cloud-based services, there is much concern regarding the inversion of the control of the data, as users lose almost all control over their data. Our solution, called BlindIdM, constitues a privacy-preserving model for IDaaS system that guarantees user's privacy and control even when data storage and processing is performed by untrusted clouds. In this model, the cloud identity provider is able to offer an identity information service without knowing the actual personal information of the users. We believe that the approach proposed here opens up new possibilities regarding privacy in the fields of identity management and cloud computing.

Acknowledgements. This work was partly supported by the Junta de Andalucía through the project FISICCO (P11-TIC-07223). The first author has been funded by a FPI fellowship from the Junta de Andalucía through the project PISCIS (P10-TIC-06334).

References

1. Nuñez, D., Agudo, I.: BlindIdM: a privacy-preserving approach for identity management as a service. Int. J. Inf. Secur. **13**(2), 199–215 (2014)
2. Dey, A., Weis, S.: PseudoID: enhancing privacy in federated login. In: Hot Topics in Privacy Enhancing Technologies, pp. 95–107 (2010)
3. Chow, S., He, Y.J., Hui, L., Yiu, S.: SPICE – simple privacy-preserving identity-management for cloud environment. In: Bao, F., Samarati, P., Zhou, J. (eds.) ACNS 2012. LNCS, vol. 7341, pp. 526–543. Springer, Heidelberg (2012)
4. Bertino, E., Paci, F., Ferrini, R., Shang, N.: Privacy-preserving digital identity management for cloud computing. Bull. IEEE Comput. Soc. Tech. Committee Data Eng. **32**(1), 21–27 (2009)
5. Angin, P., Bhargava, B., Ranchal, R., Singh, N., Othmane, L.B., Lilien, L., Linderman, M.: An entity-centric approach for privacy and identity management in cloud computing. In: 29th IEEE Symposium on Reliable Distributed Systems, pp. 177–183 (2010)
6. Casassa Mont, M., Pearson, S., Bramhall, P.: Towards accountable management of identity and privacy: sticky policies and enforceable tracing services. In: Proceeding 14th International Workshop on Database and Expert Systems Applications, pp. 377–382. IEEE (2003)
7. Cloud Security Alliance. Top threats to cloud computing, version 1.0 (2010)
8. Agudo, I., Nuñez, D., Giammatteo, G., Rizomiliotis, P., Lambrinoudakis, C.: Cryptography goes to the cloud. In: Lee, C., Seigneur, J.-M., Park, J.J., Wagner, R.R. (eds.) STA 2011 Workshops. CCIS, vol. 187, pp. 190–197. Springer, Heidelberg (2011)
9. Fowler, G.A., Barrett, D., Schechner, S.: U.S. shuts offshore file-share 'locker'. Wall Street J. (2012)
10. OASIS Security Services TC. Glossary for the OASIS Security Assertion Markup Language (SAML) V2.0 (2005)
11. Maler, E., Reed, D.: The venn of identity: options and issues in federated identity management. IEEE Secur. Priv. **6**(2), 16–23 (2008)
12. OpenID Authentication 2.0. http://openid.net/specs/openid-authentication-2_0.html
13. Hardt, D., Bufu, J., Hoyt, J.: OpenID Attribute Exchange 1.0. http://openid.net/specs/openid-attribute-exchange-1_0.html
14. OASIS Security Services TC. Assertions and Protocols for the OASIS Security Assertion Markup Language (SAML) V2.0 (2005)
15. Nunez, D., Agudo, I., Lopez, J.: Integrating OpenID with proxy re-encryption to enhance privacy in cloud-based identity services. In: 4th IEEE International Conference on Cloud Computing Technology and Science (CloudCom), pp. 241–248. IEEE (2012)
16. De Caro, A., Iovino, V.: jPBC: java pairing based cryptography. In: Proceedings of the 16th IEEE Symposium on Computers and Communications, ISCC 2011, pp. 850–855. IEEE (2011)

Empirical Approaches for the Cloud

Metrics for Accountability in the Cloud

Carmen Fernández-Gago^(✉) and David Nuñez

Network, Information and Computer Security Lab,
University of Malaga, 29071 Malaga, Spain
{mcgago,dnunez}@lcc.uma.es

Abstract. Accountability in the Cloud is a key concept that is determined by the *accountability attributes*. For assessing how accountable an organisation is we should be able to assess or provide techniques for measuring the attributes that influence on accountability. How much or to what extent they should be measured is a key issue. One of the goals of the A4Cloud project is, therefore, to develop a collection of metrics for performing meaningful measures on the attributes that influence accountability. This paper sets up the foundations towards the elicitation of metrics for accountability attributes. We describe here a metamodel for metrics for accountability attributes, which constitutes the basis for the process of elicitation of metrics for accountability. This metamodel is intended to serve as a language for describing accountability attributes and sub-attributes and for identifying the elements involved in their evaluation. One of the key components of the metamodel is the type of evidence the attribute use.

1 Introduction

One of the important aspects behind the accountability concept is the ability of an organization to demonstrate their conformity with required obligations [6]. The goal of an organisation is therefore the demonstration of accountability through the measurement of the degree of such conformity and the provision of meaningful evidence. Thus, measurement becomes an important tool for assessing the accountability of an organization by external authorities (and organizations themselves, in the case of self-assessment). It is then crucial to find suitable methodologies for eliciting metrics for accountability attributes. Metrics can be of different types (quantitative and qualitative), and they can be supported by different kinds of evidence. Thus, for the case of accountability we need to determine which are the most suitable ones for each case of the attributes. In fact, it is not the attributes themselves that we measure but the evidence related to them. It is then of paramount importance to identify the most suitable evidence for each aspect of the accountability attributes to be measured.

The methods and models that we introduce in this paper rely on different inputs for eliciting metrics such as the context and the nature of the attribute to be measured. In order to carry out the process of elicitation of metrics we start by a review of the definitions of the basic concepts and terminology regarding

© Springer International Publishing Switzerland 2015
M. Felici and C. Fernández-Gago (Eds.): A4Cloud 2014, LNCS 8937, pp. 129–153, 2015.
DOI: 10.1007/978-3-319-17199-9_6

metrics. The concepts related to Metrology range from what is to be measured (attributes) to what is a measure, scale or measurement method. Then, we perform an analysis of the accountability attributes from the metrics perspective. This analysis will allow us to identify the aspects or dimensions involved in the definitions of the attributes that are suitable to be measured. It is worth to note that it is not possible to measure the attributes themselves as they are very general but specific aspects and dimensions that are identified for them. For instance, it might not make much sense to measure how transparent an organization is but instead we could measure more specific aspects such as whether there exists a notification process. Once the attributes to be measured are analysed we have to define a methodology for performing meaningful measures. Thus, we define a metamodel for eleicitng metrics for accountability attributes that takes as inputs evidence and criteria that follows a top-down approach for the process of elicitation of metrics. We illustrate the use of the metamodel in the case of the transparency attribute.

The paper is organised as follows. Section 2 introduces the basic concepts and definitions on measurement and Metrology and Sect. 3 their application to security properties. An analysis of the definitions of accountability attributes from the metrics point of view is performed in Sect. 4. The methodology that we propose for measuring them is introduced in Sect. 5 and an example of its application is described in Sect. 6. Finally, Sect. 7 concludes the paper and outlines the open research areas in the field.

2   Background and Basic Definitions of Metrics

In this section we will summarise the main concepts concerning metrics that will be used for defining accountability metrics. We start with some notions of Metrology within the context of information security and privacy.

Metrology is defined as the scientific study of measurement [1]. As such, there already exists a broad selection of reference material regarding metrology concepts, including standards, books, research papers and guidelines. In this section we will provide a brief review of them from the most important sources. In particular, we will use the following material as the main reference on metrology and information security measurement:

- ISO/IEC 27004:2009 (E) Information Technology Security techniques Information Security Management Measurement [5]: This standard belongs to the ISO/IEC 27000 family on information security. In particular, the 27004 standard provides guidance on the development and use of measures with respect to Information Security Management Systems (ISMS). Most of the definitions regarding measurement proposed here are extracted or adapted from this standard.
- NIST SP 800-55 (revision 1) Performance Measurement Guide for Information Security [4].

- Complete Guide to Security and Privacy Metrics [11]. As its title states, this book provides extensive guidelines for developing security and privacy metrics, as it is based on a wide selection of metrology and information security standards and guidelines.
- Software Metrics and Software Metrology [7] is another useful source of metrology concepts, in this case with a focus on the software area. It provides basic concepts for designing measurement methods.

2.1 Definitions

Taking the above documents and [3] as main references we have adapted the following definitions for the scope of our work in the A4Cloud project [2].

- **Attribute:** property or characteristic of an object that can be distinguished quantitatively or qualitatively by human or automated means [3].
- **Metric or measurement result:** a set of indicators, together with an associated interpretation, that is designed to facilitate decision-making and improve performance and accountability through collection, analysis, and reporting of relevant data (adapted from [5,11]).
- **Measure:** variable whose value is assigned as a result of measurement [3].
- **Measurement method:** logical sequence of operations, described generically, used in quantifying an attribute with respect to a specified scale [3].
- **Indicator:** measure that provides an estimate or evaluation of specified attributes derived from an analytical model with respect to defined information needs [5].
- **Evidence:** data collected to support a metric, including the data inputs necessary to calculate and validate the metric (adapted from [4]).

Note that we prefer to use the term 'attribute' rather than 'property'. This decision is based on the fact that the ISO/IEC 27004:2009 standard uses the 'attribute' term for referring to a measurable concept. In addition, the term 'property' is often used to refer to functional properties of a system. Therefore, in our case, attribute is used as a synonym of 'non-functional property'. Also, the term 'attribute' is the one used in the Conceptual Framework for describing the main concepts that comprise accountability in the A4Cloud project.

2.2 Scales of Measurement

In the classical theory of measurement [17], the scales of measurement (or levels of measurement) are a set of categories for classifying measurement methods regarding their characteristics. Identifying the scale for each particular metric is essential for interpreting and analysing its results. Moreover, since each scale has a set of permitted operations, knowing its scale allows us to assess the validity of a metric, or at least, to discard senseless metrics.

We can classify the scales of measurement as follows:

- **Nominal scales.** This type of scale is applicable for mapping entities to names or categories. It is also known as categorical scale. Values in a nominal scale are not related to each other. For this reason, only the equality operation (=) is permitted for nominal values. From a statistical viewpoint, only modes can be computed.
- **Ordinal scales.** This scale permits to assign an order relation to its values, which is used to put measured entities in order. For this reason, ordinal scales are said to have magnitude. However, there is no information for measuring the differences between values. A simple example of this scale is the set of values 'Low – Medium – High'. There is an order relation that permits to state that High is greater than Medium, which in turn is greater than Low, but it makes no sense to measure the difference between Low and Medium. Ordinal scales are also nominal. Ordinal scales therefore permit to use equality (=) and inequality (≤) operations, as well as medians and percentiles. Certain non-parametric statistical tests that only require ordinal data, known as ranking tests [17], can also be performed.
- **Interval scales.** This type of scale permits to measure differences between values. Additionally, interval scales are also ordinal scales. Thus, their values can be compared and ordered. Interval scales permit additions and substractions of their values. Therefore, means and standard deviations can also be computed. However, multiplications and divisions, and hence any other operations that depend on those, such as ratios, cannot be performed.
- **Ratio scales.** This type of scales improve interval scales by adding a meaningful zero value. Ratio scales are also interval scales. All the operations that are valid for interval scales apply here too. In addition, multiplication and division are also meaningful.

Nominal and ordinal metrics are often grouped as qualitative metrics, whereas interval and ratio metrics are quantitative. This differentiation is very important when processing the results of metrics, which will happen when aggregating and composing metrics or when producing interpretation of the results of a metric. Qualitative metrics may need to be converted to quantitative, in order to make possible complex processing, such as aggregated metrics. Note that this process often consists on defining a transformation from a qualitative domain (which at most possess a partial ordering) to a numeric one, which implies making assumptions on the validity of such transformation. On the contrary, quantitative metrics may need to be converted to qualitative ones when facing the reporting of final assessments, in order to be easily interpreted by people. For example, a numeric metric could be transformed to a simple Green-Yellow-Red label.

2.3   Guidelines for the Development of Metrics

In this section, we will provide some guidelines for the development of metrics. We set up the following steps: design of the metric, application and exploitation of the result of the metric. In the following, we will explain these steps in detail:

Design of the Metric. This is the initial phase of the life cycle of the metric, which is composed of the following steps:

1. **Definition of the scope and measurement objectives.** This first step intends to provide a clear description of the purpose of the metric and aids to isolate its context. It is composed of the following sub-steps:
   (a) **Specification of the attribute and entity to be measured.** This sub-step is related to the characterization of the measured concept. In particular, it addresses questions such as 'What do we want to measure?', 'Which attribute of which entity?', etc.
   (b) **Objectives of the metric.** In this sub-step, we will clearly define the goals of this metric and its context. It addresses questions like 'What is the purpose of this metric?', 'Who will use it?', 'Whose viewpoint is used for defining this metric?', etc.
   (c) **Relation to the requirements.** This sub-step is important when the metric is related to any non-functional requirement. As we mentioned earlier, metrics are useful to verify the compliance of such requirements.
2. **Definition of the measurement method.** In this step, a mapping from the observations to a measure is established, as well as the associated details of the measurement method. This can be done in the following steps:
   (a) **Specification of the measurement scale and measurement unit.** This step is important for realizing the admissible operations on this metric, and therefore, correctly defining it.
   (b) **Specification of the mapping from observations to measures.** This step provides means for effectuating this mapping. Note that the measure could either be numerical or nominal. The mapping could be expressed in several ways, such as a mathematical expression, an algorithm or a generic procedure.
3. **Documentation of the metric.** Metrics have to be properly documented once they are specified.

Application of the Metric. This phase corresponds to the execution of the measurement method to the observations from the real world.

1. **Input data collection.** This step gathers the data that will be used for performing the measurement procedures.
2. **Application of the measurement method.** This step comprises the execution of the measurement method to the observed data gathered in the previous step.
3. **Verification of the measurement results.** The results from the application of the metric should be verified in order to guarantee its quality. Special attention should be given to delicate steps of the application, such as mathematical operations and input data gathering.

Exploitation of the Results of the Metric. Once the result of the metrics is obtained and verified, then it has to be exploited. The steps involved in this phase are the following:

1. **Reporting of the results.** This step is intended for the presentation of the results of the application of the metric. The output of this step should be documented with the main information from the application phase.
2. **Interpretation of the results.** Interested stakeholders could interpret the results of the application in relation to the objectives of the metrics and its associated requirements. For example, the management of an organization could make use of the results of the metrics in order to support management decisions, such as the initiation of corrective actions.

3   Metrics for Attributes Relevant to Accountability

In this section we will consider some attributes (or non-functional properties) that influence accountability to a certain extent, and will mention some metrics for them that have been considered in the literature. These attributes are especially relevant in the A4Cloud framework. We categorize these attributes in three main areas:

- Privacy attributes.
- Security attributes.
- Cloud-specific attributes.

3.1   Measuring Privacy Attributes

The relation between privacy and accountability is complex and materializes in several ways. For example, digital transactions are easily recorded by service providers and third parties, leading to increasing tracking and profiling of individuals. This fact clashes with the right to be informed (in some cases, even consent is needed) and with the right of the individuals to be forgotten (in the case of the EU, this right is proposed for recognition in the proposed regulation on data protection [10]). Privacy and accountability are in this case related concepts, as providers of IT systems (i.e. data-collecting parties) should be accountable for the protection and treatment of the personal information they gather.

This aspect is a particular case of a more general relation between privacy and accountability. Organizations should be accountable for the degree of conformity with their privacy-related obligations. These obligations could be either of regulatory, contractual or ethical nature, among others. Measuring the degree of conformity with these obligations is very important in order to assess the level of accountability of an organization.

A minor instance of the relation of privacy and accountability (within the A4Cloud context) can be seen also in the trade-off between anonymity and accountability of users. If users should be accountable of their use of IT resources, some compromise must be established regarding their privacy. At one end of the spectrum, a fully anonymous system difficulties accountability, as it is not possible to trace the identity of users who misbehave. In this case, the accountability of the system will presumably be low. At the other end, a fully accountable system difficulties anonymity. Therefore, the level of users privacy in a system influences its accountability and viceversa, but it is not clear to what extent. However, this aspect is out of the A4Cloud scope.

Privacy metrics have been applied in anonymity networks, anonymity in databases, and unlinkability for individuals. One of the examples of metrics in anonymity networks is *anonymity set* [15]. This is a metric that is given by the numbers of members in a set, to whom the adversary is looking for. The adversary will take advantage of all he/she knows about the members of the set to exclude as many individuals as possible. If the adversary is able to reduce the number of members of the set to one such that there is only one individual the adversary would have been successful. Thus, the bigger the set is the better anonymity is preserved.

3.2   Measuring Security Attributes

Availability. In today's world where more and more of our every day lives rely upon automated processing, the inability to access or use personal data can have consequences that range from a minor inconvenience to life threatening consequences. For example, when a bank ATM network becomes unavailable, it will result in discontent from card owners, but if a hospital system is unable to access patient data it may have more serious effects.

It should be noted that data protection is not limited to protecting privacy, but also concerned to broader goals such as assuring that data is notably processed 'fairly and lawfully' and that this is processed in a secure manner [9]. Availability can then be as important as confidentiality and integrity of data. Additionally, data subjects generally have in the right to access, update or erase (depending on the cases) their data. For these rights to be exercised, the system supporting the data must be available. For all these reasons, the ability to measure availability of a system is relevant to accountability.

Availability can be usually defined as the **target percentage of total operational time or requests** for which a service should be considered available in a period of time [8]. It is necessary to define precisely what the service is and what constitutes an 'unavailability event'. Defining an unavailability event requires the definition of certain parameters [8]:

- Service request. This is related to the functions of the service that are included in the measurement.
- Failure of a service request. What is the criteria to determine that a service failed? Are there standards for that?
- Sample size. What is the time period where the availability criteria is applied? If the sample size is too low the measure might not be significant.

- The scope of the service. Does this apply to requests from a single customer, service-wide user requests, requests from a specific geographical region, etc.? Does the service cover end-to-end fulfilment of requests, or only as far as the nearest Internet connection point?
- The commitment period to measure availability has to be always specified. This period could be one year, one month, one week, etc.

We could measure availability based on the definition of a single request failure. Thus, the target percentage of total requests can be calculated as the ratio $\frac{T-F}{T}$, where T is the total number of requests and F the number of request failures.

Providers could define a **recovery time objective (RTO)** as the maximum acceptable delay for recovery from an availability incident. RTO can be measured against **mean recovery time (MRT)**, which is the necessary average time to recover from an unavailability event.

Incident Response. According to [8] an incident is any event which is not part of the normal operation of the service and which causes, or may cause an interruption or a reduction in the quality of the service as stated in the SLA. Usually, it is necessary to characterize incidents through the following parameters:

- A Severity level. A classification of the incident according to a severity scale.
- Time to respond. Time between the notification of the incident and the implementation of the remediation action.

Based on these parameters it is possible to define the following metrics:

- Percentage of incidents of a certain severity resolved in a period of time.
- Recovery process and expected time to recover.
- Time to report. This is the time since the occurrence of an incident and until it is reported to the user.
- Time since the last incident of a given severity level.
- Specific incident data (e.g. number of records breached, downtime, time to respond).

Data Lifecycle Management. Data lifecycle management is related to how well the practices to handle data are managed by the provider. The measurements that can be performed for it include measuring the efficiency and effectiveness of such practices: service's back up, data replication system, portability and data loss prevention systems. The following parameters can be measured:

- Back-up test frequency and results.
- Restoration speed.
- Success or failure of operational back-ups.
- Data recovery points.

- Export test results.
- Percentage of response to requests.
- Data loss protection.
- Data durability.
- Scheduled deletion failure.
- Legal disclosure of regulatory requests.

Data Confidentiality Level. We propose the following measure to indicate the level of encryption of data in a cloud-based system (see Table 1):

Table 1. Data confidentiality level

Level	Description
0	Data is not cryptographically protected by the cloud provider
1	Data is cryptographically protected in transit
2	Data is cryptographically protected at rest and in transit
3	Data is cryptographically protected even at execution time

A system with Level 0 of data confidentiality does not use any cryptographic protection. It may, however, use other types of security measures, such as access control policies. A system that achieves Level 1 protects data that is transmitted from and to the cloud provider. This kind of system achieves security against an eavesdropper, but data is in clear inside the cloud provider, and therefore, susceptible to insider attacks or security breaches. Level 2 implies that data is protected also at rest. Proper mechanisms for key management need to be used. However, data should be decrypted before processing and could be accessed by malicious software or insiders. In a system with Level 3, the cloud provider does not decrypt data prior processing because the cryptographic scheme enables the processing of encrypted data. This level could be achieved with the aid of Fully Homomorphic Encryption schemes, but current proposals are not viable in practice. However, for certain applications, such as secure auctions and e-voting, there are simpler homomorphic schemes that are efficient and usable, and could reach this level.

Confidentiality Objective. We propose a measure to indicate the level of confidentiality achieved by a system regarding client data independently of the means used to achieve this objective (see Table 2).

The last level represents the best possible protection for a cloud client, however it will limit the ability of cloud providers to process the data except for storage purposes.

Table 2. Level of confidentiality

Level	Description
0	Data confidentiality does not satisfy any of the above levels
1	Data may be accessible by the cloud provider personnel for regular operational purposes, under the control of an authentication, authorization and accounting (AAA) mechanism
2	Technical and organizational measures are in place so that data may only be accessible to privileged CSP personnel (administrators) for debugging or maintenance purposes, under the control of an AAA mechanism
3	Technical and organizational measures are in place so that data is only accessible to privileged CSP personnel to respond to law enforcement or extraordinary requests made by the client, under the control of an AAA mechanism
4	Data is encrypted by the client with cryptographic keys that cannot be ascertained by the provider

3.3 Cloud-Specific Metrics

Elasticity. Following a similar approach to [8], we propose to define the elasticity ratio, a quantitative measure of elasticity, as the ratio $\frac{T-F}{T}$, where F is the total number of failures of resource provisioning requests over a period P (the commitment period), and T is the total number of provisioning requests over period P.

Location. In a cloud environment, providing the exact location of the data center that holds the clients data is neither strictly useful nor necessarily desirable (for physical security reasons). On the other hand, there is a strong case for providing a country or regional indicator of the location of the data, since it has strong regulatory implications. In some circumstances, the data may however reside in two or more datacenters during its life cycle. In practice, it is usually impossible to strictly 'prove' that data is only in a particular location (and not elsewhere) and we must rely on the trustworthiness of the cloud providers to provide that information. We propose to define a *location indicator* as a list of pairs *(location, certainty)*, where *location* refers to the ISO 3166-1 alpha-2 country or region code where the data resides, and *certainty* refers to the probability that the data will be located in this location at least once during its lifecycle (according to the CSP). Note that identical copies of data may be simultaneously in two different locations. Additionally, the proposed 'certainty parameter' could also be expressed as the average percentage of time that the data spends in a location during its lifecycle.

Data Isolation. This property is about ensuring the confidentiality, integrity and availability of data between different cloud clients [8]. When it comes to data isolation, we can ask the following questions: can a cloud client read or modify a memory block, storage data or network packets produced by another client? Can a cloud client still read a memory block or storage data once another client has deleted it? Recent research shows the additional risk of side channel attacks, whereby a cloud client can discover information about another client, including in particular the value of secret cryptographic keys, by observing the temporal behaviour of the system [18]. To the best of our knowledge there are no metrics associated with data isolation in the cloud. As a first step, we propose to define the following indicator called *data isolation testing level*, which describes the level of testing that has been done by the cloud provider to assess how well data isolation is implemented (see Table 3).

Table 3. Data isolation testing level

Level	Description
0	No data isolation testing has been performed
1	Read/write isolation has been tested
2	Secure deletion has been tested, in addition to read/write isolation
3	Absence of known side channel attacks has been tested, in addition to read/write and secure deletion

It is important to note that in order to use such a metric, the resources in the scope of the measurement need to be well defined (storage, CPU, network, memory, database, etc.). Additionally, a standard set of tools or procedures need to be defined to establish the tests that should be conducted to assess each level.

4 A Review on Accountability Attributes from the Metrics Perspective

The accountability attributes have been defined in [16]. We remind here their definitions according to the Conceptual Framework for accountability introduced there and we will present an analysis of the accountability attributes in order to assess their usefulness with respect to metrics. Such an analysis will be carried out focusing on the following aspects:

– *Are the definitions of the accountability attributes valid from the point of view of metrics? Is there any ambiguity in the definition given by the Conceptual Framework? Is the attribute to be evaluated well identified from the definition?* These questions will help us to identify any inconsistencies, vagueness, and significant overlappings of the definitions of the attributes. Ideally, a correction should be proposed.

- *Can the attribute be decomposed in other sub-attributes?* The definitions of the attributes included in the conceptual framework are in some cases very abstract and high-level. Therefore, it might be useful to identify particular cases for each attribute depending on its nature and context that may be more concrete and useful from a metrics viewpoint.
- *Interdependencies with other attributes.*
- *What type of metrics could be defined for this attribute? Are there any requirements for a metric for this attribute?* We should identify the possible characteristics for a metric for such attribute depending on its nature and context and if possible, identify potential metrics for them.

For all of the attributes it might difficult to measure the attribute itself. For this reason, we identify dimensions of the attributes that are easier to be measured.

4.1   Transparency

Transparency is a property of an organization or a system about how well it implements and demonstrates the implementation of the following three transparency practices:

- Informing upstream stakeholders about data protection policies and their implementation practices.
- Notification in case of policy violation and other events that have been agreed upon in the policy, which includes explanation of the actions taken on such event.
- Responding to data subject access requests about data handling, e.g., data storing and processing.

A transparent organization will implement procedures for supporting these practices, and will provide means for demonstrating the existence and quality of such procedures.

From a high-level point of view, a transparency metric would measure how easy is for an external party to inspect the policies and procedures of an organisation regarding data protection.

There are several dimensions for assessing transparency that could be measured:

- Accessibility. This dimension is related to the level of easiness for obtaining the necessary information by the relevant stakeholders. The more transparent an organization is, the easier for stakeholders is to obtain the information they need.
- Effectiveness. Even if information is fully accessible, it may not be effective. It is necessary that the receptor is capable of processing, digesting and using the information [12]. This dimension is related to the usefulness of provided information. For example, the provision of excessive amounts of information, although accessible, renders it useless. The same aspect applies to the format and method of the provision of information.

- Timing. This dimension is related to assessing when the transparency actions are taken with regard to the event that triggered (this dimension has more sense with aspects such as notification). For example, it is possible to measure quantitatively the elapsed time between the event of the violation of a privacy policy and the corresponding notification.
- Other dimensions can be framed as combinations of accessibility, effectiveness, and timing. For instance, the provided information may be incomplete at the beginning (an accessibility problem) but may be completed after further user requests, which is also a timing problem.

4.2 Responsibility

Responsibility is a relationship between two entities regarding a specific Responsibility Target (policy, rules, states of affairs), such that the Responsibility Holder is responsible to the giver of the responsibility, the Responsibility Principal.

According to this definition, Responsibility should take into account any operation performed by the responsibility holder, then the policy should be used to evaluate if the performed action was according to the norm or not. As shown in Fig. 1, the important point for the responsibility attribute is that responsibilities cannot be looked at in an isolated way but must always be considered as a relationship between two agents. The Responsibility Target for which responsibilities are held may be at any level of granularity of the organization.

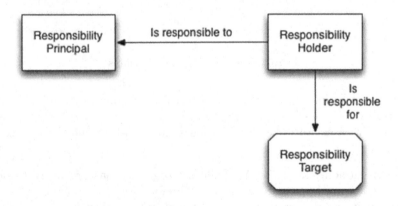

Fig. 1. Responsibility relationships

Some of the practices that we could identify for responsibility, derived from the definition given above, are:

- Responsibility granting. The process where the responsibility principal grants the actual responsibility to the responsibility holder. It should be noted that the granting of responsibility can actually involve a chain of Responsibility Holders, as shown in Fig. 2. For example, the primary Cloud Service Provider (data processor) might be responsible towards the Cloud Customer (data controller), if one of the sub-processors carrying out processing operations on his behalf do not implement the appropriate security measures for the protection of personal data.

– Responsibility assessment/attribution. The process where conformance of the Responsibility Holders performed actions is evaluated with respect to the Responsibility Target. This practice can be subdivided into the following:

 • Non-repudiation. Comprehending the unambiguous authenticity and integrity of the Responsibility Holders identity.
 • Authentication. As required to assess the identity of the Responsibility Holder. As mentioned in the example above, in a chain of Responsibility it is possible that the person responsible for a malicious action, is not the legal responsible.
 • Integrity. Needed to assess that the Responsibility Holders identity and actions have not been tampered with.

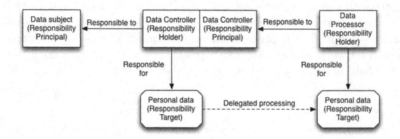

Fig. 2. Responsibility relationships

If we want to measure (either qualitatively or quantitatively) an entity's responsibility (i.e., its Responsibility Level) with respect to (i) some specific action and (ii) a set of policy/rules, then some high-level metrics to take into account are:

– Level of Authentication (LoA). Different organizations are likely to deploy different authentication mechanisms, therefore we cannot expect the same assurance in the responsible entity's (unambiguous) identification process.
– Delegation of Responsibility. This metric should assess the responsibility delegation process. It is clear that responsibility will attenuate in long delegation chains.
– Integrity. In analogy to the LoA metric(s), the inherent assurance of the adopted integrity mechanisms must be assessed to measure the organizations responsibility. For example, an organization using MD5 to protect the integrity of their log files cannot have the same Responsibility Level of other organization using SHA-512, due to the inferior integrity level offered by MD5 with respect to SHA-512.

– Duty/Role separation. The model used to split the responsibilities (e.g., n out of m), must be clearly stated in order to determine the responsible entity/ entities. Notice that this metric is somehow related to the Delegation metric.

4.3   Remediability

Remediability is a property of an organization on the quality of its internal processes for taking corrective and compensatory actions in case of failing to comply with their commitments and policies. According to this definition, remediability is supported by the following main practices:

– Notification, which implies informing the relevant stakeholders (e.g., affected data subjects, regulators, services elsewhere in the service chain) about the failure, breach or disclosure.
– Reparation, which is related to taking corrective actions and technical remedies for restoring the system to the state prior the damage, if possible. This implies restoring data and supporting forensic recording.
– Redress, which implies legal remedies due to the damage suffered. These remedies may imply that the affected part claims compensatory, or even, punitive damages.

   The Remediability concept is built upon the existence of a relation of responsibility between two entities, the responsibility holder and the responsibility principal (as described in Sect. 3.2) and the occurrence of a failure to comply with the responsibility target. Remediability also adds a fourth entity called remediation agent, such as a court or a dispute resolution entity, which may be used as a third-party by the responsibility principal and the responsibility holder in order to arbiter the remediation actions. Figure 3 shows these relationships.

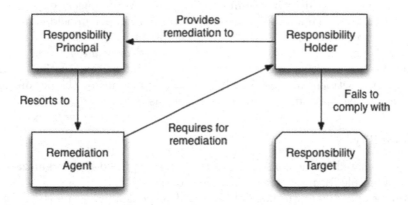

Fig. 3. Remediability relationships

   A metric for remediability would measure the quality of the remediation practices held in place by an organization. There are several aspects that can be assessed with respect to the quality of remediation of an organization:

– As notification is part of the remediation process, one can evaluate the quality of the notification procedures. More aspects to be measured are:
  • Existence and quality of the notification processes. For example, simply to assess the existence of internal policies within an organization for addressing the notification of the affected parties after any damage has occurred.
  • Timing of notification. The relevance of notification is affected by the elapsed time between the occurrence of the damage and the effective time of notification.
  • Efectiveness of the notification. Even if notification is provided, it may not be useful for the relevant stakeholder. For example, indirect notification, such as publication of a notice in a web site, is not as useful as a direct notification by email. Also, the information included in the notification should be useful enough for the affected party, such as a proper explanation of the incident and the taken actions, and a description of the possible options for seeking for remediation.
– Reparation activities. Metrics could be defined to evaluate the quality of the technical remedies and corrective actions:
  • Preparedness level. Actions intended to prepare the organization in advance to the event of a failure and the necessity of restoring to a prior state. Some of these practices are data recovery and support forensics.
  • Repairability level. Assessment of the level of reparation of an organization to restore a failure, from the perspective of the affected party. For example, restoring damaged data from a back-up can be enough, while the disclosure of personal data that has already taken place cannot be entirely corrected.
– Redress. A metric for redress could measure aspects that impact the quality of the redress actions planned and taken by the organization such as proper definition of compensations, standard vs custom compensation, number of incidents that end up with compensatory/punitive damages, expenses due to compensatory damages (e.g. average/total redress per upheld complaint), number of complaints, time to resolve a complaint, etc.
– Proactivity towards remediation. That is, an organization can take either a proactive or a reactive attitude with respect to remediation actions. Hence, remediation actions can be taken in a proactive manner by the organization, or in a reactive way, after complaints of the customer.

4.4 Liability

Liability is related to the consequences that must be faced if an organization is found responsible for not fullling its obligations.

Defining and differentiating liabililty and responsibility is pretty complex. On the one hand, responsibility is a requirement for liability to be established. On the other hand, although an entity might be responsible, it might not be considered at the end liable (for instance, due to an incident that happened, which the responsible entity could not predicted or prevented).

The first step towards eliciting relevant Liability metrics is to decide which are the actual consequences to consider. For example, if a re-definition of Liability only considers economic consequences, then we can derive a set of economic-driven metrics (EDM). State of the art works on the EDM field (like Innerhofer [13]) have studied this topic in detail.

4.5   Observability

Observability can be defined as the ability of a system to expose (part of) its operations to authorized stakeholders.

An observable system will rely on processes and procedures for supporting these characteristics, and will provide means for demonstrating the existence and quality of such procedures. In the first case, an observable system will provide 'openings' for inspection, that is, means for independent inspection by third parties. In the second case, an observable organization must demonstrate and provide evidence of the low influence of unobservable actions in the state of the system. This aspect may be more difficult to fulfill. Hence, from a high-level viewpoint, an observability metric would measure the quality and effectiveness of such procedures.

Quality and effectiveness of observability can be assessed mainly from information based in certification from third parties. Organizations may be audited and/or certified by trusted third parties, who can then assert to what extent external inspections relate to internal system functioning.

4.6   Verifiability

Verifiability is a property of a process or system describing how well it implements and demonstrates the following practices:

- Compliance of process or system behaviour with rules is documentable.
- Continuous documentation.
- Scope of documentable compliance is a balance between benefits and costs.

A verifiable process or system will implement procedures for supporting these practices, and will provide means for demonstrating the existence and quality of such procedures. Accountability evidence relates to the documentation that should be collected in relation to compliance process. The scope of accountability evidence is based on the balance between benefits and costs.

4.7   Attributability

Attributability describes a property of an observation that discloses or can be assigned to actions of a particular actor (or system element). It implies the existence of two attributability processes:

- An evidence collection process that provides data regarding the effects of the actions of an actor in the system. For example, a logging component within an information system.

– An attribution process that maps evidence to actors. Log analysis is an example of this kind of process.

According to the attributability definition, attributability is independent of regulations, i.e., the attributability processes should function whether regulations exist or not. Accountability is what extends attributability by taking regulations into consideration.

A metric for attributability should measure the quality of the attributability processes of a system in order to ascribe actions to actors. Thus, when facing the assessment of attributability within an organization, the processes of attribution and evidence collection must be identified and described. These descriptions, which are considered the evidence of attributability, are what support a metric for attributability.

The implementation of an attributability metric has to be chosen depending on the use-case and the available evidence. For instance, in legal scenarios, it could be required that the observation is unambiguously and probably attributed to a set on entities (usually one). For example, the observation of the factual circumstances of processing might lead to the attribution of the role of data controllers to two or more entities (called joint data controllers). In this case, the set notation makes sense and the evidence must be good enough to reduce the set size of the set of entities that could have caused the observation to the minimum. In other scenarios, where strong indication for attribution is required, but not unambiguity, approaches based on information theory are more likely to yield the intended results. Aspects such as Data Stewardship, Data Lifecycle Management and Log Management also affect directly the quality of attributability of an organization. Thus, metrics for these subconcepts will be very useful for deriving metrics for attributability.

5   Measuring Accountability Attributes

In this section we propose a model-driven approach that includes the definition of a metamodel for describing metrics and accountability properties [14]. The goal of this metamodel is to serve as a language for describing: (i) accountability properties in terms of entities, evidence and actions, and (ii) metrics for measuring them.

One of the main features of this metamodel is that metrics are defined to take two main kinds of inputs: **Evidence** and **Criteria**. Any assessment or evaluation (i.e., a metric) can only be made using as input some tangible and empirical evidence, such as an observation, a system log, a certification asserted by a trusted party, a textual description of a procedure, etc. That is, a metric does not directly measure a property of a process, behaviour, or a system, but uses the evidence associated with them in order to derive a meaningful measure. Evidence is the fundamental support of any evaluation method and is what gives an objective dimension to assessments. Criteria are all the elements that convey contextual input that may constrain what should be measured, such as stakeholder's preferences, regulations and policies.

Next, we will describe the elements of the metamodel, which can be seen in Fig. 4.

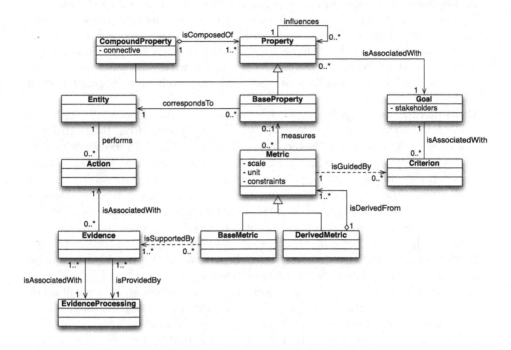

Fig. 4. Metamodel for metrics for accountability

- **Goal:** High-level description of the attribute (or family of attributes) that is modelled. These elements also contain a reference to the stakeholder (or stakeholders) for which the goal is oriented.
- **Attribute:** Attributes can be distinguished quantitatively or qualitatively by some evaluation method, however they may be defined as very-high level concepts. Thus, we consider that attributes can be further decomposed into more basic ones in some cases. In these cases, **BaseAttribute** elements can be defined in terms of entities and the actions between them, whereas **Compound Attribute** elements are defined in terms of other attributes, making possible a top-down decomposition of properties, from a high-level and abstract way to a tangible and more accessible one. In addition, attributes may also influence other attributes, not necessarily taking part of a composition relationship. The model then permits to express these influence relationships among attributes.
- **Entity:** This element is used to describe the entity that meets the modelled attribute. An entity is a physical or conceptual object that performs actions and that meets properties. For example, an organization, a process or a system can be considered as entities.
- **Action:** We define an action as a process that occurs over a period of time and it is performed by or has an effect on entities. Even though actions have

an effect in the environment, we cannot deal directly with these consequences, but with the evidence associated to them.

- **Evidence:** We define evidence as a collection of information with tangible representation about the effect of actions. Evidence is used to support a metric. That is, evidence is not an abstract concept about the consequence of activities, but actual data that can even be processed by a machine. Note, however, that evidence may come from sources with different levels of certainty and validity, depending on the method of collection or generation of such evidence.

- **EvidenceProcessing:** In our model, we assume that evidence, although it is associated to the effect of actions, does not directly stem from them. Instead, evidence is originated or collected by means of an EvidenceProcessing element. In this way, we model the fact that there may not exist a perfect correlation between the effects or consequences of actions and the evidence associated with them. The EvidenceProcessing element makes this difference explicit. With the inclusion of this element in our metamodel, we emphasise that the method of collection and processing of evidence is as important as the evidence itself. For this reason, there should also be evidence associated to each EvidenceProcessing element, describing how it works. Such evidence may be used by a metric during the evaluation process.

- **Metric:** We define it as an evaluation method for assessing the level of satisfaction of a non-functional property (or attribute in our case) in a quantitative or qualitative way, on the basis of evidence and contextual criteria. Metrics can be of two types: **BaseMetric** for metrics that use evidence as inputs for their calculations, and **DerivedMetric** for aggregated metrics that are defined as a function of other metrics. Aggregated metrics may rely on auxiliary metrics that are not associated with any attribute and that are defined solely for facilitating the definition of the parent metric. In both cases, metrics may use Criterion elements for guiding the evaluation with respect to the context of the metric. This element has the following fields:
  - Scale: This field describes the type of measurement scale used in this metric. The scale can be either nominal, ordinal, interval or ratio.
  - Unit: This field represents the measurement unit adopted as standard for measuring the property. The definition of a measurement unit is only necessary in the case of quantitative metrics.
  - Constraints: This field conveys the contextual constraints that may affect the application and validity of the metric.

- **Criterion:** This element captures all the contextual input that may constrain what should be measured by the metric, such as regulation, best practices, organisational policies and contracts, and stakeholders' preferences. It could be the case that one could define different metrics for the same attribute. The assessment methodology for each metric will depend on the contextual input given for the metrics evaluation. The Criterion element will be the responsible of conveying such contextual information.

6   Measuring Transparency

In this section we show how the metamodel presented in Sect. 5 can be applied to any of the accountability attributes. We have chosen transparency for our example. According to the definition of transparency, a metric for it would measure how an organization implements and demonstrates some practices related to how well deals with policies and procedures regarding data protection, as well as the quality of the transparency processes held in place by the organization. Figure 5 shows how transparency is modelled by using our metamodel.

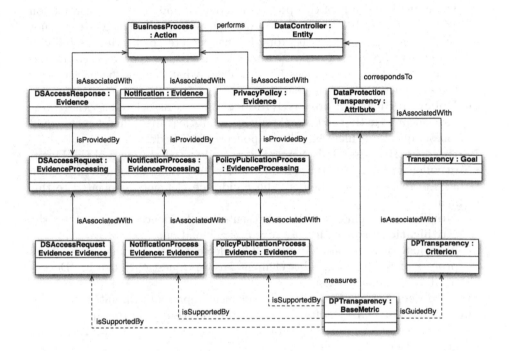

Fig. 5. Modeling transparency

The high-level goal in this example is represented by the **Transparency** element. This is a very generic goal that can have several properties associated to it. We are considering transparency with respect to data protection (**DataProtectionTransparency**). This property is defined upon an organization that acts as data controller (since it determines the purposes and means of the processing of personal data). In other words, a metric for this property would evaluate how transparent this organization (i.e., the **DataController** element) is with respect to data protection. In this example, the actions of the **DataController** are subsumed into one **Action** element and called **BusinessProcess**. One might want to be more specific and could model particular business processes, but in this case, it is not necessary.

The **DataController** must implement and demonstrate the transparency practices that we identified in Sect. 4 (informing stakeholders about data protection policies, notification of policy violations and responding to data subject access requests).

These practices are mapped to the following **EvidenceProcessing** elements:

– **PolicyPublicationProcess:** This element describes the internal procedures of the DataController with respect to the publication and communication of data protection policies to the relevant stakeholders.
  - **PrivacyPolicy:** This **Evidence** is produced by the **PolicyPublication-Process**. The result of this process is a description of the data protection policy accessible by the relevant stakeholders. This element by itself is not relevant for measuring the property that we are considering as individual policies are not assessed by a metric for transparency, as such metrics focus on making the policies known. Thus, what it could be measured is the existence of these elements.
  - **PolicyPublicationProcessEvidence:** This is associated to the transparency process that published policies and its features. This element could answer questions like 'Are all the policies published?'
– **NotificationProcess:** This element is related to the practices of the **Data-Controller** with respect to the notification of any violation of daa protection policies to relevant stakeholders. The **Evidence** elements associated to this element are:
  - **Notification:** This element represents the Evidence generated by the **NotificationProcess** in case of a policy violation.
  - **NotificationProcessEvidence:** This element describes the nature of the process of notification. This element answers questions such as 'Does a notification process exist?'
– **DataSubjectAccesssProcess:** This element represents the internal procedures of the **DataController** for permitting data subjects to request access to their data and for properly responding to such requests. The two **Evidence** elements associated to it are:
  - **DataSubjectAccessResponse:** This element is the evidence representing the response generated by the **DataSubjectAccessRequestProcess** in case of an access request from a data subject.
  - **DataSubjectAccessRequestEvidence:** This element represents a description of the characteristics of the process for permitting data subject access requests. This element answers questions such as 'Does a process for data subject access requests exist?'

It is the **Evidence** elements associated to the **EvidenceProcessing** elements, and not the evidence produced by them, the ones that are evaluated by the **DataProtectionTransparency** metric.

Based on the existence of the transparency processes identified by the definition of transparency, we could define a metric for **DataProtectionTransparency** (see Table 4).

Table 4. Naive example of a metric for transparency

Level	Description of the level
None	No transparency processes are implemented by the Data Controller
Low	One transparency process is implemented by the Data Controller
Medium	Two transparency processes are implemented by the Data Controller
High	All the transparency processes are implemented by the Data Controller

The stakeholders' criteria for this particular metric is conveyed by the **DataProtectionCriterion**. In this case the measurement is about the existence of transparency processes but the metric does not evaluate their quality.

A more complex metric could be one that counts the existence of a transparency process if it has been audited by a trusted third party. We could define an ordered scale as described in Table 5.

Table 5. Another example of a metric for transparency

Level	Description of the level
0	No transparency processes are implemented by the Data Controller
1	Only a process for data subject access requests is implemented by the Data Controller
2	Only a process for notification is implemented by the Data Controller
3	Either the process for publication of policies or the processes for notification and data subject access requests are implemented by the Data Controller
4	The processes for publication of policies and data subject access requests are implemented by the Data Controller
5	The processes for publication of policies and notification are implemented by the Data Controller
6	All the transparency processes are implemented by the Data Controller

Note that a different definition of transparency could lead to a different model; that is the reason why we consider that a first requirement towards creating metrics is agreeing on a clear, concise and stable definition of the property to be measured, so that an appropriate model can be defined.

7   Conclusion and Future Work

This paper lays the foundations for the development of metrics in the context of the A4Cloud project. This includes: (i) the definition of basic concepts for developing metrics, (ii) an analysis of the accountability attributes from the metrics perspective, and (iii) a metamodel for describing such attributes and their metrics.

The analysis of accountability attributes has helped us to refine the concepts involved in the definitions and to identify plausible sources of evidence in order to support the evaluation of such attributes. The metamodel for accountability metrics constitutes the first step in the metrics elicitation process. It serves as a language for describing the accountability attributes in terms of entities and activities among them. Moreover, it also allows us to describe the sources of evidence involved in those activities and to identify the evidence elements that can be used to support metrics. Thus, this metamodel is a valuable tool for guiding the process of defining metrics.

In the future, we intend to apply the metamodel to all the accountability attributes and not only transparency. We are also going to explore a bottom-up approach for the elicitation of metrics, as well as the top-down approach that we have introduced in this paper. In this new approach we are going to use as input for the elicitation of the metrics, control frameworks and how they influence on accountability.

Acknowledgements. This work has been partially funded by the European Commission through the FP7/2007–2013 project A4Cloud under grant agreement number 317550. The first author is funded by a FPI fellowship from the Junta de Andalucía through the project PISCIS (P10-TIC-06334).

References

1. New Oxford American Dictionary
2. The Cloud Accountability Project. http://www.a4cloud.eu/
3. ISO/IEC 15939:2007 – Systems and software engineering – Measurement process (2007)
4. NIST SP 800-55 – Performance measurement guide for information security. National Institute of Standards and Technology (2008)
5. ISO/IEC 27004:2009 – Information Technology – Security techniques – Information Security Management – Measurement (2009)
6. Implementing accountability in the marketplace – a discussion document. accountability phase iii – the madrid project. Centre for Information Policy Leadership (CIPL), November 2011
7. Abran, A.: Software Metrics and Software Metrology. Wiley, New York (2010)
8. ENISA. Procure secure – a guide to monitoring of security service levels in cloud contracts (2012)
9. EU Parliament and EU Council. Directive 95/46/EC of the European Parliament and of the Council of 24 October 1995 on the protection of individuals with regard to the processing of personal data and on the free movement of such data
10. EU Parliament and EU Council. Proposal for a regulation of the european parliament and of the council on the protection of individuals with regard to the processing of personal data and on the free movement of such data (general data protection regulation) (2012)

11. Herrmann, D.S.: Complete Guide to Security and Privacy Metrics: Measuring Regulatory Compliance, Operational Resilience, and ROI. CRC Press, Boca Raton (2007)
12. Hood, C., Heald, D. (eds.): Transparency: The Key to Better Governance?, vol. 135. Oxford University Press, Oxford (2006)
13. Innerhofer-Oberperfler, F., Breu, R.: An empirically derived loss taxonomy based on publicly known security incidents. In: International Conference on Availability, Reliability and Security, ARES 2009, pp. 66–73. IEEE (2009)
14. Nuñez, D., Fernandez-Gago, C., Pearson, S., Felici, M.: A metamodel for measuring accountability attributes in the cloud. In: 2013 IEEE 5th International Conference on Cloud Computing Technology and Science (CloudCom), vol. 1, pp. 355–362. IEEE (2013)
15. Pfitzmann, A., Hansen, M.: Anonymity, Unlinkability, Undetectability, Unobservability, Pseudonymity, and Identity Management–A Consolidated Proposal for Terminology. Version v0.31 (2008)
16. A4Cloud project. MS:C-2.2 - Initial framework description report, February 2013
17. Stevens, S.S.: On the theory of scales of measurement. Science **103**(2684), 677–680 (1946)
18. Zhang, Y., Juels, A., Reiter, M.K., Ristenpart, T.: Cross-vm side channels and their use to extract private keys. In: Proceedings of the 2012 ACM Conference on Computer and Communications Security, pp. 305–316. ACM (2012)

Models for Cloud Risk Assessment: A Tutorial

Erdal Cayirci[(✉)]

Electrical and Computer Engineering Department,
University of Stavanger, 4026 Stavanger, Norway
erdal.cayirci@uis.no

Abstract. Although the technology for cloud services has been maturing for more than a decade, many potential users still have some concerns about the security and especially privacy. Users need to analyze the risks to face prior to embracing the cloud concept. Recently, many organizations and researchers assessed the cloud risks. There are also both quantitative and qualitative models developed for this purpose. Our tutorial first introduces the definitions and then provides a survey on the results from cloud risk assessment efforts and risk models developed for cloud.

Keywords: Risk assessment · Risk analysis · Risk management · Risk modeling · Trust · Cloud · Security · Privacy · Service · ENISA · CNIL · CSA

1 Introduction

Moving business processes to the cloud is associated with a change in the risk landscape to an organization 1. Cloud Security Alliance (CSA) 2 has found that insufficient due diligence was among the top threats in cloud computing in 2013. This threat is linked to the fact that organizations which strive to adopt cloud computing often do not understand well the resulting risks. Therefore, risk, trust and accountability are critical notions for cloud services and closely related to each other. In literature, trust is stated as the main barrier for potential subscribers before they embrace cloud services. For realization of cloud computing, trust relation between the Cloud Customer (CC) and the Cloud Service Provider (CSP) has to be established. This requires an in depth understanding of risk and the accountability of the CSP.

Moreover, regulations related to data protection, financial reporting, etc. put certain requirements that should be complied with even when outsourcing business processes to 3rd parties, like CSPs. For example, EU Data Protection Directive, in particular Article 29 Data Protection Working Party 3, recommends that all data controllers (usually corporate cloud customers) perform an impact assessment of moving personal data of their clients to the cloud. However, most of the CC, especially Small-Medium Businesses (SMBs), may not have enough knowledge in performing such assessments at a good level, because they may not necessarily employ IT specialists and the lack of transparency is intrinsic to the operations of the CSPs. This makes difficult to choose an appropriate CSP based on cloud customer's security requirements, especially considering the abundance of similar cloud offerings [4].

© Springer International Publishing Switzerland 2015
M. Felici and C. Fernández-Gago (Eds.): A4Cloud 2014, LNCS 8937, pp. 154–184, 2015.
DOI: 10.1007/978-3-319-17199-9_7

Both risk and trust have been extensively studied in various contexts for hundreds of years. Risk management, and specifically risk assessment for IT has also been a hot research topic for several decades [5]. On the other hand, modelling risk and trust for cloud computing and associating it with the notion of accountability has attracted researchers only recently [6, 7, 8, 9].

Cloud computing services use autonomic mechanisms for self-configuration, self-optimization and self-healing. These mechanisms make decisions on allocating resources (i.e., physical servers, computation power and memory), and migrating data and processes among servers. Because of this autonomic nature of cloud computing, CSP may not be able to identify exactly in which physical machine data are stored or a process is hosted. In addition to this, multi-tenancy allows multiple CCs share the same software concurrently. Moreover, a software used by multiple CCs may process data owned by various CCs and data may have parts with different classification levels. Therefore, cloud computing introduce new vulnerabilities although it seems providing more secure environment at the first glance [12]. The security threats that a CSP faces are further exacerbated by the nested cloud architectures and when a cloud service federation involves multiple data centers owned by multiple CSP.

A CC has a special challenge in risk assessment comparing to conventional information technology (i.e., other than cloud) customers. CSP usually keep the locations, architecture and details about the security of their server farms and data centers confidential from CCs. Therefore, it is more difficult to a CC to assess all the threats and vulnerabilities. Additionally, CSP have to prioritize the issues to solve when risks are realized. These uncertainties increase risk and imply that the CCs have to trust CSP [13]. A CC has to rely on the autonomic procedures of CSP for managing the infrastructure appropriately according to the CCs' security dynamics, treating the CCs' issues in a timely manner, detecting, recovering and reporting the security incidents accurately. Therefore, CSP have to be accountable to their CCs, and in many cases the CCs should be able to transfer their accountability to their CSP. However, since we expect that CSP may use services by the other CSP, the transfer of accountability may end up at a CSP whose accountability does not mean anything to the CC. It is clear that the nested nature of clouds make accountability an extremely sophisticated issue and increases the risk for CCs.

Chief information officers perceives the barriers for cloud adoption [14] as vendor lock-in (i.e., to be dependent on a vendor), cloud performance and availability, security and challenges in integrating internal and external services. According to another survey among 264 non information technology executives (non-IT) and 462 information technology executives, the barriers are security, regulatory risks, business case, adapting business processes, interoperability, lack of awareness, adjusting policies and building skill sets [14].

Risk, trust and accountability should not be treated as related only to security but also QoS and GoS. The centralization of resources and sharing them increase the utilization. However, shared resources may be congested from time to time. Congestion control, service differentiation, user differentiation and prioritization are complex challenges especially for large clouds with high scalability requirements. The CCs need to be assured that their GoS and QoS requirements are fulfilled and their operations are not hampered due to congested cloud resources. Providing such an assurance, measuring and guaranteeing QoS/GoS are not trivial tasks.

The bottom-line is that accountability [9] and trust are concepts required to be realized before potential CCs embrace cloud computing approach. Therefore, "trust" with cloud computing perspective has attracted researchers recently [14, 15], and "trust as a service" is introduced to cloud business model. Standardised trust models are needed for verification and assurance of accountability, but none of the large number of existing trust models to date is adequate for the cloud environment [16]. There are many trust models which strive to accommodate some of the factors defined by [17] and others [18] and there are many trust assessment mechanisms which aim to measure them. These tend to be developed in isolation and there has been little integration between hard and soft trust solutions.

One way to increase the trust of CC to a CSP is providing them with some controls over the cloud. In [25] controls that can a CC be given are categorized into five broad classes as controls on data stored, data during processing, software, regulatory compliance and billing. The techniques that need to be developed for these controls include remote monitoring, prevention of access to residual data, secure outsourcing, data scrambling, machine readable regulations and SLA, automatic reasoning about compliance, automatic collection of real time consumption data, and make your own bill. Although these are techniques which have already been developed for both cloud computing and the other purposes, many CSP still need time for their implementation, deployment and maturity.

Recently, Accountability for Cloud and Other Future Internet Services (A4Cloud) Project conducted a one day workshop on trust and risk for cloud, called A4Cloud Risk Workshop on Sep 27, 2013. Twenty nine stakeholders including the CCs from various sectors (e.g., healthcare, banking. military, etc.) attended to the workshop. Two of the important conclusions from the workshop are as follows:

1. Many stakeholders consider data breaches and data loss as the topmost security threats for cloud computing, which are also recognized as the top two by Cloud Security Alliance (CSA). However, this is not shared by all the stakeholders. The highest priority threat is DoS attacks for the stakeholders from the telecommunications, and abuse of cloud services for the stakeholders from banking industry. Therefore, the conclusion is that the consequences and vulnerabilities related to security threats change from one sector to the other. Moreover, the importance of threats changes from one cloud service model to another (i.e., IaaS, PaaS and SaaS). Therefore, when modelling risk for cloud computing, it is not easy to include consequences of threats and vulnerabilities into the risk model. Similarly,
2. CSP may not be willing to share or to specify the technical details of its physical architecture, the locations of data and processes, and data security systems. Therefore, it is impossible for the CC to develop a risk model based on an exhaustive (or even detailed) list of threats and vulnerabilities.

This tutorial starts with a section on definitions, where we clarify the terms referred in the later sections.. In Sect. 3, we introduce some efforts mainly in Europe to analyze the threats and vulnerabilities, which include the Cloud Security Alliance (CSA) initiatives to analyze the top threats against cloud and to obtain a better insight into how well the cloud service providers (CSP) are prepared for them. CSA prepared a questionnaire called Cloud Assessment Initiative Questionnaire (CAIQ) for this purpose. In Sect. 4, a risk assessment exercise by European Network and Information Security Agency (ENISA) is presented. ENISA's risk assessment is generic and applies to all CSP and CC. It was published in 2009. A4Cloud complemented ENISA's framework by using CAIQ and a number of tools and models, which can be used to assess the risks associated with a given CSP and CC pair and supports relative risk analysis. That is called Cloud Adopted Risk Assessment Model (CARAM) and explained in Sect. 5. The National Commission on Informatics and Liberty (CNIL) is a French Board, which conducted a risk assessment for cloud more recently. CNIL's work goes further by introducing some measures to reduce the risks to acceptable levels. We elaborate on CNIL's work in Sect. 6. ENISA's and CNIL's works, as well as, CARAM can be categorized as qualitative and inductive schemes. A4Cloud has developed also a quantitative model called as Joint Risk and Trust Model (JRTM) for cloud risk assessment in 2013. JRTM is explained in Sect. 7. Finally, we conclude our tutorial in Sect. 8.

2 Definitions

Risk analysis is defined as "an attempt to envision how the future will turn out if a certain course of action or inaction is taken" [5]. Three questions are answered during a risk analysis:

- A scenario s_i (i.e., What can go wrong?)
- The probability p_i of s_i (i.e., the probability that the scenario is realized)
- The consequence x_i of s_i

Hence, the risk R is a set of triplets that answers three questions (i.e., R = {<si, pi, xi >}, i = 1, 2, …, N) for N scenarios (i.e., N represents the number of all possible scenarios) [5, 10, 11].

A risk is in essence the product of a threat, a vulnerability and the consequences (i.e., the impact of threat), and cloud computing is subject to a long list of threats and vulnerabilities [12].

Risk perception for the same scenario may be different from person to person even time to time because the probabilities and consequences may be different for different people at different times. This is called as perceived risk. On the other hand, absolute risk is the same for everyone and every time. That is not easy to compute the absolute risk because someone's absolute risk is the perceived risk for someone else. Perceived risk is also quite often named as relative risk in the literature. In our tutorial, we will use the term relative risk differently. Relative risk is the risk of a course of action comparing to another course of action. An example for relative risk is the risk of using cloud instead your own infrastructure and software. Another example is the risk of receiving services from a CSP instead of an alternative CSP.

2.1 Risk Scenario, Event and Incident

"Scenario" is a key term in the definition of risk. That is called differently in different schemes introduced in this tutorial. For example, it is called directly as risk by ENISA and feared event by CNIL. A4Cloud clarifies this term further and introduces the notions called event and incidents. A4Cloud also classifies incidents as security, privacy and service incidents as follows:

- Incident: An Incident is an event that results in a security, privacy or service violation/outage; e.g., respectively confidential data leakages after an attack, personal data collection without appropriate consent from the data subjects, or data cannot be recovered after a hardware failure. It is important not to confuse event with incident; For instance, losing an access badge is a security event. If an outsider uses the lost badge to enter a building without authorization, then it is a security incident.
- Security incident: A security incident can be defined as a single attack or a group of attacks that can be distinguished from other attacks by the method of attack, identity of attackers, victims, sites, objectives or timing, etc. It results in the violation or imminent threat of violation of computer security policies, acceptable use policies, or standard security practices.
- Privacy Incident: A privacy incident can be an intentional or unintentional violation of the consent obtained by the data controller from the data subjects, or a violation of the applicable data protection regulatory framework. A privacy incident can be the result of a security or service incident whose damage to the confidentiality of personally identifiable information (PII); e.g., a data controller uses data for purposes not originally declared, an attacker gains access to PII, personal data is transferred to third parties without consent.
- Service Incident: A service incident is an event that violates the terms of service, service level agreement, or contracts between the customer and the service provider. It may be the result of failure (e.g. power outage, natural disaster, hardware failure, or human errors), attacks, or intervention of third parties (governmental agencies or law enforcement) preventing customers to use the services as established via contracts, resulting for instance in service outages.

2.2 Trust

Definition of trust is also a starting point for modeling risk and trust. In [19] and [13], trust is defined as "the willingness of a party to be vulnerable to the action of another party based on the expectation that the other will perform a particular action important to the trusting party, irrespective to the ability to monitor or control the trusted party". This definition does not fully capture all the dynamics of trust, such as the probabilities that the trustee will perform a particular action and will not engage in opportunistic behavior [14]. There are also hard and soft aspects of trust [20, 21, 22]. Hard part of trust depends on the security measures, such as authentication and encryption, and soft trust is based on things like brand loyalty and reputation. In [23], the authors introduced not only security but also accountability and auditability as elements which impact CC trust in cloud computing, and can be listed among the hard aspects. In [24], Service Level Agreement (SLA) is identified as the only way that the accountability and auditability of a CSP is clarified and therefore a CSP can make CCs trust them. The conclusion is that "trust" is a complex notion to define.

In [15], the CC trust to a CSP is related to the following parameters:

- Data location: CCs know where their data are actually located.
- Investigation: CCs can investigate the status and location of their data.
- Data segregation: Data of each CCs are separated from the others.
- Availability: CCs can access services and their data pervasively at any time.
- Privileged CC access: The privileged CCs, such as system administrators, are trustworthy.
- Backup and recovery: CSP has mechanisms and capacity to recover from catastrophic failures and not susceptible for disasters.
- Regulatory compliance: CSP complies with security regulations, certified for them and open for audits.
- Long-term viability: CSP has been performing above the required standards for a long time.

2.3   Risk Management, Assessment and Analysis

The definitions of risk analysis, assessment and management are given as follows in [1]:

- Risk Analysis is "systematic examination of the components and characteristics of risk."
- Risk Assessment is a "product or process which collects information and assigns values to risks for the purpose of informing priorities, developing or comparing courses of action, and informing decision making."
- Risk Management is a "process of identifying, analyzing, assessing, and communicating risk and accepting, avoiding, transferring or controlling it to an acceptable level at an acceptable cost."

Therefore, we can perceive risk analysis as a sub domain to risk assessment, which is a sub domain to risk management as shown in Fig. 1. Risk assessment schemes and models are the main topic of this tutorial. When risk assessment is qualitative, a non-numeric but self descriptive value, such as low, medium or high risk, is assigned as the risk value at the end of the process. When it is quantitative, a numeric value, such as a probability, a proportion or an expected rate, is the result of the assessment.

Risk assessment schemes are quite often categorized also as inductive versus deductive. Inductive techniques are typically based on inducing all possible consequences or reasons for an unwanted outcome (i.e., event). An event tree is a good example for this category. That starts with an event. In the next phase the events that may cause the root event is analyzed. This practice is repeated at every level until reaching the events (leaves) that cannot be further partitioned. Finally, values (typically likelihood and severity) assigned to each leaves. A deductive technique uses the

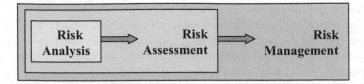

Fig. 1. Risk analysis, assessment and management.

opposite approach and starts from the reasons and continues by deducing from them until reaching the top level event.

3   CSA's Notorious Nine and Cloud Assessment Initiative

Cloud Security Alliance's (CSA) list of the top threats for cloud is an important source to start with cloud risk assessment. CSA conducts a survey among the experts and stakeholders to gain an insight into their perception on the threats against the cloud, and publishes the results in a document titled "The Notorious Nine: Cloud Computing Top Threats in 2013" For this tutorial, we used the second edition of the document, which was from February 2013. An earlier version of the same publication was in 2010.

In the document, nine threats selected as the top threats are introduced in the priority order determined by again the same experts contributed to the survey. For each threat, apart from its description, the information depicted in Fig. 2 are also given: which service models that this threat can affect, which percentage of the experts consider it as relevant, what its ranking was in 2010 survey and how its perceived as a risk, actual and/or perceived.

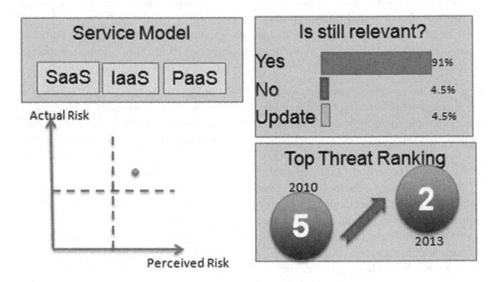

Fig. 2. The data loss threat in CSA's notorious nine.

We do not elaborate on each of the Notorious Nine further in this tutorial because the names of the threats are self explanatory and our tutorial is not about the threats but cloud risk assessment models. Further explanations on each of these threats can be found in [2]. The CSA's Notorious Nine list includes the threats below in the given order:

3. Data Breaches
4. Data Loss
5. Account or Service Traffic Hijacking
6. Insecure Interfaces and APIs
7. Denial of Service
8. Malicious Insiders
9. Abuse of Cloud Services
10. Insufficient Due Diligence
11. Shared Technology Vulnerabilities

Cloud Assesment Initiative Questionnaire (CAIQ) [30] is a questionnaire prepared for CSPs. That aims to address one of the notorious nine (i.e., CSA list of top nine threats), which is "insufficient due diligence." CAIQ includes many questions categorized into control groups listed below:

- Compliance
- Data Governance
- Facility Security
- Human Resources Security
- Information Security
- Legal
- Operations Management
- Risk Management
- Release Management
- Resiliency
- Security Architecture

The questionnaires answered by many CSPs are available to access by anyone in CSA Security, Trust and Assurance Registry (STAR) [4]. STAR Database is becoming a resource to have a better insight into how well a particular CSP is prepared to tackle with various threats. Therefore, it can be an important tool for risk assessment for the cloud services received from a given CSP.

4 Cloud Risk Assessment by ENISA

In its recommendations on risk assessment for cloud computing 1, ENISA provides a list of relevant incident scenarios, assets and vulnerabilities. It suggests estimating the level of risk on the basis of likelihood of a risk scenario mapped against the estimated negative impact, which is the essence of the risk formulation by also many others in the literature [5, 6, 7, 11, 28, 29]. Although ENISA's recommendations are specific for cloud computing, it is a generic framework that does not provide an approach to map the specifics of CSPs and cloud service customers (CSC) to the 35 risk scenarios listed in the report 1.

ENISA's risk scenarios are listed in Table 1 at the Appendix. They are grouped in four categories: policy and organizational, technical, legal and the other scenarios not specific to cloud computing. The likelihood of each of these scenarios and their business impact are determined in consultation with an expert group. The scale of probability and impact has five discrete classes between very low and very high. For example, the probability and impact of Incident Scenario P1 in "Policy and Organizational Scenarios" category (i.e., lock-in) are given as HIGH and MEDIUM relatively.

Then, the likelihood (probability) and business impact (impact) values that are determined by the experts are converted to the risk levels for each incident scenario based on a risk matrix with a scale between 0 and 8 as shown in 3. Finally, the risk levels are mapped to a qualitative scale as follows:

- Low risk: 0–2
- Medium: 3–5
- High: 6–8

ENISA also provides a list of 53 vulnerabilities (i.e., 31 cloud specific and 22 not cloud specific vulnerabilities) and 23 classes of assets that cloud customers may keep in cloud. ENISA's list of vulnerabilities and assets are given in Tables 2 and 3 at the Appendix, respectively. Each of 35 incident scenarios is related with a subset of vulnerabilities and assets. For example, the Incident Scenario P1 is related to Vulnerabilities V13 (lack of standard technologies and solutions), V31 (lack of completeness and transparency in terms of use), V46 (poor provider selection), V47 (lack of supplier redundancy) and Assets A1 (company reputation), A5 (personal sensitive data), A6 (personal data), A7 (personal data critical), A9 (service delivery – real time services), A10 (service delivery).

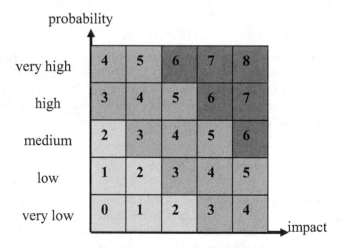

Fig. 3. ENISA estimation of risk level.

A cloud customer can assess the risk level related to a scenario qualitatively and understands what kind of vulnerabilities and assets are related to each scenario by examining [1]. However, these values represent educated guesses over a range of common cloud deployments and do not have a precise semantics. ENISA's framework can be categorized as a generic qualitative inductive risk analysis framework for cloud computing.

5 Cloud Adopted Risk Assessment Model

In practice, the risk levels are related to many factors like as the controls that CSPs provide and the assets of the specific users. Therefore, a generic value cannot be applied to all CSPs and CSCs. Although vulnerabilities and assets for each incident scenario are given by ENISA framework, it does not describe how those values can be adapted for specific CSP and CSC pair. CARAM [7] fills this gap. For that, first the qualitative scale used by ENISA as probability and impact values are mapped to a quantitative scale as follows:

- Very low $\rightarrow$ 1
- Low $\rightarrow$ 2
- Medium $\rightarrow$ 3
- High $\rightarrow$ 4
- Very high $\rightarrow$ 5

For example, probability P1 and impact I1 values for the first scenario (i.e., lock in) is HIGH and MEDIUM respectively. We map these values as follows: P1 = 4 and I1 = 3.

However, probability and impact of a risk scenario are very much dependent on the vulnerabilities and assets involved in. Therefore, these values cannot be the same for all CSP and CSC. CARAM adjusts the values from ENISA, taken as a baseline, considering additional information about the cloud service. For that, we use Eqs. 1 and 2:

$$\beta_i = P_i \times v_i \tag{1}$$

$$\delta_i = I_i \times \alpha_i \tag{2}$$

In Eq. 1, for the risk scenario i, βi is the adjusted probability, vi is the vulnerability index of a given CSP, δi is the adjusted impact and αi is the asset index for a given CSC. Note that vulnerability index of a CSP is the same for all CSC and the asset index of a CSC is the same for all CSPs. Vulnerability and asset indices are calculated as given in Eqs. 3 and 4 respectively, where vki is 1 if vulnerability k is in the list of vulnerabilities 1 for risk scenario i, and 0 otherwise. Similarly, aki is 1 if asset k is in the list of assets 1 for risk scenario i. Please note again that there are 53 vulnerabilities and 23 assets listed in 1. The other two parameters εk and γk in Eq. 3 and 4 are derived from the answers to the questionnaires (i.e., CAIQ and A4Cloud Questionnaire). The vulnerability related parameter εk is relatively more complex and elaborated on more detailed later. The asset related parameter γk is given value 0 if the CSC's answer to the question that "Does the service that you seek will involve any asset of yours that fall in the same category as asset k?" is "NO", and value 1 otherwise. We would like to highlight that CARAM is independent from the number of incident scenarios and probability, impact, vulnerability and assets assigned to the incident scenarios. Moreover, it is possible to assign weight values for each of assets and vulnerabilities if some of them are assumed as of higher importance comparing to the others.

$$v_i = \frac{\sum_{k=1}^{53} v_{ki} \times \varepsilon_k}{\sum_{k=1}^{53} v_{ki}} \qquad (3)$$

$$\alpha_i = \frac{\sum_{k=1}^{23} a_{ki} \times \gamma_k}{\sum_{k=1}^{23} a_{ki}} \qquad (4)$$

5.1   The Vulnerability Parameter for a CSP

We use CSA Consensus Assessment Initiative Questionnaire (CAIQ) [30] to assign a value to the vulnerability parameter εk. CAIQ is an effort to provide CSC with an ability to make more rational decisions on selecting CSP. The answers to CAIQ by many CSP are publicly available in CSA Security, Trust and Assurance Registry (STAR) database [4]. CAIQ aims collecting data directly from CSP on how much they comply with the regulations/standards and how secure is their infrastructure. It consists of questions grouped into the control areas explained in Sect. 3, asking about state of implementation. The CSPs are expected to answer these questions as "Yes", if the control is implemented, and as "No" otherwise. However, most of the CSP that have answered the questionnaire in STAR database used free text explanations rather than simple "Yes" or "No", which is more informative. CARAM provides the following mechanism to map the answers given to the questions in CAIQ to one of the categories in Table 4. Please note that the category "Yes" in Table 4 means the control is implemented, which is positive. The answer "Yes" to CAIQ questions do not always imply a more secure system (i.e., a control is implemented). For example, the "Yes" answer to CAIQ Question RS06-01 "Are any of your datacenters located in places which have a high probability/occurrence of high-impact environmental risks (floods, tornadoes, earthquakes, hurricanes, etc.)?" implies a negative outcome, which means the control is not implemented. Therefore, CARAM maps the answer "Yes" to this question as "No: the control is not implemented".

Given that there are about 100 of CSPs in the mentioned registry providing answer to about 200 questions each, the automation of this assessment could save significant time. For the automatic classification of the free text answers to CAIQ questions we user supervised machine learning algorithms provided by the WEKA tool 32. For that we have provided a training set representing a random sampling of around 200 classified answers out of circa 9000 answers and used it to classify the other remaining answers. The 10-folds cross-validation provided an accuracy of around 84 % of correctly classified instances, which we consider enough for our purpose.

Table 4. The categorization of the answers given to the questions in CAIQ.

Yes: The control is implemented
Yes, conditionally: The control can be implemented under some conditions
No: The control is not implemented
Not available: The answer is not given
Not applicable: The control is not applicable to the provided service

After classification of the answers to one of the categories in Table 4, the implementation value qm is assigned for each of the controls. If the answer to a question is "YES", that trivially means the control implied in question m is available (i.e., qm = 0) and hence the related vulnerabilities are mitigated. The "NO", "NOT APPLICABLE" and "NOT AVAILABLE" classes mean that the control will not be available, and therefore qm = 1. If the class is "YES CONDITIONALY", the CSC needs to be asked another question: If the conditions are acceptable for the CSC. If they are acceptable, qm = 0. Otherwise, qm = 1.

When qm is known for a CSP and a CSC, Eq. 5 gives the vulnerability related parameter ε_k for the CSP and the CSC. Please note that this value is for a specific CSP and CSC pair. In Eq. 5, n is the number of questions in CAIQ, and $r_{m,k}$ is 1 if the question m is related to vulnerability k. It is 0 otherwise.

$$\varepsilon_k = \frac{\sum_{m=1}^{n} r_{m,k} \times q_m}{\sum_{m=1}^{n} r_{m,k}} \tag{5}$$

Equation 5 requires the mapping of the CAIQ questions to vulnerabilities (i.e., $r_{m,k}$). Our recommendation for this mapping is given in Table 5 at the Appendix.

5.2   Relative Risk Assessment with Posterior Articulation of CSC Preferences

ENISA Risk Assessment Model is based on 35 incident scenarios. This is too many in number for selecting a CSP that fits best to a CSC's requirements. Therefore, we first reduce the number of criteria from these 35 incident scenarios to three fields of cloud risks: security, privacy and service [7]. For that, we compute the probability that a privacy (βr), a security (βs) and a service (βe) incident can occur and the impact of a privacy (δr), a security (δs) and a service (δe) incident by applying Eqs. 6 to 11. In Eqs. 6 and 9, ri is 1 if ENISA incident scenario i is related to privacy, and 0 otherwise. In Table 6 at the Appendix, we provide this mapping relation between ENISA scenarios and privacy incidents. ωri and αri are real numbers between 0 and 1. They are the weight factors for probability and impact relatively. The significance of every scenario may not be the same when calculating an aggregated value for privacy, security and service incidents. Moreover, the scenarios may need to be treated differently for each CSC especially when calculating the aggregated impact values. The weight factors are for making these adjustments. If the significance of each scenario is the same, then the weight factors can be assigned 1. Similar to ri, rs and re are the mapping values for security and service risks relatively. ωsi and αsi are the weight factors for security scenarios, and ωei and αei are the weight factors for service scenarios.

$$\beta_r = \frac{\sum_{i=1}^{35} \beta_i \times r_i \times \omega_{ri}}{\sum_{i=1}^{35} r_i \times \omega_{ri}} \tag{6}$$

$$\beta_s = \frac{\sum_{i=1}^{35} \beta_i \times s_i \times \omega_{si}}{\sum_{i=1}^{35} s_i \times \omega_{si}} \tag{7}$$

$$\beta_e = \frac{\sum_{i=1}^{35} \beta_i \times e_i \times \omega_{ei}}{\sum_{i=1}^{35} e_i \times \omega_{ei}} \tag{8}$$

$$\delta_r = \frac{\sum_{i=1}^{35} \delta_i \times r_i \times \alpha_{ri}}{\sum_{i=1}^{35} r_i \times \alpha_{ri}} \tag{9}$$

$$\delta_s = \frac{\sum_{i=1}^{35} \delta_i \times s_i \times \alpha_{si}}{\sum_{i=1}^{35} s_i \times \alpha_{si}} \tag{10}$$

$$\delta_e = \frac{\sum_{i=1}^{35} \delta_i \times e_i \times \alpha_{ei}}{\sum_{i=1}^{35} e_i \times \alpha_{ei}} \tag{11}$$

When probability (i.e., β) and impact (i.e., δ) values are calculated, they are mapped to the qualitative scale as follows:

- $[0, 1] \rightarrow$ Very low
- $(1, 2] \rightarrow$ Low
- $(2, 3] \rightarrow$ Medium
- $(3, 4] \rightarrow$ High
- $(4, 5] \rightarrow$ Very high

Finally, by using the same approach as shown in Fig. 3, the risk values for privacy Rr, security Rs and service Re are obtained in a qualitative scale as Low, Medium or High. Please note that these values are calculated for each CSP-CSC pair, and enumerated as Low < Medium < High.

At this stage, the CSC (the customer that needs relative risk assessment) provides CARAM with the maximum acceptable levels of risks for privacy Rrmax, security Rsmax and service Remax. CSC may also provide a set $U = \{p1,..., pn\}$ of CSP that should be excluded from the assessment due to reasons like business relations, politics, past experience, etc. When this information is available, CARAM creates a set F of feasible CSP out of the set S of all the CSP available for assessment (i.e., CSPs that have a completed CAIQ in STAR Database) such that:

$$F \subset S$$

$$p_i \in F \text{iff}(pi \notin U) \wedge \left(R_{rmax,} > R_{ri} \right) \wedge \left(R_{smax} > R_{si} \right) \wedge \left(R_{emax} > R_{ei} \right)$$

where R_{ri}, R_{si} and R_{ei} are the privacy, security and service risks for the CSP p_i.

F can be an empty set, a set with only one element or multiple elements. If F is an empty set, there is no feasible solution for the CSC. If F has only one element, that is the only feasible solution for the CSC. In both of these cases, CARAM informs the CSC directly with the result. If F has multiple elements, all CSPs in F but the non-dominated ones are removed from F. In the resulting set F' there cannot be any CSP which has all Rri, Rsi and Rei values smaller than any other CSP in F'. If the resulting F' includes only one CSP, CARAM informs the CSC about the solution that fits best to it. If there are multiple CSPs in F', the CSC is given the complete F' for the posterior articulation of the preferences.

6 The National Commission on Informatics and Liberty (CNIL)

Another qualitative inductive scheme was published by "The Commission nationale de l'informatique et des libertés" (CNIL) or in English: The National Commission on Informatics and Liberty [31] more recently. CNIL's methodology is similar to the ENISA's Framework with the following difference: It is a risk management technique focused on privacy risks in cloud computing. It is still generic and does not differentiate CSPs or cloud customers.

CNIL's Risk Management Scheme has five stages in which the follwoing are analyzed: 1. Context, 2. Feared Scenarios, 3. Threats, 4. Risks, 5. Measures. Since it includes not only an assement on the level of risk for the listed incident scenarios (i.e., feared events) but also some measures against them, we categorized CNIL as a scheme recommended for cloud risk management.

According to a CNIL, a threat uses the vulnerabilities of assets, such as computers, data storages and facilities, to affect or to gain access to the primary assets such as personal data which impacts on the owner of those primary assets. The end result is called as a feared event. This relation among the components of a risk is depicted in Fig. 4.

According to CNIL the privacy related feared events are as follows:

- Unavailability of legal processes
- Change in processing
- Illegitimate access to personal data
- Unwanted change in personal data
- Disappearance of personal data

Please note that CNIL is risk management model for only privacy related feared events. CNIL also categorizes primary assets related to these events into two classes:

- Processes: They process the personal data or are required by the processes for informing the data subjects, getting their consent, allowing the exercise of the rights of opposition, access, correction and deletion.

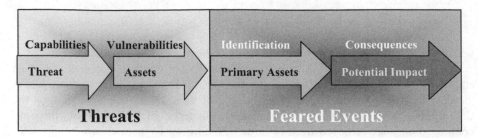

Fig. 4. CNIL components of risk.

- Personal Data: They are the data used by the processes that fall in primary asset category. Therefore, they are not only the data processed but also the data required for processing the personal data.

CNIL determines the threats against privacy in cloud as:

- Persons who belong to the organization: user, computer specialist, etc.
- Persons from outside the organization: recipient, provider, competitor, authorized third party, government organization, human activity surrounding, etc.
- Non-human sources: computer virus, natural disaster, flammable materials, epidemic, rodents, etc.

The supporting assets that the threats can exploit to create the feared events are given in [31] as:

- Hardware: computers, communications relay, USB drives, hard drives, etc.
- Software: operating systems, messaging, databases, business application, etc.
- Networks: cable, wireless, fiber optic, etc.
- People: users, administrators, top management, etc.
- Paper media: printing, photocopying, etc.
- Paper transmission channels: mail, workflow, etc.

Similar to many other risk models, CNIL computes the level of risk based on it's severity and likelihood. It actually first analyzes and assigns the values for likelihood and severity and them sum them up to find out the level of risk as given in Eq. 12. This is different from many other approaches which models the risk scenarios as a product of probability and impact but nor as a sum of them.

$$\text{Level of risk} = \text{Severity} + \text{Likelihood} \qquad (12)$$

CNIL uses a scale with four values: negligible, limited, significant, maximum. It also gives the clear definitions of what these values mean in various context (i.e., the level of identification for personal data, the prejudicial effect of feared events, vulnerabilities of supporting assets and capabilities of risk sources. For each feared event, those parameters are assigned values, and the likelihood and severity are calculated by using Eqs. 13 and 14.

$$\text{Severity} = \text{Identification} + \text{Prejudicial Effect} \tag{13}$$

$$\text{Likelihood} = \text{Vulnerabilities} + \text{Capabilities} \tag{14}$$

The results of these equations are mapped to qualitative values as follows:

- <5   Negligible
- =5   Limited
- =6   Significant
- >6   Maximum

This exercise ends with the matrix in Fig. 5, which depicts the level of risk for each feared event.

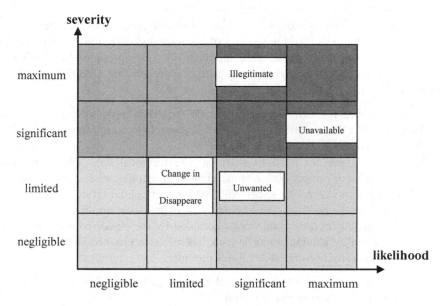

Fig. 5. Level of risks for feared events.

CNIL continues with recommendations on how to treat these risks such that they can be shifted to left and down in the level of risk matrix. After that, they reassess the level of risk, which are called as residual risk, and justify why they are acceptable after this treatment.

7 Joint Risk and Trust Model for Cloud Service Mashups

As explained before, trust definition is mainly based on the vulnerability that the trusting party is exposed to by this trust relation, and both positive and negative actions taken against this vulnerability by the trusted party. Such a trust relation is a very sophisticated notion. In this section, we introduce Joint Risk and Trust Model (JRTM) which can be used by a trust as a service (TaaS) provider. JRTM is a model developed within A4Cloud Project. Please note that it is not an architecture or mechanism to build trust but a model that can be used for deciding if a service is trustworthy enough to a CC. In other words, JRTM computes if the risks associated with a cloud service mashup are below the risks that the CC is ready to accept. It is a quantitative and inductive risk assessment model for cloud service mashups. This model can be embedded into an overarching framework such as the one introduced in [26].

7.1 Collecting Evidence for JRTM

JRTM is based on the evidence about each CSP collected by a TaaS provider. Evidence is collected (i.e., counted) for periods as shown in Fig. 6. The length of the periods depends on the CSP dynamics, such as the number of subscribers and services, and may vary from the order of hours to the order of weeks.

For collecting evidences, controls may need to be given to TaaS providers. These controls may include areas like the security of software and data stored and processed regulatory compliance and billing. This approach (i.e., giving controls to TaaS providers) may be more practical comparing to the approach that recommends giving controls to every CC [25], because:

- It is more secure for CSP comparing to the controls given to every CC. The probability that a TaaS provider makes use of controls to compromise the security or the performance of a cloud is lower.
- TaaS provider does not need to share all the technical data with every CC. Therefore, CSP can protect both commercially and security wise sensitive data.
- CC do not need to monitor or to control CSP for every cloud service. Instead, they take a recommendation from a third party who is an expert on this topic.
- When TaaS providers are organizations accepted by the cloud industry, they may act also as a quality assurance mechanism. Therefore, accredited certification third parties can naturally become also a TaaS provider.

JRTM is a practical and scalable scheme that requires collection of only the following information (i.e., evidence) in every period:

- ε_i: the number of CCs who were subject to at least one security event in period i
- ε_{ei}: the number of CCs whose all security events were eliminated before they become incidents that affect the CCs in period i
- Φ_i: the number of CCs who were subject to at least one privacy event in period i
- Φ_{ei}: the number of CCs whose all privacy events were eliminated before they become incidents that affect the CCs in period i
- ρ_i: the number of CCs who were subject to at least one service event in period i
- ρ_{ei}: the number of CCs whose all service events are eliminated before they become a service incident and hamper the operations of the CCs in period i
- u_i: the total number of CCs in period i
- D: the set of privacy event durations (i.e., the number of time periods between the time period that a privacy event starts and the time period that the privacy event is detected)

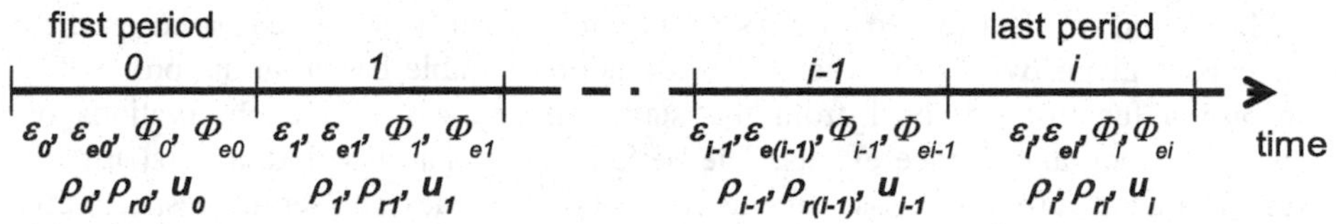

first period   last period

Fig. 6. Collecting the evidence for risks.

As implied by the evidence collected, JRTM distinguishes three types of risks: security, privacy and service. Privacy has a difference from the other two. It is very likely that a privacy event is not detected when it is initiated. It is even probable that some of them may never be detected because their effect is not directly observable. On the other hand, the potential damage of a privacy event is higher when it's duration is longer. Therefore, we collect evidence about privacy event durations and address this issue within our model. However, we cannot take undetected privacy events into account not only because they are not measurable but also because the recommendations by a TaaS provider cannot be based on speculations but evidence.

7.2 Computing Risk and Trust

In JRTM, risk and trust are modelled jointly by using these evidences. The real risk is the risk that cannot be (or is not) eliminated by the CSP. If the part of the security risk $\delta\varepsilon$, privacy risk $\delta\Phi$ and the service risk $\delta\rho$ not eliminated by the CSP is lower than the CC can take (i.e., $\tau\varepsilon$, $\tau\Phi$ and $\tau\rho$), then the cloud service is viable for the CC. We further elaborate on this relation at the end of this section. As shown in Eqs. 15 and 16, we perceive the risk as the probabilities rε, rΦ and rρ that a security, privacy or service event occurs, and trust as the probabilities tε, tΦ and tρ that the CSP can eliminate the events before they become security, privacy or service incidents.

$$\delta_\varepsilon = r_\varepsilon - (r_\varepsilon \times t_\varepsilon),$$ (15)

$$\delta_\phi = r_\phi - (r_\phi \times t_\phi),$$ (16)

$$\delta_\rho = r_\rho - (r_\rho \times t_\rho).$$ (17)

This approach to model risk fits well for the dynamics in cloud computing because of two reasons: Firstly, it does not require that the TaaS provider assesses the consequence for the realization of a risk, which is very much dependent on the CCs' functions. Instead, the consequences are represented by the thresholds $\tau\varepsilon$, $\tau\Phi$ and $\tau\rho$ given by the CCs. We discuss the selection of thresholds later. Secondly, it does not need to assess all threats and vulnerabilities. For a TaaS provider or CC, it is not practical to list all threats and vulnerabilities because it is not likely that CSP will share all the details about their physical architecture, platforms and security systems with public, their CC or even with TaaS providers.

The periodical data related to risks $r\varepsilon$, $r\Phi$ and $r\rho$ can be weighted based on their freshness as given by 18–20, where R is a random variable based on the probability distribution functions derived from the statistical analysis of the observations on security, privacy and service events. The period i is the latest period, and $r\varepsilon(i)$, $r\Phi(i)$ and $r\rho(i)$ are the current risk assessments for security, privacy and service respectively. The security, privacy and service event ratios (i.e., $s = \varepsilon/u$, $p = \Phi/u$ and $g = \rho/u$) are fit to a distribution and statistics (i.e., shape, scale and location parameters), and this analysis for distribution and the statistics is repeated at the end of every period. The random processes $R(s)$, $R(p)$ and $R(g)$ use these distributions and statistics.

$$r_{\varepsilon(i)} = (1 - \omega)R(s) + \omega\frac{\varepsilon_i}{u_i}, \tag{18}$$

$$r_{\phi(i)} = (1 - \omega)R(p) + \omega\frac{\phi_i}{u_i}, \tag{19}$$

$$r_{g(i)} = (1 - \omega)R(g) + \omega\frac{\rho_i}{u_i}. \tag{20}$$

The parameter ω in Eqs. 18–20 is the weight parameter, and can be given any value between 0 and 1 including 0 and 1 (i.e., $\{\omega \in \Re \mid 0 \leq \omega \leq 1\}$). The higher ω implies the lower level of uncertainty and the higher level of influence by the statistics in the last period. When it is 1, risk is determined based on the frequency of the incidents in the last period and there is not any uncertainty for the end result. When it is 0, risk is completely random according to the distribution and the statistics of the observations. Please note that the distribution and statistics in $R(s)$, $R(p)$ and $R(g)$ include also the data from the last period.

Trust parameters $t\varepsilon$, $t\Phi$ and $t\rho$ consists of two parts, i.e., hard $t\varepsilon h$, $t\Phi h$, $t\rho h$ and soft $t\varepsilon s$, $t\Phi s$, $t\rho s$, as shown in Eqs. 21–23. Hard part of trust is based on the architecture (i.e., the security systems and capacity) of the CSP and the content of SLA. Therefore, it is mostly related to evidence, and we calculate it purely based on the performance of CSP. On the other hand, soft trust is sensitive to the latest incidents and more sensitive to negative incidents comparing to positive incidents. Typically trust and reputation are built slowly but can be lost very quickly. We capture this relation through Eqs. 21 to 29.

$$t_\varepsilon = \begin{cases} 0, & \text{if } t_{\varepsilon h} + t_{\varepsilon s} < 0; \\ 1, & \text{if } t_{\varepsilon h} + t_{\varepsilon s} > 1; \\ t_{\varepsilon h} + t_{\varepsilon s}, & \text{otherwise.} \end{cases} \tag{21}$$

$$t_\phi = \begin{cases} 0, & \text{if } t_{\phi h} + t_{\phi s} < 0; \\ 1, & \text{if } t_{\phi h} + t_{\phi s} > 1; \\ t_{\phi h} + t_{\phi s}, & \text{otherwise.} \end{cases} \tag{22}$$

$$t_\rho = \begin{cases} 0, & \text{if } t_{\rho h} + t_{\rho s} < 0; \\ 1, & \text{if } t_{\rho h} + t_{\rho s} > 1; \\ t_{\rho h} + t_{\rho s}, & \text{otherwise.} \end{cases} \tag{23}$$

Hard trust is measured similar to risk. In Eqs. 24–26, εei, Φei and ρei is the number of subscribers whose all security, privacy and service events are eliminated before they become incidents respectively at period i. Random variable R generates random numbers according to the distributions and statistics of the ratios between the number of eliminated security events and total number of security events (i.e., se = $\varepsilon e/\varepsilon$), the number of eliminated privacy events and total number of privacy events (i.e., pe = $\Phi e/\Phi$) and between the number of eliminated service events and the total number of service events (i.e., ge = $\rho e/\rho$). In Eq. 25, we have another random variable R(D), which is assigning random values distributed according to the distributions and statistics of the values in privacy event duration set D.

$$t_{\varepsilon h(i)} = (1 - \omega)R(s_e) + \omega \frac{\varepsilon_{ei}}{\varepsilon_i}. \tag{24}$$

$$t_{\phi h(i)} = \left((1 - \omega)R(p_e) + \omega \frac{\phi_{ei}}{\phi_i}\right)^{R(D)}. \tag{25}$$

$$t_{\rho h(i)} = (1 - \omega)R(g_e) + \omega \frac{\rho_{ei}}{\rho_i}. \tag{26}$$

Soft parts of trust tεs(i), tΦs(i) and tρs(i) are calculated based on the change in the performance of CSP. In Eqs. 27–29, the slope value γ is a positive real number larger than or equal to one (i.e., $\{\gamma \in R \mid \gamma \geq 1\}$) and represents the relation of trust with the negative/positive change (i.e., trend) in performance. If the performance of the CSP gets worse, the CSP loses its credibility quickly. The sharpness of the drop in trust is related to the slope value γ. On the other hand, it takes more effort and time to gain trust as captured by Eqs. 27–29.

$$d_{\varepsilon(i)} = \frac{\varepsilon_{ei}}{\varepsilon_i} - \frac{\varepsilon_{e(i-1)}}{\varepsilon_{i-1}};$$

$$d_{\phi(i)} = \frac{\phi_{ei}}{\phi_i} - \frac{\phi_{e(i-1)}}{\phi_{i-1}};$$

$$d_{\rho(i)} = \frac{\rho_{ei}}{\rho_i} - \frac{\rho_{e(i-1)}}{\rho_{i-1}};$$

$$t_{\varepsilon s(i)} = \begin{cases} d_{\varepsilon(i)}^{\gamma}, & if\ d_{\varepsilon(i)} \geq 0; \\ -\sqrt{[\gamma]}|d_{\varepsilon(i)}|, & if\ d_{\varepsilon(i)} < 0; \end{cases} \tag{27}$$

$$t_{\phi s(i)} = \begin{cases} d_{\phi(i)}^{\gamma}, & if\ d_{\phi(i)} \geq 0; \\ -\sqrt{[\gamma]}|d_{\phi(i)}|, & if\ d_{\phi(i)} < 0; \end{cases} \tag{28}$$

$$t_{\rho s(i)} = \begin{cases} d_{\rho(i)}^{\gamma}, & if\ d_{\rho(i)} \geq 0; \\ -\sqrt{[\gamma]}|d_{\rho(i)}|, & if\ d_{\rho(i)} < 0. \end{cases} \tag{29}$$

Equations 15–17 are for a single service risk. Since cloud service mashups consist of multiple services, we need to extend them for multiple services. In Eqs. 30–32, S, P and G are the expected overall security, privacy and service risk (i.e., the risk that cannot be eliminated by the CSP) for cloud service mashups respectively. The number of services in a mashup is n, and ak is the number of alternative services available for service k in the inter-cloud (all the clouds that can be accessed for this service). It is trivial to see at Eqs. 30–31 that the higher the number of services compose a mashup, the higher the security and privacy risks become. The same relation can also be observed at Eq. 32 with a difference: the higher number of alternatives decreases the service risk.

$$S = 1 - \prod_{k=1}^{n} (1 - \delta_{\varepsilon k}) \tag{30}$$

$$P = 1 - \prod_{k=1}^{n} (1 - \delta_{\varphi k}) \tag{31}$$

$$G = 1 - \prod_{k=1}^{n} \left(1 - \prod_{m=1}^{a_k} \delta_{\rho k m}\right) \tag{32}$$

Since S, P and G are stochastic processes, their result are not deterministic (i.e., includes uncertainty through random variables). Therefore, a TaaS using our model first needs to build confidence intervals for S, P and G (i.e., $u(S)<S<v(S)$, $u(P)<P<v(P)$ and $u(G)<G<v(G)$) according to the confidence level λ given by the CC. For this, static Monte-Carlo simulation can be used.

7.3   Due Diligence and TaaS Recommendation for Selecting a Service Mashup

After building the confidence interval, the TaaS provider recommends the service mashup if and only if, $v(S) < \tau_{\varepsilon}$, $v(P) < \tau_{\varphi}$ and $v(G) < \tau_{\rho}$, where τ_{ε}, τ_{φ} and τ_{ρ} are the security, privacy and service risk thresholds given by CC. Before this, two further questions need to be answered: How can a CC determine τ_{ε}, τ_{φ} and τ_{ρ}? How can a TaaS provider assigns the distributions and statistics for R(s), R(p), R(g), R(se), R(pe) and R(ge) when a CSP is registered first time?

Answering the first question is completely a CC responsibility and based on the consequences and opportunities of the risk taken. TaaS provider's recommendation is in essence that the assessed absolute risk according to the confidence level given by the CC is below the risk acceptable by the CC. Therefore the acceptable level of risk is determined by the correct party, which is the CC, and can also be based on relative risk analysis [15]. For this, CC do not need to know the details about the technical architectures, their vulnerabilities and threats. Instead they focus on a comprehensive and abstract risk probability given based on practical evidence. Therefore, it is easier for a CC to run a risk assessment based on the consequences and opportunities of the risks taken. A number of recommendations may guide CC in the definition of their risk profiles [1, 27].

There are multiple ways to answer the second question. The TaaS provider can initialize $R(s)$, $R(p)$, $R(g)$, $R(s_e)$, $R(p_e)$ and $R(g_e)$ with the same distributions and statistics as the average of the other CSP that have a similar architecture to the CSP registered the first time. After this, the CCs may be provided with a recommendation by using larger confidence intervals than the confidence level specified by the CCs and warned about this fact.

Another difficulty in making the statistics is related to temporal and geographic correlations of the risks. For example, a law such as "the data protection act" affects not only one CSP but all CSP that have data center in the same country. Therefore, the impacts of this law should not be reflected only to a CSP that has the experience due to this law but also all the CSP that have a data center in the same country. Similarly, when this law changes or is removed, its effects should be removed from the statistics associated with all the CSP in the country. None of these change the essence of JRTM.

8 Conclusion

The cloud approach promises many advantages to IT users in any size or level. However, the potential users have difficulties in assessing the risks associated with moving to the cloud. Therefore, risk assessment for cloud has attracted many researchers from industry, government and academia. As a result, there are many techniques, schemes and approaches already available in the literature. In this tutorial, we elaborate on some of them.

In 2013, CSA published the second edition of the results from their analysis of the top threats against cloud. It is called as the Notorious Nine. CSA also prepared CAIQ, which was answered by many CSP. These answers are publicly available in STAR. Both the Notorious Nine Document and STAR are good sources of data for the cloud risk assessment. The governmental and nongovernmental organizations in Europe conducted risk assessment studies for cloud. ENISA and CNIL are the best known examples that fall in this category. A4Cloud has also developed models for risk assessment: CARAM and JRTM. CARAM is an qualitative inductive risk assessment model that complements ENISA and CAIQ. JRTM is a quantitative technique that relies on a third party which collects evidences for the risk and trust parameters.

Acknowledgments. This work was supported by EU FP7 Accountability for Cloud and Other Future Internet Services (A4Cloud) Project.

Appendix

Table 1. ENISA's list of risk scenarios and their categories.

Risk Category	Risk name
Policy & Organizational	P1. Lock-in
	P2. Loss of governance
	P3. Compliance challenges
	P4. Loss of business reputation due to co-tenant activities
	P5. Cloud service termination or failure
	P6. Cloud provider acquisition
	P7. Supply chain failure
Technical	T1. Resource exhaustion (under or over provisioning)
	T2. Isolation failure
	T3. Cloud provider malicious insider - abuse of high privilege roles
	T4. Management interface compromise (manipulation, availability of infrastructure)
	T5. Intercepting data in transit
	T6. Data leakage on up/download, intra-cloud
	T7. Insecure or ineffective deletion of data
	T8. Distributed denial of service (DDoS)
	T9. Economic denial of service (EDOS)
	T10. Loss of encryption keys
	T11. Undertaking malicious probes or scans
	T12. Compromise service engine
	T13. Conflicts between customer hardening procedures and cloud environment
Legal	L1. Subpoena and e-discovery
	L2. Risk from changes of jurisdiction
	L3. Data protection risks
	L4. Licensing risks
Not Specific to the Cloud	N1. Network breaks
	N2. Network management (i.e., network congestion/mis-connection/non-optimal use)
	N3. Modifying network traffic
	N4. Privilege escalation
	N5. Social engineering attacks (i.e., impersonation)
	N6. Loss or compromise of operational logs
	N7. Loss or compromise of security logs (manipulation of forensic investigation)
	N8. Backups lost, stolen
	N9. Unauthorized access to premises (including physical access to machines and other facilities)
	N10. Theft of computer equipment
	N11. Natural disasters

Table 2. ENISA's list of vulnerabilities.

Cloud Specific Vulnerabilities
V1. Authentication Authorization Accounting (AAA) vulnerabilities
V2. User provisioning vulnerabilities
V3. User de-provisioning vulnerabilities
V4. Remote access to management interface
V5. Hypervisor vulnerabilities
V6. Lack of resource isolation
V7. Lack of reputational isolation
V8. Communication encryption vulnerabilities
V9. Lack of or weak encryption of archives and data in transit
V10. Impossibility of processing data in encrypted form
V11. Poor key management procedures
V12. Key generation: low entropy for random number generation
V13. Lack of standard technologies and solutions
V14. No source escrow agreement
V15. Inaccurate modelling of resource
V16. No control on vulnerability assessment process
V17. Possibility that internal (cloud) network probing will occur
V18. Possibility that co-residence checks will be performed
V19. Lack of forensic readiness
V20. Sensitive media sanitization
V21. Synchronizing responsibilities or contractual obligations external to cloud
V22. Cross-cloud applications creating hidden dependency
V23. SLA clauses with conflicting promises *to* different stakeholders
V24. SLA clauses containing excessive business risk
V25. Audit or certification not available to customers
V26. Certification schemes not adapted to cloud infrastructures
V27. Inadequate resource provisioning and investments in infrastructure
V28. No policies for resource capping
V29. Storage of data in multiple jurisdictions and lack of transparency about this
V30. Lack of information on jurisdictions
V31. Lack of completeness and transparency in terms of use
Vulnerabilities not Specific to the Cloud
V32. Lack of security awareness
V33. Lack of vetting processes
V34. Unclear roles and responsibilities
V35. Poor enforcement of role definitions
V36. Need-to-know principle not applied
V37. Inadequate physical security procedures
V38. Misconfiguration
V39. System or OS vulnerabilities

(Continued)

Table 2. (*Continued*)

Vulnerabilities not Specific to the Cloud
V40. Untrusted software
V41. Lack of, or a poor and untested, business continuity and disaster recovery plan
V42. Lack of, or incomplete or inaccurate, asset inventory
V43. Lack of, or poor or inadequate, asset classification
V44. Unclear asset ownership
V45. Poor identification of project requirements
V46. Poor provider selection
V47. Lack of supplier redundancy
V48. Application vulnerabilities or poor patch management
V49. Resource consumption vulnerabilities
V50. Breach of nda by provider
V51. Liability from data loss (cp)
V52. Lack of policy or poor procedures for logs collection and retention
V53. Inadequate or misconfigured filtering resources

Table 3. ENISA's list of assets.

Assets
A1. Company reputation
A2. Customer trust
A3. Employee loyalty and experience
A4. Intellectual property
A5. Personal sensitive data
A6. Personal data
A7. Personal data – critical
A8. HR data
A9. Service delivery – real time services
A10. Service delivery
A11. Access control/authentication/authorization (root/admin v others)
A12. Credentials
A13. User directory (data)
A14. Cloud service management interface
A15. Management interface APIs
A16. Network (connections, etc.)
A17. Physical hardware
A18. Physical buildings
A19. Cloud Provider Application (source code)
A20. Certification
A21. Operational logs (customer and cloud provider)
A22. Security logs
A23. Backup or archive data

Table 5. The mapping of CAIQ questions to ENISA vulnerabilities.

Audit Planning, CO-01	V02, V03, V13, V14, V16, V23, V25, V26, V27, V29, V33, V35, V50,
Independent Audits, CO-02	V02, V03, V13, V14, V16, V23, V25, V26, V27, V29, V33, V35, V50,
Third Party Audits, CO-03	V02, V03, V13, V14, V16, V23, V25, V26, V27, V29, V33, V35, V50,
Contact/Auth Maintenance, CO-04	V14, V21, V29, V30,
Info Sys Regulatory Map, CO-05	V07, V08, V09, V10
Intellectual Property, CO-06	V34, V31, V35, V44
Intellectual Property, CO07	V34, V31, V35, V44
Intellectual Property, CO-08	V34, V31, V35, V44
Ownership/Stewardship, DG-01	V22, V23, V24, V29, V30, V31, V33, V34, V35, V42, V43, V44
Classification, DG-02	V32, V36, V37,
Handling/Labeling/Security Policy, DG-03	V01, V04, V05, V06, V08, V10, V11, V12, V19, V20, V22, V32, V37, V39,
Retention Policy, DG-04	V21, V29, V44
Secure Disposal, DG-05	V37, V42, V44, V51, V52
Nonproduction Data, DG-06	V32, V36, V37, V43, V44,
Information Leakage, DG-07	V1, V4, V5, V32, V36, V37
Risk Assessments, DG-08	V16, V22, V29, V32, V33, V34, V44
Policy, FS-01	V17, V32, V37,
User Access, FS-02	V02, V03, V17, V19, V25, V29, V32, V37
Controlled Access Points, FS-03	V17, V19, V32, V37
Secure Area Authorization, FS-04	V22, V29
Unauthorized Persons Entry, FS-05	V17, V19, V32, V37
Offsite Authorization, FS-06	V22, V29
Offsite equipment, FS-07	V6, V31, V42, V43, V44
Asset Management, FS-08	V6, V31, V42, V43, V44
Background Screening, HR-01	V17, V18, V50
Employment Agreements, HR-02	V17, V18, V32, V34, V35, V50
Employment Termination, HR-03	V17, V18, V50
Management Program, IS-01	V1, V16, V32, V33, V34
Mngt Support/Involvement IS-02	V1, V32, V33, V34
Policy, IS-03	V13, V19, V32, V33, V52
Baseline Requirements, IS-04	V1, V5, V8, V9, V11, V12, V13, V17, V19, V32, V33, V39. V40
Policy Reviews, IS-05	V03, V28, V32, V50, V52
Policy Enforcement, IS-06	V32, V34, V35
User Access Policy, IS-07	V1, V2, V3, V4, V6
User Access Rest/Auth, IS-08	V6, V42, V43, V44
User Access Revocation, IS-09	V3, V4, V17, V35

(*Continued*)

Table 5. (*Continued*)

User Access Reviews, IS-10	V1, V2, V3, V4, V17, V36
Training/Awareness, IS-11	V32, V36
Industry Knowledge/Benchmarking, IS-12	V5, V13, V32, V39, V40
Roles/Responsibilities, IS-13	V34, V35
Management Oversight, IS-14	V32, V34, V35
Segregation of Duties, IS-15	V34, V36,
User Responsibility, IS-16	V32, V34, V35
Workspace, IS-17	V06, V40, V42, V43, V44
Encryption, IS-18	V08, V09,
Encryption Key Mngt, IS-19	V08, V09, V11, V12
Vulnerability/Patch Mngt, IS-20	V02, V03, V05, V08, V16, V39, V40, V48
Antivirus/Malicio Software, IS-21	V40, V48,
Incident Management, IS-22	V34, V41, V52
Incident Reporting, IS-23	V52
Incident Resp Legal Prep, IS-24	V19, V30, V52
Incident Response Metrics, IS-25	V52
Acceptable Use, IS-26	V25, V31, V36, V43, V50
Asset Returns, IS-27	V13, V31, V50
eCommerce Transactions, IS-28	V08, V09, V10
Audit Tools Access, IS-29	V05, V06, V39, V53
Diag/Config Ports Access, IS-30	V05, V06, V39, V53
Network/Infra Services, IS-31	V02, V15, V28, V31
Portable/Mobile Devices, IS-32	V39, V48
Source Code Access Restrict, IS-33	V48
Utility Programs Access, IS-34	V04, V05, V39
Nondisclosure Agreements, LG-01	V18, V23, V24, V25, V30, V31
Third Party Agreements, LG-02	V21, V22, V23, V29
Policy, OP-01	V28, V31, V34, V35, V52
Documentation, OP-02	V15, V36, V38, V42, V43, V52, V53
Capacity/Resource Planning, OP-03	V14, V15, V27, V28, V49, V50, V53
Equipment Maintenance, OP-04	V5, V47
Program, RI-01	V51
Assessments, RI-02	V16, V24
Mitigation/Acceptance, RI-03	V16, V24
Buss/Policy Chng Impacts, RI-04	V16, V19, V24
Third Party Access, RI-05	V21, V24, V41, V47, V52
New Develop/Acquisition, RM-01	V13, V40
Production Changes, RM-02	V25, V36, V38, V50
Quality Testing, RM-03	V15, V38, V40
Outsourced Development, RM-04	V13, V40

(*Continued*)

Table 5. (*Continued*)

Unauthorized Soft Install, RM-05	V13, V40
Management Program, RS-01	V41, V52
Impact Analysis, RS-02	V16, V52
Business Continuity Plan, RS-03	V23, V24, V25, V27, V28, V41, V47
Business Continuity Testing, RS-04	V23, V24, V25, V27, V28, V41, V47
Environmental Risks, RS-05	V37, V41
Equipment Location, RS-06	V37, V41
Equipment Power Failures, RS-07	V37, V41
Power/Telecom, RS-08	V29, V45, V46
Customer Access Req, SA-01	V21, V23, V45, V46
User ID Credentials, SA-02	V1, V2
Data Security/Integrity, SA-03	V13, V32
Application Security, SA-04	V13, V48
Data Integrity, SA-05	V08, V09
Product/Nonproduction Env, SA-06	V41, V45
Rem User Multifact Auth, SA-07	V01
Network Security, SA-08	V32
Segmentation, SA-09	V06, V07, V53
Wireless Security, SA-10	V32
Shared Networks, SA-11	V32
Clock Synchronization, SA-12	V39
Equipment Identification, SA-13	V01
Audit Logging/Intru Detect, SA-14	V01, V32
Mobile Code	V32

Table 6. Mapping ENISA scenarios as privacy, security and service incidents.

ENISA Incident Scenarios	Privacy	Security	Service
P1	0	0	1
P2	1	0	0
P3	1	1	1
P4	0	1	0
P5	0	0	1
P6	1	1	1
P7	0	0	1
T1	0	0	1
T2	1	1	0
T3	1	1	1
T4	1	1	1
T5	1	1	0

(*Continued*)

Table 6. (*Continued*)

ENISA Incident Scenarios	Privacy	Security	Service
T6	1	1	0
T7	1	1	0
T8	0	0	1
T9	0	0	1
T10	1	1	0
T11	1	1	0
T12	1	1	1
T13	0	1	0
L1	1	1	0
L2	1	0	1
L3	1	1	0
L4	0	0	1
N1	0	0	1
N2	0	0	1
N3	0	0	1
N4	1	1	1
N5	0	1	0
N6	0	1	1
N7	0	1	1
N8	1	1	1
N9	1	1	0
N10	1	1	1
N11	0	0	1

References

1. ENISA, Cloud Computing; Benefits, Risks and Recommendations for Information Security, 2009 Edition, June 2014. http://www.enisa.europe.eu
2. CSA, The Notorious Nine Cloud Computing Top Threats in 2013, June 2014. https://downloads.cloudsecurityalliance.org/initiatives/top_threats/The_Notorious_Nine_Cloud_Computing_Top_Threats_in_2013.pdf
3. EU, Opinion 05/2012 on Cloud Computing (2012). http://ec.europa.eu/justice/data-protection/article-29/documentation/opinion-recommendation/files/2012/wp196_en.pdf
4. CSA, Security, Trust & Assurance Registry (STAR), June 2014. https://cloudsecurityalliance.org/star/#_registry
5. Kaplan, S., Garrick, B.J.: On the quantitative definition of risk. Risk Anal. **1**(1), 11–27 (1981)
6. Cayirci, E.: Joint trust and risk model for MSaaS mashups. In: Pasupathy, R., Kim, S.-H., Tolk, A., Hill, R., Kuhl, M.E. (eds.) Proceedings of the 2013 Winter Simulation Conference, pp. 1347–1358. Institute of Electrical and Electronics Engineers, Inc., Piscataway (2013)

7. Cayirci, E., Garaga, A., Oliveira, A.S., Roudier, Y.: Cloud adopted risk assessment model. In: International Workshop on Advances in Cloud Computing Legislation, Accountability, Security and Privacy (CLASP) (2014)
8. Jansen, W., Grance, T.: Guidelines on security & Privacy, Draft Special Publication 800-144 NIST, US Department of Commerce (2011)
9. Pearson, S., Charlesworth, A.: Accountability as a way forward for privacy protection in the cloud. In: Jaatun, M.G., Zhao, G., Rong, C. (eds.) Cloud Computing. LNCS, vol. 5931, pp. 131–144. Springer, Heidelberg (2009)
10. DHS, *DHS Risk Lexicon*. Department of Homeland Security (2008)
11. Ezell, B.C., Bennet, S.P., Von Winterfeldt, D., Sokolowski, J., Collins, A.J.: Probabilistic risk analysis and terrorism risk. Risk Anal. **30**(4), 575–589 (2010)
12. Cayirci, E.: Modelling and Simulation as a Service: A Survey. In: Pasupathy, R., Kim, S.-H., Tolk, A., Hill, R., Kuhl, M.E. (eds.) Proceedings of the 2013 Winter Simulation Conference, pp. 389–400. Institute of Electrical and Electronics Engineers Inc, Piscataway (2013)
13. Rousseau, D., Sitkin, S., Burt, R., Camerer, C.: Not so different after all: a cross-discipline view of trust. Acad. Manag. Rev. **23**(3), 393–404 (1998)
14. Pearson, S.: Privacy, security and trust in cloud computing. In: Pearson, S., Yee, G. (eds.) Privacy and Security for Cloud Computting, Computer Communications and Networks, pp. 3–42. Springer-Verlag, New York (2012)
15. Rashidi, A., Movahhedinia, N.: A model for user trust in cloud computing. Int. J. Cloud Comput. Serv. Archit. (IJCCSA) **2**(2), 1–8 (2012)
16. Li, W., Ping, L.: Trust model to enhance security and interoperability of cloud environment. In: Jaatun, M.G., Zhao, G., Rong, C. (eds.) Cloud Computing. LNCS, vol. 5931, pp. 69–79. Springer, Heidelberg (2009)
17. Marsh, S.: Formalising Trust as a Computational Concept. Doctoral dissertation, University of Stirling (1994)
18. Banerjee, S., Mattmann, C., Medvidovic, N., Golubchik, L.: Leveraging architectural models to inject trust into software systems. In: Proceedings of the SESS 2005, pp. 1–7. ACM, New York (2005)
19. Mayer, R.C., Davis, J.H., Schoorman, F.D.: An integrative model of organizational trust. Acad. Manag. Rev. **20**(3), 709–734 (1995)
20. Wang, Y., Lin, K.-J.: Reputation-oriented trustworthy computing in e-commerce environments. Internet Comput. **12**(4), 55–59 (2008)
21. Osterwalder, D.: Trust through evaluation and certification. Soc. Sci. Comput. Rev. **19**(1), 32–46 (2001). Sage Publications, Inc.
22. Singh, S., Morley, C.: Young australians' privacy, security and trust in internet banking. In: Proceedings of the 21st Annual Conference of the Australian Computer-Human Interaction Special Interest Group: Design: Open 24/7 (2009)
23. Ko, R.K.L., Jagadpramana, P., Mowbray, M., Pearson, S., Kirchberg, M., Liang, Q., Lee, B.S.: TrustCloud: a framework for accountability and trust in cloud computing. In: 2nd IEEE Cloud Forum for Practitioners (ICFP) (2011)
24. Kandukuri, B.R., Paturi, R., Rakshit, V.A.: Cloud security issues. In: IEEE International Conference on Services Computing (2009)
25. Khan, K., Malluhi, Q.: Trust in cloud services: providing more controls to clients. IEEE Comput. **46**(7), 94–96 (2013)
26. Singhal, M., Chandrasekhar, S., Tingjian, G., Sandhu, R., Krishnan, R., Gail-Joon, A., Bertino, E.: Collaboration in multicloud computing environments: framework and security issues. IEEE Comput. Mag. **46**(2), 76–84 (2013)

27. Simmonds, P., Rezek, C., Reed, A.: Security Guidance for Critical Areas of Focus in Cloud Computing V3.0 (No. 3.0) (p. 177). Cloud Security Alliance (2011). http://www. cloudsecurityalliance.org/guidance/
28. ISACA, COBIT 5: A Business Framework for the Governence and Management of Enterprise IT, June 2014. http://www.isaca.org/cobit/pages/default.aspx
29. ISO/IEC 31010, Risk Management-Risk Assesment Techniques (2009 Edition), June 2014. https://www.iso.org/obp/ui/#iso:std:iso-iec:31010:ed-1:v1:en
30. CSA, Consensus Assessment Initiative Questionnaire, June 2014. https://cloudsecurityalliance. org/research/cai/
31. CNIL, Methodology for Privacy Risk Management: How to Implement the Data Protection Act, 2012 Edition, June 2014. http://www.cnil.fr/english/publications/guidelines/
32. WEKA: Data Mining Software in Java, June 2014. http://www.cs.waikato.ac.nz/ml/weka/

Agent-Based Evidence Collection
in Cloud Computing

Philipp Ruf$^{(\boxtimes)}$, Thomas Rübsamen, and Christoph Reich

Cloud Research Lab, Furtwangen University of Applied Science,
Furtwangen, Germany
{philipp.ruf,thomas.ruebsamen,christoph.reich}@hs-furtwangen.de

Abstract. Nowadays there are many offerings of cloud services all over the world which have various security requirements depending on their business use. The compliance of these cloud services with the predefined security policies should be proven. In a cloud infrastructure this is not an easy job, because of its immense complexity. This paper proposes an architecture which uses software agents as its core components to collect evidence across the different layers of cloud infrastructures (Cloud Managment System, Hypervisor, VM, etc.) and builds a chain of evidence to prove compliance with predefined security policies.

Keywords: Cloud computing · Evidence · Persistence · Accountability · Audit

1   Introduction

This work addresses the problem of collecting, processing and persisting evidence from different sources inside a highly dynamic environment and its automation dependent on a policy describing the contract between a `costumer entity` and its `Cloud Service Provider (CSP)`. The automation aspect is addressed by an `Software Agent` (in following `agent`) and is based on the previous work "Supporting Cloud Accountability by Collecting Evidence Using Audit Agents" [1] by Prof. Dr. Christoph Reich and M. Sc. Thomas Rübsamen. For example, a `CSP` is collecting information about policy violations and storing them using the service of a second CSP. The potentially confidential captured evidence need to be persisted in a integrity-verifiable way and protected from unauthorized access. This project's expected contributions are additional control mechanisms highlighting the transparency desired by the cloud service costumers and accentuating the trust in `CSPs` and their contractual awareness.

The proposed agent-based architecture, which we describe in the following, collects evidence to allow the detection of policy violations and generates policy violation reports while protecting sensitive information and respecting costumer privacy at the same time. Thereby using an agent framework supporting strong and weak agent migration [2] was necessary for distributing and delegating tasks on demand adjusted to their different destination environments. The data to

© Springer International Publishing Switzerland 2015
M. Felici and C. Fernández-Gago (Eds.): A4Cloud 2014, LNCS 8937, pp. 185–198, 2015.
DOI: 10.1007/978-3-319-17199-9_8

collect is depending on the assured policy contract between a cloud costumer and a cloud provider which, can be statutorily regulated, defined by the service provider or created out of user specific criteria. Through periodically audits, the implemented agents are able to provide the requested claims of evidence by persisting recognized policy violations.

While a Cloud Service itself potentially contains service interdependencies with external Service Providers, the sources of evidence to be covered by a trusted service are increasing, too. A `Chain of Accountability` can be formed implementing these centrally coordinated trusted (accounting) services along the supply chain. Pointing out the exact location of a occurred policy violation depicts how trust in a `CSP` is strengthened using services implementing evidence reveal- and notify mechanisms and therefore supporting accountability (e.g. members of the architecture to propose). In a multi-`CSP` scenario with service coherences inter-`CSP` collaboration is still a fundamental requirement. Currently, there is no standardized way for a cloud service costumer to check on his own whether or not he is affected by a policy violation occurred along the supply chain. The meanwhile established usage of `Web Objects` (like for example the `Amazon Simple Storage Service AS3`) extends the `Chain of Accountability` with dynamic interaction, which (usually) is transparent to the costumer. Potential evidence sources like these connections **on demand** and their potentially scalable content must be observed as of the time a active interaction with the service occurs. Therefore, the possibility of interacting with a `CSP`'s trusted service provides the transparency needed in a complex environment like the cloud.

This paper is structured as follows: in the first chapter of this paper we discuss related work (see Sect. 2). In Sect. 3, the evidence collection and persistence architecture including used technologies and agent coherences is described. Following that, the actual collection of evidence and the different collection agent types are explained in Sect. 4 followed by the persistence mechanism in Sect. 5. Following that, Sect. 6 describes the migration of agents in a scenario, where multiple cloud providers are involved. After that, an example of how service coherences are affecting policy violation evaluation, will be discussed in Sect. 7. We conclude this paper in Sect. 8 where our perception of further work is noted, too.

2   Related Work

Reich and Rübsamen empathized the need of policy violation audits and proposed how evidence collection has to be mapped to accountability in their previous work [1]. They are proposing an *Audit Agent System* which was the groundwork for the construction of the architecture presented in this paper. This work will not focus on the mentioned audit aspects but on the storing, presenting and processing of evidence.

The idea of using `Digital Evidence Bags (DEB)` [3] plays a key role as a solid evidence persistence structure in this paper. Based on the work by Turner, Schatz and Clark propose an extension for connecting evidence composing and referencing DEBs using a `Sealed Digital Evidence Bag` [4]. This mechanism is a possible extension to this architectures persistence mechanism.

The usage of software agents also were proposed in the context of `Security Audit as a Service (SAaaS)` [5]. A related presentation layer and distributed sources of evidence are discussed in this paper but specializing on security policies and the guardedness of a source located at the input layer. Also, a *'security business flow'* modeler generating the policies to observe is differencing `SAaaS` from approach proposed in this paper.

Of course there are many tools offering a agent-based solution for monitoring network devices by collecting and analyzing a wide range of current system properties. Industry standards like `Nagios` [6] also providing an agentless monitoring solution which is a less capable but goes easy on resources. Also there are Software as a Service (SaaS) monitoring solutions like `New Relic` [7] which providing agents collecting data dependent on different scopes and devices. Besides the traditional monitoring of (network - e.g. cloud) resources it supports real-time analytics and a performance monitoring, which can be integrated into the application development process. Therefore, it is not surprising to be confronted with this system using a Platform as a Service (PaaS) like `Cloud Control` [8] or `AppFog` [9] simplifying the monitoring of scalable applications. Transmitting the current values to the cloud brings different advantages like rapid data analyzing using resources on demand. The architecture proposed in this paper also supports monitoring functions but differs by extending this aspect in focusing on active intervention like interacting with third party tools and their provided `API`s.

3   Architecture Overview

The focus of this section is the brief introduction of this works architecture design including its components and used technologies. To understand the flow and properties of the proposed architecture, we have to take a closer look at the `Java Agent DEvelopement framework (JADE)` [10] which is the technological foundation of our work (Fig. 1).

JADE complies with the `Foundation for Intelligent Physical Agents` (FIPA) specifications [11,12], which define the internal behavior on action selection and execution as well as external agent interaction. The external agent interaction refers to the interaction context and the message creation, which draws on the `FIPA ACL` (Agent Communication Language). Other specified parts of JADE are system and platform services, which can be used for agent service registration or agent migration [13].

Using this powerful framework makes creating different agent infrastructures quite simple. Every JADE instance is denoted as a `Container` while multiple `Containers` are denoted as a `Platform`. Inside a `Platform` exactly one `Main Container` exists beside the different agent implementations, which itself contain agents for infrastructural provisioning. New agents, for example, can be added transparently as needed and contacted after their registration with a platform's `Main Container`. Using the recommended design guide [14],

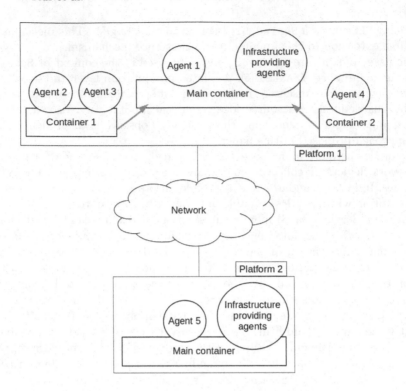

Fig. 1. JADE platforms and containers

the distributed agents are geared to each other and can be modularly extended. Also, the possibility of using JADE in Public Key Infrastructure mode is given by creating a configuration file containing the path to a Key-Store, key access password(s) and starting an agent with the configuration file as a parameter. Not only exchanged messages but also code transmission (used for agent migration - see Sect. 6) is encrypted if both participants are using the JADE Public Key Infrastructure (PKI) module/Add-On.

Being acquainted with the used agent framework lightens the contact with and comprehension of this architecture. A high level overview of the architecture is depicted in Fig. 2, revealing how distributed agents are communicating within it and in which way the different architectural components are interacting. All parts of this architecture are positioned inside one JADE Platform containing an evidence interpretation as well as a persistence agent which both interact with the distributed collection agents. Note, that additional services, which are provided out-of-the box by JADE (such as the centralized service registry and multi-platform interaction), are not pictured in Fig. 2.

To provide a chain of evidence, every trusted service of the supply chain contains a controlled agent which is responsible for evidence collection. To determine a policy violation, a variety of sources like the cloud management system, network packet data flows and storage units are browsed for conspicuous patterns. Also, external programs can be triggered to analyze their output.

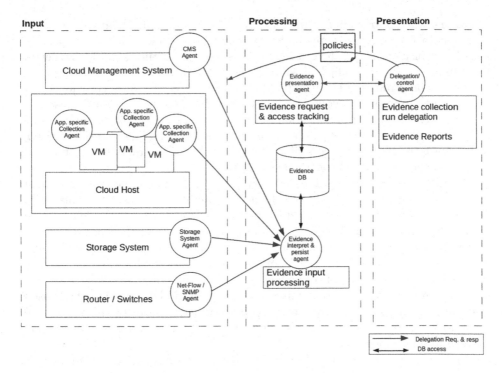

Fig. 2. High level architecture

To ensure data and therefore evidence integrity, every evidence collection run is persisted using a `Digital Evidence Bag` [3] which has been adopted for this approach (see Sect. 5). The DEB can contain raw data and diverse meta-data depending on the costumer contract or the kind of occurred policy violation, respectively. This architecture provides an interface delegating and coordinating tasks by interacting with the distributed `Evidence Collection Agents`.

The `Input Layer` contains different agents responsible for collection of evidence in their different scopes and locations. Currently covered evidence sources and their techniques are specified in Sect. 4. Each detected violation is noticed and the whole evidence including its meta- and additional control data is sent to the processing side. To guarantee information integrity, evidence is provided with a signature, which must be consistent during the evidence report process. This means, evidence integrity is ensured from the violation detection until the conversion from raw data to the output message has happened. At this point, a participating actor or an external system could be notified automatically. This automatic, transparency-strengthening process could therefore strengthen the trust in a `CSP` providing composite services [15].

The `Processing Layer` is responsible for the integrity observance and the evidence request access tracking which is expressed inside the `DEBs Tag Continuity Blocks (TCB)`, implemented as a H2 Database [16]. The `Evidence`

Interpret And Persist Agent is listening for successfully finalized or failed evidence collection records created by the Input Layer which triggers the persisting of new insights. Also, the Evidence DB is communicating with the Evidence Presentation Agent, which interacts directly with the Delegation/Control Agent. Its only purpose is the expressive presentation of requested evidence in due consideration of the requesting actor. It is also conceivable to provide a costumers exclusive evidence collection system. In this scenario, the compliance of policies (from CSP side) is possible using a separate Cloud Service Provider Agent with the required access rights, respectively the interaction with the costumers exclusive Delegation Control Agent.

The Presentation Layer is the only point of direct contact with a human actor (e.g., a customer or a trusted third-party auditor) inside this architecture. The user interaction handling and request transformation is handed over to the Delegation/Control Agent. Besides requesting meta data about currently active Evidence Collection Agents, a costumer entity is able to check the current status of the contractual compliance with its CSP. Also the explicit delegation of a evidence collection run is possible due communicating with this agent. Conveniently, the opportunity of adapting the JADE library to JSP based systems is given. Therefore, the orchestration of agent actions (which of course must follow agreed-upon policies) could be added for instance to a costumers private web interface.

Protective goals inside this forensic mechanism are integrity and confidentiality of collected data which have to be guaranteed until the evidence collection has finished and was persisted. On the other hand, collected data should only be requested by authorized auditors or other authorized entities such as cloud regulators.

4   Evidence Collection

This section is an introduction to the different evidence collecting agents, their evidence sources and the detection of policy violations. As shown in Fig. 2 the Input Layer potentially contains several distributed evidence sources located at Infrastructure as a Service (IaaS) -level. Besides the examination of log files [1] inside different systems, APIs and external applications are sources of evidence, which can be used to determine policy violations by different patterns. The evidence collection is performed either by using a so called OneShotBehaviour for a particular evidence collection initiation or by collecting evidence periodically/continuously. Currently the evidence sources are covered by the following Evidence Collection Agents:

– CMS Agent:
   This agent is able to interact directly with the central component of any cloud infrastructure. To detect policy violations, APIs provided by the Cloud Management System are used to gather needed information. In case of Open-Nebula [17] the process of evidence collection could be the request for current storage, network or virtualization orchestration and of course the analysis of

log files, where events originating from cloud operations are recorded. For example, there is this internal project working on business secrets, which is placed on a separate hypervisor. Because of its critical data, this system would claim besides other transparency increasing measures the delegation of a CMS Agent. This agent would be responsible for gathering lifecycle information, tracking of occurred snapshots (which are relevant considering the aspect of needed confidentiality) and workload information of every (reachable) node.

– Application Specific Agent:
  These agent types collect a specific kind of evidence defined by the policy. For example, a policy could look like "It is not allowed to store email addresses inside a VM". To detect evidence of non-compliance, patterns matching email addresses need to be searched and recorded. Therefore, the agent is triggering an external program searching the VMs hard disk for the given pattern. This can be done using the Cornell Spider tool [18], which generates a log file containing all file paths that possibly compromise the given pattern including additional meta data. Of course the occurrence of false positives cannot be excluded automatically from the output.

– Storage System Agent:
  This agent is communicating directly with various Storage Management APIs. Besides performance monitoring this agent is also able to determine the exact location (e.g. datacenter) of a service. This feature can be used to verify the awareness of policies requiring a geographically aspect.

– Net-Flow Agent:
  This agent's task is the investigation of different network-enabled devices inside a CSPs network. Some policies will prohibit the network communication with certain addresses and/or address-ranges for a specific network device. By analyzing NetFlow logs, the policy violating communication can be tracked and used as evidence (e.g., communication endpoints, time and duration).
  In Sect. 6 there is a description of how to use this agent type along different CSPs in case of using their XaaS as supply chain.

After the evidence collection run has finished, the executing Evidence Collection Agent generating a evidence record as basis for the corresponding DEB. In some cases the evidence is a complete file which must be sent to the Processing Layer for purposes of conservation of evidence. Working large log files containing evidence can become a performance problem because each file containing a violation must be transmitted to the processing layer. In that case the evidence file must be transmitted inside a signed Blob and persisted at the processing layer (best encrypted, too) guaranteeing tamper evident properties.

5   Evidence Persistence

This section illustrates the different data structures (Tables) of the Evidence Database and how the different attributes are mapped to and reflect a Digital

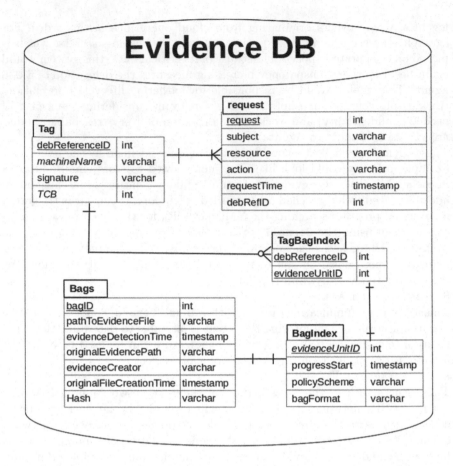

Fig. 3. Evidence database

Evidence Bag (DEB). Like mentioned before, the persistence of evidence is triggered at the processing side as soon as the `Evidence Interpret and Persist Agent` is receiving a record from an `Evidence Collection Agent` registered with its platform. After verifying the dataset's integrity and adding the current `Request` record, every evidence request is processed by automatically forming the responding `Tag` row and its underlying layers. Therefore, the `Evidence Interpret and Persist Agent` is connected to a H2 Evidence Database (Fig. 3) using JDBC.

A DEB contains a `Tag` which has a `1:N` relation to an `Index`, which in turn is related `1:1` to a `Bag`.

- The `Tag Table` containing information about each evidence collection run in all because of its relation to the particular `Bag` and their overlying `Index Tables`. At this layer, meta data about the evidence record, information about the delegating agent and a reference to the last accessing subject of this evidence collection run are stored.

- To be aware of actions performed on a specific `Tag` or `Tag`-underlying layer the `TCB` entry references a row inside the `Request Table` to detect every single corresponding evidence access.
- The `1:N` relation between the `Tag` and the `Index` is established using an intermediate table.
- Also, containing a signature of every underlying relation altogether, the `Tag` table is a robust core element of this evidence persistence mechanism. Inside the evidence database the signatures are stored as `Base64 varchar`(String) and being restored as byte array for data integrity verification using the `Java.security API`.
- Besides the `Progress start` (at the `Evidence Collection Agents` side) and the `Policy scheme`, the `Index` table contains a `bagFormat` attribute to categorize the occurred evidence. As mentioned before every evidence collection run that scored no policy violation must be persisted, too. This can be done at this point. The `bagFormat` is a first indicator of the significance of persisted evidence. It can be *'structured text'*, *'raw binary data'*, *'archive'*, *'no policy violation'* or any other suitable categorization.
- By referencing the `Bag` table by its corresponding `evidenceUnitID`, a requesting subject is able to reach a stored policy violation. If the evidence is associated with a file, the file is persisted including its signature at the processing layers storage but is not stored inside the database because of performance loss inside the signing and verifying mechanism. However the path to this evidence file is stored inside this `Bag` table besides the `evidenceDetectionTime`, original evidence meta data and an additional Hash. Therefore, using the `JAVA Security API` every Tag is signed with the `Evidence Interpret and Persist Agent`'s DSA key, while the actual bag holds the `Evidence Collection Agent`'s signature, which was created during the collection process.

6   Agent Migration

This section focuses on a distributed evidence collection scenario by illustrating the possibilities of agent migration. Wasting system resources on not currently needed services (e.g. agents) can be avoided using the JADE API and/or the JADE GUI for manual agent orchestration [2]. Figure 4 depicts the scenario of a multi/inter CSP agent distribution on demand: According to a given policy, the `A-PPL Engine (Accountable Privacy Policy Language)` enforces accountability policies, like planned in the `A4Cloud Project` [19].

Also, the reaction on an occurred event is described (e.g., the notification of a subject about the analyzed evidence scoring a specific result). The `A-PPL` is currently work in progress. It extends `PPL` which extends the `eXtensible Access Control Markup Language (XACML)` [20] which is why this part is currently emulated inside this architecture using a `XACML Parser` deciding whether a function will be executed or not (e.g. the migration function).

Because of the `A-PPL Engine`'s SaaS aspects [21] the service probably will run inside a different ISP's virtual machine, which also possibly will be stored

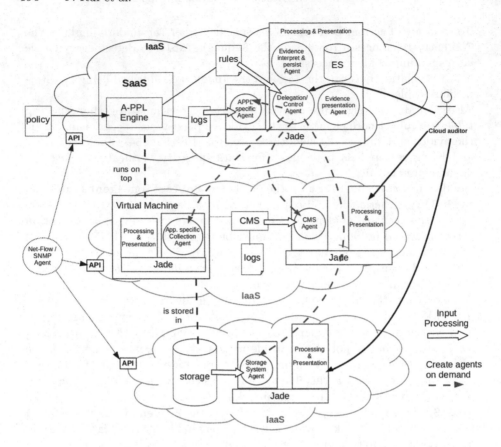

Fig. 4. Agent distribution on demand

inside a different ISP's Infrastructure. To provide a high availability the data is probably replicated to another data center, which possibly is located in another country and because of that following another juristic system [22]. Therefore, the actual avail of transparent data location in the cloud is to interpret as additional risk for a costumer.

Depending on the imported rules the `Delegation/Control Agent` distributes/ migrates the requested `Evidence Collection Agent`s to their JADE destination platform. The different scarcely spawned `Evidence Collection Agents` initially performing a service registration after noticing their corresponding `Processing Layer` to communicate with. To avoid unnecessary overloading data traffic the evidence is always persisted inside their corresponding `Evidence Store` (weak migration).

The possibilities of network analytics are given anyway if the `Net-Flow Agent` is positioned ISP-local. To implement the `Net-Flow Agent` in a CSP-comprehensive way, every CSP must offer either a standardized API to check out the necessary connection stats or executing a (continuous) `Net-Flow Agent`

by their own to communicate with. Potentially this API will implement the
Cloud Trust Protocol (CTP) [23]. To collect every available net-flow evidence
the different CSPs must report their supporting services to the requesting system
(e.g. this architecture) or respectively provide a way to check them out. While
there is no standardized API the opportunity of using a Net-Flow Agent on
every service providing CSP is given (see Sect. 7).

Also the possibility of temporary migration is given, where an agent will be
transferred to another platform and migrated back to the ordering agents platform (strong migration). In this case, not only the agents executable is transmitted between the platforms but its currently objects containing new insights, too.
Of course, distributed agents remove themselves from their corresponding platforms in case of a non-continuous evidence collection run. To collect evidence,
the corresponding agent platform must be started with the required rights to
access the resource (in most cases this is root).

7   Complex Service Provision Scenarios

A service provision chain scenario demands a correlation of evidence collected
by all involved services and their platform's Evidence Collection Agents. The
complexity of this service provision refers to the inclusion of multiple Service
Providers and different companies, respectively.

Figure 5 depicts a scenario where CSP A is offering a (potentially public)
Service A but using Service B provided by CSP B (transparent to costumers).
In this example, a network communication with a country outside the EU takes
place at the service provided by CSP B.

The agreed upon policy predicates that every processed data must been held
inside the European Union but because of the supply chain CSP interoperability
is needed, more precisely a trusted service is needed.

Both CSP A and CSP B are hosting services inside their own datacenters
located inside the EU. All necessary evidence connections are provided using
this evidence collection architecture trusting a central Locality Compliance
Agent which is aware of all service relationships used by a potential costumer.

If CSP A respects the policy by hosting a service inside the EU but is in turn
using a service provided by CSP B, CSP A alone is not able to guarantee the
compliance to this policy.

Requesting evidence reports from the affected (distributed) platforms Dele-
gation/Control Agent is how compounded evidence is come about. Depending on the data transmitted from Service A to Service B, potentially valuable
information could be transmitted to a 'forbidden' location, which is why the
Evidence Collection Agent placed at CSP B diagnoses for network communication policy violations and creates an evidence record inside its platform's
Evidence DB. Once the Locality Compliance Agent receives all necessary evidence reports from the participating CSP's Presentation Layers, the occurrence of interdependent policy violations are checked depending on the given
EU data policy. Every new insight about interdependent policy violations will be

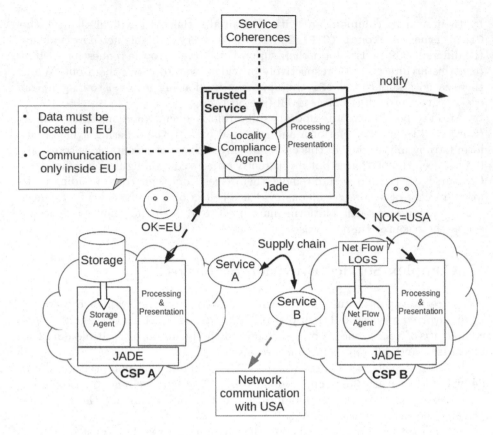

Fig. 5. Service coherences

forwarded to the A-PPL Engine which possibly will consider further steps (i.e., notifying stakeholders). Passing the new insights along the chain of accountability is relevant for a full conclusion but must go easy on network resources at the same time if this evidence architecture is applied in large datacenters. Therefore, for example a simple *'OK=EU'* or *'NOK=USA'* message on demand is sufficient for a pooled decision filling the dashboard of a customer's private web interface using the boolean product of all replies, group of replies respectively.

8   Conclusion and Future Work

This paper underlines the importance of structured evidence collection on demand running on nearly every device supporting transparency and therefore trust. The presented architecture enables distributed collecting and persisting of evidence following imported rules. Because of the possible distributed JADE platforms this construct will work in large CSP data centers without overloading the average performance.

To provide a quick evidence processing there must be a mechanism that excludes already known policy violations at **Evidence Collection Agent** side. The mentioned **Sealed Evidence Bag** [4] is a potentially evidence persistence extension. Also, the collected evidence must be presented in a convincing and distinct way at the user interface. Still existing challenges among other things are the performance evaluating of the defined architecture and scaling tests enabling the deployment of this architecture for highly dynamic services.

Acknowledgment. This research is closely related to the **A4Cloud Project**.

References

1. Reich, P.D.C., Rübsamen, M.S.T.: Supporting cloud accountability by collecting evidence using audit agents. In: 2013 IEEE International Conference on Cloud Computing Technology and Science (2013)
2. Bellifemine, F.L., Caire, G., Greenwood, D.: Developing Multi-Agent Systems with JADE. Wiley Series in Agent Technology. Wiley, Chichester (2007)
3. Turner, P.: Unification of Digital Evidence from Disparate Sources (Digital Evidence Bags). QinetiQ
4. Schatz, B., Clark, A.: An open architecture for digital evidence integration. In: AusCERT Asia Pacific Information Technology Security Conference
5. Validating Cloud Infrastructure Changes by Cloud Audits
6. Nagios. www.nagios.com
7. New Relic. http://www.newrelic.com/
8. Cloud Control. www.cloudcontrol.com
9. App Fog. www.appfog.com
10. Italia, T.: Java Agent DEvelopement framework. http://jade.tilab.com
11. Poslad, S.: Specifying protocols for multi-agent systems interaction. ACM Trans. Auton. Adap. Syst. (TAAS) **2**(4), 1–24 (2007)
12. Foundation for Intelligent Physical Agents. http://www.fipa.org/
13. Reddy, P.I.P., Damodaram, D.A.: Implementation of Agent Based Dynamic Distributed Service
14. Nikraz, M., Caireb, G., Bahri, P.A.: A Methodology for the Analysis and Design of Multi-agent Systems using JADE. Telecom Italia Lab
15. Jansen, W., Grance, T.: Guidelines on security and privacy in public cloud computing. National Institute of Standards and Technology, U.S. Department of Commerce (2011)
16. H2 Database Engine. http://www.h2database.com
17. Open Nebula. http://opennebula.org/
18. Tchamdjou, M.Y.D.E.: Agenten zur Erkennung von sensiblen Daten und deren Schutz. HFU, Technical report
19. Accountability for the Cloud. http://www.a4cloud.eu/
20. XACML - Extensible Access Control Markup Language. www.oasis-open.org/
21. Benghabrit, W., Grall, H., Royer, J.-C., Sellami, M., Azraoui, M., Elkhiyaoui, K., Önen, M., Santana De Oliveira, A., Bernsmed, K.: A cloud accountability policy representation framework. In: CLOSER - 4th International Conference on Cloud Computing and Services Science, Barcelone, Espagne (2014). http://hal.inria.fr/hal-00941872

22. Bradshaw, S., Cunningham, A., Luciano, L.D.C., Hon, W.K., Hörnle, J., Reed, C., Walden, I. In: Millard, C. (ed.) Cloud Computing Law. Oxford University Press, Oxford (2013)
23. Cloud Trust Protocol. https://cloudsecurityalliance.org/research/ctp/

Socio-Legal Aspects of the Cloud

Understanding the Cloud: The Social Implications of Cloud Computing and the Need for Accountability

Maartje G.H. Niezen$^{(\boxtimes)}$ and Wouter M.P. Steijn

Tilburg Institute for Law, Technology and Society (TILT),
Tilburg University, Tilburg, The Netherlands
m.g.h.niezen@tilburguniversity.edu,
wouter.steijn@tno.nl

Abstract. Five years ago, cloud computing was one of the top emerging new technologies, nowadays it is almost common place. This rapid introduction of cloud business models in our society coincides with critical questions on the cloud's risks, such as security and privacy. Moreover, there seems to be an increased demand for accountable behaviour in the cloud. This paper explores how society understands the cloud, its related risks and the need for accountability in the cloud. This exploration provides insight in the social implications of cloud and future Internet services and the way cloud and accountability tools will be adopted in society.

Keywords: Cloud computing · Accountability · Public understanding

1 Introduction

Five years ago, cloud computing was one of the top emerging new technologies, similar to wireless power, 3-D printing and e-book readers [1]. Currently cloud computing has gained momentum. Cloud storage has become the new standard for data sharing and storing for individual and business users (e.g. DropBox, Flickr, Google Drive, OpenDrive, JustCloud). This rapid introduction and implementation of cloud computing business models in our society, however, coincides with questions on the risks of cloud computing. Often uttered risks are the security, interoperability and reliability of cloud computing. These risks not only matter to cloud users, but might even matter to the public at large. This paper will focus on the public understanding of cloud computing, the public issues at hand and how the call for accountability in the cloud sector fits into this discussion.

Previous research on emerging new technologies has demonstrated that unfamiliarity with a technological phenomenon and related scientific, social and ethical uncertainties might give rise to public controversies [2–4]. The introduction of biotechnology is a point of example. "Cross-national stand-offs over the commercialization of genetically modified (GM) crops, the patenting of gene fragments and higher life forms, and the divergent policy regimes that have developed around research with embryonic stem cells give tangible evidence of the conflicts that can arise if tacit public expectations with respect to the management of biotechnology are not met" [2, p. 140].

© Springer International Publishing Switzerland 2015
M. Felici and C. Fernández-Gago (Eds.): A4Cloud 2014, LNCS 8937, pp. 201–225, 2015.
DOI: 10.1007/978-3-319-17199-9_9

Public resistance due to lack of understanding might thus effectively stall a new industry. Typically, these examples do not refer to innovations that are perceived as consumer goods but have an inherent public nature.

Despite being a consumer good the uncertainty surrounding cloud computing, in specific the cloud's complex, ubiquitous and opaque nature, raises questions on the distribution of responsibilities as were it a public good [5]. In fact, the inherent technological, cross-border and dynamic character of cloud computing raises special problems for its responsible governance. Think of the organized irresponsibility due to trans-boundary data transfers – as data storage is scattered all over the world and the relation between data-subjects, data-controllers and data-processors opaque, nobody feels -or is- responsible if things go wrong.

In order to deal with these uncertainties in the cloud ecosystem the notion of accountability is introduced. Accountability "broadly denotes the duty of an individual or organisation to answer someone in some way about how they have conducted their affairs" [6, p. 989]. The notion of accountability originates from the public sector and is related to good governance with main attributes as transparency, responsibility and responsiveness. Apparently, the market mechanism alone does not seem to have the ability to govern the cloud business model, vendor lock-in being a good example of this malfunction of the market mechanism. This introduction of accountability in cloud ecosystems is a wider established trend in the private sector [7]. One might even speak of a culture of accountability; the patterns, traits, and products of accountability increasingly define current governance of the private sector.

However, a one on one transfer (of the use) of the accountability notion from the public to the private sector is unfitting. The demands within the private sector might be different. The experience with accountability as a governing notion in the public sector is high, yet its use in the private sector is relatively unknown and new especially in highly competitive markets like the IT sector. Therefore, we deem it relevant to explore how the accountability notion has been transferred from the public to the private sector, and whether this might imply some reconfiguration of its operationalization in practice. Subsequently, the introduction of accountability in the cloud ecosystem is a second point of interest in this paper, mainly in relation to the governance of new emerging technologies and the public understanding of cloud computing.

This paper explores how society understands the cloud, its related risks and the need for accountability in the cloud. Such an understanding provides insight in the social implications of cloud and future Internet services and the way cloud and accountability tools will be adopted in society. Our research can be positioned within the sociological sciences, combining the discipline of science, technology and society studies (STS) on public understanding of science and risk society with the discipline of public administration on good governance and accountability. Our research departs from the idea that public perceptions of emergent technologies, like cloud computing, have become increasingly important to understand. First, because cloud computing has a deep impact on the way our society is and will be organized. Second, because the Snowden files about the NSA and PRISM reveal governments control over our data. Both reasons might cause public debates that stall further development of cloud and future Internet services sector. This means that first an identification of areas of concern is needed. Knowing the actual public concerns about cloud computing and the development of future Internet services may be important, not only the general positive/negative attitude or disposition toward cloud computing [8]. Insights in the public understanding of cloud computing will inform the discussion on the responsible governance of data in the cloud and the need for accountability. In our discussion of accountability we will take a public administration perspective, entailing governance as the creation of conditions for ordered rules and collective action [9]. It is about understanding how people and technologies are able to steer one another to certain directions, in this case handling data in the cloud in a responsible and accountable way. Subsequently, there is a need for exploring why and how the notion of accountability has been transferred from the public to the private sector, in specific cloud computing sector.

This paper will start with outlining how governing the cloud and its risks currently are understood. This outline is followed by a theoretical exploration of the transfer of the accountability notion from the public to the private sector, specifically its operationalization within the cloud ecosystem. Next, a survey among the Dutch population provides empirical insights in the actual public understanding of cloud computing, related concerns and need for governance of data. In our analysis we will focus upon the meaning of the survey's outcomes in light of the debate for eliciting the public's concerns with respect to cloud computing and how to govern accountable behaviour in the cloud. Finally, the paper will evaluate the social implications of cloud computing and the need for accountability and accountability tools.

2 Cloud as Emerging Technology in Need of Responsible Governance

Governing innovation, in a modern technological culture in which the existence of uncertainty of scientific knowledge and related societal problems are key characteristics, requires a thorough understanding of the risks that come with innovation. Cloud computing is such an innovation that might be in need of responsible governance. In this section we explore the traditional approach to the cloud's risks and risk perceptions, followed by a more publicly informed approach to governing innovation and risks.

2.1 Governing the Cloud via Risk Analysis and Management

While the cloud and future Internet creates new business opportunities it also creates a variety of new technical, organizational and regulatory "complexities" and risks. The traditional approach to understanding these complexities and risks is performing risk analysis and risk management. It focuses on identifying and assessing risks that can be captured in for example statistics due to the availability of scientific knowledge (data, information). The risk assessment aims to produce the best estimate of the physical harm that a risk source may induce [10]. The typical risk management lifecycle involves risk assessment, setting policies to mitigate these risks, implementing controls and running systems in accordance with these controls, and monitoring and auditing to ensure risks are mitigated.

Accordingly, understanding the risks of using cloud services is a fundamental issue. Despite the non-contentious financial advantages cloud computing raises questions about security and privacy. For example, cloud users simply have to rely on and trust cloud vendors experience in dealing with security and intrusion detection systems [11]. Most of the identified risks relate to security and privacy issues, for example: the way data operators handle and disclose provided data, subsequent data use by third parties, security of data provided, legality of cloud services usage, disruptions of cloud services, vendor lock-in, and violation of privacy laws by cloud service usage [12].

One of the main identified risks of cloud computing is its security. Aspects such as the lack of proper data and Virtual Machine (VM) segregation or jurisdiction concerns regarding data location are among the most regarded problems on this area. Other security concerns refer to the service-oriented architecture of cloud (the risks of various forms of attacks such as DOS, Man-in-the-Middle etc.) and multi-tenancy and the difficulties in isolation among tenants' data [13]. Despite these serious worries, the perception of security in cloud computing to be cautious has changed over the years. Moreover, the cloud does not necessarily offer less security than individuals can achieve on their own. In fact, the opposite can be argued since security is promoted as one of the cloud's advantages. Mostly because knowledge and awareness on cloud technologies and mechanisms has increased. As an illustrative example, results from KPMG surveys regarding perception of cloud computing [14, 15], based on responses from more than 650 executives from different industries, show that while in 2011 security ranked as the top challenge, in 2013 it ranked third, after integration and transition challenges. Thus, one possible interpretation is that perception of security in the cloud of decision-makers has matured from initial fear and reluctance to increased confidence and willingness to integrate. Technical issues that hinder implementation and integration of cloud computing technologies into business have taken the lead role regarding executives concerns [16].

In order to cope with these security risks or to mitigate these risks, they first have to be made measurable. Risk then is "a measure of the extent to which an entity is threatened by a potential circumstance or event, and typically a function of (1) the adverse impacts that would arise if the circumstance or event occurs; and (2) the likelihood of occurrence" [17]. Accordingly, security risks are "categorised into policy and organizational risks, technical risks, legal risks and risks not specific to the cloud. The description of each risk includes risk levels (likelihood, impact), the comparison to the baseline (non-cloud solution), affected assets and exploited vulnerabilities" [18]. Analysing these risks allows for the systematic use of information to identify sources and estimate risk. For example, the A4Cloud works on a systematic risk assessment model, including soft and hard trust measures, "to support the causal analysis of the emergence of specific threats (i.e. how threats exploit vulnerabilities and then affect assets or controls)" [17]. The resulting risk models, sometimes combined with empirical evidence or experts' judgments, support the assessment of risk in terms of likelihood and impact. After the identification of the risks, they are evaluated against established risk criteria; i.e. norms laid down by experts or in law. The comparison between the measured risks and risk criteria subsequently result in an identification of threats or risks that need to be dealt with and proposals of controls to be taken.

A second main risk relates to privacy. "Cloud computing is associated with a range of severe and complex privacy issues" [12]. These issues for example refer to the appropriate collection, use and disclosure of data, safe storage and transmission of data, term of retention, and access to data. For sure, cloud computing's omnipresent nature presses the most on these privacy issues; exposing data subjects and data processors to the diverse laws of multiple countries.

Currently, privacy issues mainly are dealt with via data protection law, such as the Data Protection Directive 95/46/EC. Although currently, there is no general EU legal requirement to conduct a Privacy Impact Assessment (PIA),[1] the PIA is seen as one of the ways to identify, analyse and assess privacy risks. A PIA is "a methodology for assessing the impacts on privacy of a project, policy, programme, service, product or other initiative and, in consultation with stakeholders, for taking remedial actions as necessary in order to avoid or minimise negative impacts" [19]. A PIA is based on a risk-management approach. Similar to dealing with security risks, privacy risks are made measurable first. PIAs provide specific guidance on how to calculate and prioritise risks, choose appropriate 'controls' (risk mitigating measures) and assess the residual risks. However, "importantly, a PIA is not a single-shot exercise, but an ongoing process from the time when a plan to process personal data is conceived throughout the entire processing. The PIA process incorporates a feedback loop, allowing to adjust both the IT-based product and the providing organisation's internal procedures depending on the PIA results" [20].

Whereas the computer scientific approach focuses upon the automatic and systematic performance of a risk model, the PIA described from a legal viewpoint seems to emphasize the need for an iterative approach and a feedback loop. Nevertheless, for both approaches goes that the identified security and privacy risks and subsequent assessments tend to focus upon issues that can be made measurable or calculable and also provide some certainty with respect to the impact they have on an organization. It is this approach to risks, risk analysis and management that is debated from a STS-perspective, since a broader, more flexible and perhaps even evolutionary approach might be needed to grasp all issues related to cloud and future Internet services. It might be that the cloud's risks are not only complex but also ambiguous in nature. This ambiguity entails "that there are different legitimate viewpoints from which to evaluate whether there are or could be adverse effects and whether these risks are tolerable or even acceptable" [10]. Accordingly a greater understanding of the issues at play might be needed.

2.2   Responsible Governance of the Cloud and Public Concerns

Increasingly it is recognized that social, ethical and economic impacts have an important role in the assessment of innovations. Identifying what uncertainties exist, what the (potential) risks are, has become core business in the analysis and assessment of innovations [21]. The research on the potential hazards and damages of the increased

---

[1] Although Article 20 of the Data Protection Directive on prior checking when data processing presents specific risks is considered a predecessor to PIA.

connectivity due to cloud computing is relatively young and the knowledge on risks is more uncertain as cloud computing is a complex, omnipresent and dynamic facilitator of the Network Society. Currently cost-benefit analysis and other positivist sciences seem to dominate the risk assessment plain. Consequently, societal and other values have less room for informing regulators in the responsible governance of innovations. When exploring the socio-economic landscape of cloud-computing it becomes obvious that concerns with respect to cloud computing not only are technical or simple problems. In fact, cloud computing: (a) is part of technological innovations that are fundamentally changing society, and (b) seems to have increased governments' capability and actual conduct to control our data.

Cloud is Changing Society's Organisation. With cloud computing the era of the network society and technological paradigm of informationalism seems to be ascertained. Early 21st century "is characterized by the explosion of portable machines that provide ubiquitous wireless communication and computing capacity. This enables social units (individuals or organizations) to interact anywhere, anytime, while relying on a support infrastructure that manages material resources in a distributed information power grid" [22]. Cloud computing has further established this network society by significantly increasing the networking capacity of distributed processing and computing power. No longer is society limited by stand-alone machines, instead a global, digitized system of human-machine interaction is established [22].

In fact, the emergence of cloud computing is drastically changing the use of information technology; it is changing computing from a personal to a public utility. "Computing is being transformed to a model consisting of services that are commoditized and delivered in a manner similar to traditional utilities such as water, electricity, gas, and telephony. In such a model, users access services based on their requirements without regard to where the services are hosted or how they are delivered" [23]. Nowadays, cloud computing has become a common delivery model for many business applications (e.g. office and messaging software, management software, accounting software, etc.). Moreover, cloud has changed the way these business applications are built and run; the hardware and software infrastructures are no longer within the company's physical space (e.g. Salesforce). It is even possible to have the entire business infrastructure in the form of server and network resources, allowing for the availability of a private cloud and virtualized local network (e.g. Amazon Web Services or Windows Azure).

Accordingly our society's organization has fundamentally changed towards the social structure of networks backed up by a new technological environment. For example, the increase in computing power in the human genome project already demonstrated how computing models and computing power coincide with scientific advancements in genetic engineering. Subsequently, what has been believed by many people to be the secrets of life now are being unravelled due to technological advancements that allow for a global networked community of various scientists (microbiologists, electrical engineers, etc.) and accompanying computing tools. Another example is the increased gap between the haves and have nots (or so-called digital divide), and subsequent exclusion of certain parts of population due to lack of access to cloud computing models. According to Castells "The network society works on the basis of a binary logic of inclusion/exclusion, whose boundaries change over time, both with the changes in the networks' programs and with the conditions of performance of these programs" [22]. Not being connected or being in the right networks simply means that people might be excluded from relevant and/or powerful networks. Although many people are not included in these networks, they are affected by the processes that take place in these global networks. Cloud computing thus has far-reaching consequences for society's organization.

Cloud and Governmental Access to Data. Controversies like the Snowden files reporting on the NSA and PRISM have fuelled public discussions on privacy, data protection and have increased the public call for transparency and accountability of governments and cloud service providers in their handling of personal information [24]. In fact, the Snowden files have changed the landscape "by single handedly unveiling a major problem with the way we store and share files". More specifically, Snowden "has exposed one of the largest issues involved with trusting all of our valuable information to the cloud — security" [25]. Whereas in the past the public did not perceive controlling their data in the cloud as an urgent matter, the PRISM controversy and increased attention to privacy of personal information likely changed the public's focus. Cloud computing creates an easier and much more manageable target from a threat-economics perspective to attack for well-equipped adversaries like nation states: data from millions of individuals located in a handful of data centres. Subsequently, individual cloud consumers' perceptions of risk seem more related to the ability to control one's information in the cloud and transparency, then related to, for example, technical risks.

Public Concerns and Cloud Adoption. Despite its widely spread use by individuals and businesses, the notion of cloud computing or the cloud remains for many an unfamiliar concept. The public at large stores its data in the cloud, but has great difficulties understanding what such data storage actually entails, what the cloud is and what implications this might have. Nevertheless, we expect to remain in control of our data. Exactly this unfamiliarity and uncertainty with cloud computing might hamper its further development and requires further understanding of public concerns.

Cloud consumers' understanding of the cloud is an important aspect in adoption of the cloud. Research by Marshall and Tang on file synching and sharing mechanisms in the cloud, for example, shows that cloud users' uncertainty and misconceptions limited their ability to fully take advantage of the service's features [26]. Users needed more accurate and robust models to be able to discover and trust cloud computing services [26]. It is reasonable to assume that cloud consumers' lack of knowledge and understanding of cloud computing influences their risk perception and subsequently their understanding of cloud computing.

Also the concerns with respect to privacy seem to depict other values and perspectives to what are believed to be risks or issues with respect to cloud computing. Previous research with regard to privacy and online behaviour demonstrates that many consumers do not trust most Web providers enough to exchange personal information in online relationships with them [27]. Not privacy but trust seems to be a quintessential element in online relations. Moreover, the public's perceptions of having little control over information privacy on the Internet have a strong influence on the consumer's willingness to engage in relationship exchanges online [28–30].

Based upon the examples and deliberation above one can assume that the concerns with cloud computing not only relate to the uncertainty of the technology itself, but also to its ethical, economic and societal impacts. Importantly, one should not assume that public issues involving risks are in fact risk issues [31]. The concerns go beyond scientific identified risks as data breaches and beyond mere compliance with data protection laws, and also relate to 'social exclusion' by not having access to the networked society or feelings of loss of control on one's data. These concerns should be elicited to encompass public expectations and policy issues that are not, or not yet, reflected in, for example, law.

2.3   Innovation and Involving the Public

The involvement of the public at large and the elicitation of public concerns is a topic heavily debated in the field of governing innovation. It is the articulation of the public issue that should steer future development of technologies and related regulations [5, 32–34]. Global innovations like cloud computing "...should respond to people's self-determined needs and aspirations, provided that certain background conditions of information and deliberation are met" [34]. In order to articulate the public issue at hand, one should ask the public for its concerns regarding the risks of cloud computing and its needs for responsible governance mechanisms to ensure that boundaries are upheld where necessary.

However, the articulation of the public issue regarding the innovations in science and technology is not a self-evident matter. Current (democratic) governing mechanisms have not kept pace with the technological developments. Then how to deal with the risks and uncertainties in a democratic and scientific informed way? A first step could be to elicit the concerns and risks not only from the scientific community, but also from other relevant stakeholders and even the general public. Such understanding of the risks might allow for collective agreements to emerge in order to cope with unavoidable residual risks, either via contracts, law, the extension of democracy or other governing mechanisms [5]. Jasanoff, for example claims that an important question of responsible governance of innovations is when and how to involve relevant stakeholders such as the general public [34]. It may be unnecessary to involve stakeholders when the drivers of the innovation can be trusted to act responsibly, but this raises the question when this is the case and how we can know? Related questions deal with who are knowledgeable actors to participate in governance mechanisms, and whether the general public even is interested in knowing every potential risk related to all innovations. Don't they have a right to remain lay and trust governments to control potential threats?

These questions with respect to cloud as an information and communication technology innovation that changes our societies' organizations and our relation with governments fits within the call for responsible innovation that entered the scientific and policy makers' debates early 2000's. This call for responsible innovation is a reaction to the variety and characteristics of emerging technologies like genetically modified foods, medical technologies and nanotechnology and the way these technologies are shaping society. Also new communication technologies like the cloud and future Internet services influence how we relate to the natural world. As cloud computing is an innovation that crosses frontiers it raises special problems for its responsible governance. For one, cloud is in essence a consumer good and not a public good. Then how to debate the responsible governance of the cloud and with whom? Moreover, in the last decade we have witnessed how the call for accountability and the responsible governance of our data in the cloud has increased due to controversies like PRISM. Subsequently, there is a need for a more reflective and deliberative role for a broad set of actors, also given the large investments that governments and private firms make in research and innovation [35]. Moreover, it is important to have insight in how responsible governance is shaped in practice, and more specifically the way this is operationalized through 'accountability' in the cloud ecosystem.

3 Exploring the Introduction of Accountability in the Cloud

Within cloud ecosystems accountability is becoming an important (new) notion, defining the relations between various stakeholders and their behaviours towards data in the cloud. However, accountability is a notion with many dimensions, different meanings to different people and different usages. For example, accountability is enshrined in regulatory frameworks like the data protection regulation, and simultaneously accountable behaviour is shaped in the relation between cloud customers and cloud providers. In our exploration of accountability in the cloud ecosystem we take a social scientific approach. Such an approach entails, for one, that we do not assume that there is a road map out there telling us how accountability works and how it will steer people to behave responsibly with data in the cloud. In fact there are many questions to ask in order to gain an understanding about accountability and the cloud: for example, what is accountability according to the different relevant stakeholders? How does accountability govern people's behaviour in general? And how does accountability govern people's behaviour in the cloud? Each of these questions requires different research approaches and different methodologies. In this paper we will focus on the way the use of the accountability notion in the private sector of cloud computing is informed by its use in the public sector, drawing upon earlier work of, for example, Bovens [36–39].

3.1 Accountability in the Public Sector

In the public sector accountability predominantly is used prescriptively; accountability of some agent to some other agent for some state of affairs. It reflects an institutional relation arrangement in which an actor can be held to account by a forum. Accountability then focuses on the specific social relation or the mechanism that involves an obligation to explain and justify conduct. Subsequently, accountability is "a relationship between an actor and a forum, in which the actor has an obligation to explain and to justify his or her conduct, the forum can pose questions and pass judgement, and the actor can be sanctioned" [36]. In an accountability relationship thus three parties can be distinguished: (a) the steward or accountor, (b) the principal or accountee or forum, and (c) the codes on the basis of which the relationship is struck. The latter are the shared framework for explanation and justification that are negotiated between the accountor (answer, explain and justify) and accountee (question, assess, and criticize). An accountability code then is a system of signals, meanings and customs, which binds the parties in a stewardship relation.

In order to do so there are different stages in accountability relations: (a) information in which explanation is given and one's conduct is justified, (b) debate, in which the adequacy of the information and/or the legitimacy of conduct is debated (answerability) and last, (c) the forum must pass judgement and sanction whether formal (fines, disciplinary measures, unwritten rules leading to resignation) or informal (having to render account in front of television cameras or disintegration of public image and career). Accountability as a mechanism thus can be used as a tool to induce reflection and learning. It provides external feedback on (un)intended effects of its policies.

However, accountability is also used in a more normative way. Bovens calls this 'accountability as a virtue' [36]. Accountability as a virtue is much defined by bad governance; what is irresponsive, opaque, irresponsible, ineffective or even deviant behaviour. Accountability as a virtue, a normative concept, entails the promise of fair and equitable governance. Behaving accountable or responsible then is perceived as a desirable quality and laid down in norms for the behaviour and conduct of actors. Moreover, accountability then is not something imposed upon someone or an organization by another actor, but an inherent feeling, the feeling of being morally obliged to be responsive, open, transparent and responsible [36].

Defining elements of accountability or the accountability relationship are: transparency, responsibility and responsiveness. *Transparency* broadly means the conduct of business in a fashion that makes decision, rules and other information visible from outside [6]. However, the relation between accountability and transparency is not as straightforward as depicted above. Transparency can have different meanings in relation to accountability. First, transparency and accountability can be inextricably intertwined: "accountability in the sense of answerability necessarily implies the answerers sharing information with those to whom they are answerable, while transparency in the sense of openness is itself a way of answering for the conduct of an individual or organisation" [6]. Second, transparency and accountability are both needed to produce good governance yet in principle are separable. This is what Hood calls the 'matching parts'. Third, the realization that "effective accountability and all variants of transparency do not always run smoothly together, and difficult trade-offs between the two principles often have to be faced" [6]. This can best be seen as the 'awkward couple' view that focuses on perverse effects of transparency in the form of e.g. box-ticking that can lead to one-way communication rather than real answerability in effective dialogue [6]. Nevertheless, in general transparency is perceived as an instrumental dimension of accountability; it is the revelation of information for purposes of accountability. *Responsibility*, though semantically not always distinguishable from accountability, is derived from the noun to respond. Yet accountability has a broader meaning: how responsibility is exercised and made verifiable. In an accountability relationship responsibility entails the stewardship of one party entrusted by another with resources and/or responsibilities. Responsibility thus refers to ownership, acknowledging being the steward or accountor with respect to certain resources and/or responsibilities. Also, it can entail an inward sense of moral obligation to explain or answer [40]. *Responsiveness* is a more evaluative dimension of accountability and refers to the aim of making governments, organisations or institutions accord with the preferences of the people [40]. Public service providers are called on to be responsive to the needs of their clients in a way analogous to private sector firms being sensitive to consumer demands [41]. However, these defining elements of accountability, transparency, responsibility and responsiveness are in themselves ideographs and umbrella concepts that are in need of operationalization themselves.

Nevertheless, in the public sector accountability often is used in relation to good governance. One can speak of good governance when the interaction between the actor and the forum has such an institutional realization it entails societal interests and moral values the best way possible. Good governance focuses upon the creation of conditions that allow collaborations, interactive processes or policy networks to function the best way possible. Moreover, these conditions do take into account the different stakeholders' responsibilities and societal interests. The driving force behind all systems of accountability, in the public services, including professional accountability is the democratic imperative for government organizations to respond to demands from politicians and the wider public [42, 43]. The use of accountability in the public sector therefore is more evaluative than descriptive and reflects upon what responsible behaviour is.

3.2   Accountability in the Cloud

The claim that accountability is relatively new in the private sector as a mechanism to govern responsible behaviour in the cloud actually is less topical than expected. First, the notion of accountability is introduced in the field of law as a data protection principle more than 30 years ago and since then more steps have been taken in the discussion on accountability in data flow and privacy protection in EU [7]. One of the main reasons for the revival of the accountability principle in the late 2000's is the globalisation of data flows [44]. Second, the equivalent of good governance, corporate governance, also dates back more than 30 years. Corporate governance entails the totality of structures, regulation and conventions that determine the way and efficiency with which a company is run and controlled. Within corporate governance the values of control and oversight of performances are embodied in the notion of accountability. The demand for more transparency in the sense of more and reliable information to inform the accountee, i.e. the share holders, allowed for more control and recommendations with respect to management and authority.

However, accountability's current use in the private cloud sector seems to point at a new perspective on accountability and good governance. Instead of focusing on control and supervision as in corporate governance, accountability now also seems to refer to a learning perspective in the sense of good governance. For example, in the A4Cloud project "[a]ccountability consists of defining governance to comply in a responsible manner with internal and external criteria, ensuring implementation of appropriate actions, explaining and justifying those actions and remedying any failure to act properly" [45]. Accountability entails an image of transparency and trustworthiness.

It holds the promise of fair and equitable governance and beholds a desirable quality of actors. Subsequently its current use seems to combine accountability as a mechanism and accountability as a virtue.

This renewed use of accountability likely is a reaction to the failure of the cloud computing market mechanism and to its governing problems due to the cloud's transborder nature. With respect to the market failure, accountability aims to address the power asymmetry between (international) corporations or cloud providers and individuals or (smaller) cloud users. The latter lacks resources and knowledge to assert their rights to information on how their data is handled in the cloud. Moreover, vendor lock-in has refrained cloud users to exit and choose other cloud vendors. In a competitive market, the main mechanism of responsiveness is consumer choice, the capacity of the consumer to exit to an alternative provider. Moreover, in the private sector accountability is mostly applied to owners and shareholders and more to the company's manager to account for the company's performance than to customers whose main right is to refuse to purchase. However, in the public sector, accountability is usually understood as a voice not an exit strategy. Including accountability in the market system of cloud computing aims to assure an increased attention of 'customer-driven' services. With respect to the transborder nature of the cloud Bennett argues that accountability in the online/Internet sector came into play when solutions were sought for governing the more complicated, networked and global environment for international data transmissions [46]. In legislative terms we see a change in focus from the legal regime to the actual protections afforded by receiving organisations. Focusing on how data is actually protected by real organisations in receiving jurisdictions rather than on the 'black letter of the law'. This means that it is not the flow of data across boundaries that should worry us, but the use of that information in ways that may harm, discriminate, deny services and so on [46, 47]. Therefore the focus should be on how to govern accountable behaviour with respect to data and personal information.

A known criticism to accountability is its connection to and implication of self-regulation. Previous Accountability Projects like the Galway Project and Paris Project have defined key requirements for accountable organisations e.g. privacy policies, executive oversight, event management and complaint handling and redress. According to Bennett [46], these elements are not significantly different from the conclusions about self-regulation in the 1990 s. What has changed is that now we have a broad consensus of what it means for a responsible organisation to protect personal data and to respect the privacy of the individual [46]. Moreover, accountability entails more than self-regulation and includes mechanisms of oversight and supportive tools and mechanisms to govern accountable behaviour.

Nevertheless, accountability in the cloud seems to be able to address data protection and privacy issues from a regulatory perspective. First, because systems are build to ensure compliance with current legal regulations for protecting privacy. Second, as it is believed that accountability can form the focus for dealing with issues of scale in regulation, privacy risk assessment, self-regulation through certification and seals and foster an environment for the development of new technologies for managing privacy. Third, accountability is a binding principle through which those who control data should on request from regulators be able to demonstrate compliance with data protection legislation as a minimum.

The renewed focus on accountability in the cloud is supposed to positively affect data controllers responsible behaviour. Since breaches of personal information may have significant negative effects both in economic and particularly in reputational terms, data controllers in both public and private sectors seem to have gained interest in minimising risks, building and maintaining a good reputation, and ensuring the trust of citizens and consumers [48].

This extension of accountability entails the extension to public dialogue. The obligation to account used to derive from the relationship between business and shareholders and between business and customers. The new approach of accountability not only focuses on the shareholder or the customer, but also to 'the other', the public at large. Accountability is seen to be a dialectical activity, requiring accountors to answer, explain and justify, while those holding them to account engage in questioning, assessing and criticizing. It thus might involve open discussion and debate about matters of public interest. The society at large has a right to information about the extent to which an organisation has complied with the (minimum) standards of law and other regulation of a quasi-legal nature. Subsequently organisations are expected to be more transparent, to make information available on behalf of an often unspecified mass audience. Importantly such an information disposal should not become a goal in itself; it is the two-way communication in which stakeholders, such as the public at large, should be able to voice their concern.

According to Gray "the empirical basis of accountability can be substantially extended from law, and quasi law to public domain matters of substance" [49]. A restriction to financial account, or legal accounts would critically limit the attempts at holism in the cloud ecosystems. Although this is not incontestable, it does lead to the specification of a community's moral and natural rights. A specification of the public domain matters of substance can be elicited via public opinion. Organisations then owe accountability to the public at large for these specified public domain matters of substance. Subsequently, the public at large has the right to information about actions that influence society, other societies, and/or future societies. The community in which the accountor operates then is the level at which information is reported, the level at which transparency must be sought. However, to what information about organisations, such as cloud vendors and cloud service providers, do communities have rights? And, to what extent does voicing concerns without a clear consequence make sense? Importantly, these public domain matters of substance should be defined and become part of an iterative process of seeking dialogue and not only providing an account. As Raab argues "[i]n any case, the audience for an organisation's or government's account must somehow be involved with the process by which the account is produced, and not only with the product" [7].

4   The Dutch Public's Understanding of the Cloud

Whereas in the previous sections we have described a normative plea for the treatment of cloud computing as a new emerging technology that requires the elicitation of public concerns and responsible governance through accountability, this section is actually exploring current public's understanding of cloud computing.

4.1 A Survey on the Public Understanding of the Cloud

In order to learn what governing mechanisms might contribute to gaining a grip on the distribution and steering of accountability in cloud computing, it is important to distinguish the underlying concerns that ideally these governing mechanisms will address. Whether the public is concerned about cloud computing and what type of concerns they have is explored based on the empirical knowledge gathered from white papers in combination with literature on the public understanding of science, risk society, accountability and related topics such as control, trust, transparency and responsiveness. These insights have been used for the design of a survey on the public understanding of cloud, their concerns and coping mechanisms.

We distributed the survey amongst a panel of LISS (Longitudinal Internet Studies for the Social Sciences), in order to obtain a representative sample of the Dutch population. The LISS panel consists of 5000 Dutch households, comprising 8,000 individuals in total. The panel is based on a true probability sample of household drawn from the population register by Statistics Netherlands (CBS). About half the LISS panel (N = 3,735) was asked to complete this survey in February 2014. In total, 2,942 individuals returned the survey, which results in a response rate of 78.8 %. From these respondents, 672 were removed from analysis. Seventy respondents were removed because they contained more than 5 % missing values, and a further 602 respondents were removed as they indicated: (a) not to have heard of the cloud and have no desire to make use of the cloud in combination with many don't knows (>95 % of 35 question-items) or neutral responses (>95 %) (N = 532), and/or (b) not to have heard of the cloud and not to use it and specifically stated not to have given a serious answer (N = 70). This left a sample of 2,270 respondents in the age range of 16 to 91 (M = 48.21, SD = 17.11). Table 1 provides an overview of some of the demographics of the sample compared to the Dutch population. Comparison shows that our sample appears representative for the Dutch population, only slightly higher educated (ISCED 5-8).

4.2 Survey Results

De obtained data is processed and analyzed using SPSS, v21. The resulting findings are depicted below.

Internet Use and Experience with the Cloud. Respondents reported to make the most use of the Internet at home, spending an average of 7 and a quarter hour per week on the Internet (M = 7.25, SD = 9.36). Next, comes work with a little over 4 hours a week on average (M = 4.14, SD = 8.75), followed by about half an hour at school (M = 0.56, SD = 2.99), and lastly respondents spend some time elsewhere on the Internet (M = 0.13, SD = 1.37). When asked whether respondents had heard of cloud computing before, 23.5 % of respondents (N = 534) reported that they had not heard of cloud computing before and 76.5 % (N = 1736) of respondents reported that they had. Of these latter respondents, 32.7 % (N = 742) indicated that they had often heard of cloud computing and the remaining 43.8 % (N = 994) had only heard of cloud computing incidentally. While 23.5 % of respondents reported not to have heard of cloud

Table 1. Sample demographics and comparison Dutch population*

		Sample	Dutch population
Gender	N	2,270	16,779,575
	Male	51.23 %	49.51 %
	Female	48.76 %	50.51 %
Age	N	2,140	12,908,802
	20 to 40	30.65 %	31.92 %
	41 to 60	50.33 %	46.20 %
	61 to 80	17.66 %	16.43 %
	81 and older	1.36 %	5.44 %
Education	N	1,751	10,883,000
	ISCED 0-1	4.00 %	8.18 %
	ISCED 2	16.33 %	22.54 %
	ISCED 3-4	41.01 %	40.71 %
	ISCED 5-8	38.66 %	28.57 %

*Age groups are based on categories used by Statistics Netherlands (Data for Age and Gender from 2013, Education from 2013). Since we did not include respondents younger than 16, we could not accurately compare our sample with the Dutch population in the age range 0 to 20. We therefore only included respondents 20-years-old and older for comparison with the Dutch population. Individuals older than 65 were excluded for education comparison as Statistics Netherlands only provides information on education for the population in the age of 15 to 65. An explanation of the ISCED levels for education can be found in [50].

computing, only 14.1 % (319) does not make use of any cloud Services. The other 85.9 % (N = 1951) indicated to make use of at least one cloud service presented to them. In appendix D all cloud services are listed with the number of respondents that make use of them. Hotmail (44.7 %, N = 993), Gmail (51.4 %, N = 1166), and Facebook (57,3 %, N = 1300) are the cloud service used by the most respondents.

Expectations of the Cloud. Expectations of cloud services can be both negative and positive. We asked respondents to respond to the following item: cloud computing comes with both benefits and concerns. What do you think about the balance between benefits and concerns? Response categories were 'the benefits outweigh the concerns', 'the concerns and benefits are about equal', and 'the concerns outweigh the benefits'. This way we were able to distinguish between cloud enthusiasts (i.e., individuals that expect the benefits to outweigh the concerns), from cloud neutrals (i.e., individuals that expect the benefits and concerns to be about equal), and cloud worriers (i.e., individuals that expect the concerns to outweigh the benefits) in our sample. We found that 28.1 % (N = 638) of our sample were cloud enthusiasts and expect the benefits to outweigh the concerns. The majority of 41.8 % (N = 948), however, was cloud neutral, expecting the benefits and concerns to be in balance, and the remaining 30.1 % (N = 684) were cloud worriers, who consider the concerns to outweigh the benefits. One sample t-test between percentages showed that there were significantly more cloud neutrals than either cloud worriers, t(2,269) = 6.64, p < .001, and cloud enthusiasts, t(2,269) = 7.91, p < .001. The number of cloud enthusiasts and worriers did not differ significantly, t(2,269) = 1.25, p = .212.

Next we investigated the concerns and benefits people may experience with regard to the cloud in more detail. Seven items assessed whether respondents expected cloud services to yield benefits for society. Responses were on a 5-point Likert Scale with (1) Completely disagree and (5) Completely agree. Reliability analysis supported combining these items into a single scale *Benefits* (α = .81). The remaining 23 items addressed general cloud concerns, data security concerns, and legal concerns. Responses were on a 5-point Likert Scale with (1) Completely disagree and (5) Completely agree. Factor Analysis with Varimax rotation appeared to verify the existence of the three scales at first glance. Based on the criteria of eigenvalues > 1, the items regarding general, data security, and cloud concerns were distinguished in three separate scales. However, factor analysis did not provide any support to distinguish between different types of concerns and instead all items were combined into a single total concern scale. Descriptive analysis showed that respondents generally shared the concerns presented to them as they scored above average (M = 3.55, SD = .74; on a scale of 1 to 5). Looking at the individual items, presented in Table 2 (see Appendix), we see that almost none of the items deviate far from the total average and each other with means ranging from 3.31 to 3.78. In other words, no specific concern appears to spring out in particular. Only the item concerning the possible incompatibility of the individuals' current data infrastructure with the requirements of the cloud instigated less concern among respondents (M = 3.01, SD = 1.07).

We subsequently looked at what benefits respondents associate with the cloud. In general, respondents did associate the cloud with the presented benefits (M = 3.35, SD = .62). Looking at the individual items, shown in Table 2b, we see that respondents appear to recognize several benefits more than others. Respondents mostly see the benefit of the cloud in the fact that it automatically organizes the backup of information (M = 3.54, SD = .92), it improves information sharing and collaboration (M = 3.92, SD = .82), and it makes more efficient use of hardware (M = 3.65, SD = .84). Respondents appear less convinced that the cloud has great beneficial effects on the economy (M = 3.11, SD = .93), allows for better security of information (M = 2.95, SD = .97), and provides individuals with more control over their personal information (M = 3.09, SD = .98).

Trust and Responsibility. In order to assess the trust and sense of responsibility, respondents have in relation to cloud services, we asked them to fill in two general trust scales, and indicate the level of trust and responsibility they place in relevant parties. The results showed that respondents were generally more inclined to believe that others are to be trusted and would be fair to them, scoring a 6.02 (SD = 2.12) and a 6.04 (SD = 2.22) respectively on a ten point scale with higher scores indicating more trust in others. Next, we look at the trust and responsibility respondents assign to the handling and supervision of their data in the cloud.

Table 3 provides an overview of how much respondents trusted the government, legal authorities, branch organizations, certification agencies, independent consumer organizations, and individual cloud providers with supervising their data in the cloud.

The results show that respondents assign most trust to legal authorities (M = 3.32, SD = .95), but the least trust in the individual cloud providers (M = 2.63, SD = .94).

Table 3. Assigned trust for supervising data in the cloud.

	Mean (S.D.)
The government	2.96 (1.04)
Legal authorities	3.32 (.95)
Branch organizations	2.90 (.90)
Certification agencies	3.04 (.92)
Independent consumer organizations	3.20 (.94)
Individual Cloud providers	2.63 (.94)

Table 4 provides an overview of how respondents ranked individual users, employers, cloud providers, independent supervisors, or legal authorities in terms of responsibility concerning the appropriate use of their data in the cloud. The table shows that the test statistics for all five c^2-analysis are significant. We can therefore reject the null hypothesis and conclude that there are statistically significant differences in how respondents rank the level of responsibility of individual users, employers, cloud providers, independent supervisors, and legal authorities. Investigating Table 4 in more detail shows that almost half of the respondents (48.7 %) rank the individual user as most responsible while a fifth of respondents (18.9 %) rank individual users as least responsible. Only 4.7 % of respondents consider employers to be most responsible and only 6.4 % consider independent supervisors to be most responsible. Over half of the respondents rank cloud providers as most responsible (29.4 %) or as second most responsible (27.1 %). Finally, over half of the respondents rank legal authorities as least responsible (32.6 %) or second least responsible (23.3 %).

Table 4. Assigned responsibility for appropriate use of data in the cloud***

N = 2209	Most responsibility <—> Least responsibility					
	5	4	3	2	1	c2
Individual user	1076	285	238	192	418	1202.57***
	48.7 %	12.9 %	10.8 %	8.7 %	18.9 %	
Employers	103	521	417	569	599	367.96***
	4.7 %	23.6 %	18.9 %	25.8 %	27.1 %	
Cloud providers	650	598	491	235	235	352.42***
	29.4 %	27.1 %	22.2 %	10.6 %	10.6 %	
Independent supervisors	142	510	621	699	237	531.32***
	6.4 %	23.1 %	28.1 %	31.6 %	10.7 %	
Legal authorities	238	295	442	514	720	329.77***
	10.8 %	13.4 %	20.0 %	23.3 %	32.6 %	

*** Individuals were asked to rank the options in order of most responsibility to least, assigning a score of 1 to 5 to each option.

Actual Behaviour. Not only did we ask about people's concerns also we inquired about their actual behaviour to cope with their previously declared cloud concerns. Inspecting the total scales, it can be concluded that respondents generally implement actual coping behaviours with respect to their concerns (M = 3.30, SD = .70). Looking at the individual items, shown in Table 5, we see that respondents are relatively less likely to check the terms and conditions before subscribing (M = 3.26, SD = 1.08), to store their information in one country only (M = 3.19, SD = .90), to check the privacy policies of the cloud service they use (M = 3.18, SD = 1.07), to ask others whether a certain cloud provider is reliable (M = 3.10, SD = 1.07). Instead, respondents were more likely to make use of certified cloud providers only (M = 3.57, SD = .95), and do not share sensitive information in the cloud (M = 3.77, SD = 1.01).

The depicted results are mainly descriptive yet give good insight whether the general public indeed has concerns, what these concerns might be, whom they trust and whom they deem responsible for the appropriate handling of data in the cloud.

Table 5. Actual coping behaviour

	M	S.D.	N
I ask others (e.g. friends/family) whether a certain cloud provider is reliable	3.10	1.07	1628
I check the terms and conditions before I subscribe to a cloud service	3.26	1.08	1752
I check the privacy policies of the cloud services I use	3.18	1.07	1710
I make sure not to store sensitive personal information in the Cloud	3.77	1.01	1755
I only make use of certified cloud providers	3.57	.95	1643
My information is stored in one country only	3.19	.90	1601
Actual Coping Behaviour Scale (Total)	3.30	.70	1403

5 Cloud's Social Implications and the Need for Accountability

In the previous sections we have argued that cloud computing is not just a new innovation like the tablet or any other regular consumer good, but is an information and communication technology innovation with a deep impact on society. Cloud computing has changed and still is changing our society's organization. Moreover, cloud computing has enabled the increased control and controlling capabilities by governments by accessing public and business data in the cloud. In order to stimulate the responsible innovation in cloud and future Internet services it is of importance to elicit potential risks and public issues with respect to the cloud's impact on society. These risks and public issues not only refer to technical, but also to social, ethical and legal issues. Moreover there is a need to govern the identified risks and public issues in order to warrant the sustainability of the cloud ecosystem.

Within cloud ecosystems accountability might be perceived as the solution in governing the responsible behaviour with respect tot data in the cloud. Accountability, especially in relation to responsible behaviour, stems from the public sector and subsequently relates to public issues. Nevertheless, this type of accountability now has entered the private cloud sector too. Cloud's impact on society by reshaping its organisation and controversies like the Snowden files are reasons to call for accountability to society at large. From a normative perspective cloud no longer is a consumer good, but has become a consumer good with public issues.

In contrast, the survey results seem to imply that the general public is not concerned much with cloud computing, nor feels the need to address its concerns actively (see actual behaviour). Cloud is a widely accepted information technology model that can expect a seamless adoption. The majority of the respondents 85.9 % (N = 1951) already use at least one cloud service presented to them of which social media services were used most. Moreover, the biggest part of the sample indicated to be either a cloud enthusiast 28.1 % (N = 638) or have a neutral feeling towards the cloud 41.8 % (N = 948). Only, 30.1 % (N = 684) are labelled as cloud worriers. In line with these findings the public assigns the most responsibility for the appropriate use of data in the cloud to the individual user. This response is in line with the perception of cloud as a consumer good.

Only the trust and responsibility results might imply that there is a need and desirability for external oversight by the in order to safeguard responsible behaviour and could plea for accountability in the cloud system. While the public generally assigns responsibility to the individual user, it also assigns most trust to legal authorities and the least trust in the individual cloud providers. These findings are in line with findings by Sjöberg and Fromm, demonstrating that individual cloud consumers (or the population at large) mainly see the benefits of cloud computing and are only to some extend aware of related risks [51].

Does this discrepancy between the normative frame in the former sections and the depicted results in the latter then demonstrate inconsistencies in the normative frame? The survey results mainly provide the picture of a consumer good for individuals, while the normative considerations plea for the public interest at stake due to cloud computing's impact on society. Some caution might be needed before drawing the conclusion that the normative considerations do not seem to hold. The survey results do indicate that currently the public is not concerned about the implications of cloud for society. Cloud computing simply is not perceived as a life altering technology accompanied with risks as genetic modified foods or xenotransplantation have been in the past. According to Warren the public most likely tends to focus on other contemporary problems that are deemed more threatening to the individual and/or society [52]. Other explanations might be that the displayed lack of interest might be caused by a general feeling of trust in the proper handling of data in the cloud, or it might be the knowledge asymmetry and the lack of knowledge on what the cloud is and why and how it should be assessed. New controversies like PRISM as well as the growth in cybercrime might, however, change this momentum of cloud computing's acceptance.

However previous research and events also demonstrate that the public sometimes realizes that public issues are at stake long after the wide spread adoption of the technology or product. An example is the use of diethylstilbestrol (DES), a medication that was used to treat morning sickness of pregnant women. Only after years of use DES was taken off national drug formularies due to the increased risk of the mother's child to rare forms of cancer and reproductive deformity due to the mother's use of DES. Another consumer good that first was widely accepted and later on perceived as having a negative societal impact is the cigarette. Cigarette smoking nowadays is related to health consequences with a negative effect on society, i.e. health costs and economic productivity.

The need for accountability might not be uttered by the general public, the business context of cloud computing does demonstrate some indications towards the need for increased transparency, responsibility and accountability. For example, Microsoft has issued several Law Enforcement Request Reports since March 2013. Microsoft explicitly states: "Microsoft receives legal demands for customer data from law enforcement agencies around the world. In March 2013, as part of our commitment to increased transparency, Microsoft began publishing details of the number of demands we receive each year in our Law Enforcement Requests Report and clear documentation of our established practices in responding to government legal demands for customer data" [53]. Similarly Apple states: "We believe that our customers have a right to understand how their personal information is handled, and we consider it our responsibility to provide them with the best privacy protections available. Apple has prepared this report on the requests we receive from governments seeking information about individual users or devices in the interest of transparency for our customers around the world" [54]. These statements indicate businesses' concerns with keeping governmental bodies like the NSA outside the data entrusted to them in order to maintain not only good business-to-business relations, but also a good reputation in the larger public. While cloud computing is not a new emerging technology like genetic modified foods, xenotransplantation or nanotechnology, it might still be considered as an innovation that needs public debate and accountability to society at large.

The facilitation of the public debate on cloud as well as accountability relations is something that does not usually origin from developments within the private sector. The private sector is less likely to seek public debate then for example scientists. However, since accountability already is introduced in the cloud ecosystem it might open up further public debate on cloud's social implications and the further need for responsible governance. Importantly, accountability in the private sector, specifically in the cloud market, is not a notion that should be used rhetorically or as a fashion accessory. Accountability as in the responsible behaviour with data in the cloud has deep implications for the relationship between cloud providers and the public at large, between data controllers and data processors, between business cloud users and (lay) end-users. Accountability is based upon certain ways of knowing and certain kinds of knowledge. Also, accountability requires the empowerment of participants who in turn require transparency as a condition of critical public discussion.

Despite the big promises of accountability in the cloud, some general warnings do remain. First, if the accountability process is to be trusted, it too must be transparent and open to accountability procedures. Even third parties or supervisory authorities need to account for their actions, results and intentions, to the wider public. Second, it is important to be aware of the accountability paradox; more accountability arrangements do not necessarily produce better governance. If the regulatory implementation merely adds administrative burdens without improving effectiveness, it will fail to deliver its stated objective. Third, accountability to the public is not straightforward, either in enhancing transparency of systems without generating more data sharing or in encouraging participation in the future direction of system development without undermining security. Fourth, scholars like Jasanoff warn for democratic participation as currently operationalized, it entails the wrong representation of the public and its views [34]. Questions to ask are to what information about organisations, such as cloud vendors and cloud service providers, do communities have rights? And, to what extent does voicing concerns without a clear consequence make sense? Subsequently there is a need for reclaiming the turf of democracy: who should be served by innovation and for what purposes. This also goes for cloud computing.

We conclude that society as a whole has an interest in accountability for cloud providers. Cloud computing is a technology that potentially has a significant impact on society. The way we structure work and leisure may change as a result of cloud services and cloud arrangements. Moreover reflection is needed on the governmental access to data in the cloud. Society thus has an interest in the responsible development of the innovations cloud and future Internet services. Accountability and the associated mechanisms and tools allow inspection of what happens in the cloud, not only for individuals, but indirectly also for society at large.

Acknowledgments.   The research leading to these results has received funding from the European Union Seventh Framework Programme (FP7/2007-2013) under grant agreement no: 317550 The Cloud Accountability Project (A4Cloud).

Appendix

Table 2. Means, standard deviation and number of respondents for each item regarding Cloud related concerns or benefits**.

2a. Cloud concerns	M	S.D.	N
Choosing reliable cloud providers	3.66	1.00	1532
My cloud provider's use of third parties for storage of my information	3.78	.97	1535
The existence of the services I use in a few years' time	3.44	1.02	1469
My options if a cloud service does not perform as promised	3.50	1.00	1473
The constant changes that cloud providers bring in their service offerings and terms and conditions	3.55	.98	1470
The potential loss of control over my information	3.70	1.04	1573
The availability of the cloud service (e.g. server down time for a prolonged period) for my own use	3.52	1.01	1528
My current data infrastructure's incompatibility with the Cloud's infrastructural requirements	3.01	1.07	1501
The low level of security	3.53	1.04	1406
Whether I can get my information out of the Cloud (e.g. customer data)	3.31	1.10	1554

(*Continued*)

Table 2. (*Continued*)

2a. Cloud concerns	M	S.D.	N
Other people might steal my information (e.g. passwords, and pictures)	3.76	.99	1615
The cloud provider uses or sells my information without my consent	3.71	1.03	1600
That my government will access my information	3.63	1.03	1603
That a foreign government will access my information	3.71	1.02	1596
That I have not properly labelled my information as sensitive when I should have	3.78	.99	1596
Governments make use of the Cloud to gain control over individuals	3.66	1.03	1593
That existing law does not sufficiently protect my personal information in the Cloud	3.74	.96	1468
There is no legal authority on the Internet whom I could turn to, if I felt that my rights were violated	3.72	.97	1460
About which country's law is applicable to my information when using a cloud service	3.77	.95	1431
About the lower security demands for information storage in the countries where my information may be stored	3.76	.96	1441
That cloud providers can disable my accounts or services	3.65	.99	1481
That I can insufficiently negotiate and customize contracts with Cloud service providers	3.56	1.00	1430
About the lack of clarity about who is responsible for the protection of my information	3.76	.96	1474
Concerns (Total)	3.55	.74	1052
2b. Benefits	M	S.D.	N
The Cloud has great beneficial effects on the economy	3.11	.93	1365
The Cloud allows for better security of information	2.95	.97	1437
The Cloud provides individuals with more control over their personal information	3.09	.98	1485
The Cloud automatically organizes the backup of information	3.54	.92	1479
The Cloud improves information sharing and collaboration	3.92	.82	1562
The Cloud makes more efficient use of hardware	3.65	.84	1469
The Cloud limits the necessity of fast hardware or allows the use of cheap hardware	3.32	.89	1396
Benefits (Total)	3.35	.62	1191

** The number of respondents varies for each item due to missing values

References

1. Fenn, J.: Inside the Hype Cycle: What's Hot and What's Not in 2009 (2009). http://my.gartner.com/it/content/1101800/1101817/august12_hype_cycle_final_jfenn.pdf
2. Jasanoff, S.: In the democracies of DNA: ontological uncertainty and political order in three states. New Genet. Soc. **24**, 139–156 (2005)

3. Marris, C., Wynne, B., Simmons, P., Weldon, S.: Public perceptions of agricultural biotechnologies in Europe. Final report of the PABE research project funded by the Commission of European Communities. Contract Number FAIR CT98-3844 DG12-SSMI (2001)
4. Mulkay, M.: The Embryo Research Debate: Science and the Politics of Reproduction. Cambridge University Press, Cambridge (1997)
5. Beck, U.: From industrial society to the risk society: questions of survival, social structure and ecological enlightenment. Theory Cult. Soc. **9**, 97–123 (1992). doi:10.1177/026327692009001006
6. Hood, C.: Accountability and transparency: siamese twins, matching parts, awkward couple? West Eur. Polit. **33**, 989–1009 (2010). doi:10.1080/01402382.2010.486122
7. Raab, C.: The meaning of the word "accountability" in the information privacy context. In: Managing Privacy through Accountability, p. 15 (2012)
8. Macoubrie, J.: Nanotechnology: public concerns, reasoning and trust in government. Public Underst. Sci. **15**, 221–241 (2006)
9. Stoker, G.: Governance as theory: five propositions. Int. Soc. Sci. J. **50**, 17–28 (1998)
10. Renn, O., Klinke, A., Asselt, M.: Coping with complexity, uncertainty and ambiguity in risk governance: a synthesis. AMBIO **40**, 231–246 (2011). doi:10.1007/s13280-010-0134-0
11. Alnemr, R.: Reputation Object Representation Model for Enabling Reputation Interoperability. Potsdam University, Potsdam (2011)
12. Svantesson, D., Clarke, R.: Privacy and consumer risks in cloud computing. Comput. Law Secur. Rev. **26**, 391–397 (2010)
13. Almorsy, M., Grundy, J., Müller, I.: An analysis of the cloud computing security problem. Presented at the Proceedings of APSEC 2010 Cloud Workshop, Sydney, Australia, 30 November 2010
14. KPMG: Embracing the cloud. Global cloud survey (2011)
15. KPMG: The cloud takes shape. Global cloud survey (2013)
16. Niezen, M., Prüfer, P., Leenes, R.E., Nuñez, D., Agudo, I., Fernandez Gago, C., Koulouris, T., Alnemr, R.: A4Cloud D:B-4.1 Interim report. Tilburg University, TILT (2013)
17. De Oliviera, A., Garaga, A., Martucci, L.A., Felici, M., Alnemr, R., Stefanatou, D., Niezen, M., Fernandez, C., Nuñez, D., Hasnain, B., Vranaki, A., Cayirci, E.: D:C-6.1: Risk and trust accountability in the cloud. SAP (2014)
18. ENISA: Cloud Computing: Benefits, risks and recommendation for information security (2009)
19. Wright, D.: The state of the art in privacy impact assessment. Comput. Law Secur. Rev. **28**, 54–61 (2012)
20. Purtova, N., Kosta, E., Koops, B.J.: Laws and reputation for digital health. In: Requirements Engineering for Digital Health and Care. Springer, New York (2014)
21. Rip, A., Misa, T.J., Schot, J.: Managing Technology in Society. Pinter Publishers London, New York (1995)
22. Castells, M.: Informationalism, networks, and the network society: a theoretical blueprint. In: Castells, M. (ed.) The Network Society: A Cross-Cultural Perspective, pp. 3–45. Edward Elgar, Cheltenham (2004)
23. Buyya, R., Yeo, C.S., Venugopal, S., Broberg, J., Brandic, I.: Cloud computing and emerging IT platforms: vision, hype, and reality for delivering computing as the 5th utility. Future Gener. Comput. Syst. **25**, 599–616 (2009). doi:10.1016/j.future.2008.12.001
24. Smith, M.: Concerns about surveillance 'fanciful,' British official says. CNN (2013). http://edition.cnn.com/2013/06/09/world/nsa-data-mining/index.html?hpt=hp_t1
25. Jain, V.: The Snowden effect, changing the course of cloud security. PandoDaily (2013). http://pando.com/2013/09/11/the-snowden-effect-changing-the-course-of-cloud-security/

26. Marshall, C., Tang, J.C.: That syncing feeling: early user experiences with the cloud, p. 544. ACM Press (2012). doi:10.1145/2317956.2318038
27. Leenes, R., Oomen, I.: The role of citizens: what can Dutch, Flemish and English students teach us about privacy? In: Gutwirth, S., Poullet, Y., Hert, P., Terwangne, C., Nouwt, S. (eds.) Reinventing Data Protection?, pp. 139–153. Springer Netherlands, Dordrecht (2009)
28. Beldad, A.D.: Trust and Information Privacy Concerns in Electronic Government. University of Twente, Enschede (2011)
29. Hoffman, D.L., Novak, T.P., Peralta, M.: Building consumer trust online. Commun. ACM 42, 80–85 (1999). doi:10.1145/299157.299175
30. Olivero, N., Lunt, P.: Privacy versus willingness to disclose in e-commerce exchanges: the effect of risk awareness on the relative role of trust and control. J. Econ. Psychol. 25, 243–262 (2004). doi:10.1016/S0167-4870(02)00172-1
31. Wynne, B.: Elephants in the rooms where publics encounter science?: A response to Darrin Durant, Accounting for expertise: Wynne and the autonomy of the lay public. Public Underst. Sci. 17, 21–33 (2008)
32. Beck, U.: The terrorist threat world risk society revisited. Theory Cult. Soc. 19, 39–55 (2002)
33. Jasanoff, S.: The Fifth Branch: Science Advisers as Policymakers. Harvard University Press, Cambridge (2009)
34. Jasanoff, S.: Governing innovation. Presented at the Knowledge in Question–A Symposium on Interrogating Knowledge and Questioning Science (2009)
35. Guston, D.H., Fisher, E., Grunwald, A., Owen, R., Swierstra, T., van der Burg, S.: Responsible innovation: motivations for a new journal. J. Responsible Innov. 1, 1–8 (2014)
36. Bovens, M.: Analysing and assessing public accountability: a conceptual framework (2006)
37. Bovens, M.: Two concepts of accountability: accountability as a virtue and as a mechanism. West Eur. Polit. 33, 946–967 (2010). doi:10.1080/01402382.2010.486119
38. Bovens, M.: Analysing and assessing public accountability: a conceptual framework. European Governance Papers (EUROGOV) No. C-06-01 (2006)
39. Bovens, M.A.P., Schillemans, T.: Handboek Publieke Verantwoording. LEMMA, Den Haag (2009)
40. Mulgan, R.: "Accountability": an ever-expanding concept? Public Adm. 78, 555–573 (2000). doi:10.1111/1467-9299.00218
41. Hughes, O.E.: Public Management and Administration: An Introduction, 4th edn. England Palgrave Macmillan, Basingstoke (2012)
42. Romzek, B., Dubnick, M.: Accountability in the public sector: lessons from the Challenger tragedy. Public Adm. Rev. 47, 227–238 (1987)
43. Romzek, B.S., Dubnick, M.J.: Issues of accountability in flexible personnel systems. In: Ingraham, P.W., Romzek, B.S. (eds.) New Paradigms for Government, pp. 263–294. Jossey-Bass, San Francisco (1994)
44. Koenig-Archibugi, M.: Transnational corporations and public accountability. Gov. Oppos. 39, 234–259 (2004)
45. Pearson, S.: Toward accountability in the cloud. In: IEEE Internet Computing, pp. 2–7 (2011)
46. Bennett, C.J.: International privacy standards: can accountability be adequate? Priv. Laws Bus. Int. 106, 21–23 (2010)
47. Bennett, C.J.: The accountability approach to privacy and data protection: assumptions and caveats. In: Guagnin, D., et al. (eds.) Managing Privacy Through Accountability, pp. 33–48. Palgrave MacMillan, Basingstoke (2012)

48. The Working Party on the protection of individuals with regard to the processing of personal data: Article 29 Data Protection Working Party, Opinion 3/2010 on the concept of accountability. 00062/10/EN WP 173 (2010)
49. Gray, R.: Accounting and environmentalism: an exploration of the challenge of gently accounting for accountability, transparency and sustainability. Account. Organ. Soc. **17**, 399–425 (1992)
50. Organisation for Economic Co-operation and Development (OECD): Classifying educational programmes: Manual for ISCED-97 implementation in OECD countries (1999)
51. Sjoberg, L., Fromm, J.: Information technology risks as seen by the public. Risk Anal. **21**, 427–442 (2001)
52. Warren, M.E.: Citizen participation and democratic deficits: considerations from the perspective of democratic theory. In: De Bardeleben, J., Pammett, J.H. (eds.) Activating the Citizen: Dilemmas of Participation in Europe and Canada, pp. 17–40. Palgrave Macmillan, New York (2009)
53. Microsoft: Law Enforcement Requests Report (2014). http://www.microsoft.com/about/corporatecitizenship/en-us/reporting/transparency/
54. Apple: Report on Government Information Requests (2013). https://www.apple.com/pr/pdf/131105reportongovinforequests3.pdf

Legal Aspects of Cloud Accountability

Brian Dziminski and Niamh Christina Gleeson[(✉)]

School of Law, Centre for Commercial Law Studies,
Queen Mary University of London, London, UK
n.gleeson@qmul.ac.uk

Abstract. This paper explores the legal aspects of Cloud accountability which are being examined in great detail in the Cloud Accountability Project. This paper first provides an overview of the basic legal framework of the US and the EU, addresses the lawmaking process, and the impact and enforcement of jurisdiction. The primary laws within the data protection framework are then further explored, as such regulations have the greatest impact on the Cloud, Cloud providers, Cloud customers, and, ultimate, Cloud users. This paper then explores the role of contracts in the Cloud. Finally, all of the analysis is pulled together in discussing how the Cloud Accountability Project is addressing these legal aspects and how such aspects should influence Cloud actors, especially Cloud providers, in their policies and legal governance.

Keywords: Cloud accountability project · A4cloud · Cloud computing law · Data protection · Cloud contracts · Cloud legal aspects

1 Introduction

An important part of the Cloud Accountability Project (A4Cloud) is the analysis of the legal and regulatory requirements that dictate how actors in the Cloud ought to behave. Such legal requirements range from terms and conditions when a user utilizes a Cloud service through contracts between businesses and Cloud providers to the various regulations, including the Data Protection Directive and e-Privacy Directive, which govern the interaction between Cloud actors. Because of the importance of those legal requirements, and in particular the constraints they impose, A4Cloud has placed a large focus on researching those legal issues, making recommendations as to future legislation and Cloud contracts, implementing such requirements into the tools being developed by A4Cloud, and providing guidance for all Cloud actors as to such legal implications. Specifically, papers have already and/or will in the future be published within A4Cloud on the evolving data protection laws, the role of standard contracts, the role of data protection audits, and the other legal and regulatory dependencies impacting the Cloud.

It is thus very difficult, especially against the vast backdrop of the legal aspects impacting Cloud Computing, to provide an all-encompassing overview of such legal and regulatory issues in a two-hour lecture and likewise within a small paper, where there are advanced degree programs with dozens of hours of lectures dedicated to these studies and multiple books and articles delving into the intricate details of the legal

M. Felici and C. Fernández-Gago (Eds.): A4Cloud 2014, LNCS 8937, pp. 226–247, 2015.
DOI: 10.1007/978-3-319-17199-9_10

aspects of the Cloud. Nevertheless, that was our task in the lecture and our task here in this paper. In doing so, we provide what is only a glimpse into some of the more important legal considerations which are being examined in A4Cloud and those using or operating within the Cloud should be most concerned.

We begin this analysis with a general overview of the lawmaking process throughout the world, with a primary focus on the EU and the US, the two primary jurisdictions impacting cloud providers and users. We then discuss the equally important issue of jurisdiction and choice of law, and how such issues impact Cloud users, customers and providers. Next we move on to what is rightfully the main focus of A4Cloud and the largest set of laws impacting the Cloud by examining the various data protection and privacy laws which impact use of the Cloud. Fourthly, we examine the role of contracts in the Cloud, an equally important legal aspect of the Cloud. Finally, we pull all of the foregoing analysis together and briefly how such issues impact the Cloud and the recommendations which A4Cloud had for legal governance, policy framework and increased accountability in the Cloud.

2   A General Overview of the Law

As referenced above, we live in a world of very complex laws. Worse yet (or better, depending on the perspective and outcome), those laws are constantly being revised and compliance with such laws one month may not mean compliance the next. Perhaps even worse, courts apply such laws inconsistently (because of the inherent difficulty of interpreting text, laws oftentimes written in a vague manner, and technology surpassing the original intent of many laws) leaving those subject to the laws to oftentimes partake in a guessing game about what the laws really mean and how they will be applied in any given situation. And, what is perhaps the proverbial frosting on the cake, the nature of the Cloud, i.e. doing business across the internet and Cloud providers being able to provide services without physically being within a jurisdiction, adds a whole new layer to the legal quagmire of which laws apply in any given transaction.

In other words, the legal landscape as it applies to the Cloud is in many ways quite cloudy itself.

2.1   The Development of Modern Law

Nevertheless, we start with the basics. Most of the laws that govern the common law world today are rooted in the Magna Carta signed 800 years ago and the human rights laws derived from that charter. The Magna Carta was drafted and imposed upon King John of England to provide certain liberties to his subjects and for the King to accept that his will was not arbitrary, but rather that people could only be punished by the rule of law. From that document, many constitutions and lesser laws have followed, establishing the laws we know today, especially the human rights laws from which the data protection laws and privacy protections find their roots.

Flash forward eight centuries, and there are now 196 countries in our world, each with its own sets of law, and many of those having different laws within the country. Within those countries, there are two primary systems: common law and civil law.

Common law jurisdictions are generally uncodified, meaning that there is no comprehensive recitation of statutes or codes, and instead law is primarily developed through judicial decisions which establish legal precedent over time. On the other hand, civil law jurisdictions follow a system of law that is codified, meaning that such jurisdictions have comprehensive recitations of codes attempting to envision the potential application of those codes to different scenarios that courts must follow. In these jurisdictions judicial decisions are less important in future applications of the codified laws. Finally, within both systems, there are different sets of laws that primarily fall into private law (for our purposes, contract and torts are the most important subsections of private law, also referred to as civil law, but not to be confused with the civil law distinction discussed above) or public law (which also encompasses criminal laws, but for our purposes also contains such laws as data protection laws).

Law, whether common law or civil law, can ultimately be summed up in two basic concepts. The first is 'complicated.' As noted, there are currently 196 countries in our world, each with its own sets of law, and many of those having different laws within the country. And ultimately, each of those nations desires those laws to protect its citizens and therefore has an inherent interest in broadly applying those protections. For example, the United States has federal laws which will generally apply to any companies doing business within the United States, i.e. targeting their activities to U.S. citizens residing in the U.S. Under that federal law system, there are hundreds of District Courts interpreting and applying those laws, thirteen Circuit Court of Appeals serving as appellate courts for appeals from those District Courts, and ultimately, the United States Supreme Court also reviewing various cases from the Circuit Court of Appeals, especially when those courts decide similar issues differently or when laws are deemed to be unconstitutional. And that is just the federal level of the United States. Concurrently with those federal laws, there are fifty states, each of which has their own set of laws. And, while many of those laws mirror the federal laws and are similar throughout the fifty states, there are nevertheless enough differences to trip up even the most savvy of businesses, users, and, oftentimes, even lawyers. Those fifty states also have dozens, sometimes hundreds, of courts, their own appellate courts, and their own courts of final jurisdiction similar to the United States Supreme Court, applying such laws, oftentimes again with little to no indication how the ultimate determinations as to any given law will be decided.

In the European Union (EU), which is the primary focus of A4Cloud, there are 28 different member states and a complicated legal framework of laws which directly apply within those states (such as Regulations), other laws which Member States are obligated to enact, but with their own interpretation (such as Directives), and other areas of the law where Member States are free to enact their own legislation or stricter legislation than otherwise required in certain areas, oftentimes with little to no guidance from the EU and such laws being solely reserved to the Member States.

The ultimate conclusion from the foregoing is it is nearly impossible for a cloud provider to comply with all of the laws that may be applicable, especially when many of those laws are in conflict. Thus, again and to say the least, laws are complicated.

The second concept to describe our international laws is "It Depends." Ask any lawyer or legal scholar a question as to a hypothetical or real situation and how the decision of law will be applied, and you most certainly will be met with a response in the vein of "it depends." Lawyers will ask more questions about the facts, want more details, and even when you have all those answers, the lawyer will generally respond that the result will depend, whether it be on other undiscovered facts, the laws which might or might not apply, the "other side of the story," how a court applies the law, and, in some jurisdictions and/or cases, how a jury views and decides the facts in question. This can be very frustrating for anyone having to deal with such laws, especially where there are serious implications in regard to such legal compliance. This becomes even more heightened in the Cloud, as not only are Cloud actors faced with trying to decide which of all the possible complicated laws they should comply with, but are then faced with uncertainty as to the application of those laws. This leads to many unintended consequences, including many companies consciously deciding to not comply with certain laws (generally making a risk assessment of where they might face jurisdiction, discussed in greater detail below, or minimal sanctions or penalties) or companies deciding to not to do business at all in some jurisdictions. But, the most common result is companies do what they can to comply in spirit in order to still conduct business, but hopefully avoid any consequences for any non-compliance with any given law.

2.2   How Laws are Generally Made

Most laws generally arise from human rights, social norms, economic necessities, and the necessary protection of society and citizens. How such laws are made in any given country or state may vary greatly, but most democratic states follow systems similar to that of the EU or US, the two most important jurisdictions in our review of Cloud Computing law. As a project that is partially funded by the European Commission, A4Cloud is primarily focused on EU law, especially the Data Protection Directive and proposed Data Protection Regulation. However, many of the companies doing business in the EU are companies organized under US law and the contracts being utilized, and/ or terms and conditions of the use of such services is oftentimes governed by US law. Thus, examination of US law, at least in relevant part, is as equally important as many of the EU laws impacting the Cloud.

In the European Union, there are three main decision-making institutions involved in the law-making process: the European Parliament, the Council of the European Union, and the European Commission. Together, those three institutions produce the policies and laws that apply in varying degrees throughout the EU Member States depending on the type of law adopted. The process is very time-consuming, complicated, and oftentimes politically charged. One prime example is the data protection laws discussed in greater detail below and the ongoing attempt to adopt a Data Protection Regulation to replace the current Data Protection Directive. The difference between a Directive and a Regulation is an important one, especially with the current posture of the data protection Framework. A Directive is a law that each Member State must enact, but the Member State has discretion in how the law is made effective and generally such laws do not need to be enacted for many years after adoption. To the contrary, a Regulation is directly applicable and enforceable in all Member States. Thus, as seen below, the EU is attempting to transform the current Data Protection

Regulation. Attempts to reform EU Data Protection law have been ongoing for a few years now, and yet remain in a relatively early stage of the process and only complicated further by elections and changes in the European institutions noted above. Oftentimes this leads to legislation being scrapped or having to be taken back to an earlier stage to essentially restart the process.

In the United States, as we saw, there are laws enacted at both the federal level and at the state level. The federal law-making process consists of three branches of government in the legislative branch (Congress), executive branch (the President and federal administrative agencies), and the judicial branch (federal courts). In its simplest of functioning, the legislative branch enacts the laws, the executive branch applies the laws, and the judicial branch interprets the laws (which as a common law jurisdiction can supplement, refine, and/or even void enacted laws). Most of the fifty states follow a similar process in adopting their own laws. Like the EU process, the US lawmaking process is very time-consuming and politically charged.

2.3   Jurisdiction

The next major factor after understanding how the laws are made, and what those laws actually provide, is how and whether those laws will apply to persons and entities. This concept can be summarized as jurisdiction, which for our purposes includes what laws will apply to any given situation and where that dispute will be adjudicated, also known as venue. Such determinations can be as complicated as the lawmaking process itself and present two general questions in respect to the Cloud: (1) can a state apply its public law to a foreign business, and if so, when and under what circumstances; and (2) in a private dispute, which laws will apply and which Court has the power to adjudicate that dispute?

Overview of Jurisdiction. In respect to the first question, a state's laws always apply to those who are within the state's geographical territory. But it is common for laws also to apply to those outside the territory if their activities affect the state in some way. Extra-territorial public law jurisdiction is guided by two overriding principles. The first is comity, in that a state should not regulate an activity where it is more appropriate for another state to do so. The second is the effects doctrine, in that a state may regulate a foreign activity which has effects in its territory. That brings us back to the basic underlying problem with the Cloud – when and where is it appropriate for a state to regulate a Cloud provider? Answering those questions leads to more questions, some of which are answered and addressed below in further examining some of the rules and regulations in respect to jurisdiction. More notably and quite problematic, is that when states are perceived to have overstepped their bounds, such excessive authority claims by states can lead to problems such as legal compliance becoming even more difficult, if not impossible, to be exercised in the future by the state; it can foster a culture of evasion by businesses and citizens of not only the laws in question, but also other laws; it can dilute the otherwise normative effect of law (again, even with other laws which were not originally the subject of the excessive authority claim); and, ultimately, it can create a conflict between states (which has been seen to some degree between the US and the EU in respect to the Data Protection Directive and some of the restrictions therein in regard to transborder transfers of data, discussed below). Again, all of these problems are especially common in the Cloud based on the nature of being able to do business over the Cloud and not having to otherwise be physically located within any given state to do so. As seen below, the Data Protection Directive purportedly answers that question in respect to EU Member States' governance of data protection issues, though it again raises more questions and the answers may not be as clear as they first seem.

EU Jurisdiction. The EU has three main regulations when it comes to the assertion of jurisdiction. The first is the Brussels Regulation, which generally applies to consumer contracts and provides that a consumer may sue within his or her own jurisdiction, regardless of what the contract otherwise states. The second is the Rome I Regulation, which decides which state's law applies to contracts, and for most situations provides that the law of a consumer's residence will apply if the merchant has directed its activities to that state, but that a choice of law provision contained within a contract is enforceable if it does not derogate from any protections provided under the consumer's national law. Finally, the Rome II Regulation applies in respect to torts (a civil wrong not otherwise controlled by a contract) and generally provides that the applicable law will be that of the state where the harm occurred. Though these regulations provide some semblance of clarity as to the exercise of jurisdiction, they are not always clear-cut. It is usually only possible to work out how they apply after the problem has arisen, rather than in advance, and difficulties can arise in answering questions like what constitutes a merchant directing their activities to a state and what constitutes harm in some cases and determining where that harm 'occurs.'

US Jurisdiction. In the United States, there are two types of jurisdiction that must be present for a federal court to exercise jurisdiction and most states follow similar principles in regard to the exercise of jurisdiction under state constitutions and laws. The first is subject matter jurisdiction, meaning that either some federal law specifically applies or that a dispute is between two citizens of different states, or a different state and different country. The second is personal jurisdiction, meaning a party must have availed itself to the protection of the laws of the U.S. and have minimum contacts with the jurisdiction in question, generally a specific state. In respect to the Cloud, the decision and test provided in *Zippo Manufacturing Co. v. Zippo Dot Com, Inc.* [1] remains rather instructive. The court in the *Zippo* case held that courts should apply a sliding scale where purely passive operators will not be subject to personal jurisdiction, whereas active websites (similar to the targeting test of the Rome I Regulation in the EU) will be subject to jurisdiction. This test, while not binding on other courts as it was decided by a Pennsylvania District Court and therefore has no impact outside of that court, has nevertheless been widely accepted in reviewing situations involving internet companies, web companies, and now the evolution into the Cloud. However, as can readily be recognized, most Cloud companies will fall somewhere in the middle, leading to a complicated and fact-intensive analysis all leading back to the answer of "it depends" discussed above.

Final Thoughts Regarding the Law, the Lawmaking Process and Jurisdiction.
This overview was not intended to scare the reader and make one avoid the Cloud
altogether. Rather, this overview introduces some of the basic concepts of law which
Cloud actors should consider and be aware of in conducting business and are which
strong building blocks in looking at some of the issues below in respect to data
protection laws and Cloud contracts. Nevertheless, as seen, some of these concepts are
quite scary and Cloud actors should proceed with caution and diligence in undertaking
business in the Cloud to ensure proper compliance. Dealing with these concepts will be
explored in greater detail in Sect. 5 in discussing effective legal governance and
accountability from a legal perspective, a concept being further explored by A4Cloud
later this year and next year in much greater detail.

3 Data Protection Laws

As noted in the Introduction, A4Cloud is most concerned with two legal areas: data
protection laws and contracts. Generally speaking, the approach to data protection varies
around the globe. The EU has taken a paternalistic approach in adopting the Data
Protection Directive in 1995 [2]. As seen below, that Directive strives to provide a
comprehensive framework to protect a person's personal information, with state-
established bodies charged with enforcing the law. Meanwhile, the US has taken a more
hands-off approach to data protection in providing very little by way of comprehensive
protections and instead generally being business-friendly. But, as seen in greater detail
below, this does not mean that the US does not provide any protections to personal data,
but rather has developed some overriding principles and sector-specific protections.
Finally, some states have followed the EU model (countries such as Canada and many
Latin American countries); other states have followed a sector-based approach like the
U.S. (countries such as Japan); other states have followed more of a self-regulatory
scheme (countries such as Australia and New Zealand); and other states have not
enacted much protection at all (countries such as China). As of mid-2013, 99 countries
had some sort of data protection framework, but over half of those nations adopted such
laws after the year 2000, showing the recent increase in such legislation [3].

3.1 The EU – the Data Protection Directive and Proposed Data
         Protection Regulation – a Comprehensive Approach

This section of the paper gives an overview of the main EU data protection legislation
and the key concepts in EU data protection law. This focuses on the current EU Data
Protection Directive 1995. It then discusses the difficulties with applying data protection law in a cloud environment.

Origins of EU Data Protection Law. As referenced above, nearly 100 countries
worldwide now have laws regulating personal data. Technological advances in the
twentieth century meant that data could be manipulated in a variety of different ways
with an increasing capacity to process, store, search and edit personal data.

Data protection laws are based on recognition of a right to privacy. All EU Member States were signatories to the European Convention on Human Rights (ECHR) that recognises in Article 8 a right to privacy. Various harmonisation measures in Europe on data protection such as the 1980 OECD guidelines and the Convention by the Council of Europe in 1981, led the European Commission to propose EU legislation to harmonise diverging data protection legislation in EU Member States. The EU data protection directive, adopted in 1995, is the key piece of legislation on data protection. This paper will focus on the current law because it is likely to remain the law until at least 2016. It is worth noting that on 25 January 2012 the European Commission unveiled a proposed legislative reform of the current data protection law in the EU that would replace the Data Protection Directive by a General Data Protection Regulation [4], but at the time of writing there is no predicted date by which the reform will be completed.

One feature of the current EU data protection law is that as it is a Directive, which means that it is addressed to Member States and not to citizens. Member States are required to implement the Directive into national law and they have discretion on how it is implemented. A minimum level of harmonisation is all that is required by the Directive. All Member States have enacted their own data protection laws based on the Directive and this means that there are different national laws in each EU Member States based on the Data Protection Directive, including some of which are stricter than that required by the Directive.

Data Protection Directive Main Concepts. The Directive regulates the processing of personal data, irrespective if such processing is automated or not.

Scope of Personal Data. Personal data means data relating to a living individual who is or can be identified either from the data or from the data in conjunction with other information that is in, or is likely to come into, the possession of the data controller. This includes any expression of opinion about the individual as set out in Article 2(a) of the DPD [2].

Sensitive personal data is a special category of personal data that is subject to stricter regulation under Article 8 of the DPD [2]. Sensitive personal data relates to specific categories of data which are defined as data relating to a person's racial origin; political opinions or religious or other beliefs; physical or mental health; sexual life; criminal convictions or the alleged commission of an offence; trade union membership. There are more safeguards for sensitive personal data – due to fear of it being used to discriminate against groups of people. In most cases a person must be asked specifically if sensitive personal data can be kept about them.

The Distinction Between Data Processors and Controllers in Data Protection Law. The law protects the rights of individuals whom the data is about, called data subjects, mainly by placing duties on those who decide how and why such data is processed, called data controllers.

A data controller is a person or company that collects and keeps data about people and 'determines the purposes and means of processing of personal data' under Article 2 (d) of the DPD [2]. The data controller has the main responsibility for complying with data protection legal obligations. A controller must ensure that processing of personal data complies with certain principles. Personal data must be processed fairly and lawfully for specified lawful purposes only. The processing must be adequate, relevant and not excessive. Personal data must also be updated as necessary, accurate and not kept longer than required. It must be processed in accordance with data subject rights.

The data processor is a 'natural or legal person, public authority, agency or any other body which processes personal data on behalf of the controller' under Article 2(e) of the DPD [2]. Processors are not normally subject directly to obligations under the Data Protection Directive.

This distinction between data controllers and data processors is an important distinction because they are treated differently under the Directive, with responsibility and liability ultimately falling upon the data controller. Data controllers must ensure that any processing of personal data for which they are responsible complies with the law. Failure to do so risks enforcement action, even prosecution, and compensation claims from individuals.

Data processors on the other hand are not subject to the law because they are presumed to be just following data controllers' instructions. Data processing means performing any operation or set of operations on data, including: obtaining, recording or keeping data, collecting, organizing, storing, altering or adapting the data, retrieving, consulting or using the data, disclosing the information or data by transmitting, disseminating or otherwise making it available, aligning, combining, blocking, erasing or destroying the data.

Data controllers remain responsible for ensuring their processing complies with the law, whether they do it in-house or engage a data processor. In law, a controller of personal data who chooses to 'outsource' data storage or processing remains a controller and responsible for complying with the Data Protection Directive. If problems arise from third party failures, the controller is still liable.

As data processing activity becomes more complex, applying the distinction between data processor and data controller has become more and more difficult [5].

Principles of Data Protection

Collection and use of Personal Data. There is a requirement in the Directive that personal data is "Processed fairly and lawfully" under Article 6(1)(a) of the Data Protection Directive. Fairness requires the data subject to be informed of the purpose of collection and intended uses. Moreover "fair" depends on one's perspective, and courts tend to interpret it from the data subject perspective. In addition, the data must be processed "for specified, explicit and legitimate and not further processed in a way incompatible with those purposes." Article 6(1)(b) of the DPD. The problem here is that nowadays purposes are constantly shifting based on the data collected.

Legitimate Processing Criteria. In order to process data in compliance with EU data protection law, Article 7 of Data Protection Directive sets out certain criteria on which a controller must base its processing activity in order to be legitimate. These criteria are consent, necessity, contract requirement, legal obligation, protection of data subject, public interest and legitimate interests of the controller. Consent of data subject is the most often cited. It is not merely consent but informed consent that is needed. It is easy now to get 'tick box' consent, particularly online, but more difficult to show informed consent.

Contractual necessity means that the processing is necessary to perform the contract, for example: billing information about the customer, the company will need to process name, address and details of payment in order to fulfil the customer's contract.

Application of the Law. The EU Data Protection Directive applies when the data controller is established within the EU, which for foreign controllers means that it has a subsidiary, branch or agency with in the EEA under Article 4(1)(a) of the DPD [2]. It also applies when the controller is in a place where national law applies by virtue of international public law (in a ship or aircraft flying a particular Member States' flag) under Article 4(1)(b) of the DPD [2]. Finally, it may apply to a controller that is not established in the EEA but that makes use of equipment situated in the EEA for the purposes of processing personal data under Article 4(1)(c) of the DPD [2]. The national laws implementing the Data Protection Directive are not harmonized and implementations differ. This means that the provisions on jurisdiction are subject to interpretation. Potentially any online business dealing with EU customers could be found to be processing personal data on EU equipment (the customers' computer) and therefore subject to EU data protection law. The proposed reform to the law proposes extending the scope of jurisdiction to anyone processing personal data of EU residents or targeting EU residents through data tracking, mining and targeted advertising. This facilitates the extraterritorial application of EU law, but is intended to ensure that EU data protection laws cannot be avoided by processing data outside the EEA.

Sending Personal Data Abroad. Personal data can be transferred freely to countries within the European Economic Area. Sending it to a country or territory outside the European Economic Area is only permitted, however, if that country or territory ensures an adequate level of protection for the rights and freedoms of individuals in relation to processing personal data.

Article 25 of the Data Protection Directive restricts the transfer of data outside the EEA. A data export or transfer is considered data 'processing' for which data subject consent is required.

This has led to complex systems for complying with this provision and ensuring that personal data can be transferred to third countries (non-EEA) countries.

First, the European Commission can declare that certain countries provide adequate protection and data can be freely exported to those countries under Article 25(6) of the DPD [2]. Relatively few countries feature on this list [6].

Effectively all exports of personal data from the EEA to third countries other than those above are prohibited unless there are special arrangements made or there is a derogation.

One of the special arrangements made for transfers of data to the US is the EU-US Safe Harbor principle, a process developed by the US Department of Commerce in consultation with the European Commission so that US companies could comply with the Data Protection Directive. This allows US organizations that import personal data from the EU to demonstrate an adequate standard of protection under Article 25 of the Data Protection Directive if they participate in this program.

Another way to comply is to use model contracts with standard contractual clauses, the terms of which have been approved by the European Commission for transfers of data outside the EEA as provided by Article 26(4) of the DPD [2]. Clauses have been issued by the European Commission for transfers of personal data from an EEA-established controller to a controller in a third country or from an EEA-established controller to a third-country processor [7].

Binding Corporate Rules (BCRs) are codes of conduct dealing with international transfer of personal data within the same group of companies, within a multinational company [8]. They are subject to approval by relevant national data protection authorities and this process can be long and costly.

Supervision and Enforcement. National data protection authorities [9] were required to be set up by Article 28 of the Data Protection Directive [2]. This gives them three core powers: investigative powers, effective powers of intervention and power to engage in legal proceedings. They are required to receive and deal with complaints and required to provide annual reports that are made public. They also play a role in giving guidance and recommending changes to the law.

Supervisory authorities on data protection law include the European Data Protection Supervisor which is an independent supervisory authority to ensure that European institutions and bodies respect data protection law. In addition, there is a body that brings together all the EU data protection bodies: the Article 29 Working Party. The Article 29 Working Party is made up of representatives of the data protection authority of each EU Member State, the European Data Protection Supervisor and the European Commission. Its main role is to give advice to the Member States on the interpretation of the data protection directive and to achieve harmonious application of the data protection directive in the EEA. It also gives the European Commission an opinion on the laws that impact on data protection law.

Although this appears to be a vast system of data protection authorities, the reality is that the variations in national implementation of the Data Protection Directive and the lack of harmonisation between Member States has meant that there is a patchy data protection regime and, in some Member States, little enforcement of data protection law.

The Cloud and Data Protection. Cloud computing raises particular questions with regard to how data protection laws apply to personal data in the cloud. The implications of data protection law on cloud computing can be analysed based on the answers to four questions: What information in clouds is 'personal data'? Who is responsible for personal data in clouds? Which Law(s) apply to personal data in clouds? How do restrictions on International data transfers work in cloud? [10] These issues are addressed briefly below but each highlights the difficulty in applying the current data protection legal framework to cloud.

Personal Data in the Cloud. The issue of what is considered as personal data in clouds is central to the application of data protection laws in the cloud [11]. The EU Data Protection Directive and the national laws based on it only apply to 'personal data'. The definition of personal data in the EU Data Protection Directive applies to data that is about an identifiable individual. This is a question of fact and may depend on context [12]. In cloud, this is complicated by whether data should be treated as personal data in various different contexts: anonymized and pseudonymized data in cloud; encrypted data in cloud; and finally sharding or fragmentation of data in cloud. These forms of data involve different processes applied to personal data but in all cases whether the data remains personal data depends on the likelihood of identifying an individual. A 'mere hypothetical possibility' to single out someone is not enough to make the person identifiable. Nevertheless, this area of law lacks clarity. The status of encrypted and anonymized data has not been clarified in the law. The DPD dates from 1995 when technologies relating to anonymization, encryption and pseudonymization were only just developing. Therefore data controllers may need to adopt a cautious approach to personal data and the risks of someone re-identifying individuals from data.

The Distinction Between Data Processors and Data Controllers in Cloud [12]. Data protection law is based on regulating the data controllers who are responsible for complying with data protection laws. In data protection law based on the EU Data Protection Directive, the distinction between the data controller and the data processor are key to applying the law. The controller has the main responsibility to comply with the law, while processors are not normally subject to data protection obligations. The complexity of this area particularly since the development of the internet has meant that the distinction between the controller and processor is not as straightforward as originally hoped [14]. The official position by the Article 29 Working Party is that cloud providers are considered data processors, unless they become data controllers because they act in a manner inconsistent with their instructions [15]. This is not the full picture and does not reflect the reality that the distinctions between data processor and data controller in cloud can be utterly blurred. For example, many cloud providers who run social networking or webmail services run advertisements based on the content of uploaded personal data and so are likely to be controllers [13]. They are not merely processing uploaded data, but they are accessing it for its own purposes, i.e. targeting advertising to cloud users based on the uploaded data and consequently these cloud providers are data controllers. Examples like this illustrate how artificial a distinction between data processor and data controller and how one entity can be both in cloud.

The position of sub-providers in the cloud computing chain of responsibility in respect of data protection also complicates matters. Guidance by Data Protection regulators [15] regarding sub-providers in cloud and the chain of contractual responsibility often reflect a traditional 'outsourcing' view of the contractual relationship between the cloud provider and sub-providers, where the cloud provider delegates processing to its sub-provider. The reality is that many providers with sub-providers have already created services based on the sub-provider's service [13]. Many cloud services are pre-packaged services build on existing sub-provider services and sub-provider terms and providers may not want to change pre-existing arrangements with sub-providers for every new contract. Therefore the degree of control of sub-providers over personal data may be as a data controller rather than a processor. Consequently, the current state of the law with its distinction between controllers and processors is less and less satisfactory in cloud.

Deciding Which Laws Apply to Personal Data in Clouds. The issue of the Data Protection Directive applying to cloud computing providers and users outside the EEA and the jurisdiction of data protection authorities to regulate them is one that creates considerable uncertainty for cloud users and providers [16]. Member States' data protection rules are not harmonized and their interpretations of the Data Protection Directive's jurisdictional scope are unclear. The fact that data processing is 'somewhere in the cloud' does not automatically exempt it from the Data Protection Directive. However, identifying when an entity falls within the jurisdiction of EU data protection law requires simplification and clarification of the current law on jurisdiction. One goal of the new proposed regulation is to clarify applicable law and to improve harmonization in the EU on this point.

Restrictions on International Data Transfer in Cloud. Cloud computing is potentially affected by restrictions on transferring personal data outside the EEA under the Data Protection Directive [17]. The Data Protection Directive when drafted did not take into account the Internet and did not envisage cloud computing. The result is that the provisions in the Directive and the national laws based on the Directive in the EU on data export are neither clear not sufficiently harmonized across the Member States. This creates legal uncertainty with using cloud. The conception of data location in particular is particularly irrelevant to data protection laws, since data can be accessed remotely. Indeed, the concept of data location may even be meaningless in cloud.

Cloud and Managing the Problems with Current Data Protection Law. Compliance with the current law is extremely difficult for cloud providers and users since it is particularly ambiguous and has not been drafted for an online world, let alone for cloud. The danger is that the uncertainty could lead to paralysis and fear of uptake of cloud by some customers.

The current proposed reform of EU data protection law is not focussed on cloud in particular. As they stand [4], the proposed reforms may help with some matters, for example clarifying the issue of jurisdiction, but may make some issues worse, for example increasing restrictions on international data transfers. One way of managing the problems with current data protection laws and cloud is by ensuring that the contractual obligations as regards data location and confidentiality as well as provisions on data transfer, security and audit rights are all addressed and well defined.

3.2   The United States – a Sectoral Approach

Quite different from the comprehensive approach undertaken by the EU, the U.S. instead largely follows a sectoral model. This means that the United States has only provided for specific protections in certain industries, though, as seen below, the U.S. has expanded general protections provided to consumers and increased scrutiny on businesses in respect to privacy policies and information security. Such areas include the healthcare sector with protection of health records, law enforcement records, consumer financial transactions, telecommunications sectors, the protection of children, and some other narrow fields.

Nevertheless, the United States, generally through the Courts and administrative actions, has also provided a more general protection for citizens' personal information, though such measures and protections have come nowhere close to the codification found in the EU through the Data Protection Directive. Instead, the Federal Trade Commission, an administrative agency generally empowered to protect trade and consumer issues in the United States, has the general authority to enforce against "unfair and deceptive trade practices." And, while it has been debated whether that phrase includes data protection and/or privacy rights, the Federal Trade Commission (FTC) has become increasingly proactive since the late nineties in protecting consumers when it comes to data protection, especially in the areas of information security, the collection and processing of data, misleading or unclear privacy notices, and the reselling of data. Such actions include:

- *In the Matter of GeoCities, Inc.* [18] – this represented the first FTC Internet privacy enforcement action in which the FTC alleged that GeoCities, which operated a website promoting an online community on which users could maintain personal home pages, misrepresented how it would use personal information in its privacy notice and also maintained children's personal information without parental consent. GeoCities settled the action and the FTC issued a consent decree, which is a judgment entered by consent of the parties in which the defendant agrees to cease and desist from the alleged illegal activity, usually without admitting any wrongdoing.
- *In the Matter of Eli Lilly & Co.* [19] – Eli Lilly & Co. is a pharmaceutical manufacturer which collected personal information from subscribers on its website, including sending updates to remind customers to take their medicine. When Eli Lilly & Co. ended that program, it inadvertently sent a mass email revealing the email addresses of all subscribers. Eli Lilly & Co. settled the enforcement action brought by the FTC, in which Eli Lilly & Co. agreed to adhere to its representations regarding the collection, use and protection of customer's data. Most notably, this also marked the first case where a defendant was also required to develop and maintain an information privacy and security program.
- *In the Matter of Gateway Learning Corp.* [20] – Gateway Learning maintained a privacy notice stating that it would not sell, rent or loan any customer's personal information without express consent of the customer. The notice also contained an opt-out provision if Gateway Learning's policy changed. Thereafter, Gateway Learning rented out customers' personal information to third-party marketers and advertisers, without providing the opt-out option to the customers. The 2004 consent decree entered against Gateway Learning provided that Gateway Learning would comply with its policy and required Gateway to relinquish all funds obtained from renting its consumers' information.
- *In the Matter of Google Inc.* [21] – this 2011 action resulted from Google's introduction of Google Buzz, a social networking service, which was integrated with Gmail, Google's email service. Gmail users were automatically enrolled in Buzz without having to provide any consent. Buzz utilized information pulled from Gmail, making such information public without disclosing such use to its customers. Such conduct conflicted with Google's own privacy notice contained on its website. The FTC alleged such conduct constituted a deceptive trade practice and that Google was in violation of the US-EU Safe Harbor framework. The consent decree was important for two reasons: (1) it represented the first time there was significant enforcement of the US-EU Safe Harbor by the FTC; and (2) it required Google to implement a comprehensive privacy program, with Google undergoing third-party privacy audits on a biannual basis.

- *In the Matter of Facebook Inc.* [22] – in 2011, Facebook settled this FTC action in which there were eight counts brought against Facebook, mostly arising from Facebook's repeated changes to its services resulting in private information being made public. Pursuant to the consent decree, Facebook was required to (1) provide users with clear notice; (2) obtain user consent before making retroactive changes to privacy terms; (3) refrain from making any further deceptive privacy claims; (4) establish and maintain a comprehensive privacy program; and (5) obtain biannual independent third-party audits of its privacy program for the next twenty years.
- *FTC v. Wyndham Worldwide Corporation, et al.* [23] – this action was brought in the United States District Court, District of New Jersey in which the FTC alleged Wyndham Worldwide Corporation, which operated hotels, failed to maintain reasonable and appropriate data security for consumers" sensitive personal information. Wyndham moved to dismiss the case, but in April of 2014 and in a 42-page opinion, the District Court held that the FTC did have the authority to bring the claims against Wyndham, thereby bolstering the FTC's right to bring privacy and data protection actions and implying security and privacy requirements for businesses that were not otherwise expressly required under law. The case remains pending and it appears likely that Wyndham will appeal the District Court's decision.

Similarly, the Obama Administration has also been more proactive in promulgating overriding principles for data protection, including, individual control, transparency, respect for context, security, access and accuracy, focused collection, and accountability in its 2012 issuance of the report "Consumer Data Privacy in a Networked World: A Framework for Protecting Privacy and Promoting Innovation in the Global Digital Economy." Reference [24] In response to that report, the Federal Trade Commission issued a report titled "Protecting Consumer Privacy in an Era of Rapid Change: Recommendations for Businesses and Policymakers" [25] guiding companies to follow three general principles of (1) privacy by design; (2) simplified consumer choice; and (3) transparency. In examining those principles, it can be seen that perhaps the US and EU are not as far apart as to data protection as it would otherwise appear in media reports and other descriptions of the two policies.

3.3   Some Other Countries' Noteworthy Approaches

As Cloud providers and customers may also be subject to other countries' laws, it is worthwhile to mention a few other approaches employed throughout the world.

One approach is the use of a more self-regulatory and/or co-regulatory approach, such as the one employed in Australia, which has adopted the Privacy Amendment Act 2000, but which otherwise encourages industry organizations to develop self-regulatory codes. Australian law also generally requires organizations to do what is reasonable under any given circumstances, as opposed to some of the bright-line rules envisioned by the EU Data Protection Directive or some of the sectoral laws in the U.S.

As noted above, other countries have adopted their own regulations, oftentimes following that of the EU, oftentimes following that of the US, and/or otherwise adopting some hybrid approach.

Finally, some countries, including China (but which does provide its citizens with a constitutional right to privacy), have yet to adopt any sort of data protection regulation, though proposed legislation is being reviewed and debated in some of those countries.

4 The Role of Contracts in the Cloud

The other important legal consideration involved in the use of cloud, and a critical method to dealing with legal risks, including the data protection risks, is to manage this by agreeing appropriate safeguards in the contract with the cloud provider. Contract law concerns the legal relationship between individuals, which includes organisations. It applies irrespective of technology and therefore there no specific terms for 'cloud contracts'. The contract establishes the 'rules' between parties and covers who does what, who pays what, what each side expects and is a feature of private law, rather than public regulatory law. We refer to this contract between the end-customer and the cloud provider as the 'cloud contract'.

Contracts can be divided into two categories: the negotiated contracts and the non-negotiated standard-form contracts. Most cloud contracts are non-negotiable standard-form contracts [10]. We will examine the main features of each below.

4.1   Standard Cloud Contracts

Standard terms and conditions contracts are often a feature of contracts between business providers and consumers or small and medium sized enterprise (SME) customers. They do not have the bargaining power of larger business customers to negotiate contract terms, nor do they have in-house legal team to help them negotiate, nor sometimes the interest in negotiating contract terms. Most cloud contracts are the providers' standard terms designed for high-volume, low-cost, standard services. Many consumer customers click to accept without even reading them.

In a survey of standard cloud contract terms [26], the results showed that many cloud providers included wide-ranging disclaimers of liability or warranty that the cloud service would operate as described and it included often included remedies only in the form of credits against future services. On the other hand, the research findings showed that there was a range of potential variations between cloud providers in their standard contracts when it concerned matters such as: the threshold for disclosing customer data to third parties, the extent to which data would be maintained by the provider at the end of the contract term and the jurisdiction and choice of law in the contract for contract enforcement. These terms could be significant and influence the choice of cloud provider.

Many consumer and SME customer did not have the know-how to assess the differences between standard cloud contracts. They often clicked their consent to these terms and conditions, without considering whether the standard contract suited them or not. Section 4.3 describes a software tool being developed as part of the Accountability for Cloud project to help consumer and SME customers assess which cloud provider standard contract is most appropriate for them.

4.2 Negotiated Cloud Contracts

Negotiated contract for cloud services are the exception rather than the rule and are often confined to large customers [27]. Contract negotiation often depends on the economic bargaining power between the respective parties and cloud contracts are no different. The starting point for cloud contracts is usually providers' standard terms and, since these do not accommodate large business users' needs, cloud users seek to negotiate.

The decision to negotiate may be driven by internal commercial issues or external issues. For example, the customer may require higher service levels for certain critical services. The decision may also depend on the need to comply with regulatory requirements and laws. A review of main terms that cloud customers seek to negotiate [27] include the following clauses:

- *limitation of liability clauses* [27] – Cloud providers' terms that limited or entirely excluded liability for data loss or for service outages were, unsurprising, the most important terms that cloud customers wanted to negotiate. It was also an area where cloud providers were most like to be intransigent, excluding or capping liability. The nature of the service was a factor in negotiations, with providers more reluctant to accept liability for cheap, commoditized services than for bespoke services. The type of customer also played a role; governments and financial institutions, for example, would insist on unlimited provider liability for certain types of loss caused by breach of regulation or security requirements.
- *clauses concerning data integrity and business continuity* – Cloud providers tend to provide backup as a separate services so that if the user pays extra, the provider will make backups. Back-up service does not mean, however, that providers will warrant data integrity or accept liability for data loss and therefore additional specific warranties need to be negotiated with providers.
- *service levels* [27] – the approach to service level agreements (SLAs) covering matters such as availability levels and performance often led to debate between customers concerning methods for measuring service levels. As standards in this area develop [28], agreeing on the key performance indicators (KPIs) will become much easier.
- *regulatory issues* [27] – clauses mainly relating to the cloud customer needing to demonstrate compliance obligations to regulators since these are often not taken into account in standard cloud contract terms. For example, cloud customers have obtained warranties from cloud providers that all data centres used for their data were in the EU or EEA so that data is kept within the EU and in this way can show data protection authorities that data are not being transferred outside the EEA.
- *confidentiality clauses* [27] – Users want to guarantee the confidentiality of their information, whether it is personal information of an individual user or business data which could even constitute a trade secret.
- *security requirements* [27] – Security requirements are a key user concern. Users may want to specify detailed security requirements, but also ask for audit rights. Some users, particularly in the regulated financial services sector, need audit rights to show to financial auditors and regulators that they are compliant with regulation.

In addition users often want security breach notifications from cloud providers, which are often not part of any standard contract terms but are required by large customers.

- *lock-in and exit* [27] – End of contract transition and exit strategy are important to cloud users and concerns about 'lock-in' are often cited as the highest user concerns, after security. Lock-in can mean various concerns but the biggest is the inability to exit a contract and, in a cloud context, the inability to retrieve data from your cloud provider, which could effectively prevent the customer switching from the cloud provider and result in them being "lock-in" to a particular cloud provider. Users want to be able to retrieve data from cloud providers at the end of the contract, or whenever they terminate the contracts. Data portability and data retention on termination of the contract, to allow the customer enough time to retrieve contract data, are key issues in negotiated contracts.
- *term and termination* [27] – the length of the contract and how the contract is terminated, whether by the passage of term, fulfilment of obligations, and/or some other event, i.e. default.

The level of success in negotiating these issues appeared to depend on the bargaining power of the customer and their insistence. Large providers generally refuse to negotiate terms and decline changes to their standard terms insisting on a 'take it or leave it' approach even when a large customer requests it [27]. Negotiated cloud contracts are as a result rare and the majority of cloud contracts are on cloud providers' standard terms.

4.3   A4Cloud Approach to Cloud Contracts

Accountability tools are intended to reassure customers and win their confidence in using cloud services. As part of the Accountability for Cloud project, a software tool called the COAT tool (Cloud Offerings Advisory Tool) is being developed that is geared towards enabling customers understand and compare various cloud provider standard contracts. This tool is aimed at consumers and SME customers. These customers do not have the ability to negotiate contract terms with cloud providers and often accept standard contract terms from cloud providers without really understanding their implications. They are customers that may not be well informed about contract terms and may not be in a position to seek specialist advice before agreeing to a contract. This tool is intended to empower these customers by acting like a comparison website, comparing the various offerings by different cloud providers and trying to match the offering that is most appropriate for the customer, based on criteria that the customer specifies.

Comparison websites have flourished particularly in regulated markets like insurance, energy and communications. Consumers seek to understand complex offering in these markets by having a comparison website provider rank different offers with explanations of the differences. Choice tools, such as comparison websites, have been praised by consumer authorities for empowering consumers to make choices, particularly in complex product and services markets [29]. This is however on condition that they respect data protection laws, are transparent about how they show search results and have clear contact details and a complaints procedure for consumers that are shown on the website [29].

The COAT tool operates like a comparison website for cloud standard contracts. The customer needs to complete a questionnaire online states its preference for particular features of cloud service. The tool compares standard cloud offerings by comparing cloud contract terms offered to consumers and SMEs - for example location of storage or jurisdiction for litigation. In addition, the tool gives 'pop-up' explanations of what the contract terms means for the consumer or SME customer so that they understand what these mean. The result is that the customer has a tool to compare the various standard cloud contracts and it can choose only from those cloud providers that have the features it requires in a cloud service.

5   Policy and Governance

As we have seen, there are numerous legal considerations for Cloud providers, Cloud customers, and Cloud users to consider in their use of the Cloud. And, while most of the strictest requirements arise from the law, in particular regulatory obligations and contractual obligations, sound legal governance also takes into consideration technological developments and tools, market and economic factors, and the cost and value of compliance. Accordingly, A4Cloud tries to take all of those factors into consideration in providing guidance and tools for Cloud providers to better achieve accountability, thereby benefitting all Cloud actors in increased security, a higher level of automated compliance, and a sound overall policy to achieve accountability. Discussion of the various A4Cloud tools which are in development, as well as comprehensive guidance as to legal and regulatory dependencies by Cloud providers, is beyond the scope of this paper. Additionally, there are approximately a dozen tools currently in various stages of development, most of which have corresponding papers detailing the issues which the tools address [30].

For Cloud providers, sound legal governance is generally viewed as effectuating safeguards to protect confidentiality, integrity and availability of data. Such protections arise from three areas: administrative steps, technical steps, and physical steps in effectuating proper safeguards within a company. Administrative steps include developing strong policies and safeguards and utilizing other administrative measures such as role-based controls to provide sound information security. Administrative steps also include policy enforcement, training, and enforcement of such policies. Technical steps include the use of technology, such as encryption, public key infrastructure, password management, authentication, tracking, non-repudiation, digital signatures and other technological tools to aid in data protection. Notably, much of the focus of A4Cloud is on the development of such tools in promoting information security, data protection, and accountability. Finally, physical steps are those steps that can be physically taken and which should not otherwise be forgotten by Cloud providers. Those steps include use of locks, perimeter controls and security monitoring. While companies are not required under any regulations to employ all measures available to them, they nevertheless should conduct a risk assessment in identifying the threat, vulnerability, and the expected loss in determining which measures should be taken and at what cost. Such an assessment and the resulting measures not only will serve to better protect the data entrusted to the Cloud provider, but it will also aid the Cloud provider in defending those measures in the event of a breach and, ultimately, to be a more accountable Cloud provider, the overriding goal of A4Cloud.

All of the foregoing takes hours of preparation, implementation, and ongoing monitoring and enforcement. Most Cloud providers should begin their compliance programs with the hiring and/or selection of a capable person as a privacy officer to oversee the entire program. This might not be a lawyer, but certainly a lawyer should be consulted to ensure that there is proper regulatory and contractual compliance and to ensure that contracts are properly negotiated and prepared. The lawyer will also be able to assist in an advisory role as to ongoing compliance, especially in tracking the evolving regulations and enforcement actions by various authorities. However, an effective policy, use of available tools, and consistent monitoring and enforcement of the policy will ensure accountability, especially when faced with a system failure and/ or data breach.

Cloud customers will want to ensure that the contracts entered into with Cloud providers provide adequate protection for service levels, audit rights, redress and remediation, and other contractual provisions to ensure that the Cloud provider is fulfilling its contractual and regulatory requirements. Again, use of a lawyer will be the best first step in such protections, especially in regard to preparing or reviewing, negotiating and finalizing any contract. But of course, consumers and SMEs may not be able to afford lawyers, and will thus need to rely on tools such as COAT.

Finally, Cloud users, i.e. individual consumers, will want to ensure that the Cloud provider and/or any business with which the user is dealing with which are conducting some business through the Cloud and collect, use or otherwise process personal information, have proper policies in place and that such companies ensure, at least through their privacy notices, terms and conditions, and/or contract that such personal information is processed for only the stated purposes and that proper remedies are in place should the Cloud provider or business utilizing the Cloud fail in their obligations.

6   Conclusion

A4Cloud is undertaking more than three years of analysis and development of the current Cloud landscape in developing guidance and tools for all cloud actors in increasing accountability throughout the Cloud. A major part of that endeavor is the analysis of the regulatory and contractual issues that oftentimes dominate account-ability. As seen herein, the legal landscape, especially as it relates to the Cloud, can be quite a quagmire of unclear and conflicting regulations, leaving Cloud providers oftentimes to guess and make what amounts to a best effort in complying. Nevertheless, by carful analysis and the consistent exercise of diligence, Cloud providers can be accountable, even when it comes to the regulatory compliance of the most relevant and controlling laws. Further, drafting of contracts and regular review of contractual terms and obligations can provide further protection to all Cloud actors. Finally, Cloud providers can increase their own accountability for the betterment of all Cloud actors by carefully considering and implementing policies and tools to increase transparency and responsibility. A4Cloud continues to research and provide guidance as to all these areas, as well as the development of tools to help automate many of the tasks necessary for Cloud providers to increase accountability. All research being conducted, all guidance being provided, and all tools being developed are scheduled to be completed by A4Cloud by the end of 2015 and we invite you to continue to follow such research and development.

References

1. Zippo Manufacturing Co. v. Zippo Dot Com, Inc., 952 F.Supp. 1119 (W.D. Pa. 1997)
2. Directive 95/46/EC of the European Parliament and of the Council of 24 October 1995 on the protection of individuals with regard to the processing of personal data and on the free movement of such data Official Journal L 281, 23/11/1995, pp. 31 – 50. (Hereafter referred to as the 'Directive' and/or the 'DPD')
3. Global Tables of Data Privacy Laws and Bills (3rd edn., June 2013), UNSW Law Research Paper No. 2013-39
4. Data protection law reform proposals published by the European Commission on 25 January 2012 are available at http://ec.europa.eu/justice/newsroom/data-protection/news/120125_en.htm
5. WP169, Opinion 1/2010 on the Concepts of 'Controller' and 'Processor', WP 169 (2010)
6. Commission decisions on the adequacy of the protection of personal data in third countries published by the European Commission available at http://ec.europa.eu/justice/data-protection/document/international-transfers/adequacy/index_en.htm
7. Commission Decision of 5 February 2010 on standard contractual clauses for the transfer of personal data to processors established in third countries under Directive 95/46/EC of the European Parliament and of the Council (2010/87/EU0), [12 February 2010] OJ L39/5
8. European Commission working papers on Binding Corporate Rules at http://ec.europa.eu/justice/data-protection/document/international-transfers/binding-corporate-rules/tools/index_en.htm
9. EU Member State data protection authorities are listed on the European Commission website at http://ec.europa.eu/justice/data-protection/bodies/authorities/eu/index_en.htm
10. Millard, et al.: Cloud Computing Law (2013, OUP Oxford) Part III Protection of Personal Data in Clouds, pp. 165–282
11. Hon, W., Millard, C., Walden, I.: What is regulated as personal data in clouds? In: Millard, C. (ed.) Cloud Computing Law, chap. 7, pp. 167–192. Oxford University Press, Oxford (2013)
12. Opinion 4/2007 on the Concept of Personal Data, WP 136 (2007)
13. Hon, W., Millard, C., Walden, I.: Who is responsible for personal data in the clouds? In: Millard, C. (ed.) Cloud Computing Law, chap. 8, pp. 193–219. Oxford University Press, Oxford (2013)
14. A29WP, Opinion 1/2010 on the Concepts of 'Controller' and 'Processor', WP169 (2010)
15. A29WP, Opinion 05/2012 on Cloud Computing, WP196 (2012)
16. Hon, W., Hörnle, J., Millard, C.: Which law(s) apply to personal data in clouds? In: Millard, C. (ed.) Cloud Computing Law, chap. 9. Oxford University Press, Oxford (2013)

17. Hon, W., Millard, C., Walden, I.: How do restrictions on international data transfers work in clouds? In: Millard, C. (ed.) Cloud Computing Law, chap. 10, pp. 254–282. Oxford University Press, Oxford (2013)
18. Decision and Order, In the Matter of GeoCities, Inc., FTC File No. 98203915, 12 February 1999. www.ftc.gov/os/1999/02/9823015.do.htm
19. Decision and Order, In the Matter of Eli Lilly & Co., FT File No. 012-3214, 10 May 2002. www.ftc.gov/os/1999/02/9823015.do.htm
20. Decision and Order, In the Matter of Gateway Learning Corp., FTC File No. 042-3047, 17 September 2004. www.ftc.gov/os/caselist/0423047/040917do0423047.pdf
21. Decision and Order, In the Matter of Google Inc., FTC File No. 102-3136, 30 March 2011. www.ftc.gov/os/caselist/1023136/110330googlebuzzagreeorder.pdf
22. Decision and Order, In the Matter of Facebook, Inc., FTC File No. 092-3184, 29 November 2011. http://ftc.gov/os/caselist/0923184/111129facebookagree.pdf
23. Federal Trade Commission v. Wyndham Worldwide Corporation, et al., Case No. 2 :13-cv-1887 (ES-JAD), United States District Court, District of New Jersey, Doc. No. 181 filed April 7, 2014
24. US Government White House 'Consumer Data Privacy in a Networked World: A Framework for Protecting Privacy and Promoting Innovation in the Global Digital Economy' February 23, 2012 available at www.whitehouse.gov/sites/default/files/privacy-final.pdf
25. Federal Trade Commission report 'Protecting Consumer Privacy in an Era of Rapid Change: Recommendations for Businesses and Policymakers' March 26, 2012 available at http://www.ftc.gov/sites/default/files/documents/reports/federal-trade-commission-report-protecting-consumer-privacy-era-rapid-change-recommendations/120326privacyreport.pdf
26. Bradshaw, S., Millard, C., Walden, I.: Standard contracts for cloud services. In: Millard, C. (ed.) Cloud Computing Law, chap. 3, pp. 39–72. Oxford University Press, Oxford (2013)
27. Hon, W., Millard, C., Walden, I.: Negotiated contracts for cloud services. In: Millard, C. (ed.) Cloud Computing Law, chap. 4, pp. 73–107. Oxford University Press, Oxford (2013)
28. Gleeson, N., Walden, I.: It's a jungle out there'?: Cloud computing, standards and the law. Eur. J. Law Technol. 5(2) (2014)
29. OFT (2012) "Price Comparison Websites. Trust, Choice and Consumer Empowerment in online markets" (November 2012, OFT 1467). European Commission 'Comparison Tools – Report from the Multi-Stakeholder Dialogue, Providing consumers with transparent and reliable information' (Report presented at the European Consumer Summit 18–19 March 2013)
30. Papers and updates on A4Cloud tools are available at the project website at www.a4cloud.eu

Definition of Data Sharing Agreements
The Case of Spanish Data Protection Law

Marina Egea[1], Ilaria Matteucci[2], Paolo Mori[2], and Marinella Petrocchi[2(✉)]

[1] Atos Research and Innovation, Madrid, Spain
[2] Istituto di Informatica e Telematica, CNR, Pisa, Italy
marinella.petrocchi@iit.cnr.it

Abstract. Electronic sharing of data among different parties, including groups of organizations and/or individuals, while protecting their legitimate rights on these data, is a key both for business and societal transactions. However, data sharing clauses are usually specified in legal documents that are far from being amenable of automated processing by the electronic platform that should enforce them. Furthermore, different parties usually pursue different interests. This may lead to conflicts that need to be solved for the agreements to succeed. Addressing this problem, in this paper we (i) discuss a proposal for the definition of a machine processable electronic data sharing multilateral contract (e-DSA); (ii) recall a controlled natural language (CNL4DSA) developed for expressing e-DSA clauses, in particular, authorizations and obligations policies on data; (iii) instantiate a resolution process that can solve potential conflicts posed by different stakeholders' clauses, e.g., legal, organizational, and end-users' clauses, according to specific criteria. We illustrate our approach on a realistic e-Health scenario derived from one described by a Spanish medical institution. The main novelty of this paper are the reference to the Spanish Data Protection Law (S)DPL as the basic source of policies regulating data exchange and the idea of a multi-step e-DSA definition phase that incrementally increases the contract granularity. To the best of our knowledge, this is one of the first attempts to investigate how a real DPL can be translated into privacy rules electronically manageable by a devoted e-DSA-based infrastructure.

Keywords: Electronic data sharing · Multilateral agreements · Data protection law · Privacy · Conflict resolution · e-Health

1 Introduction

Sharing data among groups of organizations and/or individuals is a key necessity in modern web-based society and at the very core of business and societal transactions. However, data sharing poses several problems including trust, privacy, data misuse and/or abuse, and uncontrolled propagation of data. Hence, who produces the data would like to protect them by imposing some constraints on the operations that are allowed. Often organizations use legal documents (contracts) to regulate the terms and conditions under which they agree to share data among themselves. A similar approach can be used when data is shared between

© Springer International Publishing Switzerland 2015
M. Felici and C. Fernández-Gago (Eds.): A4Cloud 2014, LNCS 8937, pp. 248–272, 2015.
DOI: 10.1007/978-3-319-17199-9_11

a user and an organisation. A key problem, in the digital world, is that the constraints expressed in such (not digital) contracts remain inaccessible from the software infrastructure supporting the data sharing and management processes and, consequently, they cannot be automatically enforced. Instead, they still need to be interpreted and translated (primarily by humans) into meaningful technical policies, to ensure degrees of enforcement and auditing. What usually happens, when end-users data are going to be processed by organisations, is that end-users are asked to accept online a series of regulatory clauses on the terms of data processing, by simply clicking on a "Review and Accept the Terms and Conditions" button, and no further controls are performed on the operations that are actually executed on such data. Neither the users receive any information about how these data are processed or stored. Namely, the processing remains completely opaque for them.

In the following, we will focus on a multi-step definition process of electronic Data Sharing Agreements (e-DSA), which can be exploited to electronically represent (and manage) traditional legal contracts, by properly defining, among other fields, the parties defining and signing the agreements, the data covered and the validity time of the agreement. In particular, the different parties will be entitled to define the privacy policies regulating the sharing of the covered data. In such a way, the resulting object will contain policies defined by distinct subjects. The e-DSA will pass a validation phase to check if the various policies could be in conflict one with each other. Upon validating the e-DSA, it will be eventually enforced (meaning that the data access requests will be subject to an access control phase, according to the policies regulating the data access and defined in the validated e-DSA).

The main novelty of this paper is the reference to the Spanish Data Protection Law as the basic source of policies regulating data exchange. Starting from the conceptualisation of the currently applicable law regulating data protection in Spain, we try to model some of the original clauses in a controlled natural language format, amenable for automatic verification. Also, we depict a scenario in which both medical organisations and patients contribute in defining the e-DSA, by expressing their own constraints and preferences on the data possibly being shared. The scenario is realistic too and it derives from a real Spanish medical institution that provided it within the European project CoCo-Cloud [10]. To the best of our knowledge, this is one of the first attempts to investigate how a real Data Protection Law can be translated into a set of privacy policies electronically manageable by a devoted e-DSA-based infrastructure. Hence, the local laws and regulations of the countries in which medical data are produced and stored impose some specific constraints on them; furthermore, the organization which produced the data may want to impose its own policies on them, and, finally, the end-users (e.g., the patients, for the scope of this paper) have also the right to define their constraints on the data referring to them. Indeed, the European Directive on Data Protection 95/46/EC, and its recent reform IP/12/46 of January 25, 2012, embraced by the legislation of different European countries, recognize the right of the individuals to consciously control the use of their personal data.

Last but not least, throughout the paper, we will show how to finalise the definition of a "conflict-free" e-DSA, by applying an appropriate conflict resolution strategy to conflicting policies possibly defined by Law, organisations, and end-users.

The Remainder of the Paper is as Follows: Section 2 reports an informal, yet quite complete conceptualization of the Spanish Data Protection Law. Section 3 introduces the notion of e-DSA, focusing on e-DSA management over its whole lifecycle and introducing the controlled natural language we have defined in the past for expressing the e-DSA privacy policies. In Sect. 4, we give examples of conflicting scenarios that could realistically arise when more than one actor define their own preferences over the same dataset. Section 5 presents a technique for solving conflicts among applicable policies evaluating to different results (i.e., one allowing data access, the other one denying it). Section 6 exemplifies the presented techniques in the healthcare scenario we refer to. Finally, Sect. 7 discusses related work and Sect. 8 draws some conclusions.

2   Conceptualizing the Spanish Data Protection Law

In this section, we provide a summary of the Spanish Data Protection Law (SDPL), i.e., Organic Law 15/1999 of 13 December on the Protection of Personal Data, as an illustration of the regulations that affect data in European member countries, with an emphasis on the regulations explicitly stated on health data processing. We cover all titles of the law but the title VI that regulates the creation and organization of the data protection agency, since this information is not relevant to the purpose of this paper. For the same reason, we skip Chap. 1 of title IV, since it regulates how Spanish public administration should handle personal data. Figure 1 depicts a conceptual metamodel that captures the main concepts handled by the law in order to concisely bring them to software and security engineers.

2.1   Summary of the SDPL

In the first title, the law specifies its subject and scope of application and also provides a list of general definitions to build the common ground. More concretely, the subject reads

> [...] this law is intended to guarantee and protect the public liberties and fundamental rights of natural persons, and in particular their personal and family privacy, with regard to the processing of personal data.

Regarding scope, the law applies to personal data recorded on a physical support which makes them capable of processing, and to any type of subsequent use of such data all over the Spanish territory. Also, it applies when data are processed by organizations that are subject to Spanish regulations and that use for the processing means established in Spain. The law does not apply to data in transit,

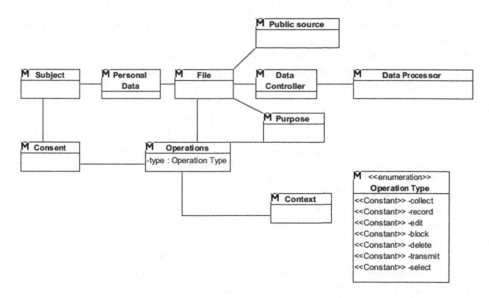

Fig. 1. SDPL conceptual metamodel

i.e., data that do not reside in Spain (neither its processing organization does) but goes across Spain in their trip to other countries.

The following definitions apply for the purposes of this law, and we have tried to capture them in Fig. 1.

- *Personal data:* any information concerning identified or identifiable natural persons.
- *File:* any structured set of personal data, whatever the form or method of its creation, storage, and digital access.
- *Processing of data:* operations and technical processes, which allow the collection, recording, storage, adaptation, modification, blocking and cancellation of data. Also, the assignments of data resulting from communications, consultations, interconnections, and transfers.
- *Data controller:* natural or legal person, whether public or private, or administrative body which determines the purpose, content, and use of data processing.
- *Data subject:* the natural person whom the personal data undergoing the processing refer to.
- *Dissociation procedure:* any processing of personal data carried out in such a way that the information obtained cannot be associated with an identified or identifiable person.
- *Data processor:* the natural or legal person, public authority, service or any other body which alone or jointly with others processes personal data on behalf of the controller.
- *Consent of the data subject:* any free, unequivocal, specific, and informed indication of wishes by which the data subjects consent to the processing of personal data relating to them.

- *Communication of data:* any disclosure of data to a person other than the data subject.
- *Sources accessible to the public:* those files which can be consulted by anyone, which are not subject to restrictive legislation, or which are subject only to payment of a consultation fee.

  More concretely, the law considers public sources the publicity register, telephone directories, and the lists of persons belonging to professional associations containing only data on the name, title, profession, activity, academic degree, address, and an indication of their membership to the association. Also, newspapers, official gazettes, and the media.

Moreover, in Fig. 2 we show how to extend the core conceptual metamodel to refine it with concepts that clearly affect the access to files, but are not present in the core definitions of the law, thus are not represented in Fig. 1. For instance, the law does not apply to domestic files, classified files, and terrorism related files. Also, a file and a data controller are linked explicitly to a right, which may turn at run time into a permission to execute operations on a file when certain authorization rules are met (e.g., explicit consent of processing to receive an economic assessment) or conditions are met (e.g., for the next 24 h). The last extension example is the subtype system below the operation meta class that tries to capture a concept that is more relevant to IT engineers than to lawyers, i.e., there may be hundreds of operations coming from different systems that could be classified using this taxonomy.

Principles of Data Protection

In this section, we outline, the principles that should govern personal data management in any processing environment subject to SDPL.

Quality of Data. Personal data may be collected for processing only if they are adequate, updated, relevant and not excessive for the legitimate purposes for which they were obtained. These data shall not be retained longer than necessary. Processing of the data for historical, statistical or scientific purposes is considered compatible with other legitimate purposes.

Consent of the Data Subject. Processing of personal data shall require the unambiguous consent of the data subject, unless laid down otherwise by law. Exceptions are public administrations (PAs) for the exercise of their functions, for business contracts or its maintenance, in the action of protecting data subject vital interest or when contained in public sources, unless rights of the data subject are jeopardized.

Right of Information in the Collection of Data. As we mentioned above, processing of personal data requires unambiguous consent of the data subject. Furthermore, the data subject from whom personal data are requested must previously be informed explicitly about existence of a file or processing operation, its purpose, the recipients of the information, and the possible consequences of sharing information, its rights of access, rectification, erasure, and objection.

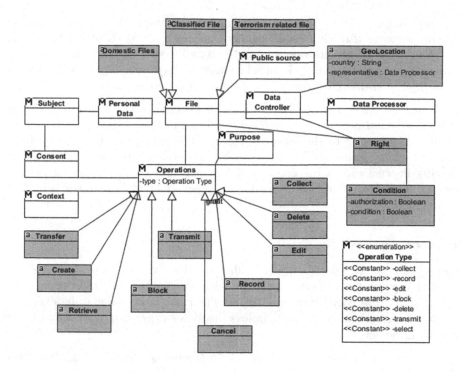

Fig. 2. SDPL extended conceptual metamodel

Data with Special Protection. Nobody may be obliged to state his ideology, religion, or beliefs. Personal data which reveal the ideology, trade union membership, religion and beliefs may be processed only with the written consent of the data subject. Exceptions shall be files maintained by political parties, trade unions, churches, religious confessions, associations, foundations, etc., as regards the data relating to their associates or members, but the communication of such data always require prior consent of the data subject. Also in the needed of medical care, the management of health care services, provided that such data is used by a health professional subject to professional secrecy.

Data on Health. Public and private health-care institutions and centers, and their professionals, may process personal data relating to the health of persons consulting them, in accordance with legislation on health care.

Data Security. The data controller and processor(s) shall adopt the measures necessary to ensure the security of the personal data and prevent their alteration, loss, or unauthorized access taking into account the context of handling.

Duty of Secrecy. The controller and processors managing personal data shall be subject to professional secrecy as regards such data and to the duty to keep them.

Communication of Data. Personal data may be communicated to third parties only for purposes directly related to the legitimate functions of the transferor and transferee with the prior consent of the data subject, except if the transfer is authorized by law, done under legal relationships, data come from public sources, or health data transfer is necessary for resolving an emergency.

Access to Data on Behalf of Third Parties. Access to data by a third party shall not be considered communication of data when such access is necessary for the provision of a service to the data controller. This processing shall be regulated in a contract and expressly laid down that the processor processes the data only following instructions of the controller, and shall not communicate them. The contract shall also set out the security measures which the processor is obliged to implement.

Rights of Persons

Right of Access. The data subject shall have the right to request and obtain free of charge information on his/her personal data subjected to processing, its origin and its (intended) communication. The right of access may be exercised only at intervals of twelve months, unless the data subject can prove a legitimate interest in the access.

Right of Rectification or Cancellation. The controller is obliged to implement the right of rectification or cancellation of the data subject within a period of ten days. Cancellation shall maintain data at the disposal of the public administrations, judges and courts, for the purpose of determining any liability. Afterwards, they shall be deleted.

If the rectified or canceled data have previously been communicated, the controller shall also notify the change so as the processor also rectifies or cancels the data.

Creation. Files in private ownership containing personal data may be created when it is necessary for the success of the legitimate activity and purpose.

Notification and Entry in the Register. Any person or body creating files of personal data shall first notify the Data Protection Agency (DPA). The notification includes the name of the controller, the purpose of the file, its location, the type of personal data, the security measures (either basic, medium or high level), any transfers intended (also to third countries). The DPA must be informed of any changes in the purpose of the computer file, the controller and the address of its location.

Communication of Transfers of Data. When making the first transfer of data, the controller must communicate this to the data subjects, indicating the purpose of the file, the nature of the data transferred and the name and address of the transferee.

Processing for the Purpose of Publicity and Market Research. Those involved in publicity, distance selling, market research, etc. shall use personal data when they feature in public sources or when they have been provided by the data subjects themselves or with their consent. In exercising the right of access, data subjects shall have the right to know the origin of their personal data. Data subjects shall have the right to ask for stop the processing of their data.

Standard Codes of Conduct. By means of sectorial agreements, administrative agreements or company decisions, publicly and privately owned controllers and the organizations to which they belong may draw up standard codes of conduct. Codes of conduct must be deposited in the General Data Protection Register.

International Movement of Data

General Rule. There may be no temporary or permanent transfers of personal data to countries which do not provide a level of protection comparable to that provided by the DPL, which is assessed by DPA.

Derogation. The provisions of the preceding paragraph shall not apply where:

- The international transfer is the result of applying agreements to which Spain is a party.
- The transfer provides international judicial aid.
- The transfer is necessary for medical care or health services management.
- Whereas the transfer of data is related to money.
- The data subject has given consent to the transfer.
- The transfer is necessary for starting or ending a contract or pre-contractual measures between the data subject and the controller.
- The transfer is necessary for ending a contract, in the interest of the data subject, between the controller and a third party.
- The transfer is necessary or legally required to safeguard a public interest, e.g. taxes.
- The transfer is necessary in legal proceedings.
- The transfer takes place at the request of a person with a legitimate interest, from a public register, and the request complies with the purpose of the register.
- The transfer takes place to a Member State of the European Union or to a country which the EU has declared to ensure an adequate level of protection.

3   Data Sharing Agreements

An electronic Data Sharing Agreement (e-DSA) is a human-readable, yet machine-processable contract, regulating how organizations and/or individuals share data. It is essentially a multilateral agreement consisting of:

- Predefined legal background information (which is usually available from a template, following, e.g., the textual template of traditional legal contracts);
- Dynamically defined information, including the definition of the validity period, the parties participating in the agreement, the data covered and, most importantly, the statements that constrain how data can be shared among the parties (such statements usually include authorization and obligation policies).

In the following, we illustrate the main phases of what we envisage to be an e-DSA definition phase, with reference to the sharing of medical data. We imagine a scenario in which the agreement draft is shown to the patient instantiating terms of law for the sharing of that kind of data, and the data sharing rules specific for that health care organization already defined by the policy experts.

In this paper, we propose a three-step phase for e-DSA definition, so that:

- (a) predefined legal background information are already filled and available in the initial e-DSA template, which encodes terms of Law for the sharing of personal data. For example, in the case of Spanish legislation, the initial e-DSA template is already filled with rules regulating the disclosure of personal data, according to SDPL (see Sect. 2);
- (b) policy experts at the hospital edit the initial e-DSA draft to set rules specific for that hospital, over covered data, according to internal regulations of the organization. It is worth noticing that editing the rules at this second step is not a frequent task, i.e., it is not requested that policy experts write a part of the e-DSA each time a patient wants to download a document. The policies internally defined at the organization are static ones and embrace categories of data, rather than the particular examination a patient may require in the future, and should be changed rarely over time. At this point of e-DSA definition, covered data are instantiated as belonging to categories of data (e.g., medical reports, payment receipts, administrative data, etc.). Also, we may envisage that e-DSA also instantiate the purpose for which it is being issued (like "clinical investigation", "publicity", "marketing", and so on).
- (c) As a third and final step in the editing phase, end-users complete the e-DSA either accepting or neglecting the previously-defined rules. In particular, the end-user has the opportunity to (1) give consent to the sharing of data, as expressed by Law and organizations-specific rules, and (2) edit some other adjustment to control her data disclosure. At this final point, the e-DSA is instantiated with the specific identifier of the end-user, and the specific identifier of the data over which the patient is expressing her sharing preferences. Given that it is unreasonable to think of end-users (e.g., patients) as policy experts, opportune authoring wizards should be designed to help the user in this last phase of e-DSA definition.

Given the three-step authoring phase depicted above, an e-DSA analysis phase is necessary before actually deploying the e-DSA. During the analysis phase, appropriate verification tools will detect possible conflicts between (1) in force law rules encoded in the initial e-DSA template at step (a), (2) organizations-specific rules, defined by policy experts at organization side at step (b), and (3) the customization of the end-user expressed in the last phase of e-DSA definition (c). However, distinct priority levels could be assigned to distinct rules. Hence, if the two conflicting rules have different priority levels, the conflict resolution is straightforward.

If the set of rules in the resulting e-DSA are conflict-free, then a deployment phase follows, where a set of enforceable policies are derived from the e-DSA and deployed within the organization IT infrastructure. E-DSA enforcement mechanisms are used to ensure that requests to access and process confidential data happen consistently with the agreed e-DSA, both during the interactions with specific services and in other contexts, including attempts of employees and/or other applications to use the data and/or disclose it to third parties.

In the following, the focus is on CNL4DSA, a controlled natural language specifically designed for expressing and analyzing e-DSA rules. We remind this language, highlighting its capability to encode some data protection principles from SPDL.

3.1 CNL4DSA

In order to be able to express e-DSA rules in a processable but, at the same time, human readable way, work in [23] has introduced a controlled natural language for electronic DSA, named CNL4DSA.

The CNL4DSA language has been thought to express *Authorizations, Prohibitions*, and *Obligations* policies referring to data and involving parties specified in the e-DSA. It expresses the rules in a way that is pretty understandable by humans, and, at the same time, it allows to derive a formal specification of the rules, that is the input for automatic analyzers.

Rules (and set of rules, i.e., policies) are expressed in terms of *subject, object* (or resource), *action*, and *environment*. Notices that these concepts are inline with those shown in Fig. 2: `Subject`, `File`, `Operation`, and `Context` (resp.). Similarly, the eXtensible Access Control Markup Language (XACML), the well known, de facto, standard for access control [27], relies on similar assumptions. We take advantage of this alignment to be able to enforce CNL clauses (in particular, SDPL originated clauses) using XACML. Hence, we consider a e-DSA policy as a set of rules that are evaluated, for each access request, to decide whether a given subject is allowed to perform a given action on a given resource, in a given environment. The features of the four elements, i.e., subjects, objects, actions, and environment, are expressed through *attributes* in XACML. Although, the enforcement of metamodel based policies would be probably different in other settings.

For each element, a (not exhaustive) list of attributes follows, especially referring to a health care scenario.

Subject. Attributes for subjects can be: ID, Role, and Organization.

- IDs express unique identifiers of the subject, e.g., "*abcde*123".
- Role specifies the functions and the capabilities of a subject in an organization. According to her role, a subject has different access privileges in a system. For example:
  - *general practitioner* is the role covered by that doctor who has a general view of the medical history of a patient;
  - *psychiatrists, orthopedists, radiologists, ...* identify doctors that are working in different medical specialty;
  - *rescue team member* provides first aids at the incident location and retrieves the first health information about the patient;
  - *patient* is used when the subject acts as a patient.

– Organization represents the organization the subject belongs to, e.g., "Red Cross" or "Hospital ABC".

Object. Attributes for objects could be: ID, Issuer, and Category.

– ID is a code that expresses the identifier of the object, e.g., "*xyz*".
– Issuer is the ID of the subject who produces that object;
– Category could be *medical*, including documents that collect medical information about the patient, and *administrative*, including documents collecting personal information, such as the patient's name, surname, address, date and place of birth, etc.

Action. We consider their IDs only, e.g., "Process", "Cancel", "Rectify", "Access".

To specify authorizations and obligations, we introduce the notion of *fragment* denoted as $f, f_1, \ldots$, and ranged over the set $\mathcal{F}$. The *fragment* is a tuple consisting of three elements, $f = \langle s, a, o \rangle$, where s is the subject, a is the action, o is the object, expressing that "the subject s performs the action a on the object o". The terms representing the action element a could be instantiated from a predefined list, e.g., as in the `Operation Type` enumerated meta-class of the meta-model represented in Figs. 1 and 2.

Referring to SPDL, examples of fragment could be "health care institutions process personal data" and "data subjects access their personal data" where "health care institutions" and "data subjects" are the subject of the fragments, "process" and "access" are actions and "personal data" represents the object.

Usually, fragments are evaluated within a specific *context*. In CNL4DSA, a *basic context* is a predicate c that characterizes the elements of the policies, like, e.g., environmental condition. Simple contexts are, e.g., temporal clauses: "within a period of ten days", or location clauses: "inside the health care centre". In order to describe complex agreements, contexts need to be composable. Hence, starting from the basic context c, we use the boolean connectors *and*, *or*, and *not* for describing a *composite context* C (ranged over the set $\mathcal{C}$) which is defined inductively as follows:

$$C := c \mid C \text{ and } C \mid C \text{ or } C \mid \text{not } c$$

As attributes of the environment we can consider, e.g.:

– Time, with the obvious meaning;
– Location, which represents a physical position (contextualizing, it could be either of the object or of the subject);
– Status, which specifies the exceptional nature of a situation, such as an emergency situation.

More complex expressions are generated by combining fragments. We refer to such expressions as *composite fragments*, and we denote them as F (ranged over the set $\mathcal{CF}$). We distinguish two disjoint sets of composite fragments: *authorization/prohibition* fragments, denoted by F_A and ranged over the set $\mathcal{AUTH}$, and *obligation* fragments, denoted by F_O and ranged over the set $\mathcal{OBL}$.

Authorization/Prohibition Fragment. The syntax of a composite authorization fragment is inductively defined as follows:

$$F_A := nil \mid can\ (cannot)\ f \mid F_A; F_A \mid if\ C\ then\ F_A \mid after\ f\ then\ F_A \mid (F_A)$$

The intuition for the composite authorization/prohibition fragment is the following:

- *nil* can do nothing.
- *can (cannot) f* is the atomic authorization (prohibition) fragment. Its informal meaning is *the subject s can (cannot) perform the action a on the object o. can f* expresses that *f* is allowed, but not required. Dually, *cannot f* expresses that *f* is not allowed, hence it is required that *f* does not happen.
- $F_A; F_A$ is a list of composite authorization fragments. The list constitutes the authorization section of the considered e-DSA. Whenever one term of the list performs a *f*-transition, then that term evolves to the correspondent derivative.
- *if C then* F_A expresses the logical implication between a composite context *C* and a composite authorization/prohibition fragment: if *C* holds, then F_A is applied.
- *after f then* F_A represents the temporal sequence of fragments. Informally, after *f* has happened, then the composite fragment F_A is applied.

Work in [23] also associates a formal semantics to CNL4DSA syntax, based on a *modal transition system* MTS [16,17], making the language amenable for automated processing and analysis, see, e.g., [22].

Example 1. The various clauses presented in Sect. 2 can be encoded in the aforementioned CNL4DSA language. As an example, we consider, from "Principles of data protection", the *Consent of the data subject* paragraph. In particular, the clauses (1) "Processing of personal data shall require the unambiguous consent of the data subject", and (2) "Exceptions are PAs for the exercise of their functions [...] in the action of protecting data subject vital interest or when contained in public sources" could be expressed in CNL4DSA as follows:

(1) **if** *hasDataCategory*(Data, Personal) and **if** *belongsTo*(Data, DataSubject) and **if** not *consentGiven*(Data, DataSubject) and **if** not *hasOrganization* (DataProcessor, PA) **then** DataProcessor **cannot** *process* Data.

(2) **if** *hasdatacategory*(Data, Personal) and **if** *belongsTo*(Data, DataSubject) and **if** *hasOrganization*(DataProcessor, PA) and **if** hasPurpose(Data-Processor, Protection) **then** DataProcessor **can** *process* Data.

Obligation Fragment. Similarly to authorisation fragments, the syntax of a composite obligation fragment is inductively defined as follows:

$$F_O := nil \mid must\ f \mid F_O; F_O \mid if\ C\ then\ F_O \mid after\ f\ then\ F_O \mid (F_O)$$

The intuition for the composite obligation fragment is the following:

- *nil* expresses no obligation.
- *must f* is the atomic obligation fragment. Its meaning is *the subject s must perform action a on the object o*. Thus, the *f*-transition is required.
- $F_O; F_O$ represents a list of composite obligation fragments. The list constitutes the obligation section of the considered DSA. Whenever one term of the list performs a *f*-transition, then that term evolves to the correspondent derivative.
- *if C then* F_O expresses the logical implication between a context C and a composite obligation fragment. It means that if C holds, then F_O is required.
- *after f then* F_O represents the temporal sequence of fragments. It means that after that *f* is performed, then F_O is required.

Example 2. In Sect. 2, we focus on the clauses about "Right of persons". If we consider the *Right of rectification or cancellation*: The controller is obliged to implement the right of rectification/cancellation of the data subject within a period of ten days. [...], this can be expressed in CNL4DSA as follows:

if *hasRole* (User, DataController) **and if** *hasDate* (RectifyRequest, Date) **and if** *timeLessThen* (CurrentDate, Date+tenDays) **then after** DataSubject *send* RectifyRequest **then** User **must** *rectify* Data

Quite obviously, if the data subject would like to cancel, the rule is similar.

4   Example Scenario

Here, we concentrate on the health care scenario, giving examples of rules that could be set through different steps of the e-DSA definition phase. As introduced in Sect. 3, rules definition occurs both statically and dynamically. First, generic rules are embedded in the initial e-DSA template according to legislation prescriptions on the protection of personal data. Then, policy experts at the medical organization set internal rules that are in force at their specific institution. Such rules will have a finer degree of granularity, with respect to the generic rules encoding terms of legislation. We may envisage that they will tell about actions allowed by subject covering roles over categories of data, e.g., "Those doctors operating at this medical institution can access medical examinations of patients in care at the same medical institution". This kind of rules is supposed to be statically defined, or, at least, we envisage they do not change very frequently over time. A third step, instead, takes place when the end-user (in the e-health scenario she will often collapse with the "patient") is going to interact with the medical institution to, e.g., book a clinical investigation, or negotiate the terms for a diagnosis collection. We envisage a scenario in which the patient is asked to accept the terms and regulations of law, as well as the internal rules previously set by the institution. The patient will also have the possibility to customize her own preferences regarding, e.g., identifiers of people allowed to collect the examinations on her stead.

It is worth noticing that, in the most general case, we envisage an e-DSA authoring phase in which the degree of granularity increases step after step. Indeed, when setting the initial e-DSA draft, generic rules regarding legislation of personal data processing are in place. Then, according to the kind of covered data, the e-DSA will increase its level of granularity since the policy experts will speak about, e.g., clinical diagnoses. Also, the agreement will have at this point one of the parties declared (i.e., the name of the medical organization which the policy experts belong to), and we may moreover suppose that various kind of e-DSA exist such that different data sharing purposes are defined. For example, specific e-DSA templates available at the hospital could be designed for "clinical investigation" purposes, while others for "marketing and publicity" or "analytics" purposes.

As a final step, after the patient has given consent to prior rules in the e-DSA and she has customized particular preferences over one (or more) of her specific documents, the patient name will be added as the other party of the agreement, and a validity time will be set up.

Hereafter, we give examples of rules that can be defined within the three-step e-DSA definition phase.

Scenario: Let us consider a radiology examination report. For the SPDL conceptualized in Sect. 2, this kind of document is classified as personal data, since it naturally contains elements that are useful to identify the data subject. Hence, the e-DSA associated to this document includes the CNL4DSA clauses imposed by the law, as for instance, the following one (that is similar to the first clause presented in previous Sect. 3):

if *hasDataCategory* (Data, Personal) and **if** *belongsTo* (Data, DataSubject) and **if** not *consentGiven* (Data, DataSubject) **then** DataProcessor **cannot** *retrieve* Data.

This clause states that the subject DataProcessor cannot perform operations on data whose category is Personal, if the DataSubject does not express her consent for the operation on such data. It is worth noticing that action *process* refers to generic actions that can be performed on a document, e.g., cancel, edit, transmit, record, etc. (as it was shown in the meta-model of Figs. 1 and 2). Legal rules are general and are introduced in the e-DSA to safeguard the Law while managing personal data.

Internal rules at a specific health care organization can be such that doctors who produces the data within the organization can ask a second opinion from doctors of the same organization, in order to provide a better diagnosis to the patient (this rule is inspired from a real case study described in [13]). Hence, in this scenario, the policy experts at the health care organization which a doctor belongs to may add, at the second level of the e-DSA draft, a rule stating that "each doctor can read the medical documents produced within the organization that doctor belongs to". This rule can be written in CNL4DSA as follows:

if *hasDataCategory*(Data, Medical) and **if** *hasRole*(DataProcessor, Doctor) and **if** *hasOrganization*(DataProcessor, Hospital ABC) and **if** *hasIssuer*(Data, Hospital ABC) **then** DataProcessor **can** *retrieve* Data.

As a third step, the radiological report is released to the patient. According to the law, the patient is the DataSubject of the report (that is the Personal data), thus the patient should give the consent to the rules regulating the management of that report by the organization. We imagine that the patient agrees (or disagrees) with the application of such rules by subscribing the e-DSA or not, e.g., by ticking the consent box.

On the one hand, if the patient does not tick the consent box, when a doctor, belonging to the same health-care organization where the report has been produced, tries to access such report, both the prohibition rule set by the law (i.e., "nobody can process the data") and the rule by the organization ("doctor can process data") apply. Obviously, such conflict must be solved to obtain an enforceable access decision. Appropriate techniques for automatically solving conflicts are described in Sect. 5. Assuming that prohibition rules set by the Law must be always enforced, in this particular case the conflict resolution strategy is straightforward, because the prohibition is prioritized during the definition phase (one could indeed set the maximum priority level for that rule).

On the other hand, if the patient ticks the consent box, the policy set by the law is not applicable (since the consent has been given). Now, the patient can express some preferences, likely though a simple authoring interface. These extra rules refine the access rights she gives on her data. Let us suppose that the patient gives her consent to access her report (whose ID is, e.g., *RadiologicalReportXY*), but she wants to allow one person only (e.g., Doctor Paul Smith) to access it. Thus, the following rules are automatically added to the e-DSA:

if *hasDataID* (Data, RadiologyReportXY) and **if** *hasRole* (DataProcessor, Doctor) and **if** *hasID* (DataProcessor, Paul Smith) **then** DataProcessor **can** *retrieve* Data.

if *hasDataID* (Data, RadiologyReportXY) and **if** *hasRole* (DataProcessor, Doctor) and **if** not *hasID* (DataProcessor, Paul Smith) **then** DataProcessor **cannot** *retrieve* Data.

For the sake of completeness, we recall that, after the third authoring step, the e-DSA will be finalized with patient name and validity time if no conflicts arise among all the set of rules defined in the three steps.

Instead, in this particular example, when a doctor who is not Doctor Paul Smith tries to access the report with ID *RadiologicalReportXY*, a conflict occurs between the rule defined by the hospital and the ones of the patient, because the former allows doctors from that hospital to retrieve the report while the rules of the patient do not allow its disclosure to other subjects but Doctor Paul Smith. Next section will introduce a technique for conflict detection and resolution.

5   Conflict Detection and Resolution

This section describes two approaches to perform, resp., analysis and resolution of conflicts among a set of policy rules.

5.1   e-DSA Analysis

The analysis process allows to detect conflicts between rules forming a policy. In particular, it checks if the rules set is conflict-free, by performing pairwise analysis over all pairs of rules in the e-DSA. The analyzer exhaustively simulates all the possible access requests, under a set of contextual conditions, defined by a policy expert (e.g., she can set date and time of the access request, the role of the subject, the data category, etc.). Thus, the analyzer checks if there exist at least two rules that, simultaneously, allow and deny the same subject to perform the same action on the same object, under the given set of contextual conditions.

The analysis tool we have proposed in [24] takes as input CNL4DSA rules. The formal engine performing the analysis of policies is Maude [5] that is an executable programming language that models distributed systems and the actions within those systems. The choice of using Maude for policy analysis was driven by the fact that rewrite rules (which Maude build upon) are a natural way to model the behaviour of distributed systems, and we see a policy exactly as a process where different subjects may interact with each other, possibly on the same set of objects. Maude comes with built-in commands allowing to search for allowed traces, i.e., sequence of actions, of a rule specified in CNL4DSA. These traces represent the sequences of actions that are authorized, or denied, by the rule. Also, exploiting the implementation of modal logic over the CNL4DSA semantics, as done in [6,33] for process algebras such as CCS [25], it is possible to prove that a modal formula, representing a certain query, is satisfied by the Maude specification of the rule (or set of rules). The analyzer shows the analysis results through a user interface deployed as a Web Application. It allows the user both to query Maude specification and visualize human-readable results.

5.2   e-DSA Conflict Resolution

Here, we describe a methodology introduced in [21] applicable to solve rules' conflicts. It is based on the Analytical Hierarchy Process (AHP), a well known multi-criteria decision system [30,31]. AHP is a multi-criteria decision making technique, which has been largely used in several fields of study. Given a decision problem, within which different *alternatives* can be chosen to reach a *goal*, AHP returns the *most relevant* alternative with respect to a set of *criteria*. The adoption of AHP to solve conflicts among rules has been described in [18,21]. Within the e-DSA scenario, the technique is applied when the conflicting rules have been defined with the same priority level.

The AHP approach requires to subdivide a complex problem (i.e., ranking conflicting rules) into a set of sub-problems, equal in number to the chosen *criteria*, and then computes the solution (i.e., choose the applicable rule) by properly merging all the local solutions for each sub-problem. In Fig. 3, we show a possible instantiation of the AHP hierarchy for conflict resolution. The goal (the box on top of the hierarchy in Fig. 3) is "select the rule" among conflicting ones, e.g., rule1 and rule2 in the boxes at the bottom of the hierarchy. As usual, rules are expressed in terms of *subject, object, action*, and *environment* and they are evaluated according to the value of these attributes in order to determine which rule can be applied to each access request.

We consider as *criteria* (second group of boxes starting from the top of the hierarchy) the *specificity* of the elements that constitute a rule: (i) *Specificity of the subject*, in which we evaluate the attributes exploited in the two conflicting rules to identify the subject, to determine which of them define a more specific set of subjects; (ii) *Specificity of the object* in which we evaluate the attributes exploited in the two rules to identify the object; (iii) *Specificity of the environment* in which we evaluate the attributes to identify the environment. Furthermore, AHP features the capability to further refine each criterion in sub-criteria, by considering the attributes that identify each element, e.g., for the subject: ID, Role, and Organization. The attributes' set depends on a given scenario.

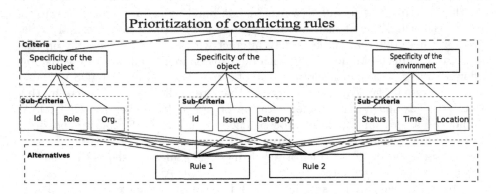

Fig. 3. AHP hierarchy for conflict resolution.

Figure 3 represents the hierarchy here considered. However, the methodology is general enough to allow the insertion of further criteria and sub criteria that may be helpful to evaluate the alternatives.

Once the hierarchy is built, the method performs pairwise comparison, from the bottom to the top, in order to compute the relevance, hereafter called *local priority*: (i) of each alternatives with respect to each sub-criteria, (ii) of each sub-criterion with respect to the relative criterion, and finally, (iii) of each criterion with respect to the goal. Note that, in case of a criterion without sub-criteria, the local priority of each alternative is computed with respect to the criterion.

Comparisons are made through a scale of numbers typical to AHP (see Table 1) that indicates how many times an alternative is *more relevant* than another.

Table 1. Fundamental scale for AHP

Intensity	Definition	Explanation
1	Equal	Two elements contribute equally to the objective
3	Moderate	One element is slightly more relevant than another
5	Strong	One element is strongly more relevant over another
7	Very strong	One element is very strongly more relevant over another
9	Extreme	One element is extremely more relevant over another

Computation of local priorities. Let the reader suppose that rule1 and rule2 are two conflicting rules. They become the two alternatives in the hierarchy and they are evaluated with respect to sub criteria. To this aim, k 2x2 pairwise comparison matrices, where k is the number of sub criteria (in our case, $k = 9$), are built according to a very simple approach, based on the presence of the attributes in the rules. Given that a_{ij} is the generic element of one of these matrices:

- rule1 and rule2 contain (or do not contain) attribute A: then $a_{12} = a_{21} = 1$.
- If only rule1 contains A, than $a_{12} = 9$, and $a_{21} = \frac{1}{9}$.
- If only rule2 contains A, than $a_{12} = \frac{1}{9}$, and $a_{12} = 9$.

Once a comparison matrice has been defined, the local priorities can be computed as the normalized eigenvector associated with the largest eigenvalue of such matrice [29].

Then, moving up in the hierarchy, we quantify how subcriteria are relevant with respect to the correspondent criterion. Hence, we evaluate how the attributes are relevant to identify the subject, the object and the environment. In particular, in our example we use the matrices in Table 2, with the local priorities shown in the last column of each matrice. As an example, in the matrice that compares the subject's attributes (the left-most one in Table 2), we write $a_{12} = 9$ since we think that the subject ID allows to identify the subject *extremely* better than the subject role. Indeed, the subject ID exactly identifies one subject. For the same reason, we put $a_{13} = 9$ (ID *vs* the organization the subject belongs to). More details are in [21].

We remark that the values in these matrices simply represent the perception of the authors on the relative relevance of the attributes. Other values could have been chosen as well.

Finally, we quantify how the three criteria are relevant for achieving the goal of solving conflicts. Without loss of generality, we hypothesize that all the criteria equally contribute to meet the goal. In this straightforward case, the pairwise comparison matrix is a 3×3 matrix with all the elements equal to 1, and the local priorities of the criteria with respect to the goal are simply 0.33 each. Hence, for the computation of the global priorities, $p_g^{c_j} = 0.33$, $j = 1,\ldots,3$ (see below).

Table 2. Comparison matrices and local priorities for subcriteria *w.r.t.* criteria

SUBJ	ID	role	organiz.	$\bar{p}_{Subj}$	OBJ	ID	issuer	category	$\bar{p}_{Obj}$
ID	1	9	9	0.818182	ID	1	5	7	0.7454
role	$\frac{1}{9}$	1	1	0.0909091	issuer	$\frac{1}{5}$	1	$\frac{4}{3}$	0.1454
org	$\frac{1}{9}$	1	1	0.0909091	category	$\frac{1}{7}$	$\frac{3}{4}$	1	0.1091

ENV	status	time	location	$\bar{p}_{Env}$
status	1	7	7	0.777778
time	$\frac{1}{7}$	1	1	0.111111
location	$\frac{1}{7}$	1	1	0.111111

Computation of global priorities. Once all local priorities are computed, the following formula computes the global priorities. For the sake of simplicity, we have in mind a hierarchy tree where the leftmost $n1$ criteria have a set of sub-criteria each, while the rightmost $n2$ criteria have no sub-criteria below them, and $n1 + n2 = n$ is the number of total criteria.

$$P_g^{a_i} = \sum_{w=1}^{n1} \sum_{k=1}^{q(w)} p_g^{c_w} \cdot p_{c_w}^{sc_k^w} \cdot p_{sc_k^w}^{a_i} + \sum_{j=1}^{n2} p_g^{c_j} \cdot p_{c_j}^{a_i} \tag{1}$$

$q(w)$ is the number of sub-criteria for criterion c_w, $p_g^{c_w}$ is the local priority of criterion c_w with respect to the goal g, $p_{c_w}^{sc_k^w}$ is the local priority of sub-criterion k with respect to criterion c_w, and $p_{sc_k^w}^{a_i}$ is the local priority of alternative a_i with respect to sub-criterion k of criterion c_w. $p_{c_w}^{sc_k^w}$ and $p_{sc_k^w}^{a_i}$ are computed by following the same procedure of the pairwise comparisons matrices illustrated above.

It is worth noticing that, in our approach, we do not consider as a decisional criterion the specificity of the action. This is because we evaluate the action only according to its ID, always present in a policy. So the evaluation of the alternative rules with respect to the criterion *action* is constant, and it does not add any meaningful information for taking the final decision.

In [18], we have developed a prototype implementation of the conflict solver based on the rules' specificity, highlighting a twofold advantage. First, the prototype is specifically based on the XACML engine and it extends the native XACML combining algorithms for conflict resolution, aiming at a finer granularity in the evaluation of conflicting rules. Secondly, we experienced good results in terms of execution time, negligible to human beings up to a quite large amount of conflicting rules (for example, execution time is 275 milliseconds with 64 conflicting rules composed by three attributes each).

6   Resolution Strategy Example

We refer to the example scenario in Sect. 4, where a doctor at Hospital ABC would like to share with another doctor a particular radiological report.

Let R_1 be the hospital rule:

if *hasDataCategory*(Data, Medical) and **if** *hasRole*(DataProcessor, Doctor) and **if** *hasOrganization*(DataProcessor, Hospital ABC) and **if** *hasIssuer*(Data, Hospital ABC) **then** DataProcessor **can** *retrieve* Data.

Instead, the patient would like to share that data with Doctor Paul Smith only (R_2):

if *hasDataID*(Data, RadiologyReportXY) and **if** *hasRole*(DataProcessor, Doctor) and **if** not *hasID*(DataProcessor, Paul Smith) **then** DataProcessor **cannot** *retrieve* Data.

If the doctor at ABC tries to show the radiology examination to a doctor different from Paul Smith a conflict occurs because both rule1 and rule2 are applicable, but with opposite effects.

According to what discussed in the previous section, each criterion is statically evaluated with respect to the goal. We recall that the local priorities of the uppermost two levels of the AHP hierarchy in Fig. 3 are stitched to the rules themselves. They are defined according to the scenario when the policies are created, and they do not change until the rules change. In our case, we hypothesize that, for the uppermost level, the local priorities are all equal to 0.33, while the local priorities for the middle level have been specified in Table 2.

Instead, the local priorities of the lowest level are evaluated at runtime, when someone tries to access the data. The evaluation is simply based on the presence, or the absence, of an attribute in the conflicting rules. In our example, we have that:

– R_1 identifies the subject through role and organization, while R_2 through role and ID.
– R_1 identifies the object through category and issuer, while R_2 through the object ID.
– Neither R_1 nor R_2 specifies constraints on the environment.

Table 3 shows an example of the simple 2×2 matrices that compare R_1 and R_2 with respect to the presence of the attribute ID of the element object. Since R_2 specifies the object through the ID, while R_1 does not, we give 9 to R_2 and $\frac{1}{9}$ to R_1.

Similar 2x2 matrices are built for evaluating R_1 and R_2 with respect to all the sub-criteria (we have 9 matrices). The global priorities are calculated according to expression 1 and instantiated as in 2:

Table 3. R_1 and R_2 evaluated w.r.t. the presence of the attribute ID of the object

ID_{Obj}	R_1	R_2	$\bar{p}_{ID_{Obj}}$
R_1	1	$\frac{1}{9}$	0.1
R_2	9	1	0.9

$$P_g^{R_1} = 0.33 \cdot ((p_{Subj}^{ID} \cdot p_{ID}^{R_1}) + (p_{Subj}^{Role} \cdot p_{Role}^{R_1}) + (p_{Subj}^{Org} \cdot p_{Org}^{R_1})) +$$
$$0.33 \cdot ((p_{Obj}^{ID_{Obj}} \cdot p_{ID_{Obj}}^{R_1}) + (p_{Obj}^{Iss} \cdot p_{Iss}^{R_1}) + (p_{Obj}^{Cat} \cdot p_{Cat}^{R_1})) + \qquad (2)$$
$$0.33 \cdot ((p_{Env}^{Stat} \cdot p_{Stat}^{R_1}) + (p_{Env}^{Time} \cdot p_{Time}^{R_1}) + (p_{Env}^{Loc} \cdot p_{Loc}^{R_1}))$$
$$= 0.34$$

where $p_{Subj}^{(-)}$, $p_{Obj}^{(-)}$, and $p_{Env}^{(-)}$ are the value of vectors of local priorities shown in Fig. 2 (rightmost column of each matrix), while $p_{ID}^{R_1}$, $p_{Role}^{R_1}$, ... are the local priorities of rule R_1 against all the subcriteria, as the result of the nine 2×2 matrices. For example, $p_{ID_{Obj}}^{R_1} = 0.1$, see Table 3. Complementary, for rule R_2 we obtain $P_g^{R_2} = 0.66$. Hence, the result of the decision strategy shows a preference for the execution of rule R_2.

7   Related Work

To the best of our knowledge, the main novelty of this paper is the translation of a real Data Protection Law, i.e., the Spanish Data Protection Law (SDPL), into privacy electronically manageable rules by a devoted e-DSA-based infrastructure. Indeed, this is the first attempt to refer to the SDPL as the basic source of the design of multi-lateral e-DSA that regulates data exchange among different entities.

On the other hand, over the last decades, researchers have investigated several solutions for (platform-independent) policy-based infrastructures, to specify, analyze, and deploy privacy, security, and networking policies. Hereafter we revise some work focused on validation and policy conflict detection and resolution.

Data protection policy analysis is essential to detect inconsistencies and conflicts before the actual enforcement. In [3], it is shown that the Event-B language (www.event-b.org) can be used to model obliged events. The Rodin platform provides animation and model checking tool set for analyzing specifications written in Event-B, thus leading to capability of obligations analysis [2]. The authors of [26] propose a comprehensive framework for expressing highly complex privacy-related policies, featuring purposes and obligations. Also, a formal definition of conflicting permission assignments is given, together with efficient conflict-checking algorithms and with a set of experimental results which show the performances of such algorithms. The Policy Design Tool [28] offers a sophisticated way for modeling and analyzing high-level security requirements in a business context and create security policy templates in a standard format. Hence, there exists generic formal approaches that could a priori be exploited for the analysis of some aspects of data protection policies. As an example, the Klaim family of process calculi [8] provides a high-level model for distributed systems, and, in particular, exploits a capability-based type system for programming and controlling access and usage of resources. Also, work in [12] exploits a static analyzer for a variant of Klaim.

Policy conflict detection is generally followed by resolutions of conflicts. Not necessarily tied to data protection, existing work concerns general conflict resolution methods for access control in various areas. The approach adopted by the eXtensible Access Control Markup Language (XACML) [27] is a very general one, defines standard rule-combining algorithms: Deny-Overrides, Permit-Overrides, First-Applicable, and Only-One-Applicable. As an example, the Deny-Overrides algorithm states that the result of the policy is Deny if the evaluation of at least one of the rules returns Deny. A classification of anomalies that may occur among firewall policies is presented in [1]. In the same work, an editing tool allows a user to insert, modify, and remove, policy rules in order to avoid anomalies.

In [14], the authors propose a conflict resolution strategy for medical policies, by presenting a classification of conflicts and suggesting a strategy based on high level features of the policy as a whole (such as the regency of a policy). If such characteristics are not sufficient for deciding which policy should be applied, the *default deny* approach is applied.

Work in [11] identifies a number of conflict types, using examples from the military and aerospace domain, and discusses how to prevent and resolve such conflicts for different classes of them.

In [19, 32] the authors deal with both the detection and resolution of conflicts. Work in [19] defines a policy precedence relationship that takes into account the following principles: *(a)* Rules that deny the access have the priority on the others; *(b)* Priorities could be explicitly assigned to policy rules by the system administrators; *(c)* Higher priority is given to the rule whose distance with the object it refers to is the lowest, where a specific function should be defined to measure such distance; and *(d)* Higher priority is given to the rule that is more specific according to the domain nesting criteria. In [32], the authors investigate policy conflict resolution in pervasive environments. They discussed different strategies for conflict detection but the part dedicated to the conflict resolution strategy just refers to quite standard strategies, i.e., role hierarchies override and obligation precedence. Also in [9], four different strategies for solving conflicts are considered. They distinguish among solving conflicts at compile-time, at run-time, in a balanced way leaving to run-time only potential conflicts, or in ad-hoc way accordingly to the particular conflicts. In general they take into account the role of the requester for deciding which policy wins the conflict. Also in this case, the strategy is based only on one criterion. The approach in [19, 32] is extended in [20]. Indeed, the authors introduce the definition and employment of the precedence establishment principals in a context-aware-manner, i.e., according to the relation among the specificity of the context. The decision criterion is a unique one that groups a set of contextual conditions.

Work in [4] presents a formal model, based on deontic logic, to detect and, possibly, solve conflicts among security policies. An implementation of the model is left as future work. In [7], the authors present *Or BAC*, a methodology to manage conflicts occurring among permissions and prohibitions. Within this approach, rules are grouped according to the organizations that emit them. The advantage of this proposal is to reduce the problem of redundant policies.

The procedure known as *Break the Glass* [15] may be applied in extraordinary situations, bypassing all the existing applicable rules. As an example, by applying this methodology, rescue team members can access patient medical documents in an emergency situation, whatever the policies related to those documents are. A proper audit support should be used to monitor the accesses.

8   Conclusions

Protecting personal data from unauthorized disclosure to third parties is an issue regulated by the legislation of different European countries, with the support of common European directives. Technically, data access, processing, and sharing can be regulated defining (and enacting) appropriate machine processable data sharing multilateral contracts, named e-DSA. Based on the protection of data, an e-DSA is written by all the entities that have a jurisdiction on that data. It collects rules that cover several aspects, from legal constraints to user-preferences.

Hence, in this paper we provided an overview of the incremental construction phases of an e-DSA. These phases follow the agreement procedure that takes into account clauses coming from a default template stating the legislation of application; the clauses introduced by an organization, e.g., a health-care company, and finally, the decisions of the end-users with respect to the use of their data (e.g., including consent, purpose, restrictions, ...). As an e-DSA construction process evolves, the clauses specified in the e-DSA reach a finer granularity. The main novelty of this paper is the reference and conceptual modelling of the Spanish Data Protection Law (S)DPL as the basic source of policies regulating data exchange. To the best of our knowledge this is also the first attempt of specifying rules of SPDL as clauses for electronic processing in a controlled natural language (CNL4DSA).

The e-DSA construction procedure is not restricted to the authoring procedure but it also includes a conflict detection and, eventually, resolution phase. We also introduce an e-DSA validator and illustrate its usage and the conflict detection and resolution process through a realistic e-Health scenario, based on a real one described by a Spanish medical institution.

In the immediate future, we will expand our studies about the conceptualization and formal analysis of the SPDL. In particular, we will validate them using scenarios of data exchange in different settings and domains where they may be classified at different sensitive levels. In this way, we will also get further feedback about the practical application of the methodology presented in this paper.

Acknowledgments. The research leading to these results has been partially funded by the European Union Seventh Framework Programme (FP7/2007-2013) under grant no. 610853 (Coco Cloud).

References

1. Al-Shaer, E.S., Hamed, H.H.: Firewall policy advisor for anomaly discovery and rule editing. In: IFIP/IEEE Integrated Network Management, pp. 17–30 (2003)

2. Arenas, A.E., Aziz, B., Bicarregui, J., Wilson, M.D.: An event-B approach to data sharing agreements. In: Méry, D., Merz, S. (eds.) IFM 2010. LNCS, vol. 6396, pp. 28–42. Springer, Heidelberg (2010)
3. Bicarregui, J., Arenas, A., Aziz, B., Massonet, P., Ponsard, C.: Towards modelling obligations in event-B. In: Börger, E., Butler, M., Bowen, J.P., Boca, P. (eds.) ABZ 2008. LNCS, vol. 5238, pp. 181–194. Springer, Heidelberg (2008)
4. Cholvy, L., Cuppens, F.: Analyzing consistency of security policies. In: IEEE Symposium on Security and Privacy, pp. 103–112 (1997)
5. Clavel, M., Durán, F., Eker, S., Lincoln, P., Martí-Oliet, N., Meseguer, J., Talcott, C. (eds.): All About Maude. LNCS, vol. 4350. Springer, Heidelberg (2007)
6. Colombo, M., Martinelli, F., Matteucci, I., Petrocchi, M.: Context-aware analysis of data sharing agreements. In: Advances in Human-Oriented and Personalized Mechanisms, Technologies and Services, pp. 99–104 (2010)
7. Cuppens, F., Cuppens-Boulahia, N., Ghorbel, M.B.: High level conflict management strategies in advanced access control models. ENTCS **186**, 3–26 (2007)
8. De Nicola, R., Ferrari, G.-L., Pugliese, R.: Programming access control: The KLAIM experience. In: Palamidessi, C. (ed.) CONCUR 2000. LNCS, vol. 1877, pp. 48–65. Springer, Heidelberg (2000)
9. Dunlop, N., Indulska, J., Raymond, K.: Methods for conflict resolution in policy-based management systems. In: Enterprise Distributed Object Computing, pp. 98–109. IEEE (2003)
10. EU FP7 grant no. 610853. Confidential and Compliant Clouds (Coco Cloud) project (2013). http://www.coco-cloud.eu
11. Hall-May, M., Kelly, T.: Towards conflict detection and resolution of safety policies. In: International System Safety Conference, pp. 687–695 (2006)
12. Hansen, R.R., Nielson, F., Nielson, H.R., Probst, C.W.: Static validation of licence conformance policies. In: ARES, pp. 1104–1111 (2008)
13. Hewlett-Packard Italiana (ed.): Coco-Cloud Deliverable 7.1: Definition of pilot requirements (2014). http://www.coco-cloud.eu/deliverables
14. Jin, J., Ahn, G.-J., Hu, H., Covington, M.J., Zhang, X.: Patient-centric authorization framework for electronic healthcare services. Comput. Secur. **30**(2–3), 116–127 (2011)
15. Joint NEMA/COCIR/JIRA Security and Privacy Committee (SPC). Break-glass: An approach to granting emergency access to healthcare systems (2004)
16. Larsen, K.G.: Modal specifications. In: Sifakis, J. (ed.) CAV 1989. LNCS, vol. 407, pp. 232–246. Springer, Heidelberg (1990)
17. Larsen, K.G., Thomsen, B.: A modal process logic. In: LICS, pp. 203–210 (1988)
18. Lunardelli, A., Matteucci, I., Mori, P., Petrocchi, M.: A prototype for solving conflicts in XACML-based e-health policies. In: Computer-Based Medical Systems, pp. 449–452. IEEE (2013)
19. Lupu, E.C., Sloman, M.: Conflicts in policy-based distributed systems management. IEEE Trans. Softw. Eng. **25**(6), 852–869 (1999)
20. Masoumzadeh, A., Amini, M., Jalili, R.: Conflict detection and resolution in context-aware authorization. In: Security in Networks and Distributed Systems, pp. 505–511. IEEE (2007)
21. Matteucci, I., Mori, P., Petrocchi, M.: Prioritized execution of privacy policies. In: Di Pietro, R., Herranz, J., Damiani, E., State, R. (eds.) DPM 2012 and SETOP 2012. LNCS, vol. 7731, pp. 133–145. Springer, Heidelberg (2013)
22. Matteucci, I., Mori, P., Petrocchi, M., Wiegand, L.: Controlled data sharing in E-health. In: STAST, pp. 17–23 (2011)

23. Matteucci, I., Petrocchi, M., Sbodio, M.L.: CNL4DSA: a controlled natural language for data sharing agreements. In: SAC: Privacy on the Web Track, pp. 616–620. ACM (2010)
24. Matteucci, I., Petrocchi, M., Sbodio, M.L., Wiegand, L.: A design phase for data sharing agreements. In: Garcia-Alfaro, J., Navarro-Arribas, G., Cuppens-Boulahia, N., de Capitani di Vimercati, S. (eds.) DPM 2011 and SETOP 2011. LNCS, vol. 7122, pp. 25–41. Springer, Heidelberg (2012)
25. Milner, R.: A Calculus of Communicating Systems. Springer-Verlag New York Inc., Secaucus (1982)
26. Ni, Q., Bertino, E., Lobo, J., Brodie, C., Karat, C.-M., Karat, J., Trombetta, A.: Privacy-aware role-based access control. ACM Trans. Inform. Syst. Secur. **13**(3), 24:1–24:31 (2010)
27. OASIS. eXtensible Access Control Markup Language (XACML) Version 3.0, January 2013
28. Policy Design Tool (2009). http://www.alphaworks.ibm.com/tech/policydesign tool
29. Saaty, T.L.: A scaling method for priorities in hierarchical structures. J. Math. Psychol. **15**(3), 234–281 (1977)
30. Saaty, T.L.: Decision-making with the AHP: why is the principal eigenvector necessary. Eur. J. Oper. Res. **145**(1), 85–91 (2003)
31. Saaty, T.L.: Decision making with the analytic hierarchy process. Int. J. Serv. Sci. **1**(1), 83–98 (2008)
32. Syukur, E.: Methods for policy conflict detection and resolution in pervasive computing environments. In: Policy Management for Web (WWW 2005), pp. 10–14. ACM (2005)
33. Verdejo, A., Martí-Oliet, N.: Implementing CCS in Maude 2. ENTCS **71**, 282–300 (2002)

Cloud Standards

Standards for Accountability in the Cloud

Alain Pannetrat[(✉)] and Jesus Luna

Cloud Security Alliance, Edinburgh, Scotland, UK
{apannetrat, jluna}@cloudsecurityalliance.org

Abstract. This paper examines the role of standards in the cloud with a particular focus on accountability, in the context of the A4Cloud Project (Accountability for the Cloud). To this end, we first provide a general overview of standards, what they are and how we can categorize them, as illustrated by a few cloud-specific examples. Next, we examine the intersection between standards and accountability, by highlighting how standards influence the A4Cloud Project and reciprocally how the A4Cloud Project aims to influence accountability related standards. We argue that *specification* standards can foster interoperability for the purpose of accountability, thereby making accountability more automated and pervasive. Finally, we take a closer look at a particular accountability requirement: the continuous monitoring of the compliance of cloud services. This is an area of great interest for standardization, which faces many research challenges.

Keywords: Cloud · Standards · Accountability · Interoperability · Security · Monitoring

1 Introduction

The IEEE standards glossary[1] describes a standard as "*a document that defines the characteristics of a product, process or service, such as dimensions, safety aspects, and performance requirements*". This work provides an overview of *standards* with a particular focus on their role for accountability in the cloud, based largely on the latest research we conducted in the context of the A4Cloud European Research Project (http://www.a4cloud.eu/).

1.1 The Importance of Standards

Standards are important in many different ways in IT. First and foremost, as we will see, standards create common vocabularies and interoperability, thereby enabling different organization to follow common and comparable processes, exchange and interpret data in a unified way. For service providers, interoperability enables automation and cost reduction. For customers, it enables choice between "compatible" offerings, avoiding vendor lock-in. In some domains, it also increases quality assurance with the adoption of standardized criteria of evaluation for products or services.

---

[1] https://www.ieee.org/education_careers/education/standards/standards_glossary.html.

© Springer International Publishing Switzerland 2015
M. Felici and C. Fernández-Gago (Eds.): A4Cloud 2014, LNCS 8937, pp. 275–288, 2015.
DOI: 10.1007/978-3-319-17199-9_12

Standards are also notorious battlegrounds for competing economic interests. In some sectors, companies lobby strongly for the adoption of standards that match their own products or services as closely as possible: it provides them with a strong advantage over their competitors, which will need to adapt to the new adopted norm. The classic example of a standards war is the videotape format[2] war between VHS and BetaMax in the 80 s.

Finally, while policymakers often influence the definition of standards in order to promote open markets or customer safety, for example, there is also evidence of the opposite: existing standards influence policy makers, as illustrated by current EU cloud standardization initiatives.[3] In this respect, *fundamental standards* (see Sect. 1.2) play a key role by establishing the scope and terminology in a field, in way that is later difficult to change completely.

1.2   The Main Categories of Standards

While there are many ways to classify standards, we propose to adopt the 4 general categories of standards defined by CEN-CENELEC[4] to structure the discussion of this work. If we restrict ourselves to the IT domain, these 4 categories can be expressed as follows:

1. **Fundamental standards** - *which concern terminology, conventions, signs and symbols, etc.*;
2. **Organization standards** - *which describe the functions and relationships of a company, as well as elements such as quality management and assurance, maintenance, value analysis, project or system management, etc.*
3. **Specification standards** - *which define characteristics of a product or a service, such as interfaces (APIs), data formats, communication protocols and other interoperability features, etc.*;
4. **Test methods and analysis standards** - *which measure characteristics of a system, describing processes and reference data for analysis*;

Examples of standards in the first 3 categories are provided in Sect. 2 where we illustrate some key cloud standards. The last category can be exemplified through software testing standards such as [1]. Since it is less relevant to our work on accountability, we do not discuss this 4th category further.

1.3   Organization of This Work

The rest of this paper is organized as follows.

In Sect. 2, we offer a few illustrative examples of standards that play a key role in the cloud, some of which are likely familiar to the reader.

---

[2] https://en.wikipedia.org/wiki/Videotape_format_war.

[3] http://eur-lex.europa.eu/LexUriServ/LexUriServ.do?uri=COM:2012:0529:FIN:EN:PDF.

[4] http://www.cencenelec.eu/research/innovation/standardstypes/Pages/default.aspx.

In Sect. 3, we examine the intersection between accountability and standards. First, we look at the role of standards from a research project perspective. Next, we focus on the use of standards to foster interoperability as a means to increase accountability.

The last section of this paper is devoted to the continuous monitoring of the security of cloud services. We argue that this is still largely an area of ongoing research where standardization has a key role to play.

2 Examples of Key Standards in the Cloud

In this section, we provide examples of *fundamental* standards, *organization* standards, and (de facto) *specification* standards, which play an important role in the cloud.

2.1 The NIST Cloud Computing Reference Architecture

The NIST Special Publication 500-292, better known as the NIST Cloud Computing Reference Architecture [5] is a good example of a *fundamental standard*. The initial goal of this standard was to create "*a level playing field for industry to discuss and compare their cloud offerings with the US Government*". This standard essentially proposes:

(1) A taxonomy of cloud actors.
(2) Key architectural components of cloud service deployment and orchestration.

The 5 main cloud actors proposed are *Cloud Consumers, Cloud Providers, Cloud Brokers, Cloud Auditors* and *Cloud Carriers*. We will not details the key architecture components proposed in the standard, but we note that they include the ubiquitous terminology for service deployment models such as *public, private, community* and *hybrid* clouds, concepts related to *management, responsibility, security, privacy, business support*, service orchestration including the *IaaS/PaaS/SaaS* deployment models. As such, it's easy to understand that this standard has been very influential in shaping the discussion about cloud ecosystems as well as following cloud standards,[5] way beyond the US government domain.

From the point of view of accountability, we note that the roles described in this standard do not provide a fully satisfactory tool to describe accountability scenarios in the cloud. The NIST model defines a Cloud Provider as an entity "*responsible for making a service available to interested parties*" and a Cloud Consumers as an entity "*that maintains a business relationship with, and uses service from, Cloud Providers*". It is tempting to consider the person (data subject) whose data is processed by a cloud as a *cloud customer*, but this approach excludes many scenarios. Consider for example the case of a hospital that stores some heath data with a cloud provider: the hospital is a *cloud customer* but the patient cannot be attributed any role in the NIST model despite being the entity to which all others are accountable to in the supply chain.

---

[5] See for example the ISO/IEC 27017 or ISO/IEC 17788 discussed in Sect. 3.1.

In the A4Cloud project, to deal with this limitation, rather than creating a new role taxonomy specifically for accountability, we chose to reuse and extend the NIST taxonomy, adding relevant accountability actors (as described in Sect. 3.2). This was done for pragmatic reasons in order to facilitate the dissemination of our work outside the project, illustrating again the importance of fundamental standards in setting the terminology in a field.

2.2   ISO/IEC 27001 and CSA CCM

Information security often tends to be based on a set of ad hoc security controls and "best practices checklists[6]" (e.g. *"update your antivirus frequently"*). While such approaches may work in small organizations, they do not scale to larger ones, because they often miss crucial issues such as governance and compliance.

ISO/IEC 27001 [3] is an *organization standard* for information security management systems (ISMS). This standard aims to bring a formalized and managed approach to information security. As such, it directs organizations to: (i) establish an information security governance process, (ii) conduct a risk analysis, (iii) apply adequate risk treatment notably by selecting relevant controls, and (iv) monitor and update the information security process through time.

IT services, including cloud services, can be certified against ISO/IEC 27001 after being audited by an independent third-party. By receiving such a certificate, the service provider demonstrates the adoption of a managed holistic approach to information security. Many prominent cloud services have achieved this certification recently (e.g. Amazon AWS, Microsoft Azur, Google Apps, etc.).

One of the key elements of the establishment of an ISMS is the selection of adequate controls, i.e. measures that mitigate identified risks and enforce the proper management of the information system. ISO/IEC 27001 (and it's companion standard ISO/IEC 27002 [2]) proposes a non-limitative catalogue of controls objectives for companies to choose from. Unfortunately, while this catalogue of control objectives is well suited for traditional IT systems, is does not fully address cloud specifics (e.g. multi-tenancy and virtualization).

In 2010, the Cloud Security Alliance (CSA, *employer of these authors*) started developing a control framework called the Cloud Control Matrix[7] (CCM) that specifically addresses cloud security issues. In the end of 2013, CSA introduced the STAR Certification[8]: the first cloud security specific certification scheme, based on ISO/IEC 27001 but extending it with several features, including the use of the CCM as the main control framework, as opposed to the traditional approach.

The example of CSA's pragmatic re-use of ISO 27001 is yet another illustration of the influence and importance of established standards, as already highlighted with the reference architecture of the NIST in the previous section.

---

[6] For example http://www.asd.gov.au/publications/Mitigation_Strategies_2014.pdf.

[7] https://cloudsecurityalliance.org/research/ccm/.

[8] https://cloudsecurityalliance.org/star/.

2.3   Amazon EC2 and S3 APIs

Amazon EC2[9] and S3[10] APIs are application programming interfaces for virtualized computing and storage facilities, respectively. Some competitors of Amazon and open-source cloud IaaS projects,[11] including OpenStack, Eucalyptus, OpenNebula or Cloud-Stack, have adopted these APIs for their IaaS offering. While they are not standards by design, these APIs have become an interesting example of de facto *specification standards*.

2.4   Gathering Cloud Standards

There are many more cloud standards beyond the previous few examples.

Some of these standards are not cloud specific but provide one of many building blocks for cloud services, such as JSON, XML, XACML [8], OpenID,[12] AMPQ [12], SSH [13] or Remote Frame Buffer[13] just to name a few examples.

On the other hand, some standards are being developed for cloud specific needs, such as:

- OVF [14]: a standard for packaging virtual "appliances" in portable containers.
- OCCI[14]: an API standard for the management of IaaS and PaaS.
- CDMI [15]: an API specification standard for managing virtual storage.

These examples of cloud specific *specification* standards generally aim to foster portability across cloud services. In the following sections we will also discuss relevant cloud *organizational* standards mainly from ISO/IEC.

For more detailed overview of standards in the cloud we refer the reader to [16].

3   Standards and Accountability

The A4Cloud Project proposes the following definition for accountability: *Accountability consists of defining governance to comply in a responsible manner with internal and external criteria, ensuring implementation of appropriate actions, explaining and justifying those actions and remedying any failure to act properly.* Putting this definition in practice through concepts, mechanisms, tools and standards is the central goal of the project as described in [23].

In 2013, ETSI (the European Telecommunications and Standards Institute) was tasked to perform a gap analysis of cloud standards through their Cloud Standards

---

[9] https://aws.amazon.com/ec2/.

[10] https://aws.amazon.com/s3/.

[11] See http://www.openstack.org/, https://www.eucalyptus.com/, http://opennebula.org/ and https://cloudstack.apache.org/.

[12] http://openid.net/.

[13] http://www.realvnc.com/docs/rfbproto.pdf.

[14] http://occi-wg.org/.

Coordination taskforce (CSC), to which A4Cloud contributed. The results [17] of this gap analysis highlight the lack of cloud accountability-related standards, by concluding that *"...our analysis has shown that cloud computing governance and assurance standards specifically developed for and aimed at the cloud already exist (e.g., cloud controls framework, security cloud architectures, continuous monitoring of cloud service provider's) and some of them are considered as sufficiently mature to be adopted. Further standardization work may be helpful as a supplement to best practices in areas such as incident management, cloud forensics, and cloud supply chain accountability management."* In this section we show how standards can play an important role in bridging this conspicuous gap, first by describing A4Cloud initiatives to include accountability in on-going cloud related standards, and second by discussing how we could create specification standards to further bolster accountability through interoperability and automation.

3.1   A Project Strategy for Putting Accountability in Standards

From a project point of view, the relationship between accountability and standards is a two-way street. On one hand, A4Cloud aims to develop a set of practices, processes and tools that can be reused and extended by cloud providers and researchers. To maximize the success of such an approach, it is necessary to reuse existing standards as much possible to facilitate interoperability with existing systems and the dissemination of project results. On the other hand, many of these practices, processes and tools contain a degree of novelty that is not covered by any existing standard. It is therefore important for us to also consider how we can influence the design of existing and future standards to cover accountability requirements. ETSI highlighted [17] *"the need for further standardization efforts in the area of accountability and cloud incident management (e.g., related with a SLA infringements)."* They further added that *"such work would greatly benefit the whole cloud supply chain, although once again the main challenge is trust/security assurance among the involved stakeholders."*

There is a very large potential for standardization work related to accountability, which extends way beyond the resources available to a single European research project such as A4Cloud. We therefore decided to build a standardization strategy that would focus on a pragmatic approach. As part of this strategy, we classified cloud related standards in the following categories:

- **Adopted standards:** Standards that are adopted in the project without any change (e.g. XACML [8]).
- **Missing standards:** Standards that are fully missing with regards to accountability, and could not be realistically created within the timeframe of the project.
- **Partial standards:** Standards that are strongly related to accountability, but that would require some modifications or extension.

As detailed in [16], we have focused our attention to standards in the third category where there is furthermore an *opportunity to contribute*, either because the standard is still in an incubating stage or because it is ongoing a revision. We will describe a few examples of these standards as an illustration.

ISO/IEC 17788 & 17789. ISO/IEC 17788 [18] is a *fundamental standard* titled "Cloud Computing Overview and Vocabulary" and aims to provide a terminology for other standards related to cloud computing. The companion ISO/IEC 17789 [19], which is titled "Cloud Computing Reference Architecture", is also a fundamental standard that aims to provide a reference architecture for cloud computing, describing cloud computing roles, activities, functional components and their relationships, much like the NIST did (see Sect. 2.1).

Our main goal from the A4Cloud perspective is to add accountability as a cross-cutting aspect in these two standards, thereby increasing the chance that accountability will be part of the discussion in future standardization processes that will reference these two fundamental standards as a foundation.

ISO/IEC 19086. This standard [9] titled "Service Level Agreement (SLA) Framework and Terminology" provides a set of building blocks for SLA, through the definition of some fundamental concepts and terminology, with an aim to set a common framework for customers and providers. It is therefore again a *fundamental standard*, rather than a standard describing SLA templates and formats, despite its title.

Whereas traditional SLAs tend to focus on performance objectives only (e.g. uptime), our main goal is to influence the wording of the standard to make additional room for the inclusion of privacy, security and governance objectives in SLAs, as these are needed to support accountability.

NIST CSC. As part of their ongoing work on a Cloud Reference Architecture and Taxonomy (RATax) NIST has began examining how to define metrics applicable to the monitoring of security properties described in an SLA [11]. As a starting point this fundamental standard will likely define core concepts such as *metrics, measurements, measurement units* and *measures* in order to build a sound SLA metric architecture.

The goal pursued by A4Cloud is again to try to influence this work to allow room for the inclusion of metrics that apply not only to performance but also to accountability related objectives, such as security, privacy and governance. As further discussed in Sect. 4.3, such a framework needs to be flexible enough to address the complexity of security measurements.

3.2 Interoperability as an Enabler of Accountability

One of the attractive aspects of the cloud ecosystem is the ability to build new cloud services and applications from other pre-existing cloud services and applications. This is typically exemplified by cloud services like Dropbox [20], which builds upon Amazon storage, or more complex services like Netflix,[15] which combine IaaS, PaaS, and content distribution networks across the globe. The ability to make services work together seamlessly across complex supply chains is made possible by two largely intertwined features: interoperability and automation. Interoperability describes[16] the

---

[15] http://techblog.netflix.com/search/label/cloud%20architecture.

[16] From the IEEE Standards Glossary. https://www.ieee.org/education_careers/education/standards/standards_glossary.html.

"ability of a system or a product to work with other systems or products without special effort on the part of the customer" and is *"made possible by the adoption of standards"*. Formal or de facto standards specify common data formats, semantics and communication protocols adopted by actors in the cloud supply chain. The adoption of standards in turn facilitates automation of the processes involved in the provisioning of cloud services, unleashing the efficiencies that make the cloud successful. We believe that with adequate automation, we can reduce *real* or *perceived* costs associated with providing accountability in the cloud can be reduced. In turn, by reducing the cost of accountability we can encourage the greater adoption of best practices for data stewardship.

As described in the next paragraphs, in order to support automated mechanisms to enable accountability provision in the cloud, we first identified all actors typically involved in cloud accountability interactions. Next, we found that their accountability-related interactions could be classified in 4 general subgroups, which in turn could be used to shape requirements for interoperability for the purpose of accountability.

As described in Sect. 2.1, the well-known NIST cloud supply chain taxonomy has shortcomings when it comes to the description of accountability actors. Nevertheless, because of its popularity, we chose to modify and extend their model rather than create a new one, creating the following cloud accountability taxonomy composed of 7 main roles:

1. **Cloud Subject:** An entity (individual or organisation) whose data are processed by a cloud provider, either directly or indirectly.
2. **Cloud Customer:** An entity (individual or organisation) that (1) maintains a business relationship with, and (2) uses services from a Cloud Provider.
3. **Cloud Provider:** An entity responsible for making a [cloud] service available to Cloud Customers.
4. **Cloud Carrier:** The intermediary entity that provides connectivity and transport of cloud services between Cloud Providers and Cloud Customers.
5. **Cloud Broker:** An entity that manages the use, performance and delivery of cloud services, and negotiates relationships between Cloud Providers and Cloud Customers.
6. **Cloud Auditor:** An entity that can conduct independent assessment of cloud services, information system operations, performance and security of the cloud implementation, with regards to a set of requirements, which may include security data protection, information system management, laws or regulations and ethics.
7. **Cloud Supervisory Authority:** An entity that oversees and enforces the application of a set of rules.

Next, we found that we could classify the accountability interactions between any pair of those 7 actors into 4 main subgroups:

1. **Agreement** covers all interactions that lead to one actor taking legal responsibility for the handling of certain data provided by another party according to a certain policy. These interactions may include a negotiation phase. A policy may *express* requirements that apply to all 7 core accountability attributes, and contributes to the *implementation* of the attributes of *responsibility* and *liability*.

2. **Reporting** covers all interactions related to the reporting by an actor about current data handling practices and policies (e.g. reporting security breaches or providing security/privacy level indictors). This type of interaction mainly supports the implementation of the accountability attributes of *transparency* and *observability*.

3. **Demonstration** covers all interactions that lead to one actor demonstrating the correct implementation of some data handling policies. This includes external verifications by auditors or cryptographic proofs of protocol executions, for example. This type of interaction mainly supports the *implementation* of the accountability attributes of *verifiability* and *attributability*. We emphasise that *Demonstration* differs from *Reporting* in that it implies some form of proof or provision of evidence.

4. **Remediation** covers all interactions that lead one actor to seek and receive or offer remediation for failures to follow data handling policies. This mainly supports the *implementation* of the accountability attribute of *remediability*.

By cross matching these 4 subgroups of interactions with the cloud accountability roles above, we identified 31 key interoperability requirements for accountability in the cloud. While we refer the reader to [21] for the details, we can highlight two key elements of this analysis. First and foremost, an essential requirement for enabling interoperability for the purpose of accountability in the cloud is the ability of 2 communicating parties to share a common understanding of security and data protection policy *semantics* and their associated *metrics*, be it for the purpose of *agreement*, *reporting*, *demonstration* and/or *remediation*. Unfortunately, this common ground for semantics hardly exists today [4]. For example, all major cloud providers use different semantics and metrics for availability [6]. The same can be said if two interacting actors use different technical standards to interpret properties such as "consent", "confidentiality level" or "user information" (independently of their legal meaning), just to give a few examples.

Second, interoperable accountability mechanisms have to be interoperable across the cloud supply chain. For example, if a cloud provider needs to report data stewardship information to a customer, it may need itself to obtain information from other providers acting as its sub-providers, while still preserving a common understanding of policy semantics.

With so many actors and interactions, we need to set priorities in attempting to automate accountability interactions in the cloud. The logical step is to focus first on the most frequent and necessary interactions and later on the more uncommon ones. In this respect, *Information* and *Agreement* are the two subgroups of interactions we should start with, focusing in particular on Cloud Customers, Cloud Providers, and Cloud Subjects (*data subjects*). At the other end of the spectrum, we expect *remediation* interactions and more generally interactions with supervisory authorities and auditors to be rarer and therefore less of a priority for automation.

There are currently some significant initiatives that could provide interoperability and automation supporting accountability in the cloud. To begin with, the A4Cloud project itself is proposing a policy language A-PPL, which is an extension of the PPL language [7], itself based on XACML [8]. More broadly, the A4Cloud project will produce a set of novel tools that will aim to tackle the interoperability issues highlighted above. The Cloud Security Alliance is developing two relevant RESTful APIs:

CloudAudit to access audit data from cloud provider, and the Cloud Trust Protocol for constant monitoring of security properties of cloud services, both contributing to automated *Information* and *Demonstration* interactions. As described in Sect. 3.1, the NIST has begun examining how to define metrics applicable to the monitoring of security properties described in an SLA. Also in Sect. 3.1, we noted that ISO is developing a new standard for cloud SLAs. The European Commission is investigating model terms for cloud SLAs [22]. As these initiatives mature and related standards begin to be developed, we hope to see *accountability as a service* become a reality in the cloud in the next few years.

4   Standardization Challenges in Continuous Monitoring

As we argued in the previous section, information (and agreement) interactions should be priority for interoperability efforts. In fact, many cloud customers hesitate to adopt the cloud because of a perceived loss of control and lack of transparency.[17] By allowing customers to frequently query and receive up-to-date information about the security and compliance level of a cloud provider, we could create a path towards greater transparency and trust.

In this section we therefore focus our attention on one particular type of accountability interactions described in the previous section: *information* interactions between Cloud Customers and Cloud Providers. More specifically, we look at the continuous monitoring of security *attributes* of cloud providers.

4.1   Defining Continuous Monitoring

We consider "continuous monitoring" as the *automated* gathering of *up-to-date* machine-readable information related to information security & privacy compliance.

By *automated*, we do not mean that the data is not produced by humans but rather that it is made available by automated means. By *up-to-date*, we mean that the information is based on periodic assessments done at reasonably short time internals. The time internals between "checks" can be seconds, hours, days, weeks, and it is supposed to be the shortest interval that would allow the collection of up-to-dated information for the purpose of monitoring the relevant security attributes of a cloud service. Such an approach is meant to complement traditional audits, which are limited to annual or bi-annual assessments, as in ISO/IEC 27001 certification (see Sect. 2.2).

4.2   The Scope of Constant Monitoring: Security Attributes

In theory, many things are susceptible to continuous monitoring as defined above, but in practice providing access to relevant *up-to-date* security information in an *automated* way is usually challenging, unless the data is related solely to system performance (e.g.

---

[17] http://ec.europa.eu/digital-agenda/en/european-cloud-computing-strategy.

availability, throughput, etc.). In the field of security, the notion of "continuous monitoring" has been tentatively applied both to high-level "control objectives" and "controls" or lower-level objects such as "service level objectives", "performance indicators" and "security properties".

By nature, *control objectives* proposed in control frameworks such as ISO/IEC 27002 or the Cloud Control Matrix (CCM) are a mix of compliance, governance and technical aspects (see Sect. 2.2). As such, most controls objectives contain elements that cannot be assessed by automated means on a reasonably short timeframe or continuous basis. For example, many control objectives in the CCM v. 3.0 refer to *"documented procedures"*, *"applicable legal obligations"* or generic functional requirements such as *"support forensic investigative capabilities"*. These elements require human assessment and no automated process would be capable of monitoring their effective implementation in an up-to-date fashion with current technology.

Controls, as instantiations of control objectives into precise mechanisms and policies, lend themselves better to "continuous monitoring". Still many controls contain elements that require human evaluation that may not be feasible on a continuous basis. Often, what we can really monitor is specific individual characteristics of a control, or characteristics that show that a control has failed. In some cases we will monitor the existence/effectiveness of a control by inferring information collected through the checking of other similar controls or security attributes. For example, we might define a control that requires the implementation of a documented backup policy, which includes monthly testing of backup restorations associated to recovery point objectives (RPO). We may not be able to *constantly monitor* that the policy is up-to-date or that the technical backup mechanisms are in alignment with the policy, but we may monitor backup restoration frequency, success rate, simulated restoration point actual (RPA) and contrast it with the RPO.

We broadly define a *security attribute* as any non-functional security characteristic of a system that can be assessed quantitatively or quantitatively. Security attributes therefore encompass elements typically called elsewhere *security properties, performance indicators,* or (improperly) *service level objectives*.

Continuous monitoring seems to be more applicable to the notion security attributes because of their more focused scope. Security attributes may include for example "monthly uptime", "encryption level in transit/at rest", "key length", "incident response time", "data erasure quality", "country level anchoring", etc.

These simpler characteristics we call "security attributes" are often –but not always– represented by values in a restricted domain and associated with specific metrics (i.e. a standard of measurement along with a measure unit). Attributes come in many "flavors": some attributes are largely *declarative* (e.g. processing location) while others are *computative*, requiring large calculations over system events (e.g. monthly uptime).

4.3   Standardizing the Measurement of Security Attributes

We next turn our attention to the necessity of standards for security attributes and their metrics.

In it's simplest form, continuous monitoring could rely on a simple API that would allow Cloud Customers to securely query Cloud Providers about a set of security attributes, as part of an automated accountability-based approach. Defining such an API is one of the goals of the Cloud Trust Protocol[18] that is currently being developed by CSA. Describing constraints on security attributes in machine-readable format can also serve as a basis for the definition of Security Level Objectives[19] in SLAs or automated monitoring-based certificate generation.[20] However, to achieve these goals, both the Cloud Customer and the Cloud Provider need to have a common interpretation of the definition and the measurement of the security attributes. Furthermore, if we want to allow Cloud Customers to compare different service offerings, this common interpretation should extend to multiple cloud customers and providers, thereby becoming a *standard*.

Defining standards for the measurement of security attributes is however a challenging endeavor as we can illustrate with 3 examples:

Uptime. We can note that all major cloud providers define at least one security attribute: availability, usually expressed as a percentage of uptime. Many IaaS providers claim a monthly uptime of at least 99.95 %. Yet as shown in [6] they all use a different method to calculate that number, making comparisons largely impossible.

Processing location. The location of data processing on a country or regional level of granularity is an important declarative attribute for regulatory compliance. However, consider the scenario where data is stored in a datacenter in Belgium but accessed for remote administration purposes form the US. Data protection authorities will typically consider that the data processing took place in Belgium and the US, while businesses will typically advertise where the data is stored, namely in Belgium.

Incident management. The quality of incident management can be measured in several complementary ways, such as the percentage of incidents reported/mitigated within a certain contractually agreed timeframe and the number of incidents over a period. As broadly discussed in [4], this requires defining precisely what an "incident" is, and expressing measurements by differentiating incidents into normalized categories (e.g. severe/medium/low) otherwise we risk comparing apple and oranges.

With these 3 examples, we can easily imagine the challenges of properly standardizing other attributes that are relevant to data stewardship, such as *confidentiality level*, *vulnerability management*, *data deletion level*, *durability or recovery point objective*, *retrievability*, etc.

While the measurement of security attributes still offers many opportunities for research, there are several standardization initiatives that are currently trying to tackle this problem. These include previously mentioned work from CSA on CTP and SLA metrics, work form NIST on metrics for SLAs (see Sect. 3.1), and effort form ISO to develop a foundation for SLA metrics (see Sect. 3.1).

---

[18] https://cloudsecurityalliance.org/research/ctp/.

[19] See the SPECS Fp7 project. http://specs-project.eu/.

[20] See the CUMULUS FP7 project. http://www.cumulus-project.eu/.

5   Conclusion

Walking through standards related to the cloud may seem like walking through a dense forest, with many paths, intersections, and opportunities to get lost. In fact, the key action in the European Commission's cloud strategy[21] is to "cut through the jungle of standards". One may feel that there are already too many standards for the cloud. Yet, many standards related to cloud service interfaces, portability, quality and management are still in their infancy. Furthermore, as this paper has shown, the cloud needs many more standards in order to enable "plug-and-play" accountability, security, and compliance. The approach developed by A4Cloud to standardization, seeks to provide meaningful contributions to relevant standardization/technical recommendations bodies in order to start bridging the identified accountability gaps.

This is just the beginning.

References

1. ISO/IEC/IEEE 29119-1:2013, Software and systems engineering—Software testing—Part 1: Concepts and definitions, Aug 2013
2. International Organization for Standardization. ISO/IEC 27002: Information Technology, Security Techniques, Code of Practice for Information Security Management. ISO/IEC 2005
3. International Organization for Standardization. ISO/IEC 27001:2013 Information technology—Security techniques—Information security management systems-Requirements. ISO/IEC 2013
4. Hogben, G., Dekker, M. (eds.) Procure Secure, A guide to monitoring of security service levels in cloud contracts, ENISA 2012
5. Liu, F., Tong, J., Mao, J., Bohn, R., Messina, J., Badger, L., Leaf, D.: NIST cloud computing reference architecture. NIST special publication, 500, 292 (2011)
6. Hogben, G., Pannetrat, A.: Mutant Apples: A critical examination of cloud SLA availability definitions. In: IEEE 5th international conference Cloud Computing Technology and Science (CloudCom), Dec 2013
7. Ardagna, C.A., Bussard, L., De Capitani Di Vimercati, S., Neven, G., Paraboschi, S., Pedrini, E., Preiss, S., Raggett, D., Samarati, P., Trabelsi, S., Verdicchio, M.: Primelife policy language (2009). http://www.w3.org/2009/policy-ws/papers/Trabelisi.pdf
8. OASIS Standard. eXtensible Access Control Markup Language (XACML) Version 3.0, 22 Jan 2013. http://docs.oasis-open.org/xacml/3.0/xacml-3.0-core-spec-os-en.html
9. ISO/IEC NP 19086, Information technology – Distributed application platforms and services – Cloud computing – Service level agreement (SLA) framework and terminology, under development, Nov 2013
10. European Commision: Cloud Service Level Agreement Standardisation Guidelines. Technical Report, Cloud Select Industry Group (C-SIG), June 2014. https://ec.europa.eu/digital-agenda/en/news/cloud-service-level-agreement-standardisation-guidelines
11. National Institute of Standards and Technology: NIST Cloud Computing: Cloud Service Metrics Description (RATAX). Working document 2014

---

[21] http://eur-lex.europa.eu/LexUriServ/LexUriServ.do?uri=COM:2012:0529:FIN:EN:PDF.

12. International Organization for Standardization. ISO/IEC 19464:2014 Information technology – Advanced Message Queuing Protocol (AMQP) v1.0 specification. ISO/IEC, 2014
13. Network Working Group of the IETF, Jan 2006, RFC 4252, The Secure Shell (SSH) Authentication Protocol
14. International Organization for Standardization. ISO/IEC 17203:2011 "Open Virtualization Format". ISO/IEC 2011
15. Storage Networking Industry Association, "Cloud Data Management Interface", Version 1, 12 April 2010
16. A4Cloud: Deliverable D:A-5.1 Report on A4Cloud contribution to standards, Sept 2014
17. ETSI: Cloud Standards Coordination – Final Report, Version 1, Nov 2013
18. International Organization for Standardization. ISO/IEC DIS 17788: Information technology—Cloud computing—Overview and vocabulary, Under development. ISO/IEC JTC 1/SC 38
19. International Organization for Standardization. ISO/IEC DIS 17789: Information technology – Cloud computing – Reference architecture, Under development. ISO/IEC JTC 1/SC 38
20. Drago, I., Mellia, M., Munafo, M.M., Sperotto, A., Sadre, R., Pras, A.: Inside dropbox: Understanding personal cloud storage services. In: Proceedings of the 2012 ACM Conference on Internet Measurement Conference (IMC 2012), pp. 481–494. ACM, New York (2012)
21. Alain, P., Vasilis, T., Daniele C. D:C-3.1 Requirements for cloud interoperability. A4Cloud public deliverable. Nov 2013
22. European Commission: Cloud Service Level Agreement Standardisation Guidelines. Technical Report, Cloud Select Industry Group (C-SIG), June 2014
23. Massimo, F., Theofrastos, K., Siani, P.: Accountability for data governance in cloud ecosystems. In: 2013 IEEE 5th International Conference on Cloud Computing Technology and Science (CloudCom), vol. 2, pp. 327–332, 2–5 Dec 2013

Accountability Glossary of Terms and Definitions

Cloud Accountability: Glossary of Terms and Definitions

Massimo Felici[(✉)]

Security and Cloud Lab, Hewlett-Packard Laboratories,
Long Down Avenue, Bristol BS34 8QZ, UK
massimo.felici@hp.com

Abstract. The Glossary of Terms and Definitions captures a shared multidisciplinary understanding within the EU FP7 Cloud Accountability Project (A4Cloud). It consists of the key terms that have been identified by the A4Cloud's Accountability Conceptual Framework. The definitions in the glossary have been drawn from relevant research literature, standards or domain specific references (e.g. data protection, cloud computing, information security, privacy, etc.). The A4Cloud's Accountability Conceptual Framework has proposed (or revised) definitions of those terms that are central to concept of accountability (and related attributes). The glossary is the result of a collaborative effort of the A4Cloud project. The final glossary consists of over 150 terms (drawn from an initial list of over 700 terms) selected for their relevance to accountability. It consists of the core accountability terms that have been defined and used across the A4Cloud project.

Term/Acronym	Brief Description/Definition	Reference
A4Cloud	Accountability for Cloud and Other Future Internet Services	[2]
Access Control	*"The process of granting or denying specific requests: 1) for obtaining and using information and related information processing services; and 2) to enter specific physical facilities (e.g., Federal buildings, military establishments, and border crossing entrances)."*	[9]
Access Control Policy	*"The set of rules that define the conditions under which an access may take place."*	[28]
Accountability Attributes	Conceptual elements of accountability as used across different domains.	[1]
Accountability Evidence	Accountability Evidence as collection of data, metadata, routine information and formal operations performed on data and metadata which provide attributable and verifiable account of the fulfilment of relevant obligations with respect to the service and that can be used to support an argument shown to a third party about the validity of claims about the appropriate and effective functioning (or not) of an observable system.	[1]
Accountability Mechanisms	Diverse processes, non-technical mechanisms and tools that support accountability practices.	[1]

(Continued)

© Springer International Publishing Switzerland 2015
M. Felici and C. Fernández-Gago (Eds.): A4Cloud 2014, LNCS 8937, pp. 291–306, 2015.
DOI: 10.1007/978-3-319-17199-9_13

(Continued)

Term/Acronym	Brief Description/Definition	Reference
Accountability Model	Accountability attributes, practices and mechanisms.	[1]
Accountability Practices	Emergent behaviour characterising accountable organisations.	[1]
Accountability, Conceptual Definition	Accountability consists of defining governance to comply in a responsible manner with internal and external criteria, ensuring implementation of appropriate actions, explaining and justifying those actions and remedying any failure to act properly.	[1]
Accountability, for Data Stewardship in the Cloud Definition (A4Cloud Definition)	Accountability for an organisation consists of accepting responsibility for data with which it is entrusted in a cloud environment, for its use of the data from the time it is collected until when the data is destroyed (including onward transfer to and from third parties). It involves the commitment to norms, explaining and demonstrating compliance to stakeholders and remedying any failure to act properly.	[1]
Accountability-based Approach	*"An accountability-based approach to data governance is characterised by its focus on setting privacy-protection goals for organisations based on criteria established in current public policy and on allowing organisations discretion in determining appropriate measures to reach those goals."*	[8]
Accountable Organisation	*"An accountable organisation demonstrates commitment to accountability, implements data privacy policies linked to recognised outside criteria, and establishes performance mechanisms to ensure responsible decision-making about the management of data consistent with organisation policies."*	[8]
Appropriateness	The extent to which the technical and organisational measures used have the capability of contributing to accountability.	[1]
Assessment	see Security Control Assessment	
Asset	*"Any item that has value to the organisation."*	[24]
Assurance	*"Grounds for confidence that the other four security goals (integrity, availability, confidentiality, and accountability) have been adequately met by a specific implementation. "Adequately met" includes (1) functionality that performs correctly, (2) sufficient protection against unintentional errors (by users or software), and (3) sufficient resistance to intentional penetration or bypass."*	[33]
Attributability	The possibility to trace a given action back to a specific entity.	[1]
Attribution	In case of a deviation from the expected behaviour (fault), an accountability system reveals which component is responsible (attribution).	[14]
Audit	*"Independent review and examination of records and activities to assess the adequacy of system controls and ensure compliance with established policies and operational procedures."*	[9]

(Continued)

(Continued)

Term/Acronym	Brief Description/Definition	Reference
Audit Log	*"A chronological record of system activities. Includes records of system accesses and operations performed in a given period."*	[9]
Audit Trail	*"A chronological record that reconstructs and examines the sequence of activities surrounding or leading to a specific operation, procedure, or event in a security relevant transaction from inception to final result."*	[9]
Authenticity	*"The property of being genuine and being able to be verified and trusted; confidence in the validity of a transmission, a message, or message originator."*	[9]
Authorization	*"A prescription that a particular behaviour shall not be prevented."*	[23]
Availability	*"The property of being accessible and usable upon demand by an authorized entity."*	[9]
Behaviour	The actual data processing behaviour of an organisation.	[1]
Binding Corporate Rules (BCRs)	*"Binding corporate rules (BCRs) are a legal tool that can be used by multinational companies to ensure an adequate level of protection for the intra-group transfers of personal data from a country in the EU or the European Economic Area (EEA) to a third country. The use of BCRs requires, in principle, the approval of each of the EU or EEA data protection authorities from whose country the data are to be transferred."*	[12]
Broad Network Access	*"Capabilities are available over the network and accessed through standard mechanisms that promote use by heterogeneous thin or thick client platforms (e.g., mobile phones, tablets, laptops, and workstations)."*	[32]
Chain of Evidence	*"A process and record that shows who obtained the evidence; where and when the evidence was obtained; who secured the evidence; and who had control or possession of the evidence. The "sequencing" of the chain of evidence follows this order: collection and identification; analysis; storage; preservation; presentation in court; return to owner."*	[9]
Cloud Auditor	An entity that can conduct independent assessment of cloud services, information system operations, performance and security of the cloud implementation, with regards to a set of requirements, which may include security, data protection, information system management, regulations and ethics.	[1]
Cloud Broker	An entity that manages the use, performance and delivery of cloud services, and negotiates relationships between Cloud Providers and Cloud Customers.	[30]
Cloud Carrier	An intermediary that provides connectivity and transport of cloud services from Cloud Providers to Cloud Customers.	[30]

(Continued)

(Continued)

Term/Acronym	Brief Description/Definition	Reference
Cloud Computing	*"Cloud computing is a model for enabling ubiquitous, convenient, on-demand network access to a shared pool of configurable computing resources (e.g., networks, servers, storage, applications, and services) that can be rapidly provisioned and released with minimal management effort or service provider interaction."*	[32]
Cloud Consumer	see Cloud Customer	
Cloud Customer	An entity that (a) maintains a business relationship with, and (b) uses services from a Cloud Provider. When necessary we may further distinguish: a) Individual Cloud Customer, when the entity refers to a person; b) Organisational Cloud Customer, when the entity refers to an organisation.	[1]
Cloud Distribution	*"The process of transporting cloud data between Cloud Providers and Cloud Consumers."*	[30]
Cloud Ecosystem	*"A cloud computing business ecosystem (cloud ecosystem) is a business ecosystem of interacting organisations and individuals - the actors of the cloud ecosystem - providing and consuming cloud services."*	[15]
Cloud Governance	*"Cloud governance encompasses two main areas: internal governance focuses on a provider's technical working of cloud services, its business operations, and the ways it manages its relationship with customers and other external stakeholders; and external governance consists of the norms, rules, and regulations which define the relationships between members of the cloud community and attempt to solve disputes between them."*	[36]
Cloud Provider (CP)	An entity responsible for making a [cloud] service available to cloud customers.	[1]
Cloud Service Management	*"Cloud Service Management includes all of the service-related functions that are necessary for the management and operation of those services required by or proposed to cloud consumers."*	[29]
Cloud Service Provider (CSP)	see Cloud Provider	
Cloud Subject	An entity whose data are processed by a cloud provider, either directly or indirectly. When necessary we may further distinguish: a) Individual Cloud Subject, when the entity refers to a person; b) Organisational Cloud Subject, when the entity refers to an organisation.	[1]
Cloud Supervisory Authority	An entity that oversees and enforces the application of a set of rules.	[1]
Cloud User	see Cloud Customer	
Community Cloud	*"The cloud infrastructure is provisioned for exclusive use by a specific community of consumers from organisations that have shared concerns (e.g., mission, security requirements, policy, and compliance considerations)."*	[32]

(Continued)

(Continued)

Term/Acronym	Brief Description/Definition	Reference
Compliance	Compliance entails the comparison of an organisation's actual behaviour with the norms.	[1]
Confidential	*"Class of information that is sensitive and/or business critical and therefore needs to be protected to a reasonable extent. It is intended for limited distribution within the organisation or to specially designated third parties, on a need-to-know ('default deny') basis."*	[26]
Confidentiality	*"Preserving authorized restrictions on information access and disclosure, including means for protecting personal privacy and proprietary information."*	[34]
Control	*"Means of managing risk, including policies, procedures, guidelines, practices or organisational structures, which can be administrative, technical, management, or legal in nature."*	[24]
Data Controller	*"The natural or legal person, public authority, agency or any other body which alone or jointly with others determines the purposes and means of the processing of personal data; where the purposes and means of processing are determined by national or Community laws or regulations, the controller or the specific criteria for his nomination may be designated by national or Community law."*	[11]
Data Integrity	*"The property that data has not been changed, destroyed, or lost in an unauthorized or accidental manner."*	[20]
Data Processor	*"A natural or legal person, public authority, agency or any other body which processes personal data on behalf of the controller."*	[11]
Data Protection Agency (DPA)	see Data Protection Authority	
Data Protection Authority (DPA)	*"A data protection authority is an independent body which is in charge of: monitoring the processing of personal data within its jurisdiction (country, region or international organisation); providing advice to the competent bodies with regard to legislative and administrative measures relating to the processing of personal data; hearing complaints lodged by citizens with regard to the protection of their data protection rights. According to Article 28 of Directive 95/46/EC, each Member State shall establish in its territory at least one data protection authority, which shall be endowed with investigative powers (such as access to data, collection of information, etc.), effective powers of intervention (power to order the erasure of data, to impose a ban on a processing, etc.), and the power to start legal proceedings when data protection law has been violated."*	[12]
Data Protection Impact Assessment (DPIA)	*"A systematic process for evaluating the potential impact of risks where processing operations are likely to present specific risks to the rights and freedoms of data subjects by virtue of their nature,*	[4]

(Continued)

Term/Acronym	Brief Description/Definition	Reference
	their scope or their purposes to be carried out by the controller or the processor acting on the controller's behalf."	
Data Protection Officer (DPO)	*"Each Community institution and body shall [...] have a data protection officer (DPO). The DPO shall ensure the internal application of the Regulation and that the rights and freedoms of the data subjects are not likely to be adversely affected by the processing operations. The DPO shall also keep a register of processing operations that have been notified by the controllers of the institution or body where he or she works."*	[12]
Data Security	*"Protection of data from unauthorized (accidental or intentional) modification, destruction, or disclosure."*	[9]
Data Subject	An identified or identifiable natural person ('data subject') to whom 'personal data' relate to; *"an identifiable person is one who can be identified, directly or indirectly, in particular by reference to an identification number or to one or more factors specific to his physical, physiological, mental, economic, cultural or social identity."*	[11]
Data Subject Consent	*"Any freely given specific and informed indication of his wishes by which the data subject signifies his agreement to personal data relating to him being processed."*	[5]
Data Transfer	*"Data transfer refers to the transmission / communication of data to a recipient in whatever way."*	[12]
Directive 2009/136/EC	Directive 2009/136/EC of the European Parliament and of the Council of 25 November 2009 amending Directive 2002/22/EC on universal service and users' rights relating to electronic communications networks and services, Directive 2002/58/EC concerning the processing of personal data and the protection of privacy in the electronic communications sector and Regulation (EC) No 2006/2004 on cooperation between national authorities responsible for the enforcement of consumer protection laws.	[10]
Directive 95/46/EC	European Parliament and Council Directive 95/46/EC of 24 October 1995 on the protection of individuals with regard to the processing of personal data and on the free movement of such data. This directive defines the overall concept of data protection in the Europe. Under this directive, individual personal data has to be collected openly and fairly with a clear explanation of the purpose for its collection.	[11]
Due Process	A moral claim to provide fair and equal treatment, and incorporates rights to full information, the right to be heard, to ask questions and receive answers, and the right to redress.	
Effectiveness	The extent to which the technical and organisational measures used actually contribute to accountability.	[1]
Ethical Accountability	It is the practice of taking responsibility of own's actions and to be accountable to one's self not only to others. It ensures: 1) the	[1]

(Continued)

Term/Acronym	Brief Description/Definition	Reference
	practice of sustainable development, 2) democratic accountability where all stakeholders are involved in the decision making process, 3) self-monitoring and self-auditing.	
Event	*"Any observable occurrence in a system and/or network. Events sometimes provide indication that an incident is occurring."*	[9]
Evidence	An accountability system produces evidence that can be used to convince a third party that a fault has or has not occurred (evidence).	[14]
Governance	*"Governance implies control and oversight by the organisation over policies, procedures, and standards for application development and information technology service acquisition, as well as the design, implementation, testing, use, and monitoring of deployed or engaged services."*	[31]
Hybrid Cloud	*"The cloud infrastructure is a composition of two or more distinct cloud infrastructures (private, community, or public) that remain unique entities, but are bound together by standardized or proprietary technology that enables data and application portability (e.g., cloud bursting for load balancing between clouds)."*	[32]
Individual Cloud Customer	see Cloud Customer	[1]
Individual Cloud Subject	see Cloud Subject	[1]
Information Accountability	*"Information accountability means that information usage should be transparent so it is possible to determine whether a use is appropriate under a given set of rules."*	[37]
Information Security	*"The protection of information and information systems from unauthorized access, use, disclosure, disruption, modification, or destruction in order to provide confidentiality, integrity, and availability."*	[9]
Information Technology (IT)	*"IT encompasses all technologies for the capture, storage, retrieval, processing, display, representation, organisation, management, security, transfer, and interchange of data and information."*	[29]
Infrastructure as a Service (IaaS)	*"The capability provided to the consumer is to provision processing, storage, networks, and other fundamental computing resources where the consumer is able to deploy and run arbitrary software, which can include operating systems and applications."*	[32]
Integrity	see Data Integrity	
Liability	The state (of an organisation or individual) of being legally obligated or responsible in connection with failure to apply the norms.	[1]
Measured Service	*"Cloud systems automatically control and optimize resource use by leveraging a metering capability at some level of abstraction*	[32]

(Continued)

(Continued)

Term/Acronym	Brief Description/Definition	Reference
	appropriate to the type of service (e.g., storage, processing, bandwidth, and active user accounts)."	
Multi-tenancy	*"A characteristic of cloud in which resources are shared amongst multiple cloud tenants."*	[15]
Non-repudiation	*"The property whereby a party in a dispute cannot repudiate or refute the validity of a statement or contract."*	[13]
Norms	The obligations and permissions that define data practices; these can be expressed in policies and they derive from law, contracts and ethics.	[1]
Obfuscation	*"The production of misleading, ambiguous and plausible but convincing information as an act of concealment or evasion."*	[6]
Obligation	*"A prescription that a particular behaviour is required."*	[22]
Obligation, Legal	A legal duty.	
Observability	The extent to which the behaviour of the system is externally viewable.	[1]
On-demand Self-service	*"A consumer can unilaterally provision computing capabilities, such as server time and network storage, as needed automatically without requiring human interaction with each service provider."*	[32]
Organisational Cloud Customer	see Cloud Customer	[1]
Organisational Cloud Subject	see Cloud Subject	[1]
Permission	*"A prescription that a particular behaviour is allowed to occur."*	[22]
Person Pseudonym	*"A substitute or alias for a data subject's civil identity (name) which may be used in many different contexts."*	[35]
Personal Data	*"'Personal data' shall mean any information relating to an identified or identifiable natural person ('data subject'); an identifiable person is one who can be identified, directly or indirectly, in particular by reference to an identification number or to one or more factors specific to his physical, physiological, mental, economic, cultural or social identity."*	[11]
Personally Identifiable Information (PII)	*"Information which can be used to distinguish or trace an individual's identity, such as their name, social security number, biometric records, etc. alone, or when combined with other personal or identifying information which is linked or linkable to a specific individual, such as date and place of birth, mother's maiden name, etc."*	[9]
Platform as a Service (PaaS)	*"The capability provided to the consumer is to deploy onto the cloud infrastructure consumer-created or acquired applications created using programming languages, libraries, services, and tools supported by the provider."*	[32]
Policy	*"A set of rules related to a particular purpose."* A rule can be expressed as an obligation, an authorization, a permission, or a	[23]

(Continued)

(Continued)

Term/Acronym	Brief Description/Definition	Reference
	prohibition. Not every policy is a constraint. Some policies represent an empowerment.	
Policy Enforcement	*"The execution of a policy decision."*	[19]
Policy Violation	see Violation	
Primary Service Provider (PSP)	see Cloud Provider	
Privacy	*"The claim of individuals, groups, or institutions to determine for themselves when, how, and to what extent information about them is communicated to others. The ability to control the collection and sharing of information about oneself."*	[38]
Privacy by Design	*"Privacy by Design (PbD) is an approach to protecting privacy by embedding it into the design specifications of information technologies, accountable business practices, and networked infrastructures, right from the outset."*	[7]
Privacy Enhancing Tool (PET)	*"It refers to a coherent system of information and communication technology (ICT) measures that protect privacy by eliminating or reducing personal data or by preventing unnecessary and/or undesired processing of personal data, all without losing the functionality of the information system."*	[12]
Privacy Impact Assessment (PIA)	*"An analysis of how information is handled 1) to ensure handling conforms to applicable legal, regulatory, and policy requirements regarding privacy; 2) t determine the risks and effects of collecting, maintaining, and disseminating information in identifiable form in an electronic information system; and 3) to examine and evaluate protections and alternative processes for handling information to mitigate potential risks."*	[9]
Privacy Impact Audit	*"Systematic evaluation of a cloud system by measuring how well it conforms to a set of established privacy-impact criteria."*	[30]
Private Cloud	*"The cloud infrastructure is provisioned for exclusive use by a single organisation comprising multiple consumers (e.g., business units)."*	[32]
Processing of Personal Data	*"Any operation or set of operations which is performed upon personal data, whether or not by automatic means, such as collection, recording, organisation, storage, adaptation or alteration, retrieval, consultation, use, disclosure by transmission, dissemination or otherwise making available, alignment or combination, blocking, erasure or destruction."*	[11]
Processor Agreement	*"Transfers of personal data from a data controller to a data processor must be secured by a contractual agreement. [...] The contract must stipulate that the data processor shall act only on instructions from the data controller. The data processor must provide sufficient guarantees in respect of the technical security measures and organisational measure governing the processing*	[12]

Term/Acronym	Brief Description/Definition	Reference
	to be carried out, and must ensure compliance with such measures."	
Prohibition	*"A prescription that a particular behaviour must not occur."*	[22]
Proof of Retrievability (POR)	Protocol that allows a client that has stored data at an untrusted store to verify in an efficient way that has means to retrieve the original data without actually retrieving it.	[27]
Pseudonym	*"A pseudonym is an identifier of a subject other than the subject's civil identity."*	[35]
Public Cloud	*"The cloud infrastructure is provisioned for open use by the general public."*	[32]
Rapid Elasticity	*"Capabilities can be elastically provisioned and released, in some cases automatically, to scale rapidly outward and inward commensurate with demand."*	[32]
Recipient	*"A natural or legal person, public authority, agency, or any other body to whom data are disclosed, whether a third party or not; however, authorities which may receive data in the framework of a particular inquiry shall not be regarded as recipients."*	[11]
Relationship Pseudonym	*"A pseudonym that is used in regard to a specific communication partner (e.g., distinct nicknames for different communication partners)."*	[35]
Remediability	The property of a system, organisation or individual to take corrective action and/or provide a remedy for any party harmed in case of failure to comply with its governing norms.	[1]
Remediation	*"The act of mitigating a vulnerability or a threat."*	[9]
Remedy(ies)	Any of the methods available at law for the enforcement, protection or recovery of rights or for obtaining redress for their infringement (judicial/administrative).	
Reputation	*"An expectation about an entity's behaviour based on information about or observations of its past behaviour."* It is a form of social control in the context of trust propagation. In a multi-agent system, reputation is the voice the agent is spreading which is not necessarily the truth while image is the actual reputation the agent has for the subject.	[3]
Resource Pooling	*"The provider's computing resources are pooled to serve multiple consumers using a multi-tenant model, with different physical and virtual resources dynamically assigned and reassigned according to consumer demand."*	[32]
Responsibility	The property of an organisation or individual in relation to an object, process or system of being assigned to take action to be in compliance with the norms.	[1]
Responsiveness	The property of a system, organisation or individual to take into account input from external stakeholders and respond to queries of these stakeholders.	[1]

(Continued)

Term/Acronym	Brief Description/Definition	Reference
Right of Access	It is *"the right for any data subject to obtain from the controller of a processing operation the confirmation that data related to him/her are being processed, the purpose(s) for which they are processed, as well as the logic involved in any automated decision process concerning him or her."*	[12]
Right of Information	*"Everyone has the right to know that their personal data are processed and for which purpose. The right to be informed is essential because it determines the exercise of other rights. The right of information refers to the information which shall be provided to a data subject whether or not the data have been obtained from the data subject. The information which must be provided relates to the identity of the controller, the purpose(s) of the processing, the recipients, as well as the existence of the right of access to data and the right to rectify the data. The right of information for the person concerned is limited in some cases, such as for public safety considerations or for the prevention, investigation, identification and prosecution of criminal offences, including the fight against money laundering."*	[12]
Right of Rectification	*"Right to obtain from the controller rectification without delay of inaccurate or incomplete personal data."*	[12]
Right to Object	*"The right to object has two meanings. First, it is the general right of any data subject to object to the processing of data relating to him or her, except in certain cases such as a specific legal obligation. Where there is a justified objection based on legitimate grounds relating to his or her particular situation, the processing in question may no longer involve those data. It also refers to the specific right of any data subject to be informed, free of charge, before personal data are first disclosed to third parties or before they are used on their behalf for the purposes of direct marketing, and to object to such use without justification."*	[12]
Risk	*"A measure of the extent to which an entity is threatened by a potential circumstance or event, and typically a function of 1) the adverse impacts that would arise if the circumstance or event occurs; and 2) the likelihood of occurrence."*	[9]
Risk Analysis	*"Systematic use of information to identify sources and to estimate risk."*	[24]
Risk Assessment	*"Overall process of risk analysis and risk evaluation."*	[24]
Risk Estimation	*"Activity to assign values to the probability and consequences of a risk."*	[24]
Risk Evaluation	*"Process of comparing the estimated risk against given risk criteria to determine the significance of the risk."*	[24]
Risk Management	*"Coordinated activities to direct and control an organisation with regard to risk."*	[24]

(Continued)

(Continued)

Term/Acronym	Brief Description/Definition	Reference
Role Pseudonym	*"A pseudonym that is chosen for the use in a specific role (e.g., patient or customer)."*	[35]
Role-Relationship Pseudonym	*"A pseudonym that is used for a specific combination of a role and communication partner."*	[35]
Rule	*"A constraint on a system specification."*	[22]
Sanction(s)	A measure taken against an entity to compel it to obey to data protection legislation or to punish it for a breach of a contractual clause.	
Security	see Information Security	
Security Breach	*"A breach of security occurs where a stated organisational policy or legal requirement regarding information security has been violated. However, every incident which suggests that the confidentiality, integrity or availability of the information has been compromised can be considered a security incident. Every security breach will always be initiated by a security incident which, only if confirmed, may become a breach."*	[12]
Security Control Assessment	*"The testing or evaluation of security controls to determine the extent to which the controls are implemented correctly, operating as intended, and producing the desired outcome with respect to meeting the security requirements for an information system or organisation."*	[34]
Service Level Agreement (SLA)	*"An SLA represents the understanding between the cloud consumer and cloud provider about the expected level of service to be delivered and, in the event that the provider fails to deliver the service at the level specified, the compensation available to the cloud consumer."*	[31]
Software as a Service (SaaS)	*"The capability provided to the consumer is to use the provider's applications running on a cloud infrastructure."*	[32]
Stakeholder	*"Any individual, group, or organisation who may affect, be affected by, or perceive itself to be affected by a decision or activity."*	[25]
Standard Contractual Clauses	*"Standard contractual clauses are legal tools to provide adequate safeguards for data transfers from the EU or the European Economic Area to third countries. The European Commission has adopted three Decisions declaring Standard Contractual Clauses to be adequate, and therefore, companies can incorporate the clauses into a transfer contract. In principle no authorization is required from data protection authorities to be allowed to use these clauses. A formal notification to the authority might nevertheless be necessary."*	[12]
Third country	*"A third country is a country which has not adopted a national law for the implementation of Directive 95/46/EC - as opposed to the 28 Member States of the EU and the three European Economic Area (EEA) countries Norway, Liechtenstein and Iceland. Third*	[12]

(Continued)

(Continued)

Term/Acronym	Brief Description/Definition	Reference
	countries need to ensure an adequate level of protection for personal data in order to enable transfers of personal data from the EU and EEA Member States to them. The effect of such a decision is that personal data can flow from the EU and EEA Member States to that third country (within the limit of the material scope as described by each Decision) without any further safeguards."	
Third Party	*"Any natural or legal person, public authority, agency or any other body other than the data subject, the controller, the processor and the persons who, under the direct authority of the controller or the processor, are authorized to process the data."*	[11]
Threat	*"Potential cause of an unwanted incident, which may result in harm to a system or organisation."*	[24]
Transaction Pseudonym	*"A pseudonym that is used for a specific transaction only, i.e., for each transaction, a different pseudonym is used."*	[35]
Transparency	The property of a system, organisation or individual of providing visibility of its governing norms, behaviour and compliance of behaviour to the norms.	[1]
Transparency, ex ante	It is concerned with *"the anticipation of consequences before data is actually disclosed (e.g. in the form of a certain behaviour)."*	[16]
Transparency, ex post	It is concerned with informing *"about consequences if data already has been revealed."*	[16]
Trust	*"Trust (or, symmetrically, distrust) is a particular level of the subjective probability with which an agent assesses that another agent or group of agents will perform a particular action, both before he can monitor such action (or independently of his capacity ever to be able to monitor it) and in a context in which it affects his own action."*	[17]
Trustworthiness	*"The attribute of a person or enterprise that provides confidence to others of the qualifications, capabilities, and reliability of that entity to perform specific tasks and fulfil assigned responsibilities."*	[9]
Unauthorized Disclosure	*"An event involving the exposure of information to entities not authorized access to the information."*	[9]
Unauthorized Information Disclosure	see Unauthorized Disclosure	
Usability	*"The extent to which a product can be used by specified users to achieve specified goals with effectiveness, efficiency and satisfaction in a specified context of use."*	[21]
Usage control	*"Usage control is an extension of access control that covers not only who may access which data, but also how the data may or may not be used afterwards."* Thus it comprises: managing, reading, writing and other operations we could do on data, controlling	[18]

(Continued)

Term/Acronym	Brief Description/Definition	Reference
	data distribution in the network, and furthermore constraining what happens after redistribution to the data.	
Validation	An accountability system allows users, operators and third parties to verify a posteriori if the system has performed a data processing task as expected (validation).	[14]
Verifiability	The extent to which it is possible to assess norm compliance.	[1]
Violation	*"A behaviour contrary to that required by a rule."*	[23]
Vulnerability	*"Weakness of an asset or control that can be exploited by a threat."* Any circumstance or event with the potential to adversely impact an asset through unauthorized access, destruction, disclosure, modification of data, and/or denial of service.	[24]

Acknowledgements. This glossary of terms and definitions consists of the A4Cloud terms defined and introduced in [1]. It also includes terms drawn from standards and other references – for such terms if the definition is an exact quotation from the reference given, quotation marks and an italics font are used to indicate this; otherwise the provided definition is derived from a close adaptation of the text within the referenced source. This work has been partly funded by the European Commission's Seventh Framework Programme (FP7/2007-2013), grant agreement 317550, Cloud Accountability Project – http://www.a4cloud.eu/ – (A4CLOUD). I would also like to thank all project colleagues who contributed to this glossary of terms and definitions, in particular, Rehab Alnemr, Monir Azraoui, Karin Bernsmed, Simone Fischer-Hübner, Bushra Hasnain, Eleni Kosta, Theofrastos Koulouris, Ronald Leenes, Christopher Millard, Maartje Niezen, David Nuñez, Melek Önen, Alain Pannetrat, Nick Papanikolaou, Siani Pearson, Daniel Pradelles, Chris Reed, Christoph Reich, Jean-Claude Royer, Anderson Santana de Oliveira, Dimitra Stefanatou, Vasilis Tountopoulos, Tomasz Wiktor Wlodarczyk.

References

1. Felici, M., Pearson, S. (eds.): D:C-2.1 Report detailing conceptual framework. Deliverable D32.1, Version Final, A4CLOUD (2014)
2. A4CLOUD: Accountability For Cloud and Other Future Internet Services, Annex I - Description of Work, Grant agreement 317550 (2012)
3. Abdul-Rahman, A., Hailes, S.: Supporting trust in virtual communities. In: Proceedings of the 33rd Annual Hawaii International Conference on System Sciences, vol. 1, pp. 1–9 (2000)
4. Article 29 Data Protection Working Party: Opinion 04/2013 on the Data Protection Impact Assessment Template for Smart Grid and Smart Metering Systems ('DPIA Template') prepared by Expert Group 2 of the Commission's Smart Grid Task Force, 00678/13/EN WP205 (2013)
5. Article 29 Data Protection Working Party: Opinion 15/2011 on the definition of consent, 01197/11/EN WP187 (2011)

6. Brunton, F., Nissenbaum, H.: Political and ethical perspectives on data obfuscation. In: Hildebrandt, M., de Vries, K. (eds.) Privacy, Due Process and the Computational Turn, pp. 164–188. Routledge, New York (2013)
7. Cavoukian, A.: Privacy by Design in Law, Policy and Practice: A White Paper for Regulators, Decision-makers and Policy-makers, Information and Privacy Commissioner, ON, Canada (2011)
8. CIPL: Accountability: A Compendium for Stakeholders, The Centre for Information Policy Leadership (2011)
9. CNSS: National Information Assurance (IA) Glossary, Committee on National Security Systems (CNSS), CNSS Instruction No. 4009 (2010)
10. Directive 2009/136/EC of the European Parliament and of the Council of 25 November 2009 amending Directive 2002/22/EC on universal service and users' rights relating to electronic communications networks and services, Directive 2002/58/EC concerning the processing of personal data and the protection of privacy in the electronic communications sector and Regulation (EC) No 2006/2004 on cooperation between national authorities responsible for the enforcement of consumer protection laws, Official Journal of the European Communities L 337/11 (2009)
11. Directive 95/46/EC of the European Parliament and of the Council of 24 October 1995 on the protection of individuals with regard to the processing of personal data and on the free movement of such data, Official Journal of the European Communities L 281/31 (1995)
12. EDPS: European Data Protection Supervisor (EDPS) Glossary - accessed online
13. Catteddu, D., Hogben, G. (eds.): Could Computing: Benefits, risks and recommendations for information security, European Network and Information Security Agency, ENISA (2009)
14. ENISA: Privacy, Accountability and Trust – Challenges and Opportunities (2011)
15. ITU-T, FG Cloud TR, Part 1: Introduction to the cloud ecosystem: definitions, taxonomies, use cases and high-level requirements, Version 1.0 (02/2012), ITU (2012)
16. Hildebrandt, M. (ed.): D 7.12: Behavioural Biometric Profiling and Transparency Enhancing Tools, FIDIS (2009)
17. Gambetta, D. (ed.): Trust: Making and Breaking Cooperative Relations. Basil Blackwell, Oxford (1988)
18. Hilty, M., Pretschner, A., Basin, D., Schaefer, C., Walter, T.: A policy language for distributed usage control. In: Biskup, J., López, J. (eds.) ESORICS 2007. LNCS, vol. 4734, pp. 531–546. Springer, Heidelberg (2007)
19. IETF: Terminology for Policy-Based Management, RFC 3198, Internet Engineering Task Force, IETF (2001)
20. IETF: Internet Security Glossary, Version 2, RFC 4949, Internet Engineering Task Force, IETF (2007)
21. ISO 9241-11:1998 Ergonomic requirements for office work with visual display terminals (VDTs) – Part 11: Guidance on usability (1998)
22. ISO/IEC 10746-2:2009 Information technology - Open Distributed Processing - Reference Model: Foundations (2009)
23. ISO/IEC 15414:2006 Information technology - Open distributed processing - Reference model - Enterprise language (2006)
24. ISO/IEC 27000:2009(E) Information Technology - Security techniques - Information security management systems - Overview and vocabulary (2009)
25. ISO/IEC 38500:2008 Corporate governance of information technology (2008)
26. ISO27 k implementers' forum, Hyperlinked information security glossary (2007)
27. Juels, A., Kaliski, B.S. Jr.: Pors: proofs of retrievability for large files. In: Proceedings of the 14th ACM Conference on Computer and Communications Security (CCS 2007), pp. 584–597. ACM, New York (2007)

28. Hu, V.C., Ferraiolo, D.F., Kuhn, D.R.: Assessment of Access Control Systems, NIST Interagency Report 7316 (2006)
29. Hogan, M., Liu, F., Sokol, A., Tong, J.: NIST Cloud Computing Standards Roadmap Working Group, NIST Cloud Computing Standards Roadmap, NIST Special Publication, 500–291 Version 1.0 (2011)
30. Liu, F., Tong, J., Mao, J., Bohn, R., Messina, J., Badger, L., Leaf, D.: NIST Cloud Computing Reference Architecture, NIST Special Publication 500–292 (2011)
31. Jansen, W., Grance, T.: Guidelines on Security and Privacy in Public Cloud Computing, NIST Special Publication, 800–144 (2011)
32. Mell, P., Grance, T.: The NIST Definition of Cloud Computing, NIST Special Publication, 800–145 (2011)
33. Stoneburner, G., Hayden, C., Feringa, A.: Engineering Principles for Information Technology Security (A Baseline for Achieving Security), NIST Special Publication, 800–27 Rev. A (2004)
34. NIST: Joint Task Force Transformation Initiative, Guide for Assessing the Security Controls in Federal Information Systems and Organizations: Building Effective Security Assessment Plans, NIST Special Publication 800–53A, Revision 1 (2010)
35. Fischer-Hübner, S., Hedbom, H. (eds.): Framework V3, D14.1.c, PRIME (2008)
36. Reed, C.: Cloud governance: the way forward. In: Millard, C. (ed.) Cloud Computing Law, Oxford University Press (2013)
37. Weitzner, D.J., Abelson, H., Berners-Lee, T., Feigenbaum, J., Hendler, J., Sussman, G.J.: Information accountability. Commun. ACM 51(6), 82–87 (2008)
38. Westin, A.F.: Privacy and Freedom. Atheneum, New York (1967)

Author Index